THE SPORTS REVOLUTION

THE TEXAS BOOKSHELF

Other books in the series

The publication of this book was made possible by the generous support of the following:

Christine and Charles Aubrey
Roger W. Fullington
Jeanne and Mickey Klein
Marsha and John Kleinheinz
Lowell H. Lebermann, Jr.
Joyce and Harvey Mitchell
Office of UT President William Powers, Jr.
Ellen and Ed Randall
Jean and Dan Rather
Tocker Foundation
Judith Willcott and Laurence Miller
Suzanne and Marc Winkelman

THE SPORTS REVOLUTION

*How Texas Changed the Culture
of American Athletics*

FRANK ANDRE GURIDY

University of Texas Press
Austin

The Texas Bookshelf

Requests for permission to reproduce material from this work should be
sent to:
  Permissions
  University of Texas Press
  P.O. Box 7819
  Austin, TX 78713-7819
  utpress.utexas.edu/rp-form

♾ The paper used in this book meets the minimum requirements of
ANSI/NISO Z39.48-1992 (R1997) (Permanence of Paper).

LIBRARY OF CONGRESS CATALOGING-IN-PUBLICATION DATA

Names: Guridy, Frank Andre, author.
Title: The sports revolution : how Texas changed the culture of American
    athletics / Frank Andre Guridy.
Other titles: Texas bookshelf.
Description: First edition. | Austin : University of Texas Press, 2021. |
    Series: The Texas bookshelf | Includes bibliographical references and
    index.
Identifiers: LCCN 2020028196
ISBN 978-1-4773-2183-6 (cloth)
ISBN 978-1-4773-2184-3 (library ebook)
ISBN 978-1-4773-2185-0 (ebook)
Subjects: LCSH: Professional sports—Social aspects—Texas—History—
    20th century. | Professional sports—Political aspects—Texas—History—
    20th century. | Professional sports—Social aspects—United States—
    History—20th century. | Minorities in sports—Texas—History—20th
    century. | Feminism and sports—Texas—History—20th century. | Civil
    rights movements—United States—History—20th century.
Classification: LCC GV584.T4 G87 2021 | DDC 796.09764—dc23
LC record available at https://lccn.loc.gov/2020028196

doi:10.7560/321836

Contents

THE SPORTS REVOLUTION

Introduction

// THE CROWD BEHIND ME ROARING! POM-POMS ARE EVERYWHERE ON DIS-
play," bellowed sports announcer Howard Cosell to a national television audience at the beginning of what turned
out to be a memorable ABC *Monday Night Football* telecast on
November 20, 1978.[1] The matchup that evening featured two of
the top teams in the National Football League (NFL). The Houston Oilers, led by their popular coach O. A. "Bum" Phillips and
their star rookie tailback Earl Campbell, faced off against the Miami Dolphins, led by their veteran quarterback Bob Griese and
their legendary coach Don Shula. The two teams were fighting
for a place in the NFL playoffs; the postseason tournament featured teams with the best regular season records to compete in
the league championship game.

That championship game was dubbed the "Super Bowl" by Lamar Hunt, the son of a millionaire oilman who exemplified the
profound impact of Texas sports entrepreneurs on the expansion of professional sports in the United States. Along with Oilers
owner K. S. "Bud" Adams, Hunt founded the American Football
League (AFL) in 1960, which successfully challenged the NFL's
supremacy over professional football. In 1966, Hunt, along with
Dallas Cowboy general manager Tex Schramm and Southern
California–native NFL commissioner Pete Rozelle, negotiated the
merger of the AFL and the NFL. This agreement created the new

1

National Football League, the most powerful sports enterprise in the country. Entrepreneurs like Hunt, Adams, and Clint Murchison Jr. were among a cadre of Texas-based businessmen who changed the face of big-time sports in the United States.[2]

The Oilers-Dolphins game on that Monday night in 1978 featured many of the elements that catapulted Texas to the forefront of US sporting culture. The setting was the Houston Astrodome, America's first indoor stadium, which was the brainchild of the visionary political leader Roy Hofheinz. Hofheinz, often nicknamed "the Judge," was a former Harris County judge and mayor of Houston who saw the Astrodome putting his city on the map for occasions just like this one. After it opened its doors in 1965, the Dome changed stadium architecture with its innovative climate-controlled environment, luxury boxes, and artificial turf: the perfect symbol of technology overcoming the hostile Texas climate.[3]

The game was televised on *Monday Night Football*, the hit television series created by then head of ABC Sports, Roone Arledge. Arledge's program, with its paradigm-shifting three-man announcing team of Frank Gifford, Howard Cosell, and Texan Don Meredith, made pro football on Monday nights "must-see TV." Football, the sport that had long been a Texas obsession, became a national sensation during the 1960s and '70s, when the game overtook baseball as the country's most popular spectator sport. This transformation was catalyzed by television and especially by networks like Arledge's ABC Sports, which televised and dramatized the game for millions of viewers. Arledge's Saturday NCAA college football and *Monday Night Football* telecasts frequently featured Texas's collegiate and professional teams, such as the University of Texas Longhorns, the Dallas Cowboys NFL franchise, and, by the mid-1970s, another emerging pro football team from the Lone Star State, the Houston Oilers.

The game also featured Earl Campbell, arguably the first black Texan sports superstar in a state where most of its black athletes had previously left their home state to pursue possibilities in the North and West. Known as the Tyler Rose, Campbell's easygoing demeanor, slow country drawl, and affinity for "cowboy" fashions made him undeniably *black* and *Texan*. He was part of a generation of talented African Americans who were able to play on racially integrated teams because civil rights activists in the state pushed for opportunities for black athletes in the 1960s. At the same time, a new generation of white coaches and team owners realized that they needed black male players to compete on the state and national levels. Some coaches were slower to ascertain where the arc of history was headed than others, but by the 1970s, black male athletes emerged as stars on integrated sports teams in a state where the sporting culture, like everything else, had been governed by legal and customary racial segregation, a system popularly known as Jim Crow. The fact that these newly emerging integrated teams were often on national television meant that this profound social and cultural revolution was televised for all the nation to see.

The technology of the Astrodome created a noise level that reverberated through the television set. Though the contest was a professional football game, the raucous Astrodome crowd of fifty thousand fans created an enthusiastic "college-like setting" in the words of play-by-play man Frank Gifford. The Oilers faithful shook the Dome with loud cheers and multiple renditions of the Oilers fight song—"We're the Houston Oilers! Houston Oilers! Houston Oilers, number one!"—after the home team scored touchdowns as fans waved Columbia blue-and-white pom-poms and "Luv Ya Blue" signs all night.

In the 1970s, Houston certainly felt like a place that was rising to the top of the heap of cities in the United States. It was arguably becoming the capital of the Sunbelt, the region of the country that was experiencing dramatic population expansion and economic growth. While the rest of the country was suffering through the oil crisis, Houston was in the midst of yet another oil boom, which produced money and good times for the rapidly growing city. The Oilers personified the possibilities Houston presented for upwardly mobile Texans during the 1970s, as did the cross-racial Anglo, black, and Mexican American crowd that was remaking the former Jim Crow city into a socially integrated, economically prosperous society. At one point in the telecast, Howard Cosell, in his characteristic hyperbolic fashion, exclaimed to the millions who watched the telecast, "Look out, America, here comes Houston! America's fastest growing city, and right now . . . in this arena . . . America's football team!"

*   *   *

In the following pages, I tell the story of Texas's impact on the expansion of collegiate and professional sports in the United States during the "Second Reconstruction," the era that roughly corresponds to the civil rights and second-wave feminist movements as well as to the sexual revolution. I offer an interpretative history of sport and society in the state from the 1960s to the 1980s, showing how sport catalyzed social change and how it did not. Where the first Reconstruction created unprecedented understandings of citizenship and belonging for the formerly enslaved, the civil rights and second-wave feminist movements one hundred years later created another transformation, in which understandings of equality extended beyond the privileged position of white men. The Second Reconstruction, like the first, entailed more than the passage of landmark federal legislation that granted new rights to previously disenfranchised groups. The *Brown v. Board of Education* Supreme Court ruling (1954), the passage of the Civil Rights and Voting Rights Acts of the 1960s, and the adoption of the Educational Amendments Act of 1972, among other landmark legislative changes, provided unprecedented opportunities for people of color and women while prompting fierce struggles over what their advancement would mean for the United States.[4]

The consequences of these legal and political transformations vividly played out in the world of sports. The influx of athletes of color and women athletes in previously prohibited spaces in the 1960s and '70s meant that sport became an arena where battles over the meanings of Americanness, blackness, whiteness, manhood, and womanhood were fought over and reimagined. Sport simultaneously catalyzed new visions of belonging and shut off other possibilities for more substantial forms of change and inclusion. The changes catalyzed by the sports revolution were propelled by the deepening commercialization of sports at all levels. By the mid-1980s, the innovation and transformation of the previous decades were overrun by commercialism and stripped of the potential for more radical visions of sport and social change.

Texas played a key role in these changes in US society because it was also a catalyst of the emergence of the so-called Sunbelt, a region that stretched from the Deep South into the Southwest that grew rapidly due to the influx of federal funds and private capital and millions of migrants. In this period, Texas was at the center of the South's movement from the rural society of the Cotton Belt to the new suburban Sunbelt.[5] With the rise of the Sunbelt came the creation of new professional sports franchises, along with the expansion of intercollegiate sports during the 1960s and '70s, and Texas played a decisive role in this transformation. Fueled by a booming energy economy, a group of imaginative sports entrepreneurs teamed up with a host of talented athletes from the laboring classes to usher in an unprecedented era of inclusion and popularity. But like all revolutions, the sports revolution also set in motion a series of contradictions that blunted its impact and revealed the negative consequences of sport's outgrowth in Texas and in the United States in general. This book shows how, for better and for worse, Texas was central to the nation's expanding political, economic, and emotional investment in sport.

Texas's sports entrepreneurs, including Lamar Hunt, Roy Hofheinz, and even Houston Cougar basketball coach Guy Lewis, used their ingenuity to create opportunities to expose athletes to a broader public, but these opportunities set in motion the precise forces that have undermined the promises of sport: skyrocketing revenues for the new sport management class and a tiny sector of the most talented players, hyper-profiteering from college athletes, and the misallocation of public dollars for costly stadium construction projects that did little more than enrich private sports interests.

The first drafts of the story that appears in the following pages were written by the state's impactful sports media, whose writings and sports commentary in newspapers and in front of the television cameras popularized the exploits of the state's athletes and teams to millions of Americans. Texas-based sportswriters, such as Blackie Sherrod, Mickey Herskowitz, Sam Blair, Skip Bayless, and many others, enjoyed large readerships. After television insinuated itself into the coverage of collegiate and professional sports, networks such as ABC Sports broadcast many games featuring Texas college and professional football teams. As television become a dominant communication and entertainment medium, many broadcasters who had connections to Texas sports became announcers for major networks, including "Dandy" Don Meredith, Kyle Rote, Verne Lundquist, Frank Glieber, and Phyllis George. All were nationally recognized announcers who narrated the state's sports story to a broader national audience. Even as it was shaped by the designs of television executives in Midtown Manhattan in the 1960s and 1970s, the national sports media bore the undeniable imprint of Texas sporting cultures.

Texan sporting cultures not only transformed the United States for better and for worse, but they also helped change the Lone Star State itself, which was built on the violence of conquest, slavery, colonization, and Jim Crow segregation. The expansion of big-time professional and collegiate sports helped transform a largely rural society to one with large, suburbanized metropolises in whose development and national visibility sports played a major role. Sports also had a profound impact on the region's historical social hierarchies. These social changes accelerated by sport had both racial *and* gender implications. Talented male athletes of color, especially black men, and, to a lesser extent, white women managed to create spaces for themselves as athletic laborers in a period when the commercialization of sport made possible new careers in a world that was previously dominated by white elite and working-class men. But white men also found greater opportunities in the growing industries of sports management and sports journalism. Women of color benefitted the least from these changes, and their struggle for inclusion would become visible years later.

In this regard, this book is more than a history of social change in sports. It exposes core understandings of what equality meant in the era when the black freedom and feminist movements were making their most significant gains. More often than not in the sport world, equality meant "integration," meaning that formerly marginalized populations achieved a degree of unprecedented inclusion, but they did so under the supervision of more powerful white male team owners, general managers, and coaches. Athletes from marginalized communities could occupy spaces on team rosters and even become superstars, but they did not ascend to the level of management, where the benefits of their labor were ultimately determined. Revisiting the sports revolution of the 1960s and 1970s invites us to rethink what we mean by integration in our time, when the limits of the victories of that era are painfully clear every day.

* * *

The story begins in the Jim Crow era, when sports arrived from the Northeast and were remade in an environment that was deeply embedded in a rigid system of racial and gender segregation. The world that Jim Crow sports made started to collapse in the late 1950s and early 1960s when a coterie of sons of wealthy oilmen spearheaded the creation of professional sports franchises in the Lone Star State. Lamar Hunt, Bud Adams, Clint Murchison, and civic boosters and visionary political leaders like Roy Hofheinz and later Tom Vandergriff made Houston and Dallas big league sports cities. In the early 1970s, other sports entrepreneurs, such as Gladys Heldman, Joe Cullman, and, again, Lamar Hunt, also sought to harness commercial interests to propel a revolution in professional tennis. Other businessmen like Bob Short and Brad Corbett merely sought to cash in on the growing market for spectator sports, even as they bungled their way through their ownership of the Texas Rangers, the Major League Baseball franchise in Dallas–Fort Worth. Meanwhile, another group of basketball entrepreneurs led by Angelo Drossos channeled the renegade spirit of the American Basketball Association (ABA) into building the San Antonio Spurs into a pro sports franchise that reflected the working-class Mexican American cultures of South Texas. Oil money fueled the sports revolution, but so did advertising dollars and, in the case of women's tennis, tobacco money. The sports revolution of the 1960s and 1970s contained the contradictions of sport in a capitalist society whereby greater opportunities were made possible by corporate interests that profited from toxic commodities.

But these sports entrepreneurs did not carry out the revolution alone. They could not have realized their dreams of linking professional sports with their aspirations as civic leaders without the abundant athletic talent from the region's rural and urban laboring classes, who were unleashed, in part, by the efforts of the freedom fighters knocking down racial and gender barriers during the 1960s. These movements had a profound impact on the sports world. In turn, the sports world had an undeniable impact on them. This book's title is inspired by these movements and the ways they were chronicled by athletic activists such as Harry Edwards, Jack Scott, and Billie Jean King.[6] Much of the impact of those movements was evident in the sporting realm, where activists, journalists, and even some athletes insisted on equal access to the opportunities created by the sports industry in the 1960s. Some were calling for much more: a radical restructuring of big-time sports away from the corrosive effects of commercialization. Farsighted Texan sportsmen understood that they could not be competitive at the regional and national levels without the athletic labor power of African Americans, Latinos, and, by the 1970s, athletic women, including cheerleaders.

The bulk of this story is set in the 1970s, when many of the social and cultural ramifications of the Second Reconstruction came into fuller view, albeit in a contradictory fashion. The metropolitan areas of Dallas and Houston take center stage in this story, since these were the areas where the expansion of professional and collegiate sports were most palpable, followed by San Antonio and Austin. Texans played and excelled at all sports, but it was baseball, basketball, tennis, and especially football where their impact was the greatest. Most of the time, these stories appear in biographies of famous sports figures or in team histories. In the following chapters, I put the Doak Walker touchdown run, the Jerry LeVias kick return, the Muhammad Ali shuffle, the Billie Jean King backhand, and the Clyde Drexler tomahawk dunk inside the history of a dynamic region in a revolutionary time.

* * *

In retrospect, I now see that this book began to be written when I furtively stayed up late to watch that thrilling Oilers-Dolphins Monday night game as a seven-year-old in a cramped apartment in New York City. And watching the game on YouTube forty years later, one can see why. The two teams produced the best drama football can provide.[7] The Dolphins and Oilers waged a seesaw battle as each team's offense marched up and down the field and scored all night long. The Dolphins, led by Griese and their Houston-native tailback, Delvin Williams, jumped out to a 7–0 lead on their first possession of the game. A few drives later, the Oilers tied the score on an Earl Campbell touchdown run. Campbell, the thickly muscled five-foot, eleven-inch, 220-pound star, showed his unusual speed for a running back his size by rambling over Dolphins defenders all night.

By the fourth quarter, the game's exhausting pace began to show itself on the Miami sideline. The Oilers offense, propelled by its powerful running game led by Campbell, began to wear down the tiring Miami defense. After the Dolphins took a 23–21 lead on a safety, the Oilers embarked on a time-consuming eighty-yard drive. The Oilers possession culminated in a beautiful touchdown run by the Tyler Rose. Taking a toss from quarterback Dan Pastorini, he followed his blockers as he ran toward the sideline, then cut sharply to his left into a hole opened up by textbook-perfect blocks by tight end Richard Caster and fullback Tim Wilson, and scurried past lunging defenders for another touchdown to put the Oilers back in the lead, 28–23. As the Astrodome crowd roared, Frank Gifford exclaimed to the television audience, "What a show this man is putting on tonight!"

Miami responded with a drive toward yet another score, but a Griese pass was intercepted deep in Houston territory. The Oilers now had possession of the ball with 3:05 remaining in the game. All they had to do was get some first downs and run the clock out until the game was over. On second down and eight yards to go from the Oilers nineteen-yard line, Campbell exploded out of his three-point stance in the Oilers backfield and took a pitch from Pastorini, his twenty-eighth carry of the night. Once again, the Tyler Rose showed his uncanny agility by immediately sidestepping an onrushing tackler who nearly tripped him behind the line of scrimmage. After a block by Ken Burrough cleared another Miami tackler from his path, Campbell broke into the clear and outran the entire defensive pursuit. As he raced past linebacker Steve Towle down the sideline, fifty yards of Judge Hofheinz's Astroturf stood between the Tyler Rose and a game-clinching touchdown. "He's gone! He's gone!" yelled Cosell as Campbell bolted toward the end zone and the Luv Ya Blue faithful began to roar. When Campbell steamrolled past the Miami forty-yard line, Dolphins cornerback Curtis Johnson seemed to have the speed and the angle to chase him down or shove him out of bounds. Cornerbacks like Johnson are usually the fastest players on a defense, with the speed to run down most running backs. But Earl Campbell was no ordinary running back. As he reached the ten-yard line, all Johnson could do was fruitlessly dive for the running back's legs to no avail. Seconds later Campbell crossed the goal line, scoring his fourth touchdown of the night. The Lucite panels on the Astrodome's roof had failed to allow sunlight to grow grass when the building opened in 1965, but on this night they helped amplify the thunderous roar by the sellout crowd when the Tyler Rose crossed the goal line after an extraordinary eighty-one-yard touchdown run to clinch the game for Houston's team.

After Campbell's electrifying run, which capped off an eventual Oilers 35–30 victory, Cosell, completely swooped up in the excitement of the moment, yelled to his viewers in his characteristic staccato manner, "What you have seen tonight, ladies and gentlemen, is a *truly* great football player, in the late moments, take *total, personal command* of a game!" Indeed, fans did see a memorable performance by an extraordinary football player, the son of a poor, black, rose-farming father and a domestic working mother from early post–Jim Crow Tyler, Texas, a talented running back who combined power and speed in a manner rarely seen in professional football.

Yet Campbell's performance was more than a great football player taking total personal command of a game. Performances like this one, and others by black athletes, exemplified the possibilities sports could provide for marginalized groups in Texas and the United States during the 1960s and '70s. On the field of play, black athletes, and to some extent white women athletes, could dramatize their aspirations for freedom, equality, and recognition in spaces from which they had been previously excluded. And with more sports on television, these performances had a greater impact on spectators who saw their aspirations and understandings widened in an unprecedented manner. The skill and craft of Campbell and his teammates communicated more profound meanings than simply an Oilers victory or defeat. Black male athletes were now an integral part of the new society emerging in Texas and the United States in the 1970s.

But as Cosell and the fans got carried away with a game that represents perhaps the best that football can offer, they overlooked the underside of the sport, which reared its ugly head even on that remarkable night. The skill of the athletes and the national television coverage helped generate enormous revenue for the unlikable Bud Adams, who, like the rest of the NFL owners, was raking in unprecedented profits from television network deals negotiated by NFL commissioner Pete Rozelle. The unpopular owner frequently complained about the beloved Astrodome, and he alienated fans with his many questionable management decisions during the team's years in Houston. In 1996, he moved his franchise to Tennessee, and few Houstonians wept when the Oilers left town.

The extraordinary success of *Monday Night Football* games, artfully called by Cosell, Gifford, and Meredith along with their colleagues at CBS and NBC Sports during the 1970s, facilitated the growing power of television networks in shaping the production, reception, and consumption of collegiate and professional football. In the process, television also showcased and glorified the violence of the sport, which we now know destroys the brains and bodies of the athletes who decide to sign up for the football life. Indeed, the Astrodome helped facilitate the destruction of players' bodies when it introduced Astroturf. The synthetic grass produced by the Monsanto subsidiary Chemstrand promised easy field maintenance and fewer injuries to players, but in fact it had the opposite effect. Astroturf produced its own maintenance costs and more injuries to players who had the unpleasant experience of being crushed by head-knocking tackles on the concrete-like floor or who ripped up ligaments on zippered seams that stitched the carpet together.

Herein lies the sports revolution of the 1960s and 1970s in all of its glories and contradictions. This book revisits many such moments on the field, in the stands, and even in the broadcast booth. Lingering on key moments in the performance of sport enables one to appreciate the enormous skill and expertise that athletes and coaches exemplify in competition. Descriptions of memorable wins and losses, touchdown runs and passes, finger rolls and jump shots, fastballs and curveballs, and backhands and volleys show up frequently in the following pages. These accounts highlight the captivating quality of sports for the performer, the spectator, and even the historian. Ultimately, this is a story about the multifaceted impact of sports—on a region's political economy; on the country's popular culture; on the ways manhood, womanhood, whiteness, blackness, and *social belonging* were understood and reimagined. It is a story of a unique industry that facilitated the creativity and self-expression of talented athletes in the 1960s and 1970s, many of whom emerged from the shadows of colonialism, Jim Crow segregation, and patriarchy to provide glimpses of a better Texas, and by extension, a better United States of America.

CHAPTER 1

Sports in the Shadow of Segregation

VISITORS TO DALLAS, TEXAS, ON NEW YEAR'S DAY 1951 WERE TOLD THAT they would be in for a treat. The city was getting ready for the annual Cotton Bowl Classic, the college football post-season game entering its fifteenth iteration that holiday season. The game was quickly becoming one of the most popular post-season football games in the nation, and it was bringing fame and some fortune to the city of Dallas and the colleges and universities in Texas. This particular contest featured two powers of college football in the South: the Texas Longhorns, the champions of the Southwest Conference (SWC), and the Tennessee Volunteers of the Southeastern Conference (SEC). Though both states had a plethora of talented African American football players, none would be suiting up for either school on that day in Dallas.

The game was only a part of the day's festivities. The Cotton Bowl Association promised a lineup of events "unparalleled in gridiron shows," according to the *Dallas Morning News*. The pre-game and halftime activities featured performances from a four-hundred-piece band from high schools across the state, including Abilene, Odessa, Waco, Palestine, Texarkana, and San Antonio, as well as a showing by the Texas Longhorns band. Also performing that day were the Kilgore Rangerettes, the famous junior college women's drill team that dazzled the crowd with their patented high leg kicks, Charleston dance routine, and rope-spinning skills, which left fans wondering about the "prettiest girl on the Rangerette line." Black Texans were not allowed to play in the game, but they did play a part in the festivities. "As an added touch of atmosphere," the *Dallas Morning News* reported, "Negro orchestras in minstrel costumes" performed jazz and "Old South songs" at various locations in the fairgrounds on bandstands made of bales of cotton. The cotton theme was ever present, as even the yard markers on the football field were made of bales of cotton, in celebration of the commodity that generated so much wealth for the East Texas landed elites and so much misery for the ancestors of many of those who performed in the "Negro orchestras" that day. The festivities, which were sponsored by the Texas Cotton Association, the Texas Cotton Ginners Association, and the Dallas Cotton Exchange, were more than a college football game. Rather, they were a romanticized staging of the "Old South."[1]

The 1951 Cotton Bowl in Dallas took place when the state's sporting scene was ascending on the national stage. Texas had developing traditions in baseball, basketball, and other sports, but it was football that was most popular and impactful. The New Year's bowl game was becoming an annual holiday ritual as Dallas joined Pasadena, Miami, and New Orleans as hosts of college football's most popular postseason classics. But as the *Dallas Morning News* story on the 1951 game and festivities shows, the state's sporting cultures were deeply entangled in the broader history of colonization, slavery, and racial exclusion. African Americans and women participated in these major sporting events, but only as segregated and subordinate partners in the re-creation of the South's racial and gender hierarchies.

In the decades after the abolition of slavery, white Texan elites went about the business of re-creating a new order of racial and gender exclusion. In the 1870s, the legislature began to pass laws that disfranchised black voters and segregated them into second-class citizens. The Terrell Election Law of 1903 began a series of state electoral rules whose stated intent was to prevent voter fraud but whose real design was to disenfranchise black, Mexican

American, and poor voters. When the Terrell Law was contested by black activists, new stipulations were passed that barred African Americans and Mexican Americans from voting in the primary election as Democrats, the most powerful political party in the state until the realignment of Texas politics in the 1970s and '80s. At the same time, the Texas state legislature worked to ensure that the "two races [would] always be taught in separate public schools."[2] When the historic *Plessy v. Ferguson* Supreme Court decision of 1896 legalized racial segregation, state and local officials further codified racial exclusion into the law and daily practices. This ensured that physical education and popular recreation practices like sport would be entrenched in a system of nonwhite subordination and exclusion. But as schools and entrepreneurs discovered sport's lucrative possibilities as a business during the first half of the twentieth century, they also realized that it could not be easily aligned with the state's commitment to Jim Crow segregation.

* * *

In the late nineteenth century, baseball was the first sport to catch on in Texas, and with the founding of the Texas League in 1888, it became the first to professionalize. The league in its multiple iterations was the main professional baseball circuit in the state until the 1950s. During that time, many eventual Major League Baseball stars got their start in the Texas League, including Dizzy Dean, Tris Speaker, Hank Greenberg, Duke Snider, and many others. The franchise in Fort Worth, known as the Panthers or the Cats, won several league titles. The Dixie Series, which featured the champions of the Texas League playing the representative team from the Southern Association, was popular among southern baseball fans from 1920 to 1958. And as national professional baseball leagues abided by the "gentlemen's agreement" of racial segregation, black Texans sought to create their own opportunities to play baseball. Various black teams enjoyed short-lived existences throughout the state, but most often, aspiring black professional baseball players found more opportunities to play in other parts of the United States and in Latin America. Indeed, one of the pioneers of Negro League baseball was Rube Foster, a Calvert, Texas, native, baseball player, and entrepreneur who founded the Negro National League in Kansas City in 1920. Meanwhile, players such as the Austin native Willie Wells were prominent stars in the US black baseball world and in the non-segregated baseball leagues in Latin America, particularly Cuba and Mexico.[3]

While baseball became the "national pastime" in many parts of the country, Texas's national pastime was football. The game arrived from the Northeast in the late nineteenth century. Since the first high school football game, a contest between Ball High School and the Galveston Rugbys on Christmas Eve 1892, the game had evolved into a state obsession. A century later, while Buzz Bissinger saw high school football under the Friday night lights as the quintessential sport of small-town America, in reality, Texas had developed its own unique manifestations of football performance and spectatorship. The marching bands, drill teams, and extensive press coverage created a large following among Texans. The spread of football in Texas was part of a broader pattern in the United States. "Football power shifted westward from the Northeast in the 1920s, then southward in the 1930s, with the Midwest and the Big Ten emerging as the premier football region and conference, the Pacific Coast just behind, and the South periodically upsetting the accustomed order," writes the historian Michael Oriard.[4] By the 1920s, schools all across the state—from El Paso in West Texas to the Golden Triangle area of Beaumont, Port Arthur, and Orange—fielded football teams. The violence and militarized culture of the sport easily harmonized with the region's legacy of conquest and colonization.

The emergence of big-time high school and intercollegiate sports occurred because there was a wealth of talent throughout the state. Football became an increasingly important part of the state's physical education programs, though the "educational" component of football was—and is—frequently questioned. High school sports competitions began in the nineteenth century, and eventually schools imposed an organizational structure on the growth of sport in Texas schools. In 1910, the University of Texas created the University Interscholastic League (UIL) to organize all recreational activities for high schools. And like all of the state's educational and recreational institutions, the UIL bore the stamp of Jim Crow segregation. Beginning in 1913, the UIL stipulated that league membership was open only to "any public white school."

By the 1930s, Texas college football was starting to achieve national notoriety due to the exploits of "Slingin'" Sammy Baugh, the record-breaking quarterback from Sweetwater, Texas, who starred at Texas Christian University (TCU) and later as a Hall of Famer in the pros. But it was in the 1940s, particularly after World War II, when Texas college football achieved national attention. It is impossible to capture the exploits of the many athletes in the state at this time, but few Texas athletes of the era exemplify the enormous national impact of Texas sports than the uniquely talented Doak Walker. His illustrious athletic career began when he was a high school star in Highland Park on the outskirts of Dallas in the early 1940s, where he lettered in five sports: football, basketball, track, swimming, and baseball. On the school's football team, he paired up with quarterback Bobby Layne to make the Highland Park Scots state championship contenders. It was widely assumed that the highly sought-after Walker would follow Layne to the University of Texas. But the athletic department of nearby Southern Methodist University (SMU) employed a trick that many athletic programs use to recruit star high school athletes: it hired Walker's high school coach, Rusty Russell, which enabled them to snatch Walker away from the Longhorns. And one could certainly surmise that the SMU Mustangs boosters also played a key role in convincing the young star to attend their university, as they would with other blue chip talents in subsequent decades.

Walker's decision to enroll at SMU was well timed. In the 1920s and '30s, the Mustangs arose as a state and national football power. Indeed, the rise of the Mustangs illustrates the synergies developing among schools and sports entrepreneurs across the Sunbelt from Texas to California. In 1935, SMU finished the regular season undefeated, earning it an invitation from the Tournament of Roses Association to play Stanford in the Pasadena Rose Bowl. Dallas city boosters quickly capitalized on the team's success. Bill Hitzleberger, a Pacific Railway executive and big SMU football supporter, helped transport six trains full of Mustangs fans to Pasadena.

Though the Mustangs lost 7–0, the game had a lasting impact on both SMU and Dallas. On his way back from watching the Rose Bowl, another oilman booster, J. Curtis Sanford, envisioned Dallas having its own New Year's bowl game. The experience in Pasadena convinced Sanford and others that a college football postseason game could promote Dallas as an up-and-coming city. The city had just outbid Houston and San Antonio to host the 1936 Texas Centennial Exposition. Thus, the time was right for Sanford to capitalize on SMU's success on the gridiron. He used his connections to the Texas Exposition Centennial and the Texas State Fair to stage a postseason college football game at Fair Park Stadium, which would be renamed the Cotton Bowl (not to be confused with the Cotton Bowl Classic). The stadium's new name revealed the city's relationship to the East Texas plantocracy and its exploitation of black labor under slavery and in the decades since emancipation. The bowl game became one of the country's showcase postseason college football games for the remainder of the twentieth century. The Cotton Bowl Classic organizers were among a host of those from other cities in the South who tried to copy the Rose Bowl formula to promote their cities through football and tourism. These bowl games, in turn, incentivized schools to field competitive teams to promote their schools on a national level.

The SMU Mustangs were one of the athletic powers of the Southwest Conference, the premier intercollegiate athletic entity in Texas and one of the most powerful in the United States. Beginning with the University of Texas in 1893, colleges and universities began fielding football teams in the 1890s. Paralleling the process high schools were using to standardize competitions, Texas's leading collegiate athletic programs chose to regulate and standardize competition by creating a league. Founded in 1914, the SWC governed collegiate competitions among the more powerful schools in Texas and in neighboring states. In addition to the University of Texas, Texas A&M, Rice, Baylor, the University of Oklahoma, Oklahoma A&M, Southwestern University, and the University of Arkansas participated. Oklahoma A&M and Southwestern dropped out of the conference, while Southern Methodist University joined in 1918, Texas Christian University joined in 1923, and Texas Tech joined in 1958. The participating schools composed the dominant athletic conference in the region, producing many legendary athletes throughout the first half of the twentieth century, including Davey O'Brien, Doak Walker, Sammy Baugh, Bobby Layne, Tom Landry, Kyle Rote, and later Don Meredith, among many others. While the conference governed many intercollegiate sports, football was the most important. The SWC also strictly adhered to Jim Crow segregation. When schools in second-tier athletic programs in the state began to desegregate in the 1950s and '60s, the Southwest Conference remained all white.

Meanwhile, the Cotton Bowl facility gained more notoriety as the stage for the exploits of All-American Doak Walker. Walker's extraordinary talents included running, passing, and kicking, and his play as a defensive back propelled the Mustangs to national stardom. In the era when players played multiple positions on offense and defense—unlike the specialized positions in subsequent decades—the Highland Park High School star epitomized the "all-purpose" football player. Walker took the league by storm in his very first season, when he returned from the merchant marine in October 1945 and almost led the Mustangs to a win over the Texas Longhorns, led by his former high school teammate turned college rival Layne, before losing 12–7. After a year in the US Army, Walker returned in 1947 and embarked on the beginning of a remarkable sophomore season with the Mustangs. He led them to an undefeated season of nine wins, zero losses, and two ties. One of his most memorable performances occurred during another game against Layne's Longhorns, in which he gained a measure of revenge over the "Steers" with a 14–13 win in front of a crowd of fifty thousand spectators at the Cotton Bowl. "The Doaker" exhibited his many talents that day: breathtaking running, timely kicking, and alert defense. In addition to a key interception, he made a clutch fifty-four-yard reception to set up the Mustangs' second touchdown.[5]

A few weeks later, during the last regular season game against the TCU Horned Frogs in Fort Worth, Walker pulled off perhaps the greatest performance in his college career. With the Mustangs trailing 12–0, the All-American almost single-handedly led his team back into the game. In the second quarter, he dropped back to pass. After finding no receivers open, he raced out of the pocket and outmaneuvered the TCU defense for a sixty-one-yard touchdown run. Another Walker touchdown run put SMU up 13–12, but TCU regained the lead with its own touchdown to go back in front 19–13 with ninety seconds left on the clock. The Horned Frogs missed the extra point, which gave SMU a chance to win with a touchdown and a point-after conversion. This was more than enough time for Walker to propel himself from a 1940s-era All-American to a Texas football legend. On the ensuing kickoff, Walker faked a handoff to a teammate, then raced down the sideline for a fifty-six-yard kickoff return before he was forced out of bounds at the TCU thirty-six-yard line. After yet another clutch Walker play, a leaping catch to give the Mustangs a first down on the TCU nine-yard line, quarterback Gilbert Johnson fired a touchdown pass to tie the score. The Doaker proved he was human after all when he missed the extra point, which forced SMU to settle for a 19–19 tie. Still, SMU's undefeated season and SWC title were preserved, giving the team a berth in the Cotton Bowl Classic.

In his junior year, the golden boy Walker did even better. He played in all eleven of SMU's games, rushed for 598 yards, averaged an impressive 4.9 yards per rushing attempt, caught 16 passes for 284 yards, passed for 383 yards, returned 10 punts and

5 kickoffs, scored 12 touchdowns, and kicked 24 extra points. For this extraordinary all-around performance, he was awarded the coveted Heisman Trophy, which is awarded annually to the best college football player in the country. During his senior season, despite suffering numerous injuries he was nominated for the All-America team, an honor he felt was undeserved due to his injury-riddled season.

Doak Walker was the right man at the right time, as far as SMU and Dallas boosters were concerned. Even before he brought his magic to the gridiron, state fair commission officials were seeking to expand the seating capacity of the Cotton Bowl. The excitement generated by SMU's and Walker's exploits in his sophomore and junior years gave city boosters the justification they needed to convince the Dallas citizenry to finance the expansion of the facility. In 1948, more seats and a second deck were added to the stadium. After the 1948 bowl game, the boosters convinced Dallasites to finance another upper deck to bring the stadium's capacity to seventy-five thousand. The stadium became known as the House that Doak Built. By the late 1940s, Dallas not only was becoming a commercial capital but also had become the "home of the Mustangs" and a national sporting destination, thanks to the athletic labor of Walker and his teammates. The Cotton Bowl became a hallowed home for college football and one of the preeminent football venues in the country. For the next forty-five years, the Cotton Bowl New Year's bowl game became one of the showcase college football postseason games in the country, along with the Rose, the Sugar, and the Orange Bowls.

But as subsequent Texan sports entrepreneurs found out, putting your city on the national map through sports necessitated bending the rules and customs of racial segregation. The Cotton Bowl Association departed from its adherence to prohibiting integrated sports teams when it decided to invite Penn State to play SMU in the 1948 Cotton Bowl Classic. The Penn State Nittany Lions had Wallace Triplett and Dennie Hoggard, two African American players, and the school had already shown that it would not capitulate to southern segregation practices. The pre-

Dennie Hoggard and his Penn State Nittany Lions teammates at a postgame affair on the SMU campus. Courtesy Heritage Hall and Southern Methodist University Archives, DeGolyer Library, SMU Libraries, Southern Methodist University.

vious year, Penn State had made it clear that it would no longer abide by gentlemen's agreements with southern schools when it refused to play the University of Miami after the latter refused to let its black team members play in the game. Black high school and college teams had been playing in all-black segregated affairs in Fair Park for decades, but never had an integrated outfit played in the stadium. Thus, the 1948 Cotton Bowl Classic was the first major integrated college football game to be played in the state of Texas. Though years later Triplett spoke of the hostile energy in the crowd, the tightly contested game seemingly came off without incident, even after he scored the game-tying touchdown in the third quarter.

Perhaps this is why the Cotton Bowl Association was comfortable enough to invite the Oregon Ducks to play SWC champ SMU in the New Year's Day bowl game the very next year. The Ducks had three black players on its roster, including Woodley Lewis, the team's starting left halfback. The Ducks also had the future Hall of Fame quarterback Norm Van Brocklin and future legendary coach John McKay, but they fell to Walker's Mustangs 21–13. The Cotton Bowl Classic organizers even allowed a small section for black fans. As historian Charles Martin has written, "the Cotton Bowl's willingness to breach the color line for one day each year gave it a competitive advantage over the Sugar Bowl and the Orange Bowl in recruiting nonsouthern teams."[6] The organizers of the latter bowls stubbornly upheld black exclusion until the mid-1950s.

The breaking of the gentlemen's agreement by the Cotton Bowl Classic organizers showed that segregation could not be easily harmonized with the commercialization of sport. The then-fledgling National Football League came to the same realization when it tried to put a pro football franchise in Dallas a few years later. In 1952, the Dallas Texans NFL franchise played one inglorious season in Dallas with two black players on its roster, Buddy Young and George Taliaferro. The Texans played in front of segregated crowds in the Cotton Bowl, a fact that drove local black fans to stay away from their games and the league to eventually transfer the franchise to Baltimore the next season.[7] Still, the occasional presence of a small number of black players on the Cotton Bowl gridiron was a crack in the wall of segregation that would topple a decade later. As boosters saw the potential revenues and visibility that sports could bring, they realized that the laws and customs of Jim Crow could not synchronize with the profitability of sport.

*   *   *

One cannot help but be compelled by Doak Walker's achievements after watching tapes of his memorable performances on grainy black-and-white films. And yet, as great as the Doaker was, he, like all the white players of his generation, benefitted enormously from the exclusion of black players from competition and from the attention lavished upon him by the sports media hungry for white stars in the years after World War II. He appeared on over fifty magazine covers in 1948 and 1949. "Always he was portrayed as an unassuming, clean-living, idealistic young man who didn't drink or smoke. He was a model and hero for boys everywhere," writes historian Darwin Payne.[8] The SMU Athletics Department did its part in promoting this image by dutifully churning out numerous press releases with his impressive array of statistics and inspiring stories of their star. Jim Laughead, one of the leading sports photographers in the country, who had a studio just down the street from SMU's campus, provided many posed and in-game photos of Walker. The publicity-makers' efforts paid off as Walker was on the cover of *Look*, *Collier's*, *Life*, and many other magazines. The 1948 issue of *Life* magazine was particularly indicative of the ways the press represented Walker, SMU, and, by extension, Texas football: "Down in Texas where, as every schoolboy knows, football players throw touchdown passes from Fort Worth to Waxahachie and think nothing at all of kicking field goals from Texarkana to El Paso, the Dallas fans this year are whooping it up for Southern Methodist University as just about the slickest football team in the country."[9]

The accompanying photo spread portrayed Walker as the star of a group of white southern "boys" hard at work in practice. In a section of the article entitled "Texas Football Is Sultry Work," the magazine showed muscular Mustangs players practicing shirtless in the stifling Texas heat. The celebration of Walker in these publications shows how he was the perfect football hero of the post–World War II Jim Crow America: a white, conventionally attractive, innocent-looking man who was small in stature by football standards but was tough enough to hang with the big bruisers. Though Walker was among many football stars who were celebrated by the press, his star text was a model for subsequent football men. A young multisport athlete from tiny Mount Vernon, Texas, named Don Meredith, who became an SMU Mustangs star a decade after Doak Walker, also made his mark on the game as a player and as a media personality. And a rich young man named Lamar Hunt, who tried out for the varsity team at SMU, would leave his own imprint on football history.

* * *

The packaging of Walker by the local and national press illustrates the unique contribution Texans made to the white masculine football hero image in the years after World War II. Yet Texas also produced an athlete who actively blurred the line between masculine and feminine fifteen years before Doak Walker burst onto the national sporting stage. On August 7, 1932, a twenty-one-year-old Beaumont native arrived to a hero's welcome in Dallas. Mildred Ella "Babe" Didrikson, the star of the 1932 Olympic Games in Los Angeles, had topped her competition as she said she would. She had become the first woman to win multiple medals at an Olympic Games. She was hailed as "America's Girl Star of the Olympics" by the *New York Times* and "Iron Woman" by another publication. The ruffian working-class hero was honored at multiple luncheons and ceremonies. She received an equally enthusiastic welcome in her hometown. When the pomp and circumstances ended, the enterprising Didrikson, like all aspiring women athletes, faced the daunting challenge of making a life for herself in an environment that was hostile to women's independence. Babe Didrikson did better than most.[10]

Mildred Ella Didrikson remains arguably the best woman athlete of the twentieth century. She was brash, she was talented, and she was from Texas. Known as the "Texas Tomboy," she was a hustler who loved to exaggerate her feats and obscure key details of her life story. She was born in 1911, not 1913 or 1914, as she claimed, in Port Arthur to Norwegian immigrants. When she was three years old, they moved to Beaumont, where she developed a ruffian, rough-around-the-edges persona. She rejected dominant ideas of femininity, but she was not a feminist. Didrikson was a "me first" personality who sought to promote herself whenever she could, often at the expense of other women. Her historic athletic feats and braggadocio made her a darling of the sporting press, though some male sportswriters and critics ridiculed her as an Amazon woman–type freak. Still, she managed to charm Grantland Rice, the legendary sportswriter, who championed her and spun stories about her athletic prowess.[11]

Didrikson excelled at many sports and liked to tell everyone how great she was, but she first became a news item as a basketball player. She benefitted from the growing interest in women's basketball in the 1920s and '30s. Texas was a region where women's basketball was increasingly accepted, even in the face of objections from physical educators who insisted that women's bodies were too frail for competitive team sports. This was the heyday of industrial league women's basketball, when companies such as the Sunoco Oil Company and Employers Casualty Company created women's teams as a way to advertise their services and products. In Dallas, Employers Casualty and Sunoco were the most popular teams, and they played games at the Fair Park Auditorium in front of crowds of three to four thousand spectators, which were substantial attendance figures at the time. In the pre–Title IX era, these semipro leagues gave working-class women opportunities to play basketball. Melvin McCombs, the Employers Casualty coach, offered Didrikson a job and a chance to play basketball in Dallas. McCombs's team, called the Golden Cyclones, went on to dominate competition for a brief period in the late 1920s and early 1930s.[12]

Didrikson's basketball exploits for Employers Casualty set the stage for her ascendance as a national sporting star in the summer of 1932. At the 1932 AAU track and field championships in Evanston, Illinois, she competed as a one-woman team for Employers Casualty against two hundred women in eight events and won six of them. She broke records in the shot put, the baseball throw, and the eighty-meter race. She tied her rival, Jean Shiley, in the high jump. Unbelievably, she earned more points by herself (thirty) than the entire second-place team representing the Illinois Athletic Club (twenty-two).[13]

Her extraordinary performance primed the sporting press for

more greatness and storylines at the Olympic Games in Los Angeles later that year. After she survived the lengthy opening ceremonies in the hot California sun in a dress, suffocating stockings,
and heeled shoes, she went on to set more world records during
the Olympiad. She won one gold medal by throwing the javelin
143 feet, 4 inches, a toss that resembled a bullet-like throw of a
catcher to second base. And, as always, Didrikson generated controversy. During the eighty-meter hurdles, she was declared the
winner over Evelyn Hall even though many observers felt Hall actually won the race. In her third event, Didrikson tied with Jean
Shiley in the high jump, but the latter was declared the gold medal
winner on a technicality. Officials ruled that Didrikson had used
an improper technique by diving over the bar rather than clearing
it with her feet first.

Even without a third gold medal, Babe Didrikson was the un-
disputed star of the 1932 Olympic Games. Didrikson continued
her pathbreaking ways by becoming a pioneering golfer during
the 1940s and '50s before she succumbed to cancer at the age of
forty-five on September 27, 1956. Didrikson was a pioneer, but
she was also a singular figure. Few women athletes occupied the
national stage while defying gender conventions and maintaining a tomboy image in the manner she did. She was way before
her time. It wouldn't be until the era of the second-wave feminist
movement when women athletes actively challenged gender conventions and dominant ideas of sexuality. Perhaps not surprisingly, it was a group of women athletes who made Texas the site of
another sports revolution in the 1970s.

Babe Didrikson was not the model of womanhood Gussie Nell
Davis had in mind when she arrived from Greenville, Texas, in
1939 to take a position as physical education teacher at Kilgore
Junior College in East Texas. Her formative experiences growing
up in Farmersville had profoundly shaped her educational philosophy. "All my life, I had wanted to dance on stage," she said on
the eve of her retirement in 1979, "and in Farmersville you didn't
dance. You would have been thrown out of church—ANY church."
She went on to study at Texas State College for Women in Denton,

Babe Didrikson Plaque, Los Angeles Memorial Coliseum. Author photo.

where she graduated at age nineteen. Then she obtained a master's degree in 1938 from the University of Southern California, which was developing its own football and marching band traditions, before returning to Texas to teach in Greenville. There, she remade Greenville High School's pep squad team into an eye-catching group of baton twirlers called the Flaming Flashes. When Kilgore Junior College dean B. E. Masters hired her to create a halftime show that would truly entertain fans, she told him confidently, "We're going to dance on that football field and every one of those girls out there is me and if they make a mistake I will have made a mistake and if they do perfect I will have done perfect and I'm gonna do a great job."[14]

Gussie Nell Davis made good on her promise. Kilgore, which

was known for the oil derricks that dotted its landscape, was re-branded as the home to arguably the most famous drill team in the country. From the moment the Rangerettes took the football field in the fall of 1940, they were a hit. Davis liked to claim she invented many of the team's drills, but they had existed before she popularized them with her squad. The Jefferson High School Lassos of San Antonio and Kay Teer Crawford's Edinburg High School Sergeanettes had run drill team–like lines at or around the same time as Davis. Male fans and—as important—female fans found a new reason to attend football games.

But the Rangerettes also became a phenomenon through sheer luck; they emerged in post–World War II America when tele-vision made it possible for the nation to experience Texas foot-ball pageantry. They also benefitted from their ability to land appearances at the Sugar Bowl in New Orleans, the College All-Star Game in Chicago, and all of the Cotton Bowl Classic festivi-ties. The Rangerette routines entailed a wide variety of steps and dance moves, but during the 1950s and '60s, they typically en-tailed shoulder shakes and their characteristic high kicks. They donned the patriotic Texan (and American) colors: red blouses, blue skirts with white belts, and white cowboy boots. Davis told filmmaker Elliott Erwitt in 1971, "That's our flag and that's every-thing concerned with our nation, the most beautiful nation in the world." The skirts were a scandal-producing length of two inches above the knee. "We were devils then," Davis liked to tell report-ers. Over time the length of the skirts grew shorter and shorter. The Rangerettes were "cute" and "wholesome" young women who tantalized male onlookers and inspired young women across the country.[15]

But Davis's squad of disciplined young women soon had com-petitors right in their own backyard. In 1947, nearby Tyler Ju-nior College created another drill team called the Apache Belles, which also performed at halftime shows at the school's football games. Their uniforms were a form of "playing Indian," a long-standing tradition of white performances of Native American ste-reotypes.[16] Though they never achieved the national visibility of

The Kilgore Rangerettes performing at the 1964 Cotton Bowl Classic. Photo by Neil Leifer.

the Rangerettes, the Apache Belles became a state institution and another drill team for aspiring young junior college women. They also became fixtures at Fair Park in Dallas. They were one of the main attractions during East Texas Day at the state fair every October, and they regularly performed at Dallas Cowboys games when the team played at the Cotton Bowl.

Gussie Nell Davis saw herself as a missionary of sorts: a mother hen–like physical educator who was helping society by fashioning the young, aspiring-class girl into a "lovely, poised, young lady." Davis's young ladies were expected to possess "values that are morally sound and that fit with society as long as it does not curve them to such a degree that they can't be individuals."[17] Being conventional and normative was the Rangerette Way. Davis saw herself teaching young women to be skilled performers, but she also saw herself bestowing life skills that prepared her team to adhere to the conventions of a patriarchal society. She was a drill sergeant who demanded the very best from her protégés. "If you can't be the best," she told *Dallas Morning News* columnist Sam Blair in 1958, "you should get out."[18] Indeed, Rangerette practices were notoriously grueling affairs run in a militaristic manner. Rangerettes were expected to respond to Davis's edicts with the obedient reply "Yes, Ms. Davis." During their annual two-week tryout boot camps in August, Davis and her lieutenants ran the contestants ragged. Their practices weren't much different than the two-a-days that football players had to suffer through in training camp. The brutal conditions were designed to toughen the Rangerettes up to perform in all weather conditions: from the brutal heat of Texas summers to the cold and muddy conditions of New Year's Days at the Cotton Bowl. And all of it had to be done with smiles on their faces, even as they were choked by thick leather belts that were two inches shorter than their waists. The fanatical emphasis on smiles was meant to convey the myth of the flawless female beauty queen. "Beauty knows no pain" was a slogan Davis liked to preach to her flock. "Beautiful girls *never* have any pain with anything that makes them beautiful," she was fond of saying to all who would listen. And yet this was a lie that even loyal adherents acknowledged. "You're supposed to have your belt at least two inches smaller than your waist," a young blonde Rangerette told filmmaker Elliott Erwitt in 1971, "and they are stiff leather. You might end up with a few welts, but you are supposed to keep smiling through everything."[19] Upholding the image of white femininity necessitated suffering enormous amounts of physical and even emotional pain.

The Rangerettes personified the strangling of athletic women into a white feminine ideal. Davis's women epitomized the gender conventions of the pre–Title IX era. Athletic women steered toward conventional roles as cheerleaders or members of dance teams. The lessons of femininity were literally pounded into their bodies. During the late segregation era of the 1950s and '60s, the Rangerettes and the Apache Belles became iconic Texan drill teams. They were pretty. They were athletic. And they were white, very white, for many decades. Even as other drill teams and cheerleading squads were diversifying their lines across the state, Davis remained loyal to her East Texan racial sensibilities. It wouldn't be until 1973 that the Rangerettes allowed a black woman to become part of their famed drill team lines.

If white women weren't athletic enough to survive the rigors of the drill teams of the Rangerettes and the Apache Belles, and if they were deemed "pretty," they could still find a place for themselves in the gender-segregated sports world as cheer-leaders or beauty queens. And once again, SMU's history illus-trates the central role of white femininity in Texan and American football culture. In the 1930s, Betty Bailey wowed fans when she strutted onto the field with Peruna, the team's mascot, and the Mustang band. After SMU beat the UCLA Bruins in the fall of 1935, *Los Angeles Times* sportswriter Bill Henry praised Bailey as "the quick steppin' little blonde" who was the "sweetheart of the band."[20] Bailey eventually married Bobby Wilson, the star quarterback of the 1935 Mustangs team, which went to the Rose Bowl. Years later, Norma Peterson became a celebrity when she appeared on magazine covers in the late 1940s with her boyfriend and future husband, Doak Walker. A decade later, when Don Meredith became an SMU football star, he, too, married college beauty queen Lynne Shamburger. "When Mustang Don Meredith is not using his arm to hurl those fabulous football passes," Ann Draper reported for the *Dallas Morning News* in 1959, "likely it's around the waist of Lynne Shamburger."[21]

The rise of the white football hero and the white beauty queen was a national phenomenon, but these social and cultural dynamics were also products of the unique regional histories of sport throughout the country. Texas had its own brand of white masculine and white feminine ideals. Both were entangled in racial and colonial ideologies of the US South and the American West, regions whose prosperity were embedded in systems of racial and gender subordination. As we'll see, the popular Texan beauty queen was uppermost in the minds of sports television executives decades later when she made football attractive to millions of fans watching at home.

The image of the Texas football hero and the beauty queen "coed" remained popular in subsequent decades and continues to be, even to this day. But as the civil rights and feminist movements were revitalized in the 1960s and '70s, these gender roles would come under scrutiny by a younger generation of women who challenged the rigid norms and hierarchies that were celebrated on the athletic fields of Texas in the 1950s.

Doak Walker and Norma Peterson. Courtesy Heritage Hall and Southern Methodist University Archives, DeGolyer Library, SMU Libraries, Southern Methodist University.

On October 13, 1958, thousands of black Texans congregated in Fair Park in Dallas to participate in Achievement Day (formerly known as Negro Achievement Day) at the Texas State Fair. Ten years after Wally Triplett and Dennie Hoggard breached the color line at the 1948 Cotton Bowl, the state fair remained, like everything else in Texas at the time, racially segregated. But the local Negro Chamber of Commerce had pushed state fair authorities to designate two days for African American programming at the event. By 1958, Achievement Day had a full slate of events: New Farmers and Homemakers Award ceremonies; a beauty contest sponsored by KNOK, a local black radio station; performances by the Prairie View A&M University marching band; and a football doubleheader at the Cotton Bowl. Since at least 1908, local black colleges and high schools had organized football games during the state fair. Local high schools such as Dallas-Lincoln and Booker T. Washington would often play each other, while black college teams from Wiley College and Prairie View A&M would also battle on the gridiron. Even the local white press publicized Achievement Day's football attractions. Using the demeaning language characteristic of the Jim Crow South, the *Dallas Morning News* previewed a 1931 game by noting to readers that the "Negro Eleven" of Booker T. Washington High School "never have defeated the Cowtown darkies" from Fort Worth High.[22] Still, white fans would often show up at the black high school and at college football games in separate sections at the Cotton Bowl even as the local white press tried to dismiss these affairs as little more than "negro gaiety." By the late 1950s, Achievement Day was attracting celebrity black performers, including LaVern Baker, the Buddy Johnson Orchestra, and vocalist Sam Cooke. And yet it was precisely at that moment that a younger generation of black Dallasites questioned the logic of Achievement Day at the fair. In 1955, NAACP activists picketed the fair and demanded access to the fair on any night they chose, rather than only on the designated "Negro day."

Retrospective accounts of segregated activities during the Jim Crow era often portray them as manifestations of black oppression, designed in part to exalt the black and white integrationist heroes of the civil rights era. But one could also view accounts of black sporting events during Jim Crow as exemplifying the importance of sports to African American communities in that period. As sports competitions grew in popularity in black communities throughout the state, educators and coaches saw the need to create an organization that would serve the function of the all-white UIL. Thus, the entity that became known as the Prairie View Interscholastic League (PVIL) was created. The original governing structure was founded by a group of black high school coaches who met in Houston in 1920 to organize black athletic and academic competitions, a black UIL of sorts. They originally called themselves the Texas Interscholastic League of Colored Schools (TILCS), which organized track meets of more than fifteen black high schools from different parts of the state. High school football coaches such as Pat Patterson of Houston's Yates High School helped spearhead further organizational efforts in the late 1930s and early 1940s, receiving institutional support from arguably the most important black college in the state, Prairie View A&M. The league provided an organizational structure for a generation of black students from high schools throughout Texas. Black high schools waged intense competitive competitions all over the Lone Star State, from the "Golden Triangle" region in the Gulf Coast; to larger urban areas like Houston, Austin, and Dallas; to smaller towns like Kilgore, Marshall, Texarkana, Wichita Falls, and Conroe.

The long list of athletic alums of PVIL schools from the Jim Crow era is truly impressive. Black football players from Jim Crow Texas could field multiple all-star teams. "Mean" Joe Greene, Otis Taylor, Dick "Night Train" Layne, Bubba Smith, Ken Houston, Gene Upshaw, and Cliff Branch are just some of the many NFL greats who came out of segregated black schools in Jim Crow Texas.[23] Though, as for the rest of Texas, football was the dominant sport in black Texan sporting culture, African American Texan athletes distinguished themselves in other sports as well. In basketball, David Lattin from Worthing High School in Houston went on to star on Texas Western's 1966 national championship team. James Cash starred on Robert Hughes's successful basketball teams at I. M. Terrell High School in Fort Worth. He, too, was an integration pioneer who became the first black men's basketball player in the Southwest Conference when he suited up for TCU in 1966.

Then there were the talented college track and field athletes who ran in the nationally impactful men's track program at Texas Southern University (TSU). In 1951, TSU hired Stan Wright to teach physical education and coach the school's track team. All Wright did was create one of the most successful college track and field programs in the country, even as he struggled to field teams with the limited resources allocated to black schools. By the late 1950s and early 1960s, the TSU Tigers were setting world records and winning track events across the country, including the Modesto Relays and Coliseum Relays in California, the Drake Relays in Iowa, and the Kansas Relays. Charlie Frazier, Homer Jones, Lester Milburn, Barney Allen, and Ray Saddler were among the school's many record-breaking sprinters. Wright himself went on to receive national and international recognition by coaching US Olympic teams and track teams in other parts of the world.[24]

As in other parts of the Jim Crow South, African Americans "turned segregation into congregation."[25] Black sporting events were community happenings, even if their scheduling had to be subject to the whims of white segregationist authorities. When their high schools couldn't play football on Friday nights, when the white schools played, they played on Thursdays or other nights when fields could be found. In addition to the rivalry football games, events such as the TSU Relays were well-attended affairs that received extensive coverage in the black press. In many of these towns, some of the biggest social events in black communities were the football games between rival high schools, such as the famous "turkey game" battles between Yates and Wheatley High Schools in Houston. While white athletes like Bobby Layne and Doak Walker, and even Babe Didrikson, received accolades from the mainstream white press and opportunities for athletic scholarships in their home state, black athletes performed behind the veil of segregation.[26]

While most black athletes who played college ball had little choice but to attend Prairie View, Wiley, Bishop, or, after 1947, Texas Southern University, others were recruited by predominantly white universities in the Midwest and West with integrated athletic teams. As football programs embarked on more elaborate searches for players, they found untapped reservoirs of talent in Texas. Bubba Smith and Tody Smith, star defensive linemen for Charlton-Pollard High in Beaumont played football at Michigan State and USC respectively. Another pair of talented brothers, Mel and Miller Farr, left Texas to play college football elsewhere. Still, black high school and college athletes received ample coverage in the state's black press. Indeed as in other parts of the country, black sportswriters were the chief advocates—and suppliers of the first drafts of black athletic history—in the Lone Star State.[27] On the sports pages of the black Texan press, one could read about the exploits of a staggering number of talented athletes during the Jim Crow era, many of whom became Hall of Fame athletes in the era when black football players were integrating professional football.

As in white schools, black high school and college sports centered on the pageantry and spectacle of marching bands and cheerleaders. Many schools had robust music instruction. Indeed, many black high schools, such as L. C. Anderson in Austin and I. M. Terrell in Fort Worth, produced scores of talented musicians and performers. From Terrell alone came jazz legends Ornette Coleman, Dewey Redman, and many others. In Austin, Benjamin L. Joyce was a legendary band master at Anderson High from 1933 to 1955, and he led the band to multiple PVIL state championships. Among Anderson's distinguished music alums are jazz great Kenny Dorham and Motown arranger Gil Askey. Football games also centered on black beauty queens, such as Miss Yates, who arrived with her court in a helicopter during halftime of the annual Yates-Wheatley Thanksgiving game in 1958.

Black high schools turned out talented athletes and musicians and exemplary citizens in spite of the obstacles imposed on them by white elite authorities. But African Americans were not the only racially marginalized group in Texas who found opportunities in the realm of sports.

* * *

In a high school gym on the South Side of San Antonio, Texas, the Sydney Lanier High School basketball team pulled off a stunning victory. The Voks, as they were called, short for Vocationals, beat their crosstown rivals, the Brackenridge Eagles, 28–26 to win the district high school basketball championship in dramatic fashion. Lanier's star guard, Tony Cardona, hit the game-winning shot in overtime. But Brackenridge fans could not handle the defeat. Immediately after the game ended, one of them charged the court and hit Cardona on the head, spawning a full-scale riot that spilled outside the gym. A team of Mexican American basketball players had defeated the all-white Eagles. Conceived as a school to educate the Mexican American kids of the barrio to become good workers for Anglo elites, Lanier High produced kids who could accomplish more than being pliant workers for white employers. Lanier's victory illustrated that Mexican Americans could excel at a supposedly American sport and create their own athletic cultures in the barrios of the state. Mexican Americans, indeed, could "play ball."[28] Coaches and school administrators saw sport as a tool of Americanization, but in fact sport was simply another form of transculturation, the making of new cultures from two or more preexisting ones. Texas Mexicans, like all ethnic groups, made supposedly foreign cultural practices their own. Years later, when the San Antonio Spurs were created as a new professional basketball franchise in 1973, the team hired native son Rudy Davalos to be one of the team's assistant coaches. Davalos played at Wharton County Junior College before starring at Southwest Texas State College and leading the Bobcats to the NAIA championship in 1960. Davalos went on to have a long career coaching and serving as athletic director at the University of Houston and the University of New Mexico.[29]

Lanier High's victory in the Brackenridge gymnasium in 1939 shows how sport in South Texas both mirrored and altered the racial landscape of the region. The Texas-Mexico borderlands depended on the exploitation of Mexican labor, social and economic order that was the colonial legacy, and Anglo domination after Texas declared its independence from Mexico. Though legally considered "white" by law, Mexican-origin Texans experienced discrimination in their daily lives. The sentiment "No dogs and no Mexicans allowed" and strict racial segregation determined life in the region. Yet Mexican American young men could carve out spaces for themselves in local high school sports teams. Some could even manage to gain the honor of being high school football coach. In the Rio Grande Valley, Bob Martin coached Mission

High School to the city championship. His star quarterback was Thomas Wade Landry, better known as Tom Landry. Landry was the South Texas borderland boy who remade himself into a Dallas sophisticate, the dapper "man with the funny hat" who was head coach of the Dallas Cowboys for twenty-nine years. Martin, who was half white and half Mexican American but whose "mother's ancestry was evident in his features and his dark complexion" taught the future football genius the game. "For the next four years I was to spend more time with Coach Martin than any other person," Landry recalled years later. "His word would become my law, his approval my inspiration. And football would become my life." And Landry's own biography shows how the fictions of Jim Crow could be enforced and altered. "Prejudice ran deep in South Texas," Landry recalled. Though the railroad tracks separating Mexicans from Anglos was enforced in Mission as in all towns in the Rio Grande Valley, Martin lived two doors down from the Landry family. His hiring as head football coach "undoubtedly caused a lot of talk around town and meant Bob Martin had far more to prove than most young coaches."[30]

A similar dynamic was emerging up the road in El Paso. Bowie High School's football team in El Segundo Barrio was coached by Buryl Baty, a former football star from Paris, Texas, who became Bowie's beloved head coach in 1950. El Segundo was not unlike the West Side of San Antonio, a neighborhood of poor and exploited Mexican American laborers. But Baty was undeterred. The former star quarterback at Texas A&M turned Bowie into a winning team before his tragic death in a car accident in 1954.[31]

Bowie High also attracted another winning coach around this time. William Carson "Nemo" Herrera, the man who coached the Lanier High basketball team, left San Antonio for El Paso in 1945. Herrera was the son of a Mexican father and a Mexican American mother whose class position helped him navigate the perilous terrain of Jim Crow. The upheavals of the Mexican Revolution prompted his family to migrate to Brownsville, Texas. They eventually wound up in San Antonio, where Herrera starred in baseball and basketball. Herrera coached Bowie's baseball and basketball teams to numerous winning seasons during his fifteen years in El Paso. His 1949 baseball team won the state championship even as segregation laws forced them to sleep in cots under the stands of Memorial Stadium in Austin, rather than in one of the local hotels. In the border region, some Mexican Americans could ascend to the "pigskin pulpit," the hallowed position of the high school coach who would be not only a football coach, but also a patriarch, public servant, and community leader. This was a status usually reserved for white men, and a perusal of football coaches in our current time reveals how racially restricted that title remains.[32]

Though the color line set stringent parameters on the sporting cultures of South Texas, the practice of sport chipped away at the structure of white supremacy. The experiences of Texas Mexicans blurred the color line in a manner similar to Latino experiences in other segregated contexts. In the gyms and ballfields of the borderlands, the fictions of white supremacy were established, but they were also altered and challenged.

* * *

On New Year's Day 1964, the University of Texas Longhorns took the field before more than seventy-five thousand fans in the Cotton Bowl Classic in Dallas against the Navy Midshipmen. The game took place only six weeks after the city and the nation were stunned by the assassination of President John F. Kennedy. Kennedy's murder, and the vocal local right-wing political movement that had made loud noises leading up to it, led many to brand Dallas as a "city of hate." Led by their young coach, Darrell Royal, the Longhorns distinguished themselves with an undefeated regular season. Still, on the national stage, they were seen as representatives of the state that had assassinated a beloved president. Their opponents were seen as the nation's team; the Midshipmen were led by their talented Heisman Trophy–winning quarterback and future Dallas Cowboys legend, Roger Staubach. Before the kickoff, both coaches were interviewed on national television.

Navy coach Wayne Hardin issued a challenge by saying, "When the challenger meets the champion and the challenger wins, then there's a new champion." When the cameras turned to Royal, the young coach confidently and stoically told the nation, "We're ready."

The Longhorns were indeed ready for the Midshipmen on that bright and sunny afternoon in Dallas. They raced off to a 28–0 lead after three quarters, and their defense shut down Staubach and the Navy offense. Scott Appleton, David McWilliams, and the sophomore linebacker Tommy Nobis thwarted the Navy attack all afternoon. The star of the game turned out to be Texas's less heralded quarterback Duke Carlisle, who threw two long touchdown passes and scored another. Royal's team convincingly beat Navy 28–6. The game cemented the Longhorns' position as the number-one team in the country and gave Royal the first of three national championships over the next seven seasons.

Royal's Longhorns were ready for the Midshipmen at the 1964 Cotton Bowl Classic, but they were not ready for the decision the university's board of regents made to desegregate all student activities at the school on November 19, 1963, only a few days before the Kennedy assassination. The Supreme Court's 1950 landmark *Sweatt v. Painter* decision compelled the university to desegregate its law school, but the institution had dragged its feet on integrating the rest of the campus, including the athletic program. Though Royal claimed that "any bona fide student who is qualified academically and athletically is welcome to try out for a team," he didn't seem to be in a hurry to recruit prospective black athletes to come to his program. "There are none we are interested in at this time," he stated after the regents gave the go-ahead to integrate.[33]

But this turned out to be the unofficial position of the UT athletic program, especially its football team, for several more seasons, even though a significant portion of the student body and faculty supported integration.[34] Royal could stall integration because he was in the midst of a string of winning seasons for Longhorns football. Though it narrowly lost the Southwest Conference championship to rival Arkansas in 1964, the team scored a dramatic victory over the Alabama Crimson Tide in the 1965 Orange Bowl. Eventually, Royal led the Longhorns to eleven conference titles and three national championships during his twenty years coaching in Austin.

The wildly successful Royal became the university's athletic director in 1963 when he was, unbelievably, also given a tenured professorship at the same time. Royal arguably had more job security than any successful college coach today. By the late 1960s, it was clear that Royal's intransigence on the question of integration ensured that Texas would follow the lead of other schools. Not unlike Major League Baseball's New York Yankees, who were able to postpone the inclusion of black players because they kept winning as an all-white outfit, the Longhorns remained at the top of the SWC. Royal's 1969 Longhorns, filled with white players from rural Texas, turned out to be the last all-white team to win an NCAA football national championship. Royal remained ready for his all-white SWC foes, but he wasn't ready for the coming social and sports revolution that would transform the state and the country.

While Royal made the Longhorns a regional and national power, the Arkansas Razorbacks were also surging to the top of the Southwest Conference. Arkansas's football program had a very similar trajectory under head coach Frank Broyles. Born in Decatur, Georgia, in 1924, Broyles became a star athlete in basketball and football at Georgia Tech, where he met his mentor, coach Bobby Dodd. Broyles eventually embarked on his own coaching career when he served as an assistant to Dodd. After one season as head coach at Missouri, he was hired away by the University of Arkansas in 1958. Broyles was Royal's main rival in the Southwest Conference, and he, too, made his team a national power by winning multiple conference titles and a national championship in 1964. Though, like Royal, he had coached black scholarship players before his arrival to the SWC, in Fayetteville

Broyles was also reluctant to integrate his football program. Like the Longhorns, the Razorbacks were among the last teams to integrate their athletic programs in the South.

Broyles and Royal were Southern gentlemen who were granted an enormous amount of power and prestige as their programs churned out winning seasons throughout the 1960s. They played the role of leaders of men because of their success on the field, but they were reluctant to demonstrate leadership on the question of segregation, even as some of their coaching peers did. Their programs represented the persistence of Jim Crow athletics as the world around them was changing rapidly.[35]

* * *

Heman Sweatt wanted to go to law school. But there were no places in Texas for aspiring African American lawyers in the 1940s to study. As part of the NAACP's national campaign to challenge *Plessy v. Ferguson*'s legal doctrine of "separate but equal," the civil rights group convinced Sweatt to sue the University of Texas Law School in 1946. What became known as the historic *Sweatt v. Painter* case was eventually ruled in his favor four years later, setting the stage for the protracted process of desegregation at the state's flagship institution. A few years later in El Paso, Thelma White was also eager to challenge the state's system of segregated higher education. Though she had been the Douglass High School valedictorian, she was not permitted to enroll at Texas Western College, the local campus of the University of Texas system. In 1955, she filed a lawsuit against the university. She ultimately decided to attend New Mexico A&M, but her suit was another trigger for the University of Texas system to begin its process of desegregation. These cases, along with the landmark 1954 *Brown v. Board of Education* Supreme Court ruling, signaled that a new day was arriving in Texas and in the broader segregated South. The rulings also would have major consequences for high school and intercollegiate athletics in the state. Soon after White's lawsuit, Texas Western began to integrate its athletic program; Tyler native Charlie Brown enrolled at the school in 1956. Ten years later, Texas Western shocked the college basketball world by beating Adolph Rupp's all-white Kentucky Wildcats with an all-black starting lineup in the 1966 NCAA college basketball championships.

Meanwhile, another sign of change was occurring in Denton when North Texas State (now the University of North Texas) was forced to desegregate its undergraduate program. In 1955, Joe Atkins, a protégé of Dallas NAACP leader Juanita Craft, sued the school for admission and won his case. The next year, the school's football team allowed Abner Haynes and Leon King, two black students from Dallas, to try out for the football team. When they walked onto the practice field for the first time, some white team leaders shook their hands and welcomed them to the team.[36] Haynes went on to star for the North Texas State Eagles, and he eventually had a successful pro career for the Dallas Texans of Lamar Hunt's newly formed American Football League. A new day was arriving in Texas, and a group of wealthy sports enthusiasts, and some college coaches, administrators, and entrepreneurs like Lamar Hunt, knew it.

CHAPTER 2

Spaceships Land in the Texas Prairie

O N DECEMBER 8, 1960, A SOUTHWEST AIRLINES DC-7 WITH SIXTY-EIGHT "NEWS-paper, radio, and television men as well as public officials, prominent citizens and assorted other gentlemen" from Houston, Texas, landed at the Los Angeles International Airport.[1] Organized by the Houston Sports Association (HSA), the group, which was recently awarded a Major League Baseball (MLB) franchise, arrived on a mission to see some of the newest sports facilities in the United States. They embarked on a whirlwind three-day trip to Los Angeles and San Francisco, where MLB teams the Dodgers and the Giants had recently relocated from their previous homes in New York City for the newly emerging West Coast market. They called it the Rain or Shine tour to promote their idea of an indoor stadium that would enable their team to play games regardless of the weather conditions.

For the next few days, the prominent Houstonians visited stadiums in both cities. They started in Los Angeles, where they studied the pros and cons of the immense Los Angeles Coliseum, the iconic sports stadium that had accomplished what the Houstonians wanted to do: put their city on the map. The Coliseum had served as home to the 1932 Olympics, college and pro football, and the recently arrived Los Angeles Dodgers, who were playing there temporarily while they awaited completion of their new stadium. The visitors then stopped in next door at the brand-new

Sports Arena, the site of a recent Democratic National Convention and the new home of the recently arrived Los Angeles Lakers NBA franchise. They were awestruck by the site of their next stop, the then in-progress Dodger Stadium in Chavez Ravine. The massive engineering project was moving mountains, not to mention the homes of former residents, to build a new stadium on the remains of the recently displaced Mexican American community. They hobnobbed with Hollywood "starlets" who supposedly couldn't keep their hands off the rich gentlemen from Texas.

During their time in San Francisco, they were less impressed by the cold and windy Candlestick Park, the new stadium of the Giants, though they found their visit to Horace Stoneham's blunder of a ballpark instructive. Throughout the trip, Roy Hofheinz, the charismatic former Houston mayor and Harris County judge, used his rhetorical skills to promote the new state-of-the-art domed stadium the HSA was promising to build in Houston. At the end of the expedition, these investors in the new sports enterprise were giddy with excitement. Houston, Texas, was now "major league," and their trip to California announced the city's arrival on the national professional sporting stage.

As the nation's population migrated westward and southward in the decades after World War II, professional sports leagues moved along with them. California was at the center of this new sporting frontier, where national pro sports enterprises sought to intrude upon smaller-scale regional leagues. It was the then-fledgling National Football League that pioneered pro sports' westward expansion when the Rams franchise moved from Cleveland to Los Angeles. The rival All-American Football Conference also created a pro football franchise out west with the San Francisco 49ers. A decade later, Major League Baseball, the most popular pro sports league in the nation, followed suit when the Dodgers and Giants broke the hearts of their fans in Brooklyn and Manhattan to leave for promised riches on the West Coast. Sports franchises were moving to the West Coast, and now a new ambitious group of civic boosters and entrepreneurs wanted to bring them to Texas.

At the center of the movement for professional sports in the Lone Star State were the sons of oil barons who sought to convert their passion for sports into profitable businesses. As was the case in the 1930s, when Dallas boosters modeled their Cotton Bowl Classic after the Rose Bowl, in the 1960s Texas sportsmen drew upon, then sought to top, their West Coast brethren to make Texas an attractive region for professional sports teams. "America had never seen rich people like the Texas oilmen who seemingly came out of nowhere after World War II," John Eisenberg writes in *Ten Gallon War*. "Sid Richardson, Hunt, and Murchison were not Harvard men who bartered equities and lorded over boardrooms. They were chicken fried gamblers who had played a desperate zero-sum game, borrowing money they could not pay back to back, speculatively drilling operations, and when their wells spurted thick crude, they suddenly had fortunes matching those of Europe's grandest royal families."[2] And it was the sons of these oilmen who transformed the sporting culture of Texas and the country.

The names of these pioneers are well known in sport history. In Houston, Bob Smith and Craig Cullinan provided the financial backing for the tireless boosterism of Roy Hofheinz to bring MLB to their city. At the same time, Houston oilman Bud Adams partnered with Dallas's Lamar Hunt, son of oil baron H. L. Hunt, to create the American Football League. The AFL successfully challenged the establishment National Football League and eventually forced a merger between the two leagues. And finally, there was Clint Murchison Jr., another son of an oil baron who was awarded the Dallas NFL franchise, known as the Cowboys, the team that revolutionized sports management and became known as "America's Team." Other sports entrepreneurs would follow in the 1970s and '80s, but it was these members of the oil elite who championed the arrival of pro sports in Texas.

But Texas sports entrepreneurs of the 1960s did more than bring pro sports to the Southwest. They changed American sports spectating by refashioning the ubiquitous institution of the stadium from a small, functional venue to a massive, comfortable leisure space that resembled a large living room. The Rain or Shine West Coast junket reveals what they had on their minds. Attending cocktail parties and socializing with fellow elites, politicians, and celebrities, with sexualized women in arm, exuded masculine power. What the Texas sports entrepreneur figured out was how to have the cocktail party with the business partners, the clients, and the sexy ladies at the ballpark itself. It is not by accident that the first three stadiums constructed with the now-ubiquitous luxury boxes in the late 1960s and early 1970s were conceived by Texas-based professional franchise owners. The parties at the Los Angeles Coconut Grove in 1960 were to be replayed in the ballpark of tomorrow. The Texas sports entrepreneurs were determined to make their cities "big league," and they aimed to not simply join the small cartel of sports owners, but also transform the ways sports was consumed by the public. The results of these efforts were two of the most influential stadiums of post–World War II America: the Astrodome, which opened in 1965, and Texas Stadium, which was unveiled in 1971.

Making Texas big league was not an easy undertaking, even for these affluent men. Indeed, the Texas sports boosters of the 1960s had many challenges to face. They had to crack the monopolies of Major League Baseball and the National Football League. The obstacles in Texas were even more daunting. They had to loosen the hold that high school and college sports had on the Texas public. They also had to navigate the complicated terrain of Jim Crow segregation, which was an increasingly difficult task in the 1950s and '60s, when the civil rights movement was making legal gains against segregation. In other parts of the South, white segregationists were digging in by resisting desegregation at every turn, including in the sporting realm. In Louisiana, for example, segregationist politicians crafted legislation that explicitly sought to prevent the racial integration of sports facilities. Pro-segregationist forces were also strong in Texas, but an unmistakable calculation had to be made if they wanted to use sports to put their cities on the map. In order to combine their business acumen with their passion for sports, they could not simply acquiesce to the state's traditions of racial exclusion. A new social order was on the horizon, and pro sports expedited its arrival.

* * *

After the discovery of oil in the southeast Texas triangle in the early twentieth century, and the building of the ship channel in 1914, Houston became a hub in the regional Gulf Coast economy. But Houston, like the rest of the US South and much of the circum-Caribbean/Gulf region, was a former slave society that passed into a system of Jim Crow segregation. Local racial understandings were shaped not only by Anglo segregationist policies but also by the particular racial understandings of the transcultural black and Mexican American populations. Still, racial segregation in schooling and public spaces, which began after Reconstruction, became firmly established in law and custom by the 1920s.[3]

In the decades following World War II, local elites turned Houston from an oil and cattle town to a booming metropolis with new industries such as aerospace and sports. In this period, Houston played a catalyzing role in the making of the Sunbelt.[4] In 1940, the population of the City of Houston was 384,514. By 1960, the city's population grew to 938,219 and continued to increase in decades thereafter. Along with the growth of the energy economy and the advent of the space industry, the expansion of professional and collegiate sports played a significant role in this transformation. The professionalization and expansion of sports promoted the growth of the new cities in the region while also providing the prospect of jobs and avenues for upward mobility for a small and growing athletic labor force. An elite group of civic-minded boosters of oilmen and other businessmen, politicians, and sports enthusiasts led the way, touting sports and stadium construction to put their cities on the map. This meant refashioning the Bayou City from one defined by Jim Crow segregation to an urban environment that bidders for pro football's Super Bowl described as "epitomiz[ing] the growing urbanization and sophistication of the progressive Southwest."[5]

Meanwhile Dallas's political economy was also profoundly shaped by the oil industry, but it was more varied than that of the petroleum-dominated Houston. Since its beginnings, Dallas had been a regional transportation hub. Over time, it became a city based on finance and insurance, and it played a key role in the East Texas cotton industry. The Dallas Cotton Exchange financed the industry, which was predicated on the exploitation of the labor of former slaves and poor whites. Oil money flowed in a big way beginning in the 1930s. After World War II, Texas Instruments and other technology companies made the city a proto-Silicon Valley. The worlds created by the Murchisons and the Hunts manifested in opulent mansions in the Dallas area. And both Clint Murchison Sr. and H. L. Hunt were rabid right-wingers who actively sought to dismantle the New Deal coalition of southern whites and northern liberals that had carried the Democratic Party to national dominance. Ironically, their sons presided over institutions that helped integrate social life in Dallas.

The Lamar Hunts, the Bud Adamses, the Clint Murchisons, and the men of the Houston Sports Association thirsted for professional sports in Texas. They had to hoist themselves onto leagues that were not interested in franchise expansion. Indeed, neither MLB nor the NFL were looking to expand into Texas. Still, in the late 1950s, the understated Hunt, who had little of the charisma of his flamboyant father, inquired about buying a football franchise. He set his sights on the Chicago Cardinals franchise, but the team's owners refused to sell. After his subsequent efforts were ignored by the league, he learned about other entrepreneurs who desired to own a football team. He then decided to convince these businessmen to form a rival football league. The first person he approached was Bud Adams, the son of K. S. "Boots" Adams, who was president of the famed Phillips Petroleum Company. In March 1959, Hunt called Adams out of the blue and asked if they could meet in Houston. They had dinner at the Charcoal Inn, a steakhouse owned by Adams, and after some small talk, Hunt asked Adams if he had tried to buy the Cardinals. The startled Adams admitted he had, and Hunt then asked Adams if he had any interest in owning a team in a new football league he wanted to start. Adams replied, "Hell yeah!"[6] Hunt, Adams, and six other owners formed the AFL, which began play in 1960. Hunt's team was the Dallas Texans, and Adams owned the Houston Oilers.

As Hunt and Adams were forming the new league, Clint Murchison Jr. was awarded an NFL franchise in Dallas. Murchison, too, had been lobbying the NFL for a team in Texas, and he, too, was rebuffed by the closed circle of league owners. But after Hunt created some competition with the AFL, the NFL had a change of heart. A few months after Hunt announced the creation of the AFL, George "Papa Bear" Halas, the highly influential owner of the Chicago Bears, convinced his fellow owners to award a team to Murchison in Dallas and one to Max Winter in Minnesota; the latter was picked off from the AFL's original ownership group. Halas even helped Murchison find Texas Earnest "Tex" Schramm to run his new franchise, called the Dallas Cowboys. A native Southern Californian who became a transplanted Texan after he studied at the University of Texas, Schramm was a truly innovative football man. Indeed, he arguably created the category of the football executive. His experience in the front office of the Los Angeles Rams during the 1950s was decisive, as was his time working for CBS Sports soon thereafter. One of his first acts as president of the Cowboys was to hire Tom Landry, then an assistant coach for the New York Giants, to be the team's head coach. The Murchison-Schramm-Landry partnership would go on to run the Cowboys for the next twenty-five years.

Over the next three years, Hunt's Texans and Murchison's Cowboys embarked on a three-year struggle for survival in Dallas. Indeed, the entire AFL was fighting to stay afloat in its fight to crack the National Football League's monopoly over professional football. Meanwhile, Adams's Houston Oilers quickly became the best team of the upstart league by winning two consecutive league championships in 1960 and 1961. The Oilers made the AFL cham-

Three influential figures in the history of professional football: Lamar Hunt, Don Meredith, and Tex Schramm. Courtesy Heritage Hall and Southern Methodist University Archives, DeGolyer Library, SMU Libraries, Southern Methodist University.

pionship game again in 1962, but they lost to Hunt's Texans 20–17 in a dramatic overtime game. Despite winning the league championship, three years of hemorrhaging money convinced Hunt that the Texans were fighting a losing battle against Murchison's Cowboys. After three seasons of struggling for the attentions of the seemingly indifferent Dallas fanbase, Hunt decided to accept a sweetheart deal to move his team to Kansas City, Missouri. The franchise was renamed the Kansas City Chiefs. It was a wise decision. The Chiefs became one of the best teams in the AFL, and the league became a force for change when it successfully challenged the NFL's monopoly on professional football, eventually forcing a merger with the establishment league in 1966. And it was Hunt and Schramm—two football executives from Texas—

who forged the deal with NFL commissioner Pete Rozelle that changed American sports history.

But more changes were unfolding in the 1960s, and they took place not in secret meetings in the country clubs or hotel suites in Dallas, but in the neighborhoods of the Third Ward in Houston.

* * *

In the fall of 1961, African Americans in Houston were in an uproar. Spurred by the sit-in movements spearheaded by the young black students of Greensboro, North Carolina, and other parts of the South, black Houstonians created their own local direct-action protest movement against racial segregation and discrimination. Eldrewey Stearns brilliantly led an organized sit-in movement of Texas Southern University students that targeted store lunch counters at Weingarten's and other department store chains and downtown eateries. Though Stearns and other activists initially endured violent responses from white reactionaries, a number of key politicians and business leaders eventually succumbed to the demands of the courageous students, though they convinced the local white press to not publicize this historic accommodation. Desegregation in Houston was now underway, but the struggle against discrimination would continue.[7]

While TSU student activists targeted lunch counters and cafeterias, local sportswriters and other black activists zeroed in on sports venues and teams as sites of struggle against segregation. Black Houstonians played a major role in the city's sporting culture both on and off the fields of play. African Americans were a substantial numerical minority throughout the city's history, comprising one-quarter to one-third of the city's population throughout the post–World War II era. In the segregated high school scene, people of African descent created their own vibrant sporting and recreational cultures. Local black newspapers such as the Houston *Informer* and the *Forward Times* devoted substantial coverage to the city's high school sports teams, particularly their football, basketball, and track programs. As other schools through the state did, black schools in Houston cultivated a wealth of athletic talent. The annual Thanksgiving "turkey game" between Yates and Wheatley High Schools was reaching the height of its popularity in the late 1950s and early 1960s.[8] At the same time, TSU featured local black talent on all of its sports teams, especially on its nationally ranked track team, coached by the legendary Stan Wright.[9] In short, even in the under-resourced and discriminatory circumstances of Jim Crow, the local black sporting scene was thriving when Houston boosters were launching their drive to bring professional sports to the city.

In 1954, Bob Boyd became the first black player to play for the Houston Buffs, the local minor league baseball team that preceded the city's MLB franchise. However, racial segregation remained the custom in sports facilities, and black athletes remained excluded from local white teams into the early 1960s. One of the main sites of struggle in the city was Jeppesen Stadium, a public high school facility managed by the Houston Independent School District, which segregated fans along racial lines. In the summer of 1961, Texas Southern University's talented track team boycotted the Meet of Champions held by the University of Houston at the stadium due to the stadium's policy of racial segregation.

The Meet of Champions boycott generated attention, but the main target of black activists was Bud Adams's Houston Oilers. Soon after the Oilers franchise was created in 1960, black newspapers—the *Houston Informer* and even the more moderate *Houston Forward Times*—repeatedly chastised Adams for the miniscule number of black players on the team's roster and for refusing to desegregate seating at Oilers home games at Jeppesen. During games at Jeppesen, black fans were relegated to end zone seating, usually the least attractive sections in a football stadium, during games when whites were present. After a home game against the Oakland Raiders in September 1960, the *Houston Forward Times* chastised Adams for his "grand scale deceit" of relegating black fans to the segregated section of the stadium after he promised equal access to the facility. Black columnist Bud

Johnson called on black fans to give the Oilers a "thumbs down," as it was "apparent that the Houston Oilers front office does not consider the Negro fan essential to the success of the team."[10]

Protests continued the following football season as activists from a local chapter of the National Association for the Advancement of Colored People (NAACP) joined a broader national campaign to combat discrimination and segregation in sports. They targeted the Oilers' first home game of the 1961 campaign, against the Oakland Raiders. Their tactic was to picket the game outside Jeppesen Stadium and try to get fans to stay away, and also for players to boycott the game. They wrote all teams asking for their cooperation in the boycott. Outside the stadium, they chanted, "Houston Oilers, champions of the UnAmerican Football League" and "Segregation is a non-profit issue; the Oilers are too," among other slogans.[11]

The boycott continued throughout the season, though it was unable to get opposing teams to boycott Oilers games. Lloyd C. A. Wells, a flamboyant local black sportswriter, was particularly strident in his criticism of black players who crossed the NAACP picket in December 1961. Wells, who was also a photographer, published photos in the *Informer* of black players who crossed the picket line and black fans at Oilers games.[12] Wells tried to appeal to the manhood of black players to get them to respect the picket line. He pulled no punches in his sharp criticism of the black players on the Chargers. "Negroes here still argue that it is not segregation at Jeppesen Stadium and hate me for trying to get them to be men, and act like people with dignity and princip[le]," he wrote that season. "Segregation is wrong, regardless of who supports or condones it."[13] Years later, Ernie Ladd, the large three-hundred-pound defensive lineman for the Chargers and native of nearby Orange, Texas, who crossed the picket line, recalled the much smaller Wells yelling at him: "'You have no nuts. You Chargers have no nuts. Big Ernie Ladd, I see you,'" the lineman recalled Wells yelling at him and his fellow players for refusing to honor the NAACP picket.[14] In subsequent years, Wells continued to blast the Oilers in the black press, and he got a measure of revenge by becoming a scout for Lamar Hunt's Kansas City Chiefs and funneling many talented black football players from the region to the team.

Bud Adams refused to act decisively on the question of segregation, but the leaders of the Houston Sports Association did. They clearly heard the concerns of black Houstonians and decided that they needed black support to move their campaign for a professional baseball team forward. Black sports writers were quick to contrast Adams's indifference to black protest with the friendlier policies of the HSA. A few weeks after the NAACP boycott, George Kirksey, a leading member of the HSA, assured the black press that the team, called the Colt 45s, "would be Houston's team without any regard to racial preferences."[15]

The catalyst for this cultural and social transformation was the HSA's campaign to build the world's first indoor stadium. Again, the Houston Sports Association, Hofheinz in particular, played a key role. After the MLB franchise was granted to the HSA, the booster group focused their attention on building the stadium. They used what would become a standard technique of lobbying taxpayers to publicly finance the new stadium. The HSA sought to convince Houston citizens to commit $24 million in taxes to finance the construction of the Astrodome. Throughout 1961, they waged a massive campaign to secure votes for the new stadium. It was at this moment when black Houstonian activists saw an opportunity to expand upon the steady gains that were being made by the local sit-in movement.

Quentin Mease, the director of the South Central YMCA, became a key player in the campaign against discrimination in Houston. Mease was convinced that sports could play "an important role in the grand design for increasing racial understanding in Houston."[16] While Wells used the press to publicly shame those who did not stand up to segregation, Mease employed more low-key tactics by using his connections to moderate white Houstonians, particularly Hofheinz and R. E. "Bob" Smith. Neither Hofheinz nor Smith were segregationists, both men having worked for racial integration in city politics and in philanthropic affairs.

Indeed, Hofheinz had long courted support from black Houstonians. During his tenure as Houston mayor, Hofheinz appointed black Houstonians to municipal boards and committees, channeled resources into public works in black communities, and even banned the usage of "white" and "colored" signs in public facilities in City Hall.[17]

When Mease was approached by Hofheinz to secure support from black Houstonians for the Astrodome bond vote in 1961, the YMCA director skillfully used the Dome campaign to his advantage. Mease agreed to support the measure on the condition that the new stadium would be desegregated in the stands, on the field, and in hiring practices. Hofheinz consented, and his alliance with Mease, and other black leaders and activists including sit-in leader Eldrewey Stearns, accelerated the end of racial segregation in the Houston sports scene. As Stearns recalled to the historian Thomas Cole:

> I saw in the Dome Stadium that it would bring about integration. . . . We had jeeps to go out in the white community. . . . It would be a black driver and white announcer announcing, "Come vote. Don't fail to support the greatest wonder in the world, the Dome Stadium!" Out in the black neighborhoods, the white boy would be driving and a Negro doing the talking on the loudspeaker, and this is something they hadn't seen, so that got their attention. . . . We won the thing.[18]

While Bud Adams remained unresponsive to demands for equal access to Oilers games and did little to cultivate and sign the abundant black athletic talent right in his home city, Hofheinz and the HSA convinced black Houstonian sports fans that the new baseball franchise would welcome black fans and black players, and it did. Hofheinz and the HSA also understood that they could not welcome integrated National League ball clubs to Houston and house them in segregated hotels. The era of the gentlemen's agreement was coming to an end. Hofheinz's HSA saw the changes in the wind and realized that their team and

A. E. Warner, James F. Brooks, and Quentin Mease, at right in front row, at the Astrodome groundbreaking on January 3, 1962. Courtesy Special Collections Division of the M. D. Anderson Library, University of Houston.

their home field could not be successful without talented African American athletes and fans. Soon thereafter, the local black press championed the coming of the Astros and the building of the Astrodome.[19]

The optics at the groundbreaking on January 3, 1962, were indicative of the inclusive spirit of the Dome project. While most photos remembered from the event were of local white male politicians of Harris County, the photo above, buried in Quentin Mease's papers illustrates that Dome boosters invited black men to participate in the ceremony by posing with their own six-shooters.

Driven by the tireless efforts and political connections and savvy of Hofheinz, the campaign successfully secured $31 million in tax-supported bonds to finance the construction of the

Dome. Relying on public money to fund stadiums was not unusual at this time, for the 1960s was the era of massive publicly financed stadiums. Yet, skyrocketing costs and the undeniable exclusivity of stadiums in recent decades should not lead us to forget the role of stadiums like the Astrodome in urban civic and cultural life. Years later, Mease remained convinced of the merits of his strategy of activism around sports: "The bargain to trade black support of the Astrodome for a desegregated facility paid off. Sports were bringing people together, and all of this promoted better understandings. These were not isolated incidents, either; they meshed into the total fabric of how we were effecting change throughout the city."[20]

* * *

The Astrodome took three years to build while the new team played in Colt Stadium, the hot and mosquito-infested facility that was the temporary home of the Colt 45s. On opening night on April 9, 1965, the Houston ballclub, now redubbed as the Astros to fit with the team's new futuristic identity, took the field in an exhibition game against the New York Yankees, MLB's winningest team, which had won more championships than any other franchise. The Dome received the blessing of Lyndon and Lady Bird Johnson, who were sitting in Roy Hofheinz's suite. Yankee star Mickey Mantle delighted the crowd by hitting the first home run in the stadium's history. The Astros eventually won the game 2–1 in extra innings. The Astros victory would be one of the few newsworthy items produced by Houston's new major league franchise. Throughout the next several years, the Astros would be overshadowed by their new home field, which captivated the nation's imagination.

Although it offended baseball purists who were appalled by the notion of indoor baseball, in general the Astrodome was a hit from the minute its doors opened in April 1965. There was simply nothing like it. Buoyed by the over-the-top promotion efforts of Hofheinz, who combined P. T. Barnumesque kitsch with projections

Inside the Astrodome, when it had grass, 1965. Otto Bettmann Archive, Getty Images.

of space-age futurity, the Dome turned out to be a trendsetter in stadium construction, for better and for worse. From the outside, the Dome looked like a giant spaceship that had landed in the middle of a Texas prairie. But the ballpark's true innovations were evident the minute fans escaped the notorious Houston heat and humidity and walked into the nearly perfect air-conditioned confines of the arena. In addition to being the first indoor stadium in the country, it contained a host of other engineering and architectural innovations, including a steel-supported lamella roof featuring Lucite skylights that were designed to emit sunlight, which would enable the grass on the field to grow; five colorful tiers of theater-style upholstered seats; and movable lower stands that allowed the field to be converted from baseball to football in a few hours. It also pioneered what would become standard stadium amenities for fans and players, including state-of-the-art locker rooms, press boxes, cafeterias, and a two-million-dollar scoreboard, which loudly orchestrated cheers from fans. The scoreboard's most noteworthy feature was its "home run spectacular," which delighted fans and annoyed pitchers from opposing teams, who had to endure a long scoreboard show after giving up a home run. The scoreboard projected across the gigantic screen images of a baseball bursting through the roof of the Dome, followed by two cowboys kicking their heels and firing their six-shooters. Then two steer would snort and have American and Texan flags emerge from their ears. The gimmickry projected Texas's rural roots into the urban, space-age indoor environment.[21]

Perhaps the ballpark's greatest innovation, one that would be a part of nearly every major league stadium built after the Astrodome, were its skyboxes, a top tier of luxury suites for Houston's VIP crowd. The Dome was the first stadium to implement such a concept. The story goes that as the stadium was being constructed, Hofheinz saw empty space above the upper rim of the stadium. He decided to add more seating and change the area from the worst seat in the house into the best. The Dome contained fifty-three suites; each had a theme and was garishly designed in ways that would offend twenty-first-century designers. There was the wood-paneled Captain's Cabin suite, the Spanish Provano suite, and the Presidential Suite. If suite holders were looking for a more exotic look, they could rent the Imperial Orient suite or the Red Dragon suite, among others. Each box spilled into mini-apartments that contained a private bathroom, refrigerator, wet bar, and closed-circuit television monitor. The suites became places to see and be seen. The ballpark was turned into the place where business deals between oilmen and other businessmen could be hatched over drinks with the roar of the crowd in the background. Even if one quibbled with Hofheinz's design taste, the luxury boxes totally revolutionized sports spectating from one in which patrons sat outdoors on a bench or in an uncomfortable chairback seat to an enclosed private space akin a living room.

In addition to the skybox, the Dome's other lasting contribution to stadiums in America was the accidental role it played in the creation of Astroturf, a green-colored carpet of synthetic grass manufactured by the now-infamous Monsanto Chemical Company. When the Astros first started to practice in the Dome, they were horrified to discover that they could not see fly balls during the daytime hours because of the glare created by the Lucite-paneled roof. When Dome officials painted the roof to address the glare issue, they created another problem: the lack of sunlight caused the grass to die. Suddenly, the Astrodome's highly touted ecosystem had failed and the so-called Eighth Wonder of the World was looking like a colossal embarrassment. Groundskeepers used green paint and whatever else they could to make the field playable. But the enterprising Hofheinz had another answer. He contacted Chemstrand, a subsidiary of Monsanto, to produce gigantic strips of artificial grass to cover the field. Initially known as ChemGrass, the surface was brilliantly rebranded by Hofheinz as Astroturf. Within a few years, nearly all new stadiums would feature the plastic grass, which Chemstrand promised would reduce the cost of field maintenance and help prevent player injuries. Of course, this all turned out to be false. The turf's brutally hard and unforgiving texture exacerbated player injuries and was almost universally despised by players.

The adoption of Astroturf seemed to reinforce the Dome's pretentions of the power of technology to conquer nature. HSA boosters had told their colleagues in California and the rest of the country that baseball could in fact be played rain or shine, and they were right. The implementation of artificial turf enhanced the stadium's status as a monument to the region's oil and gas elite, as many of its features were due to the scientific products produced by the DuPont Company and other petrochemical companies in the region. Indeed, Gulf Oil (and years later Texaco) paid for the rights to advertise their companies with illuminated signs on each side of the gigantic scoreboard.

The Astrodome even created the phenomenon of ballpark tourism, which is now a standard practice of stadium managers eager to generate revenues to pay off the astronomical cost of their construction. By the late 1960s, the Dome became the third most visited tourist site in the country, attracting visitors from around the world. Visitors could come and be awestruck at the sight of the structure while tour guides recited all of the facts and figures from the HSA's hyperbolic script:

> You are now sitting in the largest room in the world. The distance from the field to the top of the Dome is 208 feet, the clear span of the stadium is 642 feet. We have another way of saying this. We can place the 18-story Shamrock Hilton Hotel in the center of the field and it will not touch the top. . . . Our seating capacity depends on the event here. We seat 49,000 for baseball, 52,000 for football, 60,000 for speaking engagements, and 66,000 for a boxing match.[22]

As the tour guides told visitors, the Dome was intentionally designed to be a multipurpose venue, a building that could be an athletic venue, a cathedral, and a convention center all rolled into one. Soon sports team owners and other sectors of the sports industry sought to book the Astrodome for their events. In addition to the Astros and the Oilers, the two main tenants of the Dome, the stadium also housed the Houston Livestock and Rodeo Show, which held its annual event every year in Houston. Geoff Winningham's forgotten 1975 documentary *The Pleasures of This Stately Dome* beautifully illustrates the many kinds of events that were held in the iconic stadium: Evel Knievel stunt jumps, soccer matches, conventions, political rallies, black college football games, musical concerts, and even bullfighting.[23]

The Dome was very much a product of the vision of Hofheinz, who was the sports booster par excellence. He dubbed his space-age creation the Eighth Wonder of the World, and he was into his ballpark more than anything else, a fact that undoubtedly led him to alienate many of his associates in the Houston Sports Association. He outsmarted and outmuscled virtually all of his partners in the HSA, including those who were instrumental in bringing Major League Baseball to Houston, such as Craig Cullinan, George Kirksey, and even Bob Smith. However, the Judge, as he was affectionately called, wasn't terribly interested in running his

Roy Hofheinz looking out to the field from his apartment in the Astrodome.
Photo by Mark Kauffman.

baseball franchise. Indeed, the Astros floundered in mediocrity most of its first seventeen seasons despite having a number of talented ballplayers before the club finally started to become exciting and competitive in the late 1970s. Nevertheless, Hofheinz was one of the most remarkable sports promoters in American history. Once he was brought into the HSA fold, he promoted his stadium project everywhere. The Judge lugged his miniature model of the Dome around, talking to everyone and anyone about all of its revolutionary characteristics while puffing on his cigar, securing votes for the bond initiatives to finance the costly project, and entertaining guests at his suite and apartment at the Dome.

Though the Astrodome was truly a revolutionary development in stadium design, it was, in many ways, a transitional structure in the history of stadium construction. It took stadium construction into the realm of suburban luxury and comfort while maintaining some of the hard-edge proletarian ethos of the urban stadium that preceded it. It was, as the historian Ben Lisle has written, "a site of both equality and distinction."[24] It was a place where working-class fans, the primary constituency of MLB, could not only attend games in the Eighth Wonder of the World but also enjoy the comforts of sitting in cushioned nylon upholstered seats. "This is EVERY MAN'S STADIUM," sportswriter Gary Cartwright was quoted saying in the *Inside the Astrodome* souvenir program, "from the cushioned center field section at $1.50 to the upper rim of blue suites which can be grabbed for $18,000 a year."[25] Though the Astrodome has been credited for bringing the affluent class to the ol' ball game, it also brought out the region's laboring majority across the racial spectrum. Mickey Herskowitz, a legendary Houston sportswriter, recalled former Astro Bo Belinsky telling him that while he was always struck by fans dressed in evening wear, "always in the box seats there'd be some farmer from Diboll or something with manure on his boots hanging over the box seat railing."[26] Evening furs, high heels, and business suits coexisted with manure-covered cowboy boots at the Astrodome.

The Dome assimilated the multipurpose paradigm of the 1960s and '70s, where stadiums were built for baseball, football, and other sports. From a design standpoint, the Dome's movable box seats resembled New York's Shea Stadium, which opened one year before the Astrodome. The multiple tiers of colored seats also drew from similar color configurations of Shea and Walter O'Malley's Dodger Stadium. The multipurpose so-called cookie cutter ballparks of the era, such as Busch Stadium in St. Louis, Riverfront Stadium in Cincinnati, Three Rivers Stadium in Pittsburgh, and Veterans Stadium in Philadelphia, would be criticized for their imperfect sight lines and ugly modernist aesthetics, and the Astrodome shared some of these characteristics. Many baseball fans today prefer the charm of the "retro ballparks," such as Oriole Park at Camden Yards in Baltimore and countless other ballparks that have been built since the 1990s. But many forget that the Astrodome, like many of the stadiums built in the 1960s and '70s, was largely accessible to the general public even as it was managed as a commercial operation. A key component of stadi-

Vintage multipurpose stadium: the football gridiron superimposed on the baseball diamond. Photo by Focus on Sport.

ums, perhaps their essential component, is their affordability to spectators. As Daniel Rosensweig notes, the "multi-purpose" "suburban" ballpark of the '60s and '70s was more inclusive than the stadiums built in downtown areas since the 1990s. "Cheap tickets, wide public concourses, and a lack of segregated seating enabled an unprecedented degree of fan diversity and mixing," he writes.[27] The stadiums of the era certainly reflected emerging suburban values in that they were "clean, comfortable, consumer-oriented, automobile-convenient, and family friendly."[28] Yet the Dome, like all multipurpose stadiums of the '60s and '70s, was used for various purposes, which drew different kinds of crowds to the ballpark. Hofheinz's tireless promotional efforts—and the need to keep the event calendar full to pay back the bonds that financed the facility—ensured that Houston's new stadium would be an accessible recreational and work environment for all Houstonians, whether they lived in the suburbs or not.

Indeed, the opening of the Astrodome helped catalyze a social and cultural revolution in Houston. Gone were the racially segregated worlds of Buffs and Jeppesen Stadiums. Following the lead of the Astros, other sporting programs gradually integrated their teams. In January 1965, the AFL's annual All-Star game was hurriedly moved to Houston when black players boldly refused to play after experiencing discrimination in New Orleans, where the game was originally scheduled.[29] In the college sporting scene, the University of Houston, which began admitting black students in 1962, became one of the first all-white schools in Texas to actively recruit black athletes in the mid-1960s. In 1965, head football coach Bill Yeoman signed the San Antonio–born Warren McVea, who became the first black player in the football program, while the basketball team, led by coach Guy Lewis, recruited two star players from Louisiana: Elvin Hayes and Don Chaney. By the late 1960s, the Astros showcased black frontline players, including Jimmy Wynn and Joe Morgan. Even Bud Adams's Oilers, under the direction of new general manager Don Klosterman, featured black stars, including defensive backs Miller Farr from Beaumont and Ken Houston from Lufkin, and linebacker George Webster.[30]

Hofheinz's desire to make the Dome an attractive venue for championship boxing led him to sign the polarizing figure Muhammad Ali, then known as Cassius Clay, the heavyweight champion of the world, to fight in Houston. In the summer of 1965, Ali visited the Dome and expressed a desire to fight in the new stadium. But he was not warmly received by spectators during a Houston Astros baseball game. According to one account, Astros fans booed him after he was introduced by the stadium's public address announcer. The champion was unfazed: "That booing doesn't bother me," said Ali. "I hope if I ever fight here, the place will be full and they'll all boo me. . . . That's my game . . . make 'em hate me . . . make 'em pay to see me get beat."[31]

Hofheinz's willingness to sign Ali to fight in the Dome is somewhat surprising. When Ali agreed to fight in Houston, he was already being chastised by the press for his criticism of the US war effort in Vietnam and for his conversion to Islam. Though Ali was idolized in his later years, he was despised by many Americans in the 1960s who saw him as unpatriotic. Others, especially black fans, loved him. The mixed reception from Houston fans did not stop Hofheinz from signing Ali to fight in the Dome. On November 14, 1966, approximately 35,460 fans, the largest crowd in indoor boxing history to that point, arrived to see Ali face Cleveland Williams, an aging fighter from nearby Yoakum, Texas. It was the first boxing match in the new stadium that had created a buzz in the sporting world and beyond. The Astrodome's large capacity ensured that the fight would have the largest indoor audience in boxing history. It also produced a record-setting closed-circuit television audience. Still, the cavernous Astrodome was probably not the best place to view a boxing match. The boxing ring was placed in the middle of the field, far away from the stands. Stadium workers laid down thousands of plywood tiles on top of the artificial turf to prevent damage to the field by cigarette butts. The ring was surrounded by thirty-three rows of fifty-dollar ringside seats. Behind the ring of seats was a huge gap before the stands for the rest of the spectators, who were probably not able to see much of the fight without the aid of binoculars. However, the top two tiers of the stadium, those farthest away from the action but also those that had the cheapest seats, were sold out. The imperfect setting didn't stop boxing fans from watching the young champion score a third-round knockout of the befuddled Williams. The Texan was dazzled by Ali's newly minted "Ali Shuffle" and the champion's dizzying array of punches and hand speed.

In February 1967, the heavyweight champion once again entered the ring in the Astrodome and brutalized Ernie Terrell during a fight that became known as the "What's My Name?" affair. Leading up to the fight, Terrell understandably drew Ali's ire because he continued to refer to him by his birth name, Cassius Clay, even though the champion had publicly changed his name to Muhammad Ali. Terrell paid dearly for his attempt to unnerve Ali in front of thirty-seven thousand spectators. During the fifteen-round fight, the champion frequently demanded that Terrell call him by his new name while mercilessly hitting him with an assortment of jabs and right crosses. Ali would soon be blackballed by the boxing authorities for his refusal to be inducted into the US Armed Forces, yet he remained a viable commercial commodity and a powerful symbol for black fans and anti-war activists. Ali would fight two more times in the Dome, which showed that for Hofheinz, the boxer's commercial value outweighed any potential objections Houstonians might have had to Ali's anti-racist and anti-war politics. In this way, the Dome became a space for events with social significance as much as it was an athletic venue.

The Dome staged events that no one had ever seen before, including a basketball game in a giant sports arena. On January 20, 1968, Guy Lewis's University of Houston Cougars, the number-two-ranked team in the nation, faced off against John Wooden's number-one-ranked UCLA Bruins in front of 52,693 fans, the largest crowd ever to see a basketball game up to that point. The game featured the two top players in the nation: Houston's Elvin Hayes and UCLA's Lew Alcindor (later known as Kareem Abdul-Jabbar). Playing on a court that was set upon the middle of the giant Astrodome floor forced fans to rely on their binoculars to watch the game. But it didn't matter as the large crowd watched Hayes outplay Alcindor, scoring thirty-nine points and leading his team to a dramatic 71–69 upset, stopping UCLA's forty-seven-game winning streak. The contest was the first ever college basketball game televised in prime time, and it would not be the last, showing that the game could draw a substantial crowd and television audience. The Game of the Century, as it was dubbed, was a boon to Lewis's Cougars, which became one of the region's top basketball programs, setting the stage for his well-known Phi Slama Jama teams of the early 1980s.

* * *

While the Judge was observing historic events in the air-conditioned luxury of the Astrodome, Clint Murchison Jr. was desperately trying to stay cool by sipping mint juleps while watching his Dallas Cowboys football team in the oven-like conditions of the press box at the Cotton Bowl. Since the 1930s, the Cotton Bowl had been Texas's showcase venue. The New Year's Day bowl game, the state fair, and the annual Texas-Oklahoma "Red River Shootout" gave the venue regional and national prominence. But the stadium, which was good enough for Doak Walker and the SMU Mustangs in the 1940s, wasn't good enough for the owner of the Dallas Cowboys in the 1960s. The facility resembled most stadiums built for football at the time. It was a large bowl-like structure that could accommodate large crowds. It was built for college, not professional, football. It resembled other football stadiums such as Tulane Stadium in New Orleans or Miami's Orange Bowl Stadium. It was large and functional. There were few bells and whistles. Fans sat on wooden bleachers that were exposed to the elements. The concessions were basic. Spectators went to Texas's college football cathedral to see the game, not the stadium.

Yet, it was beloved by the small but loyal group of fans who would actually come out to watch the Cowboys in its early years. When the team started to win in 1966, crowds packed the stadium on the Texas State Fairgrounds. It drew a cross-section of fans, particularly as the stands were integrating in the 1960s. In a sense, games at the Cotton Bowl were an extension of the carnivalesque atmosphere of the fairgrounds. Spectators were emotional, and they gave the Cowboys hell when they didn't perform up to expectations. Football fans throughout the country got a taste of the wrath of Cotton Bowl regulars during a memorable 1970 game when the Cowboys were humiliated by the St. Louis Cardinals 38–0 on national television. Don Meredith, the recently retired Cowboys quarterback and former SMU legend, was broadcasting the contest for ABC's *Monday Night Football*. Throughout the game, Meredith could not help but express his dismay at his former team's dismal showing that night. As the fans mercilessly booed and jeered the Cowboys' putrid performance, Meredith comically recalled the trauma of his playing days at the stadium. At one moment, after one of the team's many turnovers that night (this one leading to the Cardinals taking a

*The Cotton Bowl. Courtesy Squire Haskins Photography, Inc.
Collection, Special Collections, the University of Texas at Arlington
Libraries.*

17–0 lead), Meredith said to the television audience, sighing, "You never know what trouble is 'til you are seventeen points behind in the Cotton Bowl." The moment reflected the atmosphere of Cowboys games at the facility. As a Cowboys fan recalled to journalist John Eisenberg years later, "The stadium was blue collar. The team was blue collar. The fans were blue collar, the whole deal was blue collar."[32]

But Clint Murchison Jr. was not blue collar, and watching his team in the uncomfortable proletarian atmosphere of the Cotton Bowl was not his idea of a good time. In the 1960s, the stadium started to show its age. The bleachers were splintering, the restrooms were unseemly, the amenities were few, and the hot, non–air-conditioned press box was despised by sportswriters. Moreover, it was in a predominantly African American neighborhood that was deemed unsafe, though the stadium was hardly the only sports venue in the country that was located in an under-resourced neighborhood. After the Astrodome opened and the Cowboys started winning, Murchison's complaints about his home field were more frequent. He offered to help build a new stadium in downtown Dallas, but he was rebuffed by Mayor J. Erik Jonsson and the State Fair Commission, the entities that managed the venerable facility. The mayor dismissed the Cowboys owner's concerns, claiming that Murchison was merely suffering from the "Astrodome Syndrome." "Nobody noticed how bad the Cotton Bowl was until the Astrodome was built," the mayor quipped to the press.[33] Jonsson's relative indifference toward Murchison is understandable in retrospect. Prior to this period, pro football teams were not the primary tenants in most stadiums. Usually, they were forced to share venues built for other purposes. The Cowboys were not a major priority for Dallas officials who were more concerned with the needs of the State Fair Commission.

By January 1967, Murchison was done with Jonsson and the Cotton Bowl. The Cowboys owner boldly bought ninety acres of land in a nearby suburb called Irving, Texas, where he threatened to build his own stadium. Jonsson continued to dismiss the upstart Cowboys owner and tried to stick it in his face by helping the State Fair Commission finance a renovation of the Cotton Bowl's seats to spite the ambitious owner who dared to leave Dallas. Jonsson's confidence in his position was misplaced, because Murchison was not bluffing. The Cowboys owner hatched an agreement with Irving officials, and he broke ground on his stadium in January 1969. Murchison's stadium deal illustrated another transformation inaugurated by Texas sports entrepreneurs: the growing political power of the National Football League. In the late 1960s, pro football was no longer taking a backseat to Major League Baseball in the spectating habits of US sports fans and in the political economy of cities. Clint Murchison's move to Irving showed that the NFL could flex its muscles against unbelieving public officials and get its own stadiums designed for its own needs, not those of baseball or other entertainment enterprises. In 1971, the same year Murchison's new football palace opened, the New York Giants announced their intention to leave Yankee Stadium in the Bronx to play in a new football stadium in East Rutherford, New Jersey. The new facility, which was called Giants Stadium, was a less opulent version of Murchison's creation in Irving. In 1972, Lamar Hunt, now in Kansas City, got his own football stadium. A few years later, the Detroit Lions and the New Orleans Saints moved into their own fancy domed stadiums. Over the next two decades, nearly all NFL franchises would abandon stadiums shared with baseball teams for opulent temples designed for football.

The Cowboys' new home, dubbed Texas Stadium, was clearly inspired by Hofheinz's Astrodome. From the outside, it looked like just another domed stadium in the middle of Texas prairieland. That is pretty much where the similarities ended. Unlike the Astrodome, Texas Stadium was a "half-dome," as John Eisenberg has described it, with a ninety-thousand-square-foot rectangular hole in the middle of a steel canopy roof. This arrangement allowed games to be played in an outdoor setting while ensuring that spectators would remain dry in inclement weather. Cowboys critics liked to sarcastically claim that Murchison left the hole in the roof to allow God to watch his favorite team and his favorite head coach, Tom Landry. The roof created odd patterns of shade and light that moved throughout the game, which would wreak havoc on the players, who were forced to trace a football traveling through irregular shadow lines on sunny days. In the early fall, the players, particularly those on the visitors' side of the field, were roasted by the hot Texas sun. While the Astrodome relished in its multicolored five-tier seating design, Texas Stadium's seats were all blue, reflecting the team's and the owner's conservative sensibilities. The sixty-five thousand seats were laid out in three tiers, forming a rounded rectangular-shaped structure that hugged the football field. This was not a stadium where baseball could be played, unlike most ballparks built in this era. Texas Stadium hosted concerts, soccer, and other events, but it was fundamentally a football venue.

Murchison loved his new stadium. Tex Schramm loved it too.

Clint Murchison Jr. and Tex Schramm at Texas Stadium, 1971. Courtesy Fort Worth Star-Telegram Collection, Special Collections, the University of Texas at Arlington Libraries.

The sportswriting brethren who suffered all those years in the Cotton Bowl's hot press box also loved it. The players, however, hated it. Hall of Fame defensive lineman Bob Lilly remembered it having a "more sterile atmosphere; there just wasn't a lot of shouting and noise." Duane Thomas, the star running back of the Cowboys during their first league championship season in 1971, recalled, "It was interesting how the crowd would respond after a touchdown. It was like 'bravo,' 'bravo,' and that was the extent of it."[34] The building was eerily quiet, unlike the noisy atmosphere of the Cotton Bowl and most other stadiums at the time. "Home games were no longer emotional outpourings," John Eisenberg explains. "They were social occasions marked by reserved, 'tasteful' cheering from a crowd that felt it was above traditional football rabble-rousing."[35] Texas Stadium turned football games into elite private club social affairs.

The Astrodome set the standard for the new era of stadium

construction, but Murchison's Texas Stadium helped establish the model that dominates stadium design and financing to this day. Not only was it the first stadium built specifically for an NFL team, but it was the first to be significantly financed by a team's season ticket holders. To pay for the building of the $25 million stadium, Murchison required season ticket holders to buy $250 bonds per seat to secure the right to buy a season ticket. This was the precursor to what is known now as the personal seat license (PSL), which virtually all NFL franchises employ to extract dollars from their fans today. He also doubled down on the Judge's luxury suite concept by constructing 176 boxes, more than double the number of suites built in the Astrodome. The suite holders got a 16' × 16' box, and unlike the Judge, who forced renters to accept his outlandish taste, Murchison allowed them to decorate the suites as they wished. And they did. Some opted for the English pub look. Others went for French court with a "pale blue glazed wall, panels decorated with reclining Roman clad ladies and scenic porcelain miniatures." No orientalist kitsch at Texas Stadium—instead, one saw suites that were miniature versions of what one might see in mansions and corporate boardrooms. All of this led Jeane Barnes, the home editor of the *Dallas Morning News*, to conclude that "the glamour of the individual boxes carries on the tradition of free-wheeling, Texas big rich!"[36] If the Astrodome sought to attract the rich man from the city and the farmer from Diboll, Texas Stadium was concerned with the rich fan only.

Lyndon and Lady Bird Johnson had attended opening night at the Astrodome in 1965, and they were also present at the opening of Clint Murchison's football palace six years later on October 24, 1971. When spectators got a good look at the new stadium, they walked into an edifice that had the "air of bloodless glamour, a postmodern coolness that topped off their computerized image."[37] In the Cotton Bowl, the natural grass and the exposure to the varied climates of North Texas made it possible for spectators to appreciate the labor involved in making a football game possible. Groundskeepers struggled to make the turf playable. Players'

Comfortable spectating at Texas Stadium, 1971. AP photo/Ferd Kaufman.

uniforms got dirty and muddy, as they did in many games during those years in Fair Park. Even the Kilgore Rangerettes and the Apache Belles had to endure the dangers of laboring in the muck and mire of the Cotton Bowl turf during their many performances at the stadium.

Texas Stadium's pristine appearance, however, virtually disappeared the hard labor entailed in making a game day possible. The mirage of the clean football field was facilitated by the use of artificial turf instead of natural grass. Murchison, eager to outdo the Judge, did not choose Chemstrand's Astroturf. Instead, he opted for the supposedly softer Tartan Turf, developed by the Monsanto competitor Minnesota Mining and Manufacturing Company (3M). The turf promised cost efficiency and safety, but like the Judge's Astroturf, it produced more brutalization. Bob Lilly echoed the feelings of most players who understood the deadly nature of Texas Stadium's Tartan Turf for football players: "The turf was the worst in the world. It was a killer."[38] The turf gave the fan and player clear sight lines unobstructed by weather and heighted by the odd angles of sunlight. Gone were the muddy football fields of the past. Gone was the yellowing grass of the Cotton Bowl. Texas Stadium's turf was perfect for the television age: a green carpeted field decorated with end zones painted blue with "Cowboys" painted across it in silver paint. By contrast, the multipurpose stadiums where fields were prepared for football and baseball at least showed the dirt that playing football entailed. Even the synthetic fields in the then in-vogue cookie cutter stadiums at least exposed the dreaded seams that covered the dirt from the baseball diamond. But football stadiums like Texas Stadium presented the illusion that players were simply laboring in a giant playpen. The field was encircled by a high wall to allow spectators to see over the heads of the players. Initially, the surrounding wall was a drab gray color, and Murchison refused to let fans drape banners and signs over it, which further contributed to the sterile atmosphere. Eventually, he added some color by painting the wall royal blue with white stars on top. He also eventually let fans bring homemade signs to liven up the atmosphere. Between the wall and sidelines were the scantily clad Dallas Cowboys Cheerleaders, who were modeled on Gussie Nell Davis's Rangerettes. The stadium, the metallic blue and white uniforms, the silver helmets with the blue star, and the cheerleaders all were part of the Cowboys' new corporate image. They were no longer simply the Dallas Cowboys. They were now on their way to becoming America's Team.

* * *

Texas oilmen sports entrepreneurs and their partners in the state, as well as the athletic laboring classes, transformed American society in more ways than one. The establishment of sports franchises in Houston and Dallas nationalized MLB and the NFL by bringing pro sports to the Sunbelt. The sports entrepreneurs erected paradigm-shifting, hypermodern stadiums that radically transformed the performance and reception of big-time sports. Pro sports put Houston and Dallas on the national map in ways that were previously unimaginable. But they also set in motion forces that transformed Texas society and sporting culture. These forces facilitated the collapse of Jim Crow segregation in Dallas and Houston. In the 1960s, commercialized sport catalyzed social change by unhinging the historical hierarchies of the Jim Crow era. The revolution unleashed by pro sports would spread to other parts of the state's sporting landscape. Nowhere was this more apparent than on the hallowed gridiron of Southwest Conference football.

CHAPTER 3

The Outlaws

IT WAS A PARTLY CLOUDY SATURDAY AFTERNOON ON NOVEMBER 5, 1966, WHEN the Southern Methodist University Mustangs faced off against the Texas A&M Aggies in a regular season college football contest at the Cotton Bowl in Dallas. The two teams belonged to the Southwest Conference, which remained one of the preeminent college football conferences in the country. The Mustangs, nicknamed the "Ponies" by their fans and the local press, had languished in mediocrity for years. But, led by their sophomore sensation Jerry LeVias, the first African American scholarship football athlete in the previously all-white conference, they had won six of their first seven games with a few dramatic come-from-behind victories. Their opponents, the Aggies, were in the midst of a disappointing season with only three wins, four losses, and one tie. The previous year, when it was announced that LeVias had signed with SMU, Gene Stallings, A&M's head coach, had questioned the wisdom of white schools signing black student-athletes. "A team that will work, pull, and fight together and really get a feeling of oneness," he claimed, "I don't believe we could accomplish this with a Negro on the squad."[1] With their surprising season, the Mustangs seemed to be proving otherwise. A large crowd of fifty-five thousand fans came to the Cotton Bowl to see if the Mustangs could continue to do so.

The game turned out to be a hard-fought contest. The Aggies raced to a 14–0 lead, but the Mustangs came back to tie the score in the third quarter. With eleven minutes left in the final period, the Mustang defense forced Texas A&M to punt. Back to receive the punt was LeVias, the electrifying kick returner, who caught the ball at the seventeen-yard line. Punt returning can be a harrowing experience because players who take on the challenge have very little time to avoid onrushing tacklers, who fly down the field at top speed. But the speedy and elusive sophomore from Beaumont "wiggled and jiggled" (as *Dallas Morning News* sports editor Walter Robertson described it) to find a little running room as Aggies converged on him from all directions.[2] As he encountered more trouble at the twenty-five-yard line, he suddenly paused to let the momentum of the Aggie defenders carry them away from him as they desperately lunged to bring him down. But they couldn't. LeVias's agility won him space to operate. Now the teamwork between black and white teammates that Gene Stallings could not envision was happening before his very eyes as two of LeVias's white teammates, Pat Gibson and Mike Mitchell, helped clear defenders from the kick returner's path. After running toward the middle of the field, LeVias suddenly cut back to the left sideline, where still more menacing Aggies tacklers awaited. But one more crunching block from another white teammate, George Wilmot, a 230-pound senior defensive end, cleared the last tacklers from LeVias's path. His speed did the rest as he zipped past Aggie would-be tacklers as though they were standing still. The speedy Mustang broke into the clear, racing past the SMU bench as his teammates and coaches exulted in triumph. The Aggies realized what previous opponents that season had discovered—that no one in the conference possessed the speed to chase down the sensational sophomore from Beaumont. Touchdown Mustangs! LeVias's game-winning eighty-three-yard punt return touchdown eventually gave the Ponies a 21–14 victory.

A Jack Beers photograph captures LeVias mid-gallop, the soon-to-be all-SWC player racing toward the end zone with A&M Aggies gassed in the background and his Mustangs teammates smiling with joy. The photo is reminiscent of other racial scenar-

Jerry LeVias taking it all the way against A&M. Courtesy Heritage Hall and Southern Methodist University Archives, DeGolyer Library, SMU Libraries, Southern Methodist University.

ios in the sordid history of the US South: runaway slaves fleeing slave catchers or innocent black men running from racist law enforcement officers. In this context, LeVias wasn't simply running for a touchdown in a college football game. Here in the stadium named after cotton—the commodity that symbolized the brutal exploitation of the enslaved—one of their descendants was running from the shadows of racial slavery and Jim Crow segregation and ushering in a new moment in the region's and the country's history—a post–Jim Crow athletic order.

One year later, another black Texan athlete made headlines for a previously all-white football program. The University of Houston Cougars football team shocked college football observers by trouncing the powerful Michigan State Spartans in East Lansing, 37–7. The star of the game was a small and fleet-footed halfback named Warren McVea. "Wondrous Warren," as he was hailed by the press, had been one of the most sought-after recruits in the country when he played for Brackenridge High School in San Antonio. In 1964, head coach Bill Yeoman pulled off a coup by signing McVea to a scholarship, making him the first player to be signed by the all-white Cougars program. McVea, like LeVias, was not a bruising runner. He was a player who made a name for himself by outrunning and eluding tacklers with an agile flair that produced exciting touchdown runs. In the game against Michigan State, he ran circles around the Spartans, the school that previously had profited from the labor of star black players from Texas. The Cougars' win, like the Mustangs' victory the year before, signaled the resurgence of Texas college football led by the talents of speedy and elusive black scatbacks. In the coming years, African American football players distinguished themselves on the field, not only in the so-called speed positions of running back, wide receiver, and defensive back, but in all positions in the sport, revolutionizing the game in the process.

* * *

It is tempting to view the history of racial integration of college football as a historical inevitability, a natural outcome of the great struggles of the civil rights movement of the 1960s, when the arc of history finally seemed to be leaning toward justice for black people. And yet, such thinking minimizes the importance of the actual decisions that were made by historical actors to change what many thought to be the natural order of things. After the historic *Sweatt v. Painter* (1950) and *Brown v. Board of Education* (1954) Supreme Court cases, many southern white schools resisted desegregation at every turn. Massive resistance was particularly intense in school athletic programs, where the anxieties generated by intimate athletic body contact made desegregation seem even more intolerable. It was one thing for newly arrived professional teams to allow black players on their rosters; it was another matter entirely to allow black men to compete on an equal playing field with white men in college football, a sport that had deeper roots in the Jim Crow South. Schools that desegregated their student bodies in the late 1950s and early 1960s still sought to shut out or minimize the presence of black male athletes on their football teams until the late 1960s and early 1970s. Yet after the University of Houston and Southern Methodist University decided to integrate, a major demographic change occurred on team rosters throughout the region in less than ten years. A seemingly natural segregationist order gave way to a seemingly normal world of racially integrated football.

The abandonment of Jim Crow college football in Texas occurred, in part, because of the massive influx of capital into the realm of intercollegiate athletics. The same forces that propelled Lamar Hunt, Bud Adams, and Clint Murchison Jr. to spend their money on professional sports franchises were behind the rising popularity of college football in the 1960s and '70s. Oil money fueled the expansion of professional sports into Texas, and oil money and the finance industry provided by wealthy football enthusiasts propelled the integration of college football. The Texas oil boom enabled many businessmen to become college football boosters who poured money into athletic programs, which also helped spawn new professions in sports management and sports journalism. Indeed, the rise of televised sports, epitomized by the emergence of ABC Sports under the visionary leadership of Roone Arledge, commanded advertising dollars that popularized Texas football on a national scale. Oil companies like Humble Oil, the Texas brand of New Jersey's Standard Oil, even sponsored SWC highlight films and radio broadcasts for decades. The energy economy also changed the gridiron itself, as chemical conglomerates convinced universities and public officials to install synthetic grass on their playing surfaces. Some of these dollars also flowed into the hands of a generation of black athletes who were suddenly encountering a new coterie of college coaches, backed by energetic wealthy boosters, eager to sign them to their alma maters by any means necessary—even if it meant abandoning the practice of racial exclusion, and even if it meant bending or breaking the rules of the National Collegiate Athletic Association (NCAA). It was the deepening commercialization of intercollegiate sports, along with the freedom struggles of the 1960s and '70s, that changed the face of college football in the state, the region, and the nation.

Many accounts of the racial integration of college football in the former Jim Crow South tend to revolve around the desegregation of the dominant programs of the region, such as the Alabama Crimson Tide, coached by Paul "Bear" Bryant, and the University of Texas Longhorns, coached by Darrell Royal. But these coaches and their programs were followers, not leaders. Debating whether or not Bryant or Royal was racist detracts attention from the programs that actually did decide to initiate integration. Though the general pattern of integration started in the states of the Upper South, it was the schools of Texas—the junior colleges, followed by North Texas State and Texas Western—that broke with Jim Crow in the late 1950s.[3] A few years later, the Houston Cougars, followed by the SMU Mustangs—the first Southwest Conference school to sign a black scholarship football player—pushed the region into a post–Jim Crow athletic order. Writing in 1975, Steve Pate, the *Dallas Morning News* sportswriter, insisted that "if there were ever two schools who took bold steps in the early 60's to wipe out some of the racial nonsense, they were SMU and Houston."[4] Integration helped revitalize SMU football and launch it to the top of the SWC, and integration helped the University of Houston emerge from obscurity to join the SWC, win conference championships, and change the sport in the state of Texas and the nation.

SMU and Houston rose to prominence due to their ability to attract black athletic talent from predominantly black high schools in Dallas and Houston. In Dallas, both programs forged ties with Dallas Carter and South Oak Cliff High Schools, while in Houston, both recruited heavily from Kashmere and Yates High Schools. Of course, SMU and Houston recruited athletes from other parts of the state, but it was these urban areas that helped them overtake Texas and Arkansas as the dominant teams in the conference by the late 1970s/early 1980s. Dallas and Houston, as much as Odessa and Midland, were largely behind the revitalization of big-time college football in Texas during this period. In this way, David Whitford's "I-45 Connection," the memorable phrase he developed to describe SMU's illegal recruiting of players from the I-45 corridor between Houston and Dallas, takes on a whole new meaning.[5]

For the black student-athletes who arrived on formerly segregationist campuses of Southwest Conference schools, integration represented more than simply an opportunity to play football and get an education. Most players willingly expressed gratitude to their alma maters for granting them athletic scholarships. What is more striking is their refusal to be treated as objects of charity. While Jerry LeVias never failed to express gratitude to SMU, he also bluntly characterized his experience playing football at SMU as "strictly a job."[6] Still, for LeVias, Jon Richardson, Rodrigo Barnes, Roosevelt Leaks, Earl Campbell, and countless players thereafter, performing on the field for predominantly white schools meant greater exposure and the ability to express self-possession through their athletic skills. Black men gained the right to express a degree of freedom on the field that their ancestors could not have fathomed a generation earlier.

The University of Texas Longhorns and the University of Arkansas Razorbacks were the Southwest Conference schools that remained committed to Jim Crow football the longest. They were also the top programs in the region. From 1959 to 1973, the two schools claimed thirteen of the fifteen conference championships in football. The Longhorns and Razorbacks usually had their choice of the most talented white high school football recruits in both states. As the well-resourced flagship public institutions of Texas and Arkansas dominated, the smaller public and private schools such as SMU, Baylor, Rice, and Texas Christian struggled to keep up. During the Jim Crow era, the football labor pool was restricted by racism as black players were not recruited by the SWC. But two head football coaches—one from an aspirational public university in Houston and another from a struggling athletic program at a small Methodist university in Dallas—changed the face of major college football in the South. Bill Yeoman at

Houston and Hayden Fry at Southern Methodist both under-stood that the segregationist game was rigged in favor of Arkansas head coach Frank Broyles and Texas Longhorn head coach Darrell Royal. One way to successfully challenge their supremacy was to recruit from the untapped market of talented black high school athletes. In this way, both schools catalyzed the racial integration of college football in Texas. Both institutions used athletics—and black athletic labor power—to unseat the segregationist powers of the SWC and propel their universities to national recognition. And both schools would eventually be penalized for it.

* * *

Hayden Fry refused to be limited by the prevailing racial mentality he encountered as a boy growing up in West Texas. "My attitude about race developed early in life," he recalled. "I had black friends while growing up in Eastland and Odessa who I played with and worked with. We spent a lot of time together." As an adolescent, Fry experienced the separation from his friends created by the social world of Jim Crow. The illogic of racial segregation stayed with Fry. "By the time I was in high school, when my black friends were playing football at Dunbar instead of with me at Odessa, I made a commitment that if I was ever in a position to change that, I would."[7] Simple as that. Or perhaps it wasn't that simple. In any case, years later when Fry was offered the head coaching job at Southern Methodist, he accepted it on the condition that he could break the color barrier in the Southwest Conference and recruit black student athletes. Although SMU's administration first rejected Fry's proposal, they eventually relented because their football program was floundering and in desperate need of new leadership. Fry's reasoning was simple: "There was no question in my mind it was the right thing to do regardless of what others thought . . . and from a selfish standpoint, I wanted to win."[8]

For decades, SWC coaches refused to recruit the state's black players. This enabled predominantly white universities in the northern and western parts of the United States to benefit from the athletic labor power of black Texans by picking a few of the very best football players to help their teams win while keeping their own team racial demographic in favor of white athletes. Black schools in Texas, such as Prairie View, Wiley, Bishop, and Texas Southern, also thrived because of the talents of black athletes. Many of the best black players from Beaumont, the town that produced Babe Didrikson and one of the ends of the Golden Triangle region of Southeast Texas, wound up playing for colleges in the North and West. Members of Jerry LeVias's family illustrate this historic pattern. His brother-in-law, George Reed, played football at Washington State. So did his cousin, Clancy Williams. His older cousins, Miller and Mel Farr, played college ball at Wichita State and UCLA respectively. All of them went on to play professional football. So did the most famous football brothers in Beaumont; Bubba and Tody Smith, sons of Charlton-Pollard High School coach Willie Ray Smith, played college ball at Michigan State and in the National Football League. And UCLA was hot on LeVias's trail, competing hard against SMU for his services.

In May 1965, Hayden Fry changed the course of history when he became the first coach in the Southwest Conference to sign a black football player to an athletic scholarship. He would not be the last. That same year, John Westbrook, a black halfback from Elgin, walked on at Baylor University. He technically was the first black player to see game action, one week before LeVias did in the Bears season opener in 1966, though he struggled to overcome hostile coaches and injuries during his time at Baylor.[9]

Jerry LeVias was an unlikely figure to be the first black scholarship football player in the SWC. He was small in stature, 5'8" and 160 lbs. As a child he was often sick—suffering from polio and a stroke that limited his ability to walk. But the little scrawny kid who was picked on for being too small and left-handed found his calling, of all places, on a football field. As he entered his teenage years, LeVias began to excel in sports, especially track and field and football. At Hebert High School in Beaumont, he was an all-sport athlete. On the football team, he was a halfback, kick returner, and wide receiver. When his high school coach became aware that SMU was looking to recruit black players, he informed SMU recruiter Charlie Curtis of LeVias's exceptional talent. But SMU was competing against eighty or ninety other schools for his services. When LeVias accepted the offer to attend SMU, the UCLA coaching staff could not believe it. Head football coach Tommy Prothro, who had coached LeVias's cousin Mel Farr, literally had to be fought off by SMU coaches to keep him from kidnapping LeVias and taking him to California. Despite the eerie resonance with the slave trade, the fierce competition for the black high school star foreshadowed the recruiting wars for black athletic talent in subsequent years. Perhaps Prothro knew that LeVias's choosing of SMU over UCLA signaled a historic shift that was about to take place. Schools in the Midwest and West now had serious competition for the services of student-athletes from Texas.

During the 1966 season, his first on the varsity team, LeVias did what he was recruited to do: perform well, perhaps even better than expected. He led the SMU Mustangs to the program's first SWC championship since the days of Doak Walker. He had a remarkable season, showing many of the skills of the legendary Walker. Though he was small for a college football player, he possessed blazing speed and uncanny elusiveness, which allowed him to excel as a kick returner and wide receiver. LeVias aptly summed up his running style to *Sports Illustrated* a few years later when he noted, "I'm like a rat in a maze. I'm always searching for an opening and if I stop or pause then I'm going to get hit with the full impact of the lick and I can't afford too many of those. I never want to let them hit me when I have both feet planted, so I'm always doing something." Standard tackling techniques failed when defenders tried to employ them to bring down LeVias. "Coaches instruct tacklers to watch the ballcarrier's waist," he continued. "If they watch mine they get hypnotized. I never run more than a step without juking."[10]

The Mustangs shocked Cotton Bowl regulars and conference

prognosticators with an exciting season. Their trademark became the fourth quarter come-from-behind victory featuring big plays by their sophomore sensation from the Golden Triangle. In the fifth game of the season, against the Rice University Owls, LeVias made several important plays, including a forty-seven-yard touchdown pass on an end-around and a fake field goal that led to first down on the game's final drive. Then he made an acrobatic game-winning touchdown catch in the back corner of the end zone with nine seconds left to beat the Owls 28–24. A few weeks later, the Beaumont speedster caught another touchdown pass in a 13–12 upset win over Darrell Royal's Texas Longhorns in Austin. After the victory over Texas A&M, the Mustangs narrowly defeated Baylor 24–22 with more last-second heroics. In the final regular season game, they won the conference championship by defeating TCU in Fort Worth 21–0, with LeVias catching yet another touchdown pass. The last two performances were particularly remarkable because the integration pioneer was receiving racist verbal and physical assaults from opponents, hate mail, and death threats.

SMU earned the opportunity to play in the New Year's Day Cotton Bowl Classic for the first time since the days of Doak Walker. But they came out flat and lost to the University of Georgia Bulldogs 24–7. Still, LeVias and the Mustangs had a remarkable season. Though Fry used him in only sixty-six plays the entire season, presumably to preserve his small body, LeVias scored nine touchdowns and threw for another. He ran the ball eight times for forty-three yards, completed five of eight passes for eighty-nine yards, caught eighteen passes for 420 yards and seven touchdowns, returned fifteen kickoffs for 393 yards, and returned seventeen punts for 222 yards and another touchdown. He was named Sophomore of the Year in the Southwest Conference.[11] He also received positive coverage from the city and campus press. Bob St. John, *Dallas Morning News* sports columnist, gave him the highest praise a Mustangs observer could give when he called him the "most exciting player to perform for the Ponies since Doak Walker and Kyle Rote. Player of the Year on the field:

Maybe. Off the field? For sure."[12] Robert Morehead, columnist for the *SMU Campus* newspaper, celebrated LeVias not only for his athletic exploits but also because he was "a man—and the first of his race to boast an SWC scholarship." Indeed, Morehead used his column as an opportunity to declare that "racism has no place in life, much less athletics."[13] Press accounts such as these suggest that LeVias's first season on the varsity team was a feel-good integration story.

LeVias turned out to be more than what Hayden Fry had hoped for. During his three years at SMU, he set SWC career records with 155 catches; 2,275 yards; and twenty-two touchdowns. He was recognized as a consensus All-American in 1968, with eighty pass receptions for 1,131 yards and eight touchdowns.[14] The LeVias years were the most successful and exciting stretch of football since the golden age of Doak Walker. After a disappointing 1967 season, the Mustangs rebounded with an 8–3 record in 1968, which concluded with a 28–27 upset victory over the Oklahoma Sooners at the Astro-Bluebonnet Bowl in the Houston Astrodome. LeVias's achievements, along with those of Warren McVea at the University of Houston and John Westbrook of Baylor, initiated a new era of college football in the state of Texas. It's not hard to understand why Hayden Fry wrote years later that he "admired Jerry LeVias more than any player [he had] ever coached."[15] LeVias went on to have a productive career as a professional with the Houston Oilers and San Diego Chargers. "I still can't believe what I accomplished under the circumstances," LeVias recalled years later. "What didn't I do? I graduated on time, academic All-American, Athletic All-American." Jerry LeVias accurately summed up his life's work and achievements when he said, "I've always been an outcast: left-handed, too small, and too sick, and too black. I was too sick to play football. I was too black to play college football. And I was too small to play pro football . . . and I did it all."[16]

But the Beaumont native paid a price for doing it all. The trauma and emotional scars of doing the painful work of integrating an all-white football program in a white university remained years after he left SMU. Though his success on the field presumably won over some of his racist critics, he never gained full acceptance from the SMU community. If anything, his well-publicized successes made him even more vulnerable to abuse from racist reactionaries. Though he eventually adjusted to the SMU academic environment, he was never welcomed in social spaces and he lived alone throughout his entire tenure at SMU.

Fry's promise to LeVias that the more touchdowns he scored, the whiter he would get never quite held true for SMU's integration pioneer. Toward the end of LeVias's remarkable sophomore season, even Fry felt compelled to publicly acknowledge the mistreatment he was enduring. He decided to back up his player to the press by telling them about the mistreatment LeVias was receiving from racist fans. "He told us he had been the object of abusive words from fans," Fry admitted. He also told them that LeVias cried after one game when an opponent spat on him. Still he felt that LeVias would stick it out at SMU. "I have told him he is a symbol of his race and if he quits he will handicap the program for other people."[17]

Some sportswriters chastised Fry for bringing the racist treatment his star player was enduring to the public. "Martyrs must be stoics," wrote the *Austin Statesman* columnist Richard Boldt. "By bringing the behind the scene turbulence forward, Fry has only encouraged cranks and bigots to try intimidating the 175-pound dandy."[18] To Boldt, Fry had the audacity to entertain the notion that perhaps stopping racism was the collective responsibility of white fans and spectators, rather than of a black martyr who should silently endure such mistreatment. Fry himself was also vilified by reactionary alumni, fans, and opponents. In the first game of the 1967 season, his Mustangs came back to once again beat Gene Stallings's Texas A&M squad 20–17. The stars of the game were LeVias and Ines Pérez, the diminutive 5' 4", 149-pound backup quarterback from Corpus Christi who threw the game-winning touchdown pass to LeVias. Fry, unlike so many of his fellow southern coaches, was willing to feature a black player and a Mexican American player, a fact that was brought to his attention

Jerry LeVias with Bob Hope, Homecoming 1968. Courtesy Heritage Hall and Southern Methodist University Archives, DeGolyer Library, SMU Libraries, Southern Methodist University.

when an Aggies booster came up to him after the game and de-clared, "You should feel great, Coach Fry. You beat us, but it took a Mexican and a nigger to do it!"[19]

Like Jackie Robinson, Jerry LeVias was an ideal integration pi-oneer not only because he was talented but also because he was perceived by Fry and his recruiters as an "exemplary" Negro. The first black scholarship athlete in the Southwest Conference had to be a model citizen with a solid family background. Like other integration pioneers, LeVias could not enjoy the privilege most humans have: the right to be flawed. LeVias was, in many ways, flawless as an athlete and as a person. When he was faced with racist taunts and death threats, he followed Martin Luther King's model, exposing the illogic of white supremacy by not fight-ing back, except with his athletic ability. Indeed, when King vis-ited SMU's campus in 1966, he counseled LeVias with the words "kindness kills," echoing his own nonviolent approach to combatting white racism. The advice resonated with the deeply religious LeVias, who told interviewers years later that the Serenity Prayer helped him endure the brutalization and isolation he experienced during his years at SMU:

God grant me the serenity
To accept the things I cannot change;
Courage to change the things I can;
And wisdom to know the difference.

Jerry LeVias is part of that courageous class of black integration pioneers. They are martyr-like historical figures whom we rightfully owe a debt of gratitude. But too often the story of racial integration in big-time sports ends when the integration pioneers entered the previously lily-white institution. As was the case with Jackie Robinson, the emotional scars stayed with the integration pioneers long after they left the playing field. Though Martin Luther King advised LeVias to stay the course of nonviolence and respond with kindness, kindness nearly killed LeVias himself, stripping him of his ability to feel. "I couldn't have any emotions," he remarked in a revealing oral history years later. "I had no emotions for anything, anyone, except for close friends."[20] Still, LeVias survived and thrived even after his football career ended. Other SWC integrators were not so fortunate. John Westbrook, the first black Baylor Bear, died at age thirty-five. Jon Richardson, the first black scholarship athlete for Frank Broyles's Arkansas Razorbacks, died of a heart attack in 2002 at age forty-nine. The trauma of desegregation might not have directly led to these deaths, but the stress of enduring racism undoubtedly shaved years off the lives of these men.

The story of integration does not end with black pioneers and their white allies killing racism with kindness. The real changes of the integration era happened thereafter, when political activism, black athletic excellence, and visionary coaching transformed the world of big-time college athletics. In the Southwest Conference, and indeed in schools and athletic programs throughout the South, the immediate thereafter was the 1970s, when the terms of inclusion of black athletes—and later women athletes—were established. Black men filled up the rosters of previously white teams and occasionally ascended to the level of assistant coach, but black men did not ascend to the level of management. The growing commercialization of intercollegiate sports in a world that was governed by the NCAA's fundamentalist stance on amateurism ensured that only transcendently talented players, including those who were African American, would get a share of the revenue generated by their talents. Much of that revenue would pass into the growing class of professionals who populated the world of sports management and journalism, a domain that remained dominated by white men. The collapse of Jim Crow college football was a realignment, rather than a demolition, of social hierarchies. The heroic stories of racial progress notwithstanding, the inequities established during the integration era remain to this day.

* * *

Darrell Royal was on top of the world. On December 6, 1969, his Texas Longhorns came back from the brink of defeat to pull out a 15–14 victory over their SWC archrivals Arkansas Razorbacks. The dramatic victory was televised by ABC Sports. ABC's *NCAA Football* program popularized college football for a national audience on fall Saturday afternoons, thanks to dramatic contests like this one. The event was popular not only because of the Longhorns' dramatic fourth-quarter comeback, but also because President Richard Nixon and a coterie of politicians, including then congressman George H. W. Bush and the US senator from Texas John Tower, attended the game. Nixon took the opportunity to visit with Royal's team after the game and presented the athletes with a plaque and a ringing endorsement as the number-one team in college football. Royal, bursting with gratitude, told Nixon, "Mr. President, I've got to be the happiest man in America tonight."[21]

The Texas head football coach had reason to be the happiest

man in America on that December evening in Fayetteville, Arkansas. His dramatic win over Frank Broyles's Razorbacks secured the number-one ranking in the country. His Longhorns went on to defeat Ara Parseghian's tough Notre Dame Fighting Irish 24–17 in the Cotton Bowl Classic on New Year's Day 1970. The win clinched Royal's second national championship in seven years. The national championship occurred in the midst of the Longhorns' unprecedented run of six consecutive conference championships. The 1969 Longhorns went down in history for another reason: they were the last all-white national championship team in NCAA college football history.

UT's undefeated national championship season seemed to mark the continuation of Longhorn dominance in the Southwest Conference, but profound changes were already underway that eventually altered conference play in the years to come. These changes were partially impelled by events off the field. The radicalization of the black freedom struggle and the growing movement against the war in Vietnam in the late 1960s had a profound impact on college athletic programs across the country. Authority was being questioned everywhere, it seemed, including in the realm of athletic programs, arenas where coaches traditionally held unquestioned authority. National publications like *Sports Illustrated* were announcing a crisis in the college game. Its 1969 article "The Desperate Coach" was a tale of coaches confronting a hoard of undisciplined, rebellious, and lazy youth who did not want to work hard anymore. One coach insisted that the aim of the New Left was "to replace the athlete with the hippie as the idol of kids." He continued, "I don't know if it can be done, but it seems society is intent on destroying Horatio Alger Jr. The oddball is getting control. The good guy is outnumbered. America seems interested only in glorifying the loser."[22]

Much of the sporting establishment viewed these movements in similar alarmist terms—as a symptom of the decline of American civilization. But the athletic manifestations of the insurgency of the late 1960s and early '70s was not a mindless rebellion of undisciplined black "militants" and hippies who did not want to cut their hair and who relished in disobeying authority. Rather, it was a movement that was raising fundamental questions about the role of sport in society and about the meaning of social and political equality, questions we are still wrestling with in our time. Athletes, like the young men drafted to fight in Vietnam, need not succumb to the dictates of their authoritarian coaches. Reading even positive portrayals of football culture fifty years later could lead some to appreciate why some athletes were resisting coaches' legitimacy. One only had to read books like Giles Tippette's *Saturday's Children* to get a sense of the abuse athletes routinely experienced in college athletic programs. Tippette's account of the Rice Owls' 1971 season under coach Bill Peterson was critical of athletic "militants" like Rodrigo Barnes, but it also exposed the abusive and opportunistic system of big-time college football. His detailed description of the season opener between Rice and the University of Houston powerfully illustrated the exploitation of college football players. He vividly portrays the courage of Stahle Vincent, Rice's integration pioneer, as he was repeatedly sent out to perform on the sizzling artificial turf of Rice Stadium in September 1971 even as he suffered from concussions and heat exhaustion during the brutally hot Houston afternoon. Tippette's portrayal questioned the prevailing idea that football was educating young men into responsible citizens.[23]

The politics of late 1960s athletic protest was impelled, in part, by the larger black student movement. On the campus of the flagship university in Austin, students continued to pressure Royal's athletic program to integrate. In the fall of 1967, the Negro Association for Progress stormed his office protesting the lack of progress on integration. Though a few black athletes had attempted to try out for the program's teams, none were actively recruited by Royal and none, for one reason or another, had stuck with the team. Student pressure continued into 1970, when African American and Mexican American student groups once again questioned UT's commitment to integration. Royal's assistant, Bill Ellington, speaking on the head coach's behalf, told students, "Like Coach Royal told you, we want the good ones as fast as we can."[24] Similar student protests were happening at other schools in Texas, including Texas A&M and SMU. Students in Texas were pushing for more than the token signing of select black super athletes. At SMU, the Black League of Afro-American and African College Students (BLAACS) made a series of demands of the university, including more recruitment of black athletes in sports other than football, especially baseball and track and field. "We have proven that we are a vital part of the football program," they wrote, "and we feel that the Athletic Department should prove its sincerity not to us, but to all black people by the recruitment of blacks in the other fields of sports at SMU."[25]

The Black Power movement had a profound impact on black athletes on predominantly white campuses.[26] Tommie Smith, John Carlos, Muhammad Ali, Jim Brown, Kareem Abdul-Jabbar (then Lew Alcindor), and others were in the vanguard of what Harry Edwards chronicled in *The Revolt of the Black Athlete*. Black Texans were also influenced by the national movement of athletic activism. Most of their protests occurred at the individual level, though occasionally they happened collectively. In 1971, four black players—Larry Dibbles, Ervin Garnett, Hodges Mitchell, and future NFL player and head coach Raymond Rhodes— quit Texas Christian University's football team due to the perceived racist policies of recently hired coach Jim Pittman. Their grievances, objections to Pittman's insistence on athletes shaving their mustaches, were intertwined with other black student concerns on the campus.[27] More common resistance took the form of individual acts of noncompliance against the dictates of athletic programs and coaches. One of the more forthright critics of the college football structure was Rodrigo Barnes, the supremely talented linebacker for the Rice University Owls. Barnes, Stahle Vincent, and Mike Tyler were the first three black football players to be signed to athletic scholarships by the school. All three distinguished themselves as the best players on the team throughout their time at Rice. Barnes never pretended to play along with the myth of the "student athlete." Football, he told sportswriter John Anders, "is strictly a business. These guys who say they love football have their love values in the wrong place. It's a part of my life but it's not everything."[28] Barnes continued to critique the college football establishment in insightful terms. "My thing is Rodrigo Barnes, 'cause after this season [Rice head coach] Al Conover won't know Rodrigo Barnes."[29]

Yet the revolt of the black athlete was also part of a larger cross-racial sports activist movement that included those who were defined as white. Throughout the country, athletes were directly challenging what they saw as their exploitation. Jack Scott, who was dismissed by some because of his alleged connection to Patty Hearst, was one of the more eloquent critics of the corruption of sports by the NCAA. His lesser-known classic, *The Athletic Revolution*, documented the collective struggles of white and black student-athletes to make astute critiques of the hypocrisy of the NCAA stance promoting amateurism even as it cast a blind eye toward their exploitation by universities and their political spokespersons. Nothing short of a radical transformation of the country's educational structure, Scott argued, would allow athletics to become relevant to the education of the youth of the United States. "Simply put," Scott argued, "there cannot *be athletics for athletes* without a concomitant emphasis on *education for students*."[30]

Countering the Nixon administration's image of football players as obedient soldiers of the political establishment, the athletic insurgency actually included many college football players, who chafed at the sport's militarized authoritarian structure. Though the most radical forms of athletic activism occurred in the northern and western parts of the country, in Texas players also crafted their own forms of dissident football literature. The former Longhorn and New York Jets All-Pro wide receiver George Sauer Jr. abruptly retired in 1971 at the peak of his career, telling reporters that football coaches "treat players like children."[31] Sauer was often characterized by the befuddled football press as a troubled soul, but he actually decided to quit the game to pursue a career as a writer even as he struggled to let go of his football career. He wrote the foreword to *Meat on the Hoof*, a book authored by another Texan football player turned critic, Gary Shaw. Like Pete Gent's novel *North Dallas Forty*, perhaps the most famous title in this body of sports dissident literature, the book exposed football's toxic masculinist culture, centering on Shaw's struggles to make the varsity team in a system that was designed to dehumanize and force less talented players to quit the team. Shaw painted vivid portraits of abusive "shit drills" and "Medina sessions" (authored by Longhorn trainer Frank Medina) run by minions of the aloof Royal, who used his distance from his players to manipulate them. To Royal, Shaw's problem was simple: he didn't really "want" to play football. Wanting to play football meant succumbing to a dehumanizing physical brutalization akin to any hazing program.

Shaw's book has often been misread as merely an exposé of Darrell Royal's Longhorn program. In fact, like much of the insurgent literature by former football players, Shaw's book raised larger questions beyond the abuses he endured as a second-string lineman struggling to make it on the Longhorn roster. Shaw was more interested in exposing the consequences of the win-at-any-cost mentality that prevailed at the University of Texas and in the big-time sports world. "It's not just that football is so popular and that attacking it would endanger the enjoyment these people have on Saturday afternoons," he wrote. "No, I think it turns right to the core of the American psyche. These big shots are all 'winners' whose most basic tenet is the same motivational core of football. Only a few get to be winners, and you make it by competing and by defeating others."[32] Shaw was not merely out to debunk the Darrell Royal myth. He was more interested in highlighting the illogic of masculinity in big-time college football and in the society at large. This is why Sauer himself wrote that it would be a "poor act of deception" if readers mistakenly took *Meat on the Hoof* to be a story of one bad college football program.[33] Reading Shaw and his contemporary nearly fifty years later in light of the abundant evidence of the relationship between playing football and brain trauma, and decades of evidence that expose the hypocrisy of the NCAA, it is hard not to think that the authors of the radical athletic insurgency were right.

The Texas versions of the national sports activist movement contributed to the tarnishing of the pristine images of coaches like Darrell Royal. The integration of his football program finally began when Julius Whittier signed with the Longhorns in 1969. By 1972, Royal's recruiters had convinced eight black players to come to Austin, including his first black star player, running back Roosevelt Leaks. But they, too, refused to perpetuate the Royal myth even while they played for the legendary coach. In a widely publicized five-part series of articles published by the Associated Press, none of Royal's black players gave their coach a ringing endorsement, a remarkable thing that one rarely sees from current scholarship athletes. When asked if he thought Royal was racist, Julius Whittier replied frankly: "'Yeah,' he said, 'I think he is.'" Then he went on to give an explanation: "Royal is from Hollis, Oklahoma. And so, you know, he can't help but be what he is from his surroundings. But I think Coach Royal knows that racism is wrong. I don't think he wants to be."[34]

While Royal was miffed at his racist image, he was more disturbed by the fact that one of his rival schools was beating him consistently on the field of play with many black Texans he could not recruit. Black players were signing with other SWC schools, but they were often going to the Oklahoma Sooners, UT's chief rival in the Big Eight conference, who the Longhorns played every October at the Red River Shootout at the Cotton Bowl. Royal's teams had dominated Oklahoma throughout the 1960s. But in 1971, the Sooners overtook them with a powerful wishbone offensive scheme—which they learned from Royal's staff—and a cadre of talented athletes to run it. In the 1971 game between the two teams, led by Abilene quarterback Jack Mildren and Houstonian running back Greg Pruitt, the Sooners trounced the Longhorns 48–27. Pruitt, another small black Texan halfback with breakaway speed who was overlooked by Royal and most SWC schools, found a home in Norman, Oklahoma. Royal's defenses could not stop the offense he supposedly authored. The Sooners took the wishbone one step further than Texas by adding speed. "And that made a huge difference," Pruitt recalled to historian Wann Smith, "because even if that X looked like it could cover the O on the chalkboard, when O runs a 4.3 and the X runs a 4.7, it isn't quite so easy."[35]

Pruitt was the first of many black Texan running backs who were wooed away from Texas to join the Sooners in Norman. Barry Switzer, an eventual longtime Sooner head coach, recalled years later that under his predecessor Chuck Fairbanks, who had previously been an assistant to Bill Yeoman at the University of Houston, the Sooners decided to wage an "all-out recruiting war in Texas" by aggressively recruiting blacks at every position, not just at the so-called "speed" positions.[36] Their efforts paid off handsomely. In the 1970s, black Texan running backs Joe Washington, Billy Sims, Kenny King, and David Overstreet, among others, shunned Royal's Longhorn football program for Sooner glory. After Switzer became Oklahoma's head football coach in 1973, the Sooners continued to dominate the Longhorns on their way to multiple national championships in the 1970s and '80s. Switzer, the self-styled "Bootlegger's Boy," was outhustling the Texas football legend, and he brashly let him know about it in the newspapers. Royal was not happy. He repeatedly whined to his friends in the press and to the NCAA authorities about recruiting violations supposedly committed by his opponents, which is probably why the Sooners were put on probation for such violations in 1974. But Royal's complaints could not change the fact that after dominating his arch rivals for years, he would never manage to defeat the Sooners again.

Darrell Royal's troubles recruiting black student-athletes were partially informed by the fact that he could view them only as objects of charity, rather than as partners he needed to depend on to survive the changing recruiting landscape in Texas. His reflections on his imagined growing racial awareness in the early '70s are particularly revealing: "I wasn't doing anything to keep them from having an equal chance—but I wasn't doing anything to help 'em get an equal chance," he told his biographer Jimmy Banks. "And if I had anything to be regretful about as far as the blacks were concerned, that was it—I just wasn't concerned soon enough about trying to help them."[37] Luckily for Coach Royal, a majestically talented running back from Tyler, Texas, named Earl Campbell decided to help *him*, even if neither saw their relationship in those terms. Royal and Ken Dabbs, his chief recruiter, successfully convinced Campbell to sign with the Longhorns in 1973. And while Campbell's first three seasons did not result in SWC titles and victories over the Sooners, the Tyler Rose eventually put it all together—perhaps not by accident—after his coach retired and was replaced by Fred Akers in 1976. Akers abandoned Royal's wishbone scheme and put Campbell in an I-formation offense, where he fully realized his football potential. In 1977, Campbell led the Longhorns to an 11–1 record, including a sweet victory over the rival Sooners in the annual Red River Shootout, an SWC championship, and a return to the Cotton Bowl Classic. He also became the first Longhorn to win the Heisman Trophy, and he went on to have a Hall of Fame professional career. Campbell helped usher the Longhorns into the post–Jim Crow era, but by then the program had fallen behind not only the Sooners but the new insurgent powers of the Southwest Conference.[38]

In the early 1970s, good ol' boy coaches in the Bear Bryant and Darrell Royal mold were slowly being eclipsed by more open-minded, often younger, football men who understood that team success was contingent on the recruitment of talented black athletes. Some, like Switzer, openly embraced the social implications of black athletes playing for white universities. Others, like Houston's Bill Yeoman and Baylor University's new head football coach Grant Teaff, were relatively silent about the social impact of black athletes in their programs, though they knew they had to find ways to recruit them to their schools. Teaff proved to be a quick study. On more than one occasion, he highlighted Waco's "great black community," which he liked to claim had enhanced Baylor's attractiveness to prospective black athletes. "We're getting not only the black players, but the top black students as well and they seem to feel there's a tremendous social life here," he insisted in 1974.[39]

Royal could not embrace the changes occurring around him, but other coaches in the conference followed Hayden Fry's example and did. In addition to Teaff, Royal's former assistant Emory Bellard, the real mastermind behind his wishbone, went beyond his mentor when he became the head coach of the Texas A&M Aggies in 1972. With black standouts such as defensive backs Lester Hayes and Pat Thomas, running back Ernest "Bubba" Bean, and kick returner Carl Roaches, the Aggies of the mid-1970s fielded some of its best teams in decades. At SMU under Hayden Fry and under his successor Dave Smith, the Mustangs continued to rely significantly on black players, including Oak Cliff High graduate Wayne Morris and their first black quarterback, Ricky Wesson, whom they signed out of Dallas Carter. Though there wasn't always a direct correlation between the integration of teams and their success on the field, by the mid-1970s, it was clear to all head coaches in the Southwest Conference that the days of winning big-time football games without black labor power were over.

By 1976, both Royal and Broyles saw the handwriting on the wall as their teams struggled through subpar 5–5–1 records. Both retired at the end of the season, and both landed on their feet as athletic directors in the expanding industry of athletic sport management. Broyles also went on to a TV career with Roone Arledge's ABC Sports as the lead color commentator with play-by-play man Keith Jackson for the network's college football telecasts. As Broyles and Royal rode off into the sunset, another upstart program was on the verge of running roughshod over the historic powers of the Southwest Conference.

* * *

The sea change in SWC football could be ascertained eight years before Broyles and Royal retired to their athletic directorships. On September 21, 1968, a sellout crowd of 66,400 spectators packed Memorial Stadium in Austin to witness the showdown between the hometown Texas Longhorns and the upstart Houston Cougars. Though the Longhorns were in the midst of their historic run of conference dominance, that season they were trying to rebound from two rare mediocre seasons. Meanwhile, the Cougars, coached by Bill Yeoman, were a rising power in Texas college football. Their emergence in the mid-1960s was tied in part to their adoption of the veer offense, an innovative scheme that wreaked havoc on defenses and allowed the Cougars to put points on the scoreboard. After Yeoman fully committed to the offensive scheme in 1966, the Cougars led the nation in yards and total offense. The offense was so successful that it prompted Darrell Royal and Emory Bellard, then his offensive coordinator, to adopt a version of it for his struggling team. In fact, the new Longhorn version, which would become known as the wishbone offense, would debut that very night against the Cougars. Still, Yeoman was confident that his team would make a good showing against the traditional Texas college football power. "Now we're ready to play the football game we've been waiting to play for a long time," Yeoman told reporters before the game.[40]

Indeed, they were ready. The game began with Cougars star running back Paul Gipson "simply stuffing the ball down the Longhorns' throats on a fifty-yard drive to a touchdown," according to the *Austin Statesman*.[41] Gipson was part of the growing number of black players Yeoman recruited to UH in the years after he signed Warren McVea. He was a speedy and powerful running back who terrorized defenses throughout his college career. His touchdown in the first quarter was the first of three he would score that night, including a spectacular sixty-six-yard run down the left sideline. Meanwhile, Chris Gilbert, the Longhorns' star running back, also turned in a memorable performance with two touchdowns of his own. Yeoman's squad had more total yards and had control of the game in the fourth quarter, but they could not push through with a game-winning score and had to settle for a 20–20 tie. The Cougars failed to win the game, but their performance earned the team a measure of respect, including from Royal and the Longhorns. The game showcased the talents of the

Cougars' black players, especially Gipson, and it allowed UH to make a legitimate argument that it should join the Southwest Conference. After persistent lobbying and negotiations, three years later, the University of Houston was admitted to the exclusive club of Texas intercollegiate athletics. The school would begin competing against SWC schools in basketball and other sports in 1975 and in football in 1976.[42]

Founded in 1927 as a junior college, the University of Houston was a private institution until 1963, when it became part of the state's public higher education system. The main campus was located southeast of downtown, not too far away from the core of Houston's black community and from Texas Southern University, the black university created by the state legislature in 1947. In Harry Fouke, the university found the right person to build the program and the university's reputation. A graduate of Rice University in 1935 who then obtained a master's degree from Columbia University, Fouke became UH's first athletic director in 1945. Over the next thirty-five years, Fouke built the athletic program from scratch. He hired alum and former Cougars standout player Guy Lewis to be the head coach of the basketball team in 1956. Lewis, who was the best player on the team's first two basketball teams in the mid-1940s, went on to lead the Cougars to national prominence during the next thirty years. Fouke also hired Bill Yeoman in 1961 to be the head football coach. Born in Indiana but raised in Arizona, Yeoman excelled as a football player, becoming one of the captains of Earl "Red" Blaik's team at Army during the late 1940s. After graduating from the academy, he coached with Blaik and later with Duffy Dougherty at Michigan State from 1957 to 1961, when Fouke hired him as the Cougars head football coach.

Yeoman's first few seasons were fairly unremarkable, but history presented the coach with an opportunity. In 1962, as black Houstonians were in the midst of their own sit-in movement, the university staved off the possibility of public protest and announced that it would break with Jim Crow and admit black students. One year later, in 1963, the same year the University of Texas desegregated its athletic program, UH announced it would begin to recruit black students into its athletic program. But while Royal and UT proceeded slowly, Yeoman and Fouke actively sought out talented African American athletes. Not surprisingly, they quickly found many talented young men available, especially as most Southwest Conference schools were slow to integrate. As a young institution without the deep entanglements in powerful segregationist alumni and with no real winning tradition, Yeoman was free to forge ahead and look for black athletic talent. He sought the assistance of the local black leader Quentin Mease, who used his San Antonio connections to recruit Warren McVea, one of the most heralded high school football players in the nation. A few months later, the school staged a coup by signing McVea to a scholarship a few months before SMU signed Jerry LeVias.[43]

Yeoman eschewed any description of himself as a racial barrier breaker. "I'd like to say it took great soul-searching and courage to recruit McVea," he told reporters years later, "but it didn't take squat. I just wanted players who could win, and they knew it. My parents were color blind. The kids know I'll chew on a black as quick as a white. I'll love a black as quick as a white."[44] If the Cougars head coach professed any underlying belief system, it was his Christian faith. He, like many football coaches and players at the time, belonged to the Fellowship of Christian Athletes. "We can talk all you want about recruiting and coaching, but the real secret is that I got my personal position worked out with the Lord. If you get things right with him, you don't need to worry anymore," he once said.[45] Yeoman's comments might look like a bunch of coach double talk. Christianity and racial integration might look like an untenable contradiction in our time, when evangelical Christianity is tethered to right-wing politics even when they directly contradict Christian values. But in the 1970s, evangelical Christianity wasn't as firmly linked to right-wing racism as it would become during and after the 1980s. The Fellow-

Bill Yeoman on the sidelines. Courtesy Special Collections Division of the M. D. Anderson Library, University of Houston.

ship of Christian Athletes had a number of prominent members who were moderate to liberal in their social attitudes, including Tom Landry, Roger Staubach, and many others.

McVea's arrival in Houston was one factor that gave rise to UH as an athletic powerhouse. The second was the university's decision to play home games at the new Houston Astrodome beginning in 1965. The Dome gave the program national visibility and an attractive home stadium for potential recruits. Though McVea struggled on the field during his sophomore season, the program's fortunes improved when Yeoman devised a new offensive scheme that became known as the veer. Like many inventions, it took shape by accident. After noticing how his offensive lineman could not consistently block defenders on running plays, Yeoman had his quarterback fake handoffs to the fullback and then veer down the offensive line, where he would have a number of options available to him. He could find a hole and keep the ball and run through it, or pitch it to a halfback running alongside him. Over time, Yeoman added passing plays off the veer, which complicated matters for defenses further. More importantly, the formation forced defenders to hesitate and wait to see what the quarterback would do with the ball. The delayed reactions took the aggressiveness away from the defenders, who could no longer disrupt plays by bullying their way past inferior blockers.[46]

Soon thereafter, the Cougars began to put up points and yardage in record numbers. In 1968, the Cougars routed the University of Tulsa by the unfathomable score of 100–6. But brilliant schemes alone don't win ballgames. Players do, and UH's football program was buoyed by an influx of talented athletes. Most of them were black and were ignored by the Southwest Conference powers. Running backs Paul Gipson and Robert Newhouse compiled record rushing seasons while receivers Elmo Wright and Riley Odoms became All-Americans and future professionals. From 1966 to 1974, the Cougars compiled multiple winning seasons and four appearances in the Astro-Bluebonnet Bowl, the City of Houston's own postseason bowl game. In 1973, led by Lufkin-native quarterback D. C. Nobles and a host of talented runners, the Cougars rolled to an 11–1 record and thrashed the Tulane Green Wave in the Astro-Bluebonnet Bowl 47–7.

The Cougars were winning on the field, yet they continued to be considered by the press and by Texas football insiders as "outlaws," as a rag-tag group from an urban commuter university that was still viewed as a glorified high school. The *Houston Post* columnist Jack Gallagher summed up the prevailing attitude toward the school and its athletic program when, in *Dave Campbell's Texas Football* preview of the 1976 season, he noted that Houston was viewed as "too loud, too strident, too vocal, too pushy in the fashion of youthful challenger Cassius Clay demanding a heavyweight title shot."[47] Not academically good enough for college, these players were lured to Houston by under-the-table inducements, critics charged. After Yeoman signed McVea, his program was put on probation for three years for alleged recruitment violations. The NCAA, the governing body of big-time college sports, saw itself as protecting the integrity of the sport. That integrity was based on the principle of amateurism, that players should be compensated for their labor only with athletic scholarships. As more black players entered the sport, the NCAA grew more suspicious of programs that seemed to sign talented players, especially if they were not part of the establishment. But the mythical nature of the "student-athlete" was well known by the press and by critics of the sport, who highlighted the ways players' time was dominated by football rather than by academic pursuits. While old-guard coaches like Darrell Royal sought to cloak their programs with tales of academic integrity, the new breed of coaches unabashedly disregarded the myth. The blacker the Cougars got, the more outlawish they became in the eyes of the old-guard college football establishment.

*   *   *

On a cold New Year's Day afternoon at the 1977 Cotton Bowl Classic, the Houston Cougars' sophomore quarterback led his team from the huddle to the line of scrimmage. He surveyed the defense as the offensive linemen in front of him kneeled into their three-point stances. His team was up against it. He had led the Cougars to a 27–7 first-half lead, but his opponents, the University of Maryland Terrapins, stormed back with two touchdowns to cut the deficit to six points, 27–21. Now the Cougars offense faced a critical third down with six yards to go on their own eleven-yard line. Six minutes were left in the game. If they failed to get a first down and keep possession of the ball, they would be forced to punt the ball back to the Terrapins, who would likely get the ball in good field position to score the go-ahead touchdown. "There wasn't any pep talks or speeches in the huddle," the quarterback told the press after the game. "We all knew the situation. We had to have the first down, we had to run some time off the clock."[48]

But as the quarterback dropped back to pass, he was immediately surrounded by a group of swarming Terrapin defenders getting ready to sack him. Somehow he eluded the tacklers and threw the ball to flanker Robert Lavergne, who was open downfield. "I was running an out route, but I was about 20 yards up the sidelines," Lavergne told the press after the game. "But then I saw the pass coming. It was right on the money." LaVergne caught the ball right along the sideline and somehow stayed in bounds at the twenty-four-yard line, a thirteen-yard pass play to give the Cougars a badly needed first down. The big play enabled Houston to regain control of the game. A few plays later, they kicked a field goal to give them three more points and clinched a 30–21 victory.[49]

In the victorious locker room after the game, the quarterback was overcome with emotion. He led his team, an unlikely band of players derided as outlaws to a Cotton Bowl victory. He thought of his cousin, Dwaine Staten, a tight end who had played with him at Dallas Carter High School; he had died of meningitis at SMU during Davis's freshman year at UH. His mind flashed to another childhood friend, Lee Gary Robinson, who had been killed in Dallas. He was reminded of another death, that of his older brother from a drug overdose. "We had all talked about watching each other play in the Cotton Bowl and being together," he told reporters in the locker room. "It seemed like every time I called home, people I had told about the Cotton Bowl and that I wanted there, something bad had happened to them." All of those losses rushed through his mind as he, the quarterback who had grown up in the shadow of the stadium where his ancestors were not allowed to play with white players on the same field, now the leader of the SWC champion and Cotton Bowl Classic victors, savored the victory.[50]

The quarterback would have been unimaginable to fans of Southwest Conference football only a few years before. His name was Danny Davis, the signal caller of the Houston Cougars football team of the mid- to late 1970s. As is often the case with African Americans who achieve success despite a background of adversity, the black quarterback's triumph could not be totally di-

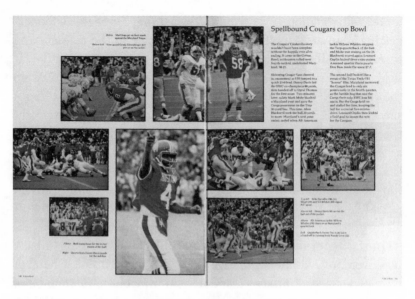

Danny Davis and the 1976 SWC Champion Cougars. Courtesy Special Collections Division of the M. D. Anderson Library, University of Houston.

vorced from the troubles of the recent and distant past, not only the nefarious forces wreaking havoc on urban America in the 1970s such as violence, material deprivation, and drugs, but also the longer history of slavery and Jim Crow segregation. Davis's was a feel-good story of Southwest Conference football in the revolutionary era of the 1970s. He was not only able to excel in the most important position, quarterback, but also to convey his genuine feelings to the press, including the griefs that he felt after his memorable performance at the 1977 Cotton Bowl Classic. He wasn't the first black quarterback in the SWC; Stahle Vincent was the first when he took snaps for Rice in 1969. Neither was Davis the first black quarterback for the Cougars. That was D. C. Nobles. However, he was arguably the first black quarterback who led an SWC team to success when he quarterbacked the Cougars from 1976 to 1978.

Danny Davis was born Danny Jones, but he changed his name after he was adopted by Sammie Davis, a prominent minister and community leader who pastored the Fellowship Baptist Church. As a kid, he sold concessions at the Cotton Bowl, hawking popcorn, peanuts, and sodas. "I remember working one Texas-OU game," said Davis, "but my real inspiration came from SMU. I remember watching Jerry LeVias and Raymond Mapps and Chuck Hixson."[51] He, like the Baylor integration pioneer John Westbrook, was the son of a minister who eventually became a minister himself after his playing days were over.

Davis was the unquestioned leader of the Cougars team that stormed the Southwest Conference during its first year in the league in 1976. The Cougars finished 7–1 in the conference and 9–2 overall, winning the title and a Cotton Bowl berth. Their most satisfying win was probably the 30–0 drubbing of the Texas Longhorns at Memorial Stadium in Austin, a game that hastened Darrell Royal's retirement. The team that helped catalyze the racial integration of college football in Texas won the conference with a majority-black playing roster. Thirty-seven of the team's sixty-five players on the 1976 roster were black. The team crashed back to earth with a 6–5 record in 1977, a disappointing season in part because Davis was sidelined with a season-ending separated shoulder injury and in part because Earl Campbell stampeded his way to his Heisman Trophy that fall. But in 1978, the Cougars came roaring back to win the conference with a 9–2 record and another trip to the Cotton Bowl. Davis, now a senior, once again led the team at quarterback. They won many of their games by close margins, showing that the team had character.

The Texas sporting press couldn't help but notice how Yeoman's Cougars had flipped the script on the Southwest Conference. "What's Yeoman doing down there in that Harlem?" Skip Bayless wrote during the season in one of his many columns about the Cougars, spoofing the white supremacists he presumed predominated in the SWC hierarchy. "There was no way this predominantly black inner-city team could sit at the front of the SWC bus. No way [Coach Yeoman] could win recruiting all those 'dumb' blacks," he continued sarcastically. "No way Yeoman can win staying as loose as he does. No way he can survive cutting practices short and giving his players Friday off."[52] In another column later that season, he wrote, "Why, people keep asking, does Houston keep winning the SWC? . . . It is because [white defensive back] Kenny Hatfield can call a teammate a 'nigger.' It is because that teammate can call Hatfield a 'slow white boy' or worse. Because, to the Cougars, bigotry is an inside joke."[53] While race tended to be a taboo subject on most teams, on the Cougars it was called out repeatedly. Hatfield, the featured player in the article, was a white cornerback on a team where seventeen of the twenty-two starters were nonwhite. Bayless thought this was noteworthy because the position was already determined to be reserved for black athletes who were supposedly faster than whites. Yeoman's team had turned the tables on the SWC, not just by fielding a near-majority black football team but by putting white players in positions that were supposedly better suited for faster blacks.

And the Cougars flipped the script in another significant way. The outlaws from "down there in that Harlem" of the Houston black community were led once again by the kid from the black community in East Dallas. What was so striking about Davis's performances, especially in the few surviving telecasts of Cougars games from that era, was the supreme confidence he showed on the field. He possessed quickness and speed, yet he was relatively short for a quarterback and wasn't the fastest player on the team. As his coach Bill Yeoman put it, "you judge a quarterback like you judge a coach—on how many games he wins. Danny is a winner."[54] Observers of the Cougars on the gridiron could hardly disagree. The quarterback ran the veer offense smartly; indeed, his coach liked to say that no one had run his offense any better. He was a *leader*—a title, like that of *winner*, that had been reserved for the white "field general" quarterback. Watching Davis discuss strategy with his head coach during a timeout in a critical moment in the first half of the 1979 Cotton Bowl Classic, one is struck by how Yeoman was listening to his quarterback more than giving instructions.[55]

Davis was among the best black quarterbacks in the 1970s, an era when they became more prevalent in college football. He also was a favorite of the local press, especially among the writers who covered college football for the *Dallas Morning News*. "I'm not fast, I'm not an All-America," he said to the press before the 1979 Cotton Bowl Classic in tongue-in-cheek fashion, purposely minimizing his talents. "All I do is hand the ball off."[56] While much discussion of the black athlete in the post–civil rights era hinges on stereotypes of black natural athleticism, Davis assumed the role that had typically been, and seemingly still is now, reserved for white quarterbacks. This is clear not only in the coverage of Davis in the Dallas press but also in the surviving telecasts of Cougars games.

The Cotton Bowl Classic on New Year's Day 1979, when the Cougars squared off against the Notre Dame Fighting Irish, should have been the storybook ending to Davis's college career. But brutal playing conditions and, more importantly, a heroic performance by a future Hall of Fame quarterback named Joe Montana unexpectedly rewrote the end of Davis's football story. The game was marred by a historic ice storm that descended on the Dallas area. Game time temperatures were twenty-two degrees Fahrenheit with an eighteen-mile-per-hour-wind and a six-degrees-below-zero wind chill. The fans, which numbered far fewer than the 32,500 listed in the official attendance figure for the game, were forced to break the ice that had covered the seats in the old stadium. The ten-year-old, threadbare artificial turf field worsened the situation, as players slipped and fell on the icy, concrete-like surface all afternoon. Still, Davis was undaunted. He directed the Houston veer offense up and down the slippery field all afternoon, leading the Cougars to a commanding 34–12 fourth-quarter lead. But unbelievably, Davis's inevitable coronation suddenly became known as the "Chicken Soup Game." Montana, who spent the third quarter under blankets in the locker room supposedly drinking chicken soup to fight off flu-like symptoms, came off the bench to lead one of the many come-from-behind victories in his legendary football career. With seven minutes, thirty-seven seconds to go, the Irish blocked a punt for a touchdown, cutting the deficit to fourteen points. Then the Irish scored two more touchdowns and a two-point conversion, the last touchdown being a scoring pass from Montana to Kris Haines with only two seconds left in the contest. The stunned Cougars watched the Fighting Irish kick the extra point to steal the game 35–34 in front of the few brave souls who stayed to watch the thrilling game. In the master narrative of college football history, the moment signified the launch of the Montana legend. It also marked the end of Danny Davis's football story. He never played pro football, but he did find a higher calling that drew on his leadership capabilities as the head pastor of Jordan Grove Baptist Church in Houston's Third Ward.[57]

The shocking loss to Notre Dame did not stop Houston's dominance of the Southwest Conference. They won the league championship yet again the very next season. Even with Davis's departure, the Cougars ran off with a 10–1 record, which gave them their third conference title in the four years they were in the league. At the 1980 Cotton Bowl Classic, under the more ideal playing conditions of a bright and sunny day, the Cougars pulled off their own dramatic last-second win over Nebraska 17–14. The outlaws from Houston had conquered the conference. Contrary to what some prognosticators feared, attendance at SWC games was reaching all-time highs and a new cadre of talented athletes were writing new chapters in the state's illustrious football story.

Yet the 1979 season marked the highpoint of Yeoman's tenure at UH. In the coming years, the program was taken down by the NCAA for recruitment violations, a fate that befell many programs in the SWC. Yeoman was unceremoniously fired amid a recruitment scandal in 1986. Somehow Bill Yeoman's Houston Cougars never quite got the recognition they rightfully deserved. Maybe they were "too loud, too strident, too vocal, too pushy," as Jack Gallagher had described them. Maybe they were too "inner-city" and "too black" to be considered a legitimate college football program. Or maybe it was because the Cougars would be eclipsed by another outlaw program at the other end of the I-45 corridor, one that made the squad in Houston seem like law-abiding citizens.

* * *

Southern Methodist University head football coach Ron Meyer and his staff of recruiters were alarmed when they opened the sports pages on February 15, 1979. Newspapers across the state reported that Eric Dickerson, arguably the most sought-after high school football running back in the country, showed up at school in little Sealy, Texas, driving a shiny new gold Pontiac Trans Am. The sighting occurred only a few weeks before Signing Day, the official day when all high school athletes were supposed to officially sign with the schools in which they would enroll to play college football. In the weeks before the Trans Am episode, Dickerson had been weighing his options between the University of Southern California, the University of Oklahoma, Texas A&M, and SMU. Though recent reports indicated that he made a verbal agreement with the A&M Aggies, Meyer and his posse thought they had the inside track on the talented running back, who many were touting would exceed the heights recently achieved by Earl Campbell. At six feet, three inches tall and 205 pounds, Dickerson possessed the power to run over tacklers, like the Tyler Rose, but he had more speed than Campbell, running the one-hundred-yard dash in only 9.4 seconds. During the Class AA state championship game in Waco a few weeks earlier, he rushed for 311 yards and four touchdowns, running past defenders as if they were standing still. Now, he was driving around Sealy in a car that SMU knew was arranged for him by Texas A&M. But the speedy tailback really didn't want to go to A&M, the preferred team for football partisans in Sealy. Desperate not to lose their prized recruit, Meyer's team of recruiters once again gave Dickerson and his family the hard sell—and a number of inducements from determined SMU boosters—that got the running back to sign with the Mustangs.

Years later, Meyer remembered that the future Hall of Famer Dickerson "bought the dream [he] sold," the promise that playing for SMU would be a stepping stone to a pro career and millionaire status.[58] Texas football observers were stunned by the Dickerson

Ron Meyer (L) and assistant coach Steve Endicott (R) posing with Eric Dickerson in Texas Stadium. Courtesy Heritage Hall and Southern Methodist University Archives, DeGolyer Library, SMU Libraries, Southern Methodist University.

signing, and they were shocked yet again when Meyer's men also signed Craig James of Houston Stratford, the second most sought-after high school running back in the state, to an athletic scholarship. Players like Dickerson and James attended Oklahoma, or Texas, or Southern Cal, not second-rate SMU. Ron Meyer had staged a coup, and everyone was put on notice that his program was on the way back after years of mediocrity. It was a new day for Southern Methodist University football, and it was a new day for talented black athletes in the state of Texas, who could now sell their services to the highest bidder—even if the bidders were operating in a system that was supposed to adhere to the principle of amateurism.[59] The era of the "Pony Express," propelled by the Dickerson and James backfield, was now at hand.

Since the Jerry LeVias years of the late 1960s, SMU's football program had fallen on hard times. Some of these troubles stemmed from unstable leadership caused by a tug-of-war between football boosters in the university's board of governors and board of trustees, and the university presidency. In 1972, Hayden Fry was unceremoniously fired by then university president Paul Hardin. Less than two years later, Hardin himself was shown the door by two influential members—and big football supporters—of the board of governors and board of trustees, Edwin Cox and C. A. Tatum, because Hardin dared to govern the football program without their approval. Though Mustangs football had a number of individual star players throughout the '70s, such as future NFL All-Pro lineman Louie Kelcher, and many African Americans, such as Alvin Maxson, Wayne Morris, Ricky Wesson, and Arthur Whittington, the team could not consistently compete with the big dogs of the conference in Austin, College Station, Lubbock, and Fayetteville. Moreover, SMU's football program was put on probation for violations when Dave Smith, Fry's successor, violated NCAA rules by providing small amounts of cash to incentivize better performance from players. Smith was eventually fired after three lackluster seasons, but the program's boosters also realized the athletic labor market was flooded with talented black athletes thanks to integration. Competition for their services was fierce, and only extra financial incentives could persuade them to come to the Hilltop to play for SMU.[60]

SMU's fortunes began to change after Ron Meyer was hired as head football coach in January 1976. The young, brash, well-dressed man from the Midwest came to Dallas eager to make a name for himself and for SMU football. Meyer's story is well known—a walk-on at Purdue University who somehow made it onto the varsity football team despite his limited skills. After a stint as a high school coach in Mishawaka, Indiana, he became a full-time assistant for Jack Mollenkopf, his former coach, back at Purdue, where he coached a number of future professionals during what was arguably one of the most successful periods in the program's history. Meyer proved himself to be a skilled recruiter even then, when he personally convinced future pros Otis Armstrong, Dave Butz, and Darryl Stingley to play at Purdue.[61]

A key moment in Meyer's professional ascent, however, was when Tex Schramm's Dallas Cowboys hired him as a scout during the franchise's first Super Bowl–winning season in 1971. The job earned him a Super Bowl ring, an object he would don over the years as evidence of his winning capabilities. The Cowboy job also put him on the radar of Dallas sports observers. From there, it was to the University of Nevada–Las Vegas, where he took a team that had finished 1–10 the year before his arrival to a 27–8 record over the next three seasons. As a head coach, Ron Meyer showed himself to be a born salesman. He was personable and bold, and he had a knack for appearing honest and sincere even when he wasn't. In Dallas, he fit in perfectly with the city's ostentatious ethos. He liked to wear three-piece suits and jewelry, and have his hair perfectly combed. "I guess if I have a basic philosophy it is to swing from the hips and let it happen," he confidently informed the Dallas media during his first press conference.[62] Like Barry Switzer, he was a young, charismatic coach who was an outsider and who refused to adhere to lingering mentalities of the Jim Crow era.[63]

But Meyer probably couldn't have pulled off his coup alone. Behind him was a visionary athletic director named Russ Potts. The Virginia native probably came to the attention of SMU president James Zumberge when the Maryland Terrapins earned a surprise bid to play Bill Yeoman's Houston Cougars in the 1977 Cotton Bowl Classic. Potts, a Tex Schramm–like figure, was an innovative force in the emerging profession of sports management. Like the famous Dallas Cowboy executive, he was a former journalist who helped revolutionize sports marketing when he worked as the Terrapins' assistant athletic director. During his six-year tenure at Maryland, the program's attendance figures shot up, radio coverage expanded, and advertising sales skyrocketed. It didn't hurt that Maryland athletics had blue chip talent that made it possible for the program to become nationally ranked, especially in basketball. Still, Potts's promotional work was revolutionary. Indeed, he might have single-handedly created a new position in sports management, the all-important sports promoter.[64]

When Potts was offered the job of SMU athletic director in June 1978, he jumped at the opportunity to run his own operation. Soon after his arrival in Dallas, he announced to the media that he hoped to make SMU athletics "profit-making, [and] spirit-oriented."[65] He, along with his assistant Brad Thomas, who had worked with Potts at Maryland, launched the Mustang Mania marketing campaign. They aggressively sought out partners among the Metroplex corporate elite. It didn't take him long to find interested parties among the city's banking and insurance community. He also found willing sponsors among companies of all types: radio stations, car dealerships, Frito Lay, and many others. A *Dallas Morning News* profile published soon after he was hired described Potts as part of a larger trend of collegiate athletic programs "selling spirit and enthusiasm, not only to established fans and potential fans, but also to business leaders for financial backing."[66] Journalists praised him not only for his marketing and public relations skills, but also for his willingness to apply Wall Street business principles to the management of SMU Athletics. "Gone are the days of the ol' football coach semi-retiring into the athletic directorship," Skip Bayless prophetically wrote in July 1980. "More and more, we'll see Wall Streeters running athletic departments."[67]

The Wall Streeter was making SMU sports seem fun and exciting. A perusal of SMU athletic publications in the 1970s shows how game programs and media guides ballooned from smallish, drab magazines with little more than black-and-white photos and football statistics, to full-color publications overflowing with advertisements from the local business community. The 1979 *SMU Football* magazine is particularly revealing, touting the achievements of Meyer's up-and-coming football program while also providing a compelling story of a Sunbelt university on the move. Images of academic excellence, an attractive campus in the midst of a bustling city, college students having fun, and sunbathing attractive coeds were undoubtedly geared toward potential recruits. Particularly noteworthy was the fact that the these "Girls of the Hilltop" included not just conventionally attractive blonde women but also attractive black women, no doubt an image that was designed to support Meyer's talking point to young black recruits that Dallas was one of the "nation's 10 best cities in which opportunities were available to blacks."[68]

During Potts's tenure as athletic director, Mustang Mania seemed to be everywhere in the Dallas–Fort Worth Metroplex: on T-shirts, on bumper stickers, at stores, and on hot air balloons. And the Dallas sports media ate it up. Potts got sportswriters to be at their boosterist best, promoting Mustang Mania all year long. News articles repeatedly appeared in the press touting the young AD's ability to promote the program and bring it into the black financially. Temple Pouncey, a sportswriter who covered the Ponies for the *Dallas Morning News*, wrote a history of the football program appropriately titled *Mustang Mania*.[69] Pouncey's book was part of a larger effort to revive the program's illustrious past, which included holding a roast for former Mustangs great and *Monday Night Football* celebrity Don Meredith, appropriately titled *Meredith Mania*.[70]

Mustang Mania was so irresistible, it could no longer be contained within the confines of the Mustangs' long-time home stadium. In a decision that resembled an "if you can't beat 'em, join 'em" maneuver, SMU decided to move its home games from the aging Cotton Bowl to Texas Stadium, the football palace of Clint Murchison's Dallas Cowboys. Since their creation in 1960, the Cowboys successfully competed for the attentions of the Dallas football fan base. The Mustangs slipped to the second football team in town. Now SMU changed course and allied itself with the professional franchise now known as America's Team. At the same time, the move put the Ponies in a more modern facility that was designed to attract corporate fans. It didn't hurt that Murchison was one of Mustang Mania's boosters due to his relationships with Bobby Stewart, the chairman of SMU's board of governors, and Ed Cox, the chairman of the university's board of trustees. The Texas Stadium move also helped with recruiting, as Meyer and his staff loved to use the facility as a prop in its publications as well as with potential recruits. Associating the program with the home stadium of the NFL's marquee franchise undoubtedly inspired visions of future Mustangs greatness.

Potts's campaign turned out to be more than mere media hype. Attendance figures, despite being somewhat puffed up by free tickets, jumped from an average of 26,635 per game in 1977 to 51,960 per game in 1978 to 56,000 per game after the move to Texas Stadium in 1979. The Mustang Club, the athletic program's main booster organization, was revitalized; Potts turned it from an operation that raised $190,000 in 1978 to one that raised more than $1 million in 1980. Meanwhile, the athletic program's revival seemed to create great public relations for the university's core mission as an academic institution, just as president James Zumberge hoped it would. SMU's endowment increased, as did applications for admission, though the athletic program continued to run at a deficit. Still, the Mustang Mania scheme had generated undeniable energy and excitement for the smallish private university with an enrollment of eight thousand students.[71]

And the team was performing better on the field. Meyer's Mustangs steadily improved from 3–8 in 1976 to 4–7 in 1977 to 4–6–1 in 1978. Injuries and inexperience kept the 1979 team at 5–6, but buoyed by Meyer's recruiting wizardry, the Mustangs turned the corner in 1980 with an 8–3 record and a trip to the Holiday Bowl in San Diego, their first postseason bowl game since the Bluebonnet Bowl bid of 1969. The highlight of the season was SMU's stunning 20–6 upset of the Longhorns in Austin, their first win over Texas since LeVias's sophomore season in 1966. Meyer unleashed the Pony Express, an offense organized around the talents of his star recruits, Dickerson and James, and freshman quarterback Lance McIlhenny. The ingenious two-back attack, in which both would alternate possessions, racked up yards and touchdowns while preserving their bodies from excessive contact. After four years of hustling and hard work, the 1980 season showed that Meyer's brash "swing from the hip" philosophy was paying off.

Meyer's Mustangs were, in many ways, patterned after Barry Switzer's Oklahoma Sooners: a racially integrated team predicated on speed. Like the Sooners, they also recruited black players at all positions, except quarterback, where Lance McIlhenny locked down the job because of his gifts of running the option offense. On defense, the Ponies featured fast and hard-hitting linemen, linebackers, and defensive backs. Harvey Armstrong, Blaine Smith, and Wes Hopkins all turned out to have productive pro careers. Meyer also started recruiting players from out of state, a novel phenomenon for a SWC program, which also attracted the attention of football observers—and the NCAA. The hustler head coach had recruited even more blue chip talent than Bill Yeoman's Houston Cougars.

At the center of the Mustangs revival in the early 1980s were the team's two star running backs, Eric Dickerson and Craig James, whom *Sports Illustrated* writer John Papanek revealingly described in a 1981 profile as "white and black and red hot": "Last Saturday night in the Astrodome the SMU tailback gained a meager 147 yards in 38 carries and scored only two touchdowns. Of course, the SMU tailback is only a junior and not merely a probable first-round draft pick, but two first-round picks. That's because the SMU tailback is two tailbacks: Eric Dickerson and Craig James."[72]

In addition to providing the tandem's impressive statistics, Papanek informed readers that James passed up baseball for football because he wanted to prove that a white player could still excel at running back, a position that was at that point dominated by African American players. "Everybody said that because I'm white, I couldn't compete," James said. "There was no doubt in my mind. I played on a state championship team just like Eric. People thought I was slow—I have never been caught from behind." Papanek's article inadvertently captured the "Dallas Way" brand of racial integration: blacks and whites playing with each other in an industry infused with capital from business and achieving racial harmony not with politics and protest, but with athletic labor employed by the local booster elite.[73]

Mustang Mania was the perfect combination of entrepreneurial spirit fueled by ambition, a booming economy, and an unprecedented influx of athletic talent. The school's boosters, many of them powerful oilmen, financiers, and real estate moguls, relished the challenge of working with Meyer to seek out and pay for the best talent money could buy. The author of Mustang Mania was celebrated as a model businessman who was combining school spirit and bottom-line profitability in new and exciting ways. Southern Methodist University was on the move, and its athletic program was seemingly leading the way.

Except for one problem: the NCAA and the college football establishment in Texas could not stand the fact that the little private university was thumbing its nose at the system of amateur athletics. Allowing Potts and Meyer to get paid was one thing; compensating student-athletes with cash, cars, and house payments in an indiscreet manner was another. While unprecedented amounts of dollars flowed into the NCAA coffers and the budgets of athletic programs, the NCAA fought to maintain the veneer of student-athletes as hard as it could, even as all of its policies ensured that the college football labor force would be made up of more "athlete-students" than student-athletes.

Soon after the 1980 Holiday Bowl, news broke that the NCAA was investigating the Mustangs program. At that precise moment, Russ Potts suddenly announced he was leaving SMU to take a position with Major League Baseball's Chicago White Sox, swearing that the NCAA investigation had nothing to do with his departure. Potts's exit was a curious move for a man who didn't have any affinity for baseball. In June 1981, the NCAA once again put SMU on probation for relatively minor recruitment violations and for buying complimentary game tickets from players, among other minor infractions.[74] The probation, which took away a bowl game and television coverage, did not stop the Pony Express from running over the competition with a 10–1 record during the 1981 season, winning their first SWC championship since the LeVias era.

But the beloved head coach who turned the Mustangs program around also decided he was ready for a new challenge. In January 1982, Meyer tearfully announced he was taking a job with the NFL's New England Patriots, one of the worst teams in the league.

Fans and journalists wondered why he would leave his team with many of his prized recruits returning for their senior seasons. But both Potts and Meyer were cut from the same cloth: they were energetic and ambitious men in sports management who were looking for fame and fortune. Though both denied their departures were due to the NCAA investigations, it was hard not to see them taking the first available flights out of town with the impending storm in sight.

*   *   *

On Saturday afternoon, October 30, 1982, the Mustangs squared off against the Texas A&M Aggies at Texas Stadium. For Mustangs fans, it was a delightful scene. A large crowd of fifty thousand—less than a sellout, but larger than most recent crowds at SMU games—turned out for the homecoming game between the undefeated Ponies and the 4–3 Aggies. The scene was reminiscent of the 1966 game between SMU and A&M. SMU was on its way to a conference title, while the Aggies were struggling. Unlike in 1966, both the Ponies and the Aggies fielded integrated teams with many black players. Like that contest sixteen years earlier, the Mustangs had the best player on the field: a player who possessed Jerry LeVias's speed, but with more size and power. That player was Eric Dickerson, who as a senior was now fully coming into this own as a running back even while he shared time with his backfield mate Craig James. The game was called by Verne Lundquist, the Cowboy radio broadcaster and local sports television personality on WFAA Channel 8 who was now moving on to his career as a play-by-play announcer on CBS Sports network television. CBS camera operators made sure to zero in on Cheryl Tiegs, the famous blonde supermodel of the early 1980s, who was attending the game as grand marshal of SMU's homecoming ceremonies. University president Donald Shields was beaming as he escorted Tiegs onto the field at halftime. SMU games now attracted not just local beauty queens, as they had during the days of Betty Bailey in the 1930s, but also nationally recognized supermodels.

But the real star of this day was Eric Dickerson. The running back was setting team rushing records while also breaking Earl Campbell's career SWC rushing mark. On this day, he bolstered his Heisman candidacy with three scintillating touchdowns runs, the last the most thrilling of them all. With the score 33–9 in favor of the Mustangs, Dickerson took a handoff, sidestepped a blocker, broke one tackle, spun out of another, then faked out yet another tackler. Rather than "wiggle and jiggle" as LeVias preferred to do, the 9.4 sprinter simply shot past Aggie defenders like a bullet down the right sideline and coasted eighty yards to a touchdown. It was a vintage Dickerson run. The Mustangs trounced the Aggies 47–9. They went on to win their second consecutive SWC championship with a 10–0–1 record. Their only blemish was an end-of-the-season tie with Arkansas. A few months later, the Ponies made their long-awaited return to the Cotton Bowl Classic and defeated the Pittsburgh Panthers 7–3. Though they were denied a national championship by pollsters who preferred the pristine image of the Penn State Nittany Lions, the Mustangs were undeniably the best team in the SWC and one of the best in the nation that year.

As Meyer's successor, Bobby Collins, was carried off the field by his players after the Cotton Bowl victory, the marriage between commercialized college football and black and marginalized players for hire never looked better. Black athletes were starring for teams across the country. Coaches and athletic directors were just beginning to earn higher salaries. Universities were drinking the Kool-Aid of college football, and blue chip players were getting "taken care of" officially with athletic scholarships and unofficially with plenty of under-the-table inducements. Yet the amateur system remained—and still remains—in college football. The "great contradiction" that Michael Oriard has eloquently described, of college football "being, at one and the same time, a commercial spectacle and an extracurricular activity," somehow remained even as it became less tenable in the 1980s and '90s.[75] Some football programs would continue to thrive in this system. SMU would not.

*   *   *

During the 1970s and early '80s, the racial integration of big-time college football in Texas and in the South was catalyzed by a monumental reconfiguration of capital and labor in a system defined by amateurism. A Texas athletic program was pushing commercialized intercollegiate athletes to its logical conclusion in football. Another Texas-inspired revolt successfully overthrew amateurism and facilitated a profound revolution in women's sports.

CHAPTER 4

We've Come a Long Way to Houston

A REVOLUTIONARY EVENT IN THE HISTORY OF AMERICAN SPORTS TOOK PLACE on September 26, 1970, in Houston, Texas. A small crowd of three hundred spectators sat in the temporary bleachers that surrounded one of the courts of the Houston Racquet Club to watch Rosemary "Rosie" Casals square off against Judy Tegart Dalton in the finals of the Virginia Slims Invitational tennis tournament. Casals, also nicknamed "Rosebud" for her smallish stature, was in a competitive match against the talented, and taller, Australian. Casals lost a close first set to Dalton, but then she roared back to decisively win the second set. Now she was in a dogfight to win the match. After nearly blowing a 4–1 lead in the third and final set, Casals finally regained control and won with a backhand winner to clinch the match and the championship in three sets, 5–7, 6–1, 7–5.

During the post-match ceremony, Casals received her winner's check of $1,600 from Delores Hornberger, the leader of the women's division of the Houston Racquet Club. Bill Cutler, a representative of Philip Morris Tobacco Company, spoke about his firm's sponsorship of the tournament. Another woman, wearing her characteristic dark sunglasses, took the microphone and thanked the club for hosting the tournament and thanked Philip Morris for providing key sponsorship money for the event. The speaker, a transplanted New Yorker named Gladys Heldman, was largely responsible for making the event happen. The Houston Racquet Club had staged a historic event in US women's sports: the launch of the first women's professional tennis tournament in the United States.[1]

Three years later, almost to the day, on September 23, 1973, another historic tennis match occurred in Houston that changed American sports history and the history of women in the United States. Instead of the intimate and exclusive Houston Racquet Club, it took place in the immense and publicly accessible Houston Astrodome in front of more than thirty thousand fans, with millions more watching on national television. On that day, the "Battle of the Sexes" was staged in a spectacular manner unequaled in the history of US sporting culture. Billie Jean King, the star tennis player and "women's libber," defeated Bobby Riggs, the former Wimbledon champion and fifty-five-year-old self-styled male chauvinist pig, 6–4, 6–3, 6–3. Houston first put women's tennis on the map; then it showed how it could be a profitable spectator sport that attracted tens of thousands of fans in person and many more on television.

In the 1960s and '70s, Texas-based transformations had revolutionized the mainstream sports of professional football, baseball, and basketball. And Texas would also become the site of a profound upheaval in the niche country club sport of tennis. A partnership between sports entrepreneurs and a group of risk-taking athletes virtually created professional tennis from the ground up, facing down fierce opposition from the tennis establishment that had profited from the unpaid labor of the world's best players for decades. The professionalization of tennis enabled the sport to achieve unprecedented popularity in the 1970s.

This golden age of tennis story has been told before, but the impact of Texas-based tennis enthusiasts tends to be overlooked. It was not by accident that the transformation of tennis took shape in the shoot-from-the-hip, risk-taking region of Texas rather than in tradition-bound New York. Certainly New York corporate money played a key role in this story, financing the unlikely convergence of tobacco and oil money with players who were fed up with tennis's fundamentalist commitment to amateurism. And it was a woman with connections to both worlds, an Upper East Side Manhattanite transplant in Houston, whose vision and boundless energy forced the world to recognize that women athletes had the ability to earn a living from sport. In the process, the sports revolution in tennis did more than democratize a country club sport. It helped usher in a new understanding of womanhood.

*   *   *

No other sport was transformed as dramatically during the 1960s and 1970s as tennis was. Like other sports, it began as a recreational activity of affluent classes, played by elite players for elite fans, confined to the country clubs of the United States, Europe, and other parts of the world. But unlike football, soccer, baseball, and even basketball, which were more accessible to a wider public of athletes and fans by the 1960s, tennis remained firmly entrenched in its elite traditions. While other sports included non-white players and players from working classes, tennis was much more resistant to the changes engendered by the civil rights and feminist movements. The sport was literally and symbolically invested in whiteness: white tennis players, white tennis outfits, and white balls were the dominant aesthetic of the sport. As Billie Jean King recalls of that era: "Everybody's wearing white shoes, white socks, white clothes, playing with white balls, everybody who plays is white. Where is everybody else?"[2]

Tennis was snobby and elitist, and it was controlled by the "Brahmins," the term Grace Lichtenstein used to characterize the white "gentlemen" who had ruled the sport in an arbitrary fashion since its emergence in the nineteenth century.[3] The gentlemen tennis stars celebrated in the sport were elegant, slender, graceful, athletic, and aggressive but not hypermasculine. Excelling at tennis does not require brute strength. Instead, one has to master subtle movements, move one's feet, and hit the ball with "touch." And of course, in mainstream tennis circles, the model sporting gentleman was a white man who wore white tennis outfits and

was competitive while exhibiting decorum and good sportsman-
ship. And unlike other sports, tennis gentlemen had to compete
for attention with women players, who played at its highest levels,
albeit in a subordinate position under the logic of gender segregation. Though all sports dominated by men are based on sexist hierarchies and exclusion, the explicit sexism of many of the game's
stars, from Jack Kramer to John McEnroe to even Arthur Ashe,
is striking. Even though they were seen by tennis authorities as
second-class citizens, women players were among the sport's biggest stars. Suzanne Lenglen, the French tennis legend, was one
of the game's most popular players in the 1920s. Tennis was also
the sport where an African American woman named Althea Gibson burst onto the international stage as a pioneering champion
in the 1950s. It is one of the great ironies of history that tennis, a
sport with some of the most pretentious and traditional cultures,
turned out to be at the forefront of the feminist movement during
the 1960s and '70s.

The rule of the tennis Brahmins was institutionalized by the
International Lawn Tennis Federation (ILTF), a conglomeration
of national federations, such as the United States Lawn Tennis
Association (USLTA) and others, that governed the sport and enforced the rules of competition. The ILTF was staunchly committed to amateurism, the notion that players should perform for fun
and personal edification, not for a living. But the gospel of amateurism was in many ways a myth: top players, usually men, received under-the-table compensation. The sport's main tournaments were the "Grand Slams": the Australian Championships;
the French Championships at Roland Garros in Paris; Wimbledon, the most prestigious tournament in England; and the US
Nationals at Forest Hills in Queens, New York. All were historically open to amateurs only. The Davis Cup, the annual competition between participating nations, was also an all-amateur
affair. Those players who were brave enough to carve out an existence as professionals were shut out of the sport's major tournaments by the amateur establishment. Jack Kramer, a star tennis
player during the 1940s, started his own pro circuits at various

points with only moderate success. He regularly fought losing battles with the USLTA until he finally ascended as a tennis promoter when the tennis authorities let professional players play in major tournaments in the late 1960s.

Tennis clubs in Texas followed this larger pattern of elitism and exclusivity that defined tennis cultures throughout the country. In cities like Dallas and Houston, tennis was played in country clubs like River Oaks Country Club, Houston Country Club, or Dallas Country Club. Schools might have had tennis programs, but they were usually peripheral in comparison to mainstream sports. Girls had even fewer opportunities to play high school tennis. Tennis's popularity paled in comparison to that of football and baseball. And the sport's elitism fit easily into the existing structure of Jim Crow segregation. Tennis clubs were solely for whites, while African American Texan enthusiasts played tennis in their own tennis associations.

By the 1960s, the pressures on the pro-amateurism establishment were becoming too strong to resist. The sport was losing popularity, and players were becoming more and more resentful of the ILTF's control of their fates. Tennis writers had been agitating for the end of the flawed amateur system for some time. Lance Tingay, the *Daily Telegraph*'s tennis correspondent, astutely sensed the winds of change that were blowing through the sport: "[The moment has] surely come for lawn tennis to rid itself of the social shackles of the nineteenth century. . . . The labourer is worthy of his hire. So is the artist. So is the great games player."[4]

Finally, in 1968, Herman David, the chairman of the All-England Club, decided to allow professionals to compete with amateurs at Wimbledon. Citing the financial rewards that so-called amateurs received from Davis Cup organizers and other events, David decided enough was enough. "The present amateur game is a living lie," he bluntly told the press.[5] After much resistance from members of the ILTF, including threats to ban the British from their events, other tennis tournaments followed suit, allowing professional players to compete with amateurs at their tennis tournaments. The great wall of amateurism finally cracked, and some powerful entrepreneurs from the Sunbelt were looking to break it open even further.

Open tennis had finally arrived. Yet male players quickly dominated the newly formed pro tournaments and the prize money they offered. The tennis federations and tournament organizers treated women players like a sideshow, the opening act for the presumed main event. Only the top players could secure semi-regular playing gigs. Jack Kramer, a longtime advocate for the professionalization of tennis, stated his feelings about the women's game plainly when he insisted: "People get up and go get a hot dog or go to the bathroom when the women come on."[6] Kramer's comments reflected the dominant mentality of the tennis establishment and the vast majority of men players, including Arthur Ashe, the black tennis star of the day. In 1970, when the women's pro tour was getting ready to be launched, he told the press: "Men are doing this for a living now. They have families, and they don't want to give up money just for girls to play. Only three or four women drew fans to a tourney, so why do we have to split our money with them?"[7] He would get an answer to his question soon enough.

* * *

Lamar Hunt was at it again. In 1960, he challenged the NFL's dominance over professional football. Now, he set his sights on the ILTF to revolutionize tennis as a spectator sport. Once Wimbledon decided to open its doors to professionals, the floodgates were open. In 1967, Dave Dixon, another Southern sports entrepreneur who helped bring the Saints NFL franchise to New Orleans, convinced Hunt to invest in World Championship Tennis (WCT), a new professional tennis circuit. Dixon and Hunt signed players who were eager to turn pro and make a living from their craft. The so-called Handsome Eight, John Newcombe, Dennis Ralston, Tony Roche, Cliff Drysdale, Earl Buchholz, Niki Pilic, Roger Taylor, and Pierre Barthes, were the first brave souls to test the waters of Open tennis.

During its first year, the WCT circuit was a financial failure, prompting Dixon to sell his share of the business to Hunt. Undaunted, Hunt, along with his nephew, fellow oilman Al Hill Jr., went to work. His goal was to sign more top male players to draw audiences, which would, in turn, attract other investors from the advertising and the television world. In September 1970, he made a big splash during the US Open (previously the US Nationals) when he announced that the WCT was going to launch a new and improved tennis tour. The Million Dollar Tour would include thirty-two players performing in twenty cities around the world. Hunt struck another blow against the tennis establishment when he announced at Club 21 in midtown Manhattan a short while later that WCT had three of the game's best players: Arthur Ashe, Charlie Pasarell, and Bob Lutz. Hunt made a splash in New York during one of the sport's biggest events.

But the tennis authorities, especially the USLTA and the ILTF, were not on board with this project, even after they allowed Open tennis to exist in the major tournaments. Their preferred pro tour was Jack Kramer's Grand Prix pro circuit. Hunt's battle to create a rival pro tennis tour was as fierce as the one he had fought against Pete Rozelle and the NFL years before. The ILTF barred his players from playing at the most prestigious tournaments, especially after Hunt had the audacity to demand fees for their services. Finally, the warring parties came to a truce in 1972. The WCT circuit would be limited to the first five months of the year, so as to not conflict with the Grand Slam tournaments. Meanwhile, Hunt's players were no longer banned from the major championships.

With the smoke from the battles between Hunt and the amateur federations finally clearing, World Championship Tennis went about establishing an international tour. The WCT tournaments featured nearly all of the top men's players. The Texan promoters chose the Moody Coliseum on the campus of SMU for the site of the championship tournament that would end the season. In the early 1970s, Dallas was not quite ready for Major League Baseball or ABA basketball, but it proved to be quite interested in professional tennis, at least for one week every spring. It didn't hurt that one of the greatest matches in the sport's history was played during the WCT finals in May 1972. Ken Rosewall defeated Rod Laver in five grueling sets, 4–6, 6–0, 6–3, 6–7, and 7–6, before a full house at the Moody Coliseum and with more than twenty million fans watching on television.

WCT became a hit thanks to the superior talents of Hunt's roster of players and his promotional wizardry, which was amply displayed at the annual WCT finals banquet, which he and his wife, Norma, hosted every year. Charlton Heston was often a celebrity guest at tournaments, and he also narrated WCT highlight films. The parties showed that WCT was very much a man's affair. In the world of WCT, men were the celebrities and the performers, while women played the role of sideline eye candy. Each year in the lead-up to the WCT finals, the *Dallas Morning News* society pages reported on the lavish poolside parties the Hunts threw for the players and celebrity guests, including "pretty blondes" and "courtmates" who posed for the cameras with the tennis stars.[8]

Despite enormous resistance from the tennis establishment, Lamar Hunt had once again shown that dollars, smart management, and talented performers could produce an entertaining sports product. Professional men's tennis was on the rise, yet women's tennis was left behind. But as WCT was taking off in Dallas, another annual tennis gathering with a different agenda began to take shape more than two hundred miles south in Houston.

* * *

Gladys Medalie Heldman was truly a tennis fanatic. She was an extraordinarily, perhaps pathologically, driven person who tirelessly promoted the sport she loved deeply. Born on May 13, 1922, Heldman was not from an athletic family. Her father, George Medalie, epitomized the phenomenon of Jewish upward mobility in early twentieth-century New York. He rose up from an impoverished childhood on the Lower East Side of Manhattan, graduated from Columbia College and Columbia Law School, and became a big-time lawyer defending mobsters and corporations. He cultivated political ties with the Republican Party establishment and was appointed US attorney for the southern district by President Herbert Hoover before dying in 1946 at the age of sixty-two.[9] Gladys's mother, Carrie "C. K." Kaplan, was an eccentric Barnard graduate who had a complicated relationship with her daughter. The Medalies were living the life of uptown Manhattan privilege, but Gladys felt stifled by the cold and neglectful atmosphere of her family. She was on her way to living the life of an East Side socialite, but circumstances and her own ambitions took her in another direction. She left the East Coast to attend college at Stanford University, where she developed an interest in medieval history.[10]

It was at Stanford where she met her future husband, Julius Heldman. Heldman was an excellent tennis player, but he could not stand the lack of financial stability in a sport with no earning potential. He eventually became an engineer, and after a tenure with the Manhattan Project, he began a long-term career with Shell Oil. Meanwhile, the energetic Gladys caught the tennis bug from her husband. She picked up the game, and her class privilege allowed her to outsource much of the care for her two daughters to her African American housekeeper. She began to play as often as she could. After moderate success on the court, she stopped playing in tournaments and created her own career as a tennis magazine publisher and a promoter.

Gladys Heldman thought of *World Tennis* as her baby. "In May of 1953, the future mother of *WT* immaculately conceived her child in a San Antonio Motel," she wrote in an editorial in 1971.[11] According to her daughter Julie's memoir, Heldman's maternal narrative about the birth and life of *her tennis magazine* is not surprising, for Gladys, like her mother, was not interested in domesticity. She was much more interested in developing her magazine and her tennis passion. In 1953, she founded *WT* and "stayed up endless nights with it and gave it endless financial resuscitation."[12] Houston turned out to be a great place for her to raise her magazine, where many tennis enthusiasts with means played at the local clubs. The most prominent was the Cork Club at the

Shamrock Hotel, built by oil tycoon Glenn McCarthy.[13] Heldman's publication chronicled all of the tennis happenings in the region and in tennis circuits around the world. Over time, she transformed what had been a mimeographed sheet called the *Houston Tennis News* into an attractive multipage publication that became *World Tennis*, the preeminent tennis magazine that she eventually sold to CBS Publications for $2.25 million in 1972.[14] But in the 1950s, Heldman was essentially producing the magazine on her own, with her bedroom becoming a mini-industrial magazine production operation while her husband and daughters provided essential labor to make the publication possible. Julius researched and wrote many pieces about tennis tournaments and tennis instruction, and provided editing on Gladys's articles, while Julie and Carrie, their daughters, and Laura, their housekeeper, did everything else—including cooking, cleaning, and endlessly serving glasses of scotch and vodka to keep the editor-in-chief fueled for her exhausting work. She inherited her own mother's quirkiness and refashioned it into a chain-smoking, energetic, brilliant woman who worked from her bed for years.

After a four-year stint in Houston, the Heldmans moved to New York City when Julius received a transfer to Shell's New York City office. During the next decade and a half, Gladys developed the unique ability to coordinate contacts and raise the money to put on successful tennis tournaments. Still, the financially secure Heldmans lost money on *World Tennis* for almost ten years before the enterprising Gladys finally captured some advertisers for her magazine. Her big catches were Pepsi Cola and Philip Morris. Neither company sold products that were healthy for tennis players—or anyone—but perhaps that was the point of going into sports advertising. The Philip Morris relationship was forged by Heldman and her close friend Joe Cullman, the company's CEO. Cullman began advertising its various brands of cigarettes in *World Tennis*. Eventually, Marlboro, the company's most popular brand of cigarettes, became the major sponsor of tennis tournaments and other sporting events.

Cullman's relationship with Gladys gave him entrée into the

*Gladys Held-
man working the
phones. Photo
by Joseph Con-
sentino,* Sports
Illustrated.

most powerful sectors of US tennis during the 1960s. In 1969, Cullman was the chairman of the US Open in Forest Hills.[15] In the 1969 US Open tennis tournament highlight film, both Held- man and Cullman briefly appear in front of the camera as for- ward-thinking tennis enthusiasts who called for better conditions for the annual tournament than what were provided by the West Side Tennis Club. "Changes that we need down the line are a bet- ter facility, better parking, more courts, and better protection for the courts in the event of rain," Cullman insisted.[16] The vision- aries seemingly summoned these changes when the tournament left the crammed West Side Tennis Club for the new and more spacious National Tennis Center in nearby Flushing Meadows in 1978, where it has been played to this day.

As Heldman consolidated her sponsorships, she continued to cover the tennis world for her magazine. She was a frequent critic of the tennis establishment's intransigent position on professionalization. She also continued to push for corporate sponsorship of tournaments, and her most steadfast ally was Cullman. In the realm of public opinion, Philip Morris was in retreat, as awareness of the relationship between tobacco and lung cancer was growing, but the company was expanding its influence in sports advertising, especially in tennis. It was not a coincidence that the new scoreboard at the West Side Tennis Club Stadium included a giant "Marlboro Country" advertisement. Thus, when the Open era had begun and women players were unable to secure regular playing opportunities, Gladys Heldman was the logical person for them to call.

*   *   *

We need not imagine locker rooms as places where male jocks boast about their sexual exploits with women. Locker rooms can also be places where a group of people forging common experiences imagine and enact social change. Such was the case in the women's locker room at the West Side Tennis Club in Forest Hills during the 1970 US Open. On August 26, 1970, thousands of women commemorated the fiftieth anniversary of the passage of the Nineteenth Amendment by launching the Women's Strike for Equality in massive demonstrations in Manhattan and other parts of the country. A few weeks later, another much smaller feminist protest took place at the US Open tennis tournament across town at the West Side Tennis club. On September 6, 1970, the locker room was transformed from one of compliant femininity to radical insurgency. Tennis stars Billie Jean King and Rosie Casals were steaming when they learned of the gross disparities between the cash prizes that would be awarded to men and women players in the upcoming Pacific Southwest tournament in Los Angeles, promoted by Jack Kramer. The Pacific offered the men's winning player of the tournament $12,500, while the women's winner was slated to receive a paltry $1,500. Moreover, the men's prize money was an $8,000 increase from the previous year, while the women's amount remained the same. And women players who did not make it through the quarterfinal round would not receive a penny for their labor. Casals and King, who were among the few women players who could earn money playing professional tennis, felt that enough was enough. They started to lobby fellow players to boycott the tournament. Nancy Richey, another top player from Texas, was also upset, and she, along with King and Casals, approached Gladys Heldman about their concerns. The mover and shaker tennis circuit impresario swung into action. She informed Kramer, the organizer of the tournament, that women players were threatening to boycott his tournament due to the paltry prize money. The promoter, who was never a fan of women's tennis, dismissed the threat, and replied, somewhat in jest: "I'll take the $7,500 and throw it in the men's singles."[17] Kramer, who liked to present himself as a magnanimous person, was no believer in women's tennis. "No matter how fast the surface, women's tennis can never become a superior spectator attraction," he succinctly put it in his autobiography written with longtime sportswriter Frank Deford. No wonder Billie Jean King recalled Heldman calling Kramer "an ass."[18]

Heldman then went through her immense list of contacts in the tennis world, and she found willing partners in Houston. As the insurgency among the women players was brewing during the US Open, she was already in the midst of moving with Julius back to the Sunbelt city where they had lived in the early 1950s. The Houston she returned to was on the verge of becoming one of the most dynamic cities in the country, with a robust sports scene of professional sports teams, successful college sports programs, and state-of-the-art stadium that was the buzz of the sports world. It also was a city with an increased appetite for tennis. She contacted Paul Pearce, the president of the Houston Tennis Association, who then wrote Delores Hornberger and Jim Hight, the incoming president of the Texas Lawn Tennis Association. Within days, Hornberger and Hight agreed to host a women's tournament with $5,000 prize money at the Houston Racquet Club to be held on September 24–27, 1970. Heldman did not tell them, however, that those dates conflicted with Kramer's Pacific Southwest tournament, which was a violation of USLTA rules.

With a deal in place to stage the tournament in Houston, Heldman went back to the players in the locker room at Forest Hills. She convinced them that a boycott would not work because they could never get the support of all the players. Then she offered them the chance to play the Houston tournament. The insurgents tossed caution to the wind and accepted her offer. Nine of the top players in women's tennis, now known as the Original Nine, agreed to forego Kramer's tournament to play in Houston: Billie Jean King, Rosie Casals, Nancy Richey, Peaches Bartkowicz, Julie Heldman, Valerie Ziegenfuss, Kristy Pigeon, Judy Tegart Dalton, and Kerry Melville.[19]

After the conclusion of the US Open, a titanic confrontation unfolded between Heldman's rebels and the USLTA's male-dominated leadership. The USLTA was able to wield influence because it reserved the power to sanction tournaments across the country. It also determined the rankings of players and their eligibility for competitions. Its pro tour head of choice, Jack Kramer, voiced his opposition to the approbation of the Houston tournament after initially claiming he would let it occur without protest. The USLTA then tried to dissuade the players from playing in Houston, threatening to ban them from playing in major tournaments. As the players descended upon Houston for the tournament organized by Heldman, the outcome of the conflict remained unclear.

In a last-ditch effort to stop the tournament, the USLTA budged a bit when it informed the Houston Racquet Club that it would approve the tournament if the club agreed not to publicize the prize money. In essence, the USLTA was asking the players and tournament organizers to perpetuate the system of "shammateurism" that precipitated the rebellion in the first place. But that wasn't good enough for the enterprising Heldman. Neither was it good enough for the players. With the fate of the tournament and the players still unclear, Heldman pulled her trump card, calling upon Joe Cullman of Philip Morris to provide sponsorship money for the tournament. "I saw the Houston tournament as a chance to support the women's game as a unique sponsorship opportunity for Philip Morris," Cullman wrote years later.[20] Instead of sponsoring with Marlboro County, the company fronted its Virginia Slims brand to sponsor the Houston tournament. Rolled out two years earlier, Virginia Slims was marketed to what the company imagined to be the young professional and liberated woman of the second-wave feminist era. Hight and Hornberger were happy to allow the tournament to be called the Virginia Slims Invitational. Though some players were understandably ambivalent about the decision to use Philip Morris as the main sponsor of the tournament, all went along with the proposal. Heldman, however, was not conflicted. She was an avid smoker who realized the corporation had the money and a skilled marketing team that could promote women's tennis.[21]

The Heldman–Philip Morris partnership turned out to be a stroke of genius. It was undoubtedly a marriage born out of convenience. The East Side socialite turned Sunbelt sports entrepreneur always had a vision for profitable tennis. Meanwhile, Cullman, himself a tennis aficionado, could cloak his deadly cigarette product under the guise of feminism with his Virginia Slims brand and slogan "You've come a long way, baby." It was a brilliant move from a business standpoint. Yet Cullman's decision was an outgrowth of his own self-fashioning as a social and political liberal. Indeed, Philip Morris had a decent track record in its support for racial integration. It donated to the National Urban League and other African American and inner city youth initiatives. He also provided jobs for tennis players who struggled to make a living during the amateur era. Cullman considered Arthur Ashe a friend, and indeed Ashe worked for Philip Morris for a number of years. Cullman noted years later, "I was not happy with the lack of diversity—racial, religious, gender, and economic—of the players and those in the stands."[22] Thus, the Philip Morris sponsorship, while driven by Cullman's desire to maximize profit, was also driven by his own personal investments in tennis, his relationship with Heldman, and his liberal politics.

With sponsorship money secured, the chain-smoking Heldman had another ace up her sleeve. She came up with the idea of signing the players as "contract professionals" for one week. The contract pro status ensured that the players could participate in a professional tournament under a sort of temporary work agreement. With the press waiting at the Houston Racquet Club for the tournament to begin, the players agreed to play for *World Tennis* for one dollar. They posed for photos holding one-dollar bills. An unlikely convergence of feminist-inspired sports activism and corporate capitalism had created an iconic moment in women's history.

But as in other professional sports, perhaps more so in tennis, capitalism was on the side of athletic labor in the early 1970s. What might seem contradictory in retrospect was what drove the expansion of professional sports during the 1960s and '70s. In football, baseball, and men's tennis, it was Texas oil money that helped finance the sports revolution and bring greater earning potential to players. Now Philip Morris cigarette money played the same role in the emergence of women's professional tennis.

The inaugural Virginia Slims Invitational in Houston was a resounding success. Even though the club could only accommodate small crowds of no more than eight hundred fans in its makeshift bleacher seats, the players' point was made. Even with Billie Jean King and Julie Heldman hampered by injuries, the hundreds of fans who showed up saw entertaining tennis. "It was surprising the girls had any strength left for fighting on the court, but their victories against the established authorities made them eager to show their worth," the *Houston Post* reported. Judy Tegart Dalton, the hard-hitting Australian, upset the second-seeded Nancy Richey in three sets, 4–6, 7–5, 6–2.[23] Meanwhile, Casals, the tournament's top seed, won a tough match against Kerry Melville in the semifinals and then a closely contested three-set final against

Dalton. Casals was awarded the winner's check for $1,600, and Dalton received the runner-up share of $1,000, which she assured the press would be used to buy a "washer dryer and a waste disposal unit" for fans who may have been concerned that these players would lose sight of their real jobs as wives and housekeepers.[24] Still, the symbolism of a women-only tournament was extremely powerful.

The inaugural Virginia Slims Invitational showed that women players could play entertaining and exciting tennis, attract a crowd, and earn prize money. "You've come a long way, babies," Philip Morris representative Bill Cutler said with pride.[25] Indeed, the rebel players would go even further during the next few years. The revolution that began at the West Side Tennis Club and was then catalyzed at the Houston Racquet Club now moved to the Heldman's new home in Houston after the tournament ended. After much deliberation, the players agreed to sign with Heldman, and a new professional women's tennis tour sponsored by Virginia Slims was born.[26]

*   *   *

Joe Cullman and Gladys Heldman were East Coast affluent, but the majority of the women who provided the athletic labor behind the tennis revolution were Sunbelt subaltern. With the notable exception of Julie Heldman (Gladys's daughter), the players who were emerging on the women's tennis scene in the late 1960s were an aspiring class of women who came largely from working and lower-middle-class backgrounds. In a sense, they were 1960s versions of Babe Didrikson, athletes who found themselves in conditions when sporting opportunities for women were now imaginable in ways they were not in the 1930s. These players were part of the broader agitation for equal opportunities and, in some cases, radical transformation. Some, like Billie Jean King, were influenced by the resurgent feminist movement that was erupting throughout the country. Others simply wanted to be treated fairly and be compensated for their talents. Many came not from establishment affluent northeast families, but from the Sunbelt. These regional and class dynamics were noted by the typically astute Casals, who told Grace Lichtenstein in 1973, "All those rich kids. They got to play tennis all the time, and yet you'd never see a top player coming out of there, from New York or Boston. The top ones, they came from Florida and California, off the public courts."[27]

Billie Jean Moffitt King was the star of the group, and her story is the most well known. Born the child of a fireman father and a homemaker mother in Long Beach, California, the Moffitts exemplified the postwar stability of the white middle class in Southern California. The ambitious and athletic young Moffitt found tennis to be the sport in which she could excel. As she continued to play in Southern California, however, she grew to resent the stuffy and elitist world of tennis in Los Angeles. Like all aspiring tennis players in Los Angeles, she had to contend with the despotic operation of Perry T. Jones, the president of the Southern California Tennis Association. "Jones was a terror to all of us junior players," King recalled years later, "because he controlled our lives totally—where we played, how much expense money we got from his association for trips outside California, or even if we got any at all."[28]

Still, King survived Jones's authoritarian brand of gentlemanly rule and made a name for herself in junior tennis circuits before breaking through at Wimbledon in the mid-1960s. She also struggled against the sport's fanatical investment in femininity. Tennis authorities and sportswriters frequently commented on her husky physique, short hair, and demonstrative nature on the court. She was not the demure woman celebrated by the tennis world. However, the harder edges of criticism were blunted after she married Larry King, a conventionally attractive man who created a role as supporting husband while developing his own career as a businessman. Still, even after she achieved her goal of being the number-one player in women's tennis, many sports writers wondered when she would quit playing and assume the expected roles of wife and mother. But Billie Jean would never submit to these rules, and by 1970, she was determined to carve out a life for herself as full-time, well-paid professional athlete.

It is fitting that one of King's partners in the women's tennis revolution was the child of Central American immigrants. Rosie Casals was a self-styled rebel tennis star. Born in San Francisco in 1948, her father was an immigrant from El Salvador. Casals's family joined the wave of migrants fleeing from the political turmoil and economic dislocation that plagued the country in the years after the Great Depression and after La Matanza, a massacre of thousands of Salvadorans by the autocratic government of Maximiliano Hernández Martínez. Immigrants from Central America and Mexico had been making San Francisco their new home since the era of the Gold Rush, and Casals found her own home on the tennis courts of San Francisco's Golden Gate Park.[29] Like King, she was first introduced to the game on public courts, not in the country club, and like King, she was keenly aware of the ways her proletarian background made her an outsider, which fueled her desire to beat the players from more privileged backgrounds. She was also aware that her tomboyish manner did not fit with the strict gender conventions of tennis.

Still, even in a world where girls were coerced to be feminine, tennis was one of the few places where an athletically inclined girl like Casals could develop her talents. Under the tutelage of her great-uncle Manuel, who raised her with her great-aunt, Maria, she played an aggressive serve-and-volley game. She also developed a hard serve, and her quickness and agility allowed her to chase down balls all over the court. She possessed touch volleys while also having the ability to hit wicked overhead smashes like a player twice her size. Casals was not the elegant player adored by the men of tennis. She was an aggressive hustler who maximized every ounce of energy her five-foot, two and a quarter-inch, 118-pound body could give.

Casals became a prodigy in the California junior tennis scene. By the late 1960s, she had paired up with King to be a formidable doubles combination. Her size and appearance were duly noted by sportswriters, who couldn't help but comment on her body and her wayward demeanor, even when they sought to be complimentary. "The only emotion she displays is an occasional slap of her substantial thighs, a quick, almost unnoticed shake of a closed fist," wrote Kim Chapin in his 1966 profile of the Salvadoran-American teenager. "Her hair, dark and close-cropped, is a bit frazzled from the moment she walks onto a court. This and her bouncy style of play give her all the color she will ever need."[30] But sportswriter portrayals such as these didn't bother the self-styled rebel. In the late '60s, even as she donned the conventional outfit of tennis whites, her short hair and demonstrative nature were all part of her rebel persona. As we shall see, after the women's pro tour was established, Casals relished pushing the envelope in tennis fashion. When she grew her hair longer in the early 1970s, she resembled, in the words of Grace Lichtenstein, "an Apache brave on the warpath" with bright colored dresses and bandanas keeping her jet black hair out of her face.[31]

Casals was a gifted athlete and an extremely sharp-witted personality. As she rose in the rankings, she embraced the life of the vagabond athlete. On the tennis circuit, she was known for drinking and smoking cigarettes, her sarcastic remarks off the court, and her all-court hustle on it. She was well liked on the tour, mixing her smarts with a self-deprecating humor, though her competitive nature was always evident on the court. Her wit and unrelenting sarcasm would be fully on display on national television when she was a guest commentator for a historic event in women's tennis a few years later.

King and Casals were joined by Nancy Richey, a Texas native who also played a significant role in the women's tennis revolution. The San Angelo–born Richey was a pioneering figure in her own right. Born in 1942, she and her younger brother, Cliff, were child prodigies groomed by their father, George, a former player whose athletic career was derailed by a car accident when he was younger. George passed on his love of tennis to his children. Nancy started playing when she was six, and Cliff followed years later. Over the next few decades, George Richey managed

Rosie Casals.
Photo by
Ed Lacey/
Popperfoto.

to secure various jobs as a tennis pro in country clubs in Dallas and Houston, which enabled him to create an environment for his children to pursue tennis. The Richeys became one of a number of successful sibling tandems in tennis history.[32]

Unlike King and Casals, who were classic serve-and-volleyers, Richey played a more composed game from the baseline, relying on a strong forehand drive to unleash on her opponents. Though she did not imagine herself as a rebel in the manner that Casals and King did, she became a de facto one through her fashion choices. She donned visors or sun hats, which covered her short brown hair. The hat also conveyed a sense of leisure and control while her opponents scurried around the court sweating with their disheveled hair. Richey also caused a stir by wearing shorts and jumpsuits instead of the traditional dress or skirt.

*Nancy Richey serving at Wimbledon, 1969. Photo by Ed Lacey/
Popperfoto.*

During the 1960s, Richey rose up in the amateur ranks to become one of the top two women's players from the United States,
along with King. Life on the road for women players like Richey
was challenging. Earning little more than expense money, staying in subpar accommodations, and cleaning her own tennis outfits, Richey did not live the glamorous life during the amateur
era. Still, she played in circuits all over the world. In 1966, she
made the finals at both Roland Garros and Forest Hills. In January 1967, she won her first major tournament at the Australian
Championships. One year later, she found herself in Paris in the
midst of the chaos unleashed by the May 1968 rebellion and won

the French Championships, her second major. The talented Texan was reaching the peak of her powers when the Open era of tennis was just beginning.[33]

Richey chafed under the authoritarianism of the USLTA, which subjected her not only to meager amounts of expense money but also to the physical incursions endured by all women. After winning a tournament, a USLTA official attempted to withhold the expense money until she gave him a kiss. Unpaid labor, personal humiliation, and vulnerability to rich and powerful men characterized the experience of women's tennis players during the amateur era. After she won at Roland Garros in 1968, she decided to skip the US Open because the USLTA had refused to give her more than expense money. This was a difficult decision; 1968 was a good year for her, and she stood an excellent chance to win at Forest Hills. The next year, she returned to Forest Hills and made it all the way to the finals before losing to Margaret Court. Richey, like King, was not enamored with the West Side Tennis Club, the hallowed grounds of the snobby USLTA ruling class. The grass was terrible, and players had to deal with the inconveniences of playing in the crammed big city. It is not surprising that the discontent that was brewing among women players surfaced at the US Open in September 1970.

Richey, King, Casals, and the other members of the Original Nine were the frontline players of the newly formed Virginia Slims Tour. Over the next few years, Heldman and her crew of tennis rebels built the separate women's tour from scratch in the face of constant USLTA opposition. They were joined by other leading women players from Europe, such as Ann Jones, the top British women's player who won Wimbledon in 1969, and Françoise Dürr, the leading French player who won Roland Garros in 1967. Others soon followed. All wore many hats on tour, playing matches, promoting the tour, and even serving as lineswomen when none could be found. In 1971, Billie Jean King became the first woman athlete to win $100,000 in prize money. Throughout the first year of the tour, she was compiling tournament wins left and right, including another $10,000 during the tour's triumphant return to Houston, which took place in the Hofheinz Pavilion at the University of Houston. The success of the tour continued to draw the ire of the USLTA, who formed a rival women's tour to compete with the Slims rebels. Still, the proverbial genie was out of the bottle. New stars including Chris Evert, Evonne Goolagong, and Martina Navratilova, among others, would come on the scene in the early 1970s. They, along with their male counterparts, pushed the game to unprecedented heights of popularity. Women's professional tennis was now here to stay.

*　*　*

The revolution in women's tennis was driven by women who perceived themselves as subordinate to the tennis Brahmins, but still the vast majority of them were white, with notable exceptions like Rosie Casals. In the early 1970s, there was no black woman player who had the name recognition of Arthur Ashe. Gladys Heldman was not unaware of this, and in her own way, she tried to bring black women players into the fold. In 1972, the Virginia Slims tour announced an agreement with the American Tennis Association (ATA), the historic black tennis circuit, to sign players to the tour. Among the better-known stars of these players was North Carolinian Bonnie Logan. Heldman's *World Tennis* covered her career and asked her to write about her little-known visit to Apartheid South Africa in 1972, an episode that has been overshadowed by Arthur Ashe's anti-apartheid activism. Logan was a pioneering tennis player, but she did not possess the resources or connections, or the tournament wins, to sustain herself on a fledgling tennis tour in the 1970s.[34]

The women's pro tennis tour was up and running, but the renegade from the Upper East Side of Manhattan would not continue to shape the movement she helped unleash. Heldman continued to clash with USLTA officials, and she lost an ill-fated lawsuit that forced her to relinquish control of the tour. In 1973, the Virginia Slims and USLTA tours merged, and Heldman was frozen out of the agreement. Years later, her dear friend Joe Cullman inexplicably erased her role from the launching of the tour and gave all the credit to Billie Jean King. Though she continued to operate on the sidelines of the tennis world, she never did return to her rightful place as a visionary tennis promoter. In 2003, she died from a self-inflicted gunshot wound in her home. Despite all her gumption and vision, she could not overcome the sexism of the tennis ruling class and her own personal demons. But in 1970, Gladys Heldman seized the moment. She did her part by using her talents and class privilege to usher in a new era of American sport history. Now the cadre of talented women athletes she brought together would use their talents and vision to carry the revolution forward. They would receive an unexpected opportunity when another representative of the male-dominated amateur era sought to capitalize on their success.

* * *

Robert Larimore Riggs always knew how to make a quick buck. The former Wimbledon champion, now a middle-aged pathological gambler, was hustling and scuffling his way through a less-than-satisfying retirement. As one of Jack Kramer's contemporaries, he had mustered all he could from the amateur order of the international tennis world. In retirement, he shuffled through life working and trying to have fun. When the Women's Pro Tour got underway in 1971, he, like many of his male contemporaries, were bemused and annoyed by the audacity of the "girls" playing tennis in their own circuit apart from the men. As the tour continued to grow, he converted his distaste into a golden opportunity to make some money from feminism. He decided to remake himself into a male chauvinist pig hustler.

It was a remarkable transformation. He played the role to the hilt, but he also saw himself as a representative of the era of gentlemanly domination of tennis. In 1971, he began to tell the press that he could beat any of the top players in the women's game. He was put off for almost two years until he finally found a taker in Australian player Margaret Court, arguably the number-one player in the women's game. Court, who never did grasp the social significance of women's sports, walked into a buzz saw. On Mother's Day 1973, the blabbermouth little man humiliated the Australian champion on national television, beating the bigger and stronger Court in straight sets, 6–2, 6–1, with his assortment of dinks, dunks, and lobs. The win gave Riggs an even bigger platform, and it seemed to discredit the claim of the feminist movement in tennis.

With his victory in hand, he set his sights on other top women players. Billie Jean King, who didn't want to give Riggs the time of day, finally agreed to play him after the embarrassment of Court's match. In July 1973, they signed an agreement for a $100,000 winner-take-all best-of-five-sets match to be promoted by Jerry Perenchio, the Hollywood promoter who had successfully promoted the Fight of the Century boxing match between Muhammad Ali and Joe Frazier on March 8, 1971. This clash would take place in the Houston Astrodome and be billed as the Battle of the Sexes. At the press conference that announced the match, Riggs began his litany of sexist pig comments, which he endlessly repeated in the months leading up to the match: "A woman's place is in the bedroom and in the kitchen, in that order," and "The male is king; the male is supreme," he recited to anyone who would listen. Retrospective renderings of the match credit much of the sexism to the tongue-and-cheek scripts of Perenchio, but the pre-match sexist rhetoric didn't just come from the blathering Riggs; it also came from the self-proclaimed male experts who relied on their status as authorities to predict a Riggs victory over the younger and athletically superior King.

* * *

Roy Hofheinz probably loved that the Astrodome would be the venue for the Battle of the Sexes. Still, Hofheinz might not have envisioned his Dome being the venue for arguably the most important tennis match in the sport's history, which also happened to be one of the most transformative social and cultural events of the 1970s. He suffered a stroke in 1970, which forced him to delegate managerial duties of his sports and entertainment empire to a host of associates in the Houston Sports Association. In the late 1960s and into the early 1970s, the "Taj Mahal of Sports" was the premier sporting and entertainment venue in the country. The Dome booked world championship boxing matches, including four bouts featuring Muhammad Ali; the famous University of Houston–UCLA college basketball game; the 1968 Major League Baseball All-Star game; the 1971 Men's College Basketball Championships; Hubert Humphrey's 1968 campaign address; the circus; concerts; and many other events. The Judge's entertainment empire expanded to include AstroWorld, an amusement park situated east of the Dome. Hofheinz had presided over the country's most dynamic entertainment complex. And Sidney Shenkler, his successor in running the Dome, bagged the premier cultural and sporting event of the 1970s when he signed the Riggs-King Battle of the Sexes for $250,000.

The Dome's carnival-like environment was the perfect setting for the overhyped Battle of the Sexes. The event combined Hofheinzian kitsch with Perenchio's boxing promotional know-how. Money was flowing everywhere. Riggs was the ringleader of the gambling spree, but he had plenty of company. He held court at the Tarzan Suite in the nearby AstroWorld Hotel and took on bets all week long in the practice bubble right next to the Dome. It seemed like every Hollywood celebrity descended upon Houston. Reporters of all types, not just the sportswriting brethren, were on hand to witness what broadcaster Howard Cosell described as a "quaint, unique event." Commentators tended to view the hype and the match as a comedic show, but what they were really experiencing was the future of professional tennis and of sports spectatorship in the United States.

But the cavernous Astrodome was not an ideal place to play or watch tennis. Like the basketball court set up for the 1968 Houston-UCLA basketball game, the tennis court was far away from the stands. The court's acrylic carpet surface, called Sporteze, had been laid out on a wooden basketball floor that was placed horizontally across the baseball infield from first to third base. The surface was not like normal hard tennis courts where balls tended to bounce higher. On the acrylic carpet, balls stayed lower than normal, making it an odd playing surface for tennis. The days before the match, King smartly toured the Astrodome to try to get accustomed to the atmosphere: "Nothing in my career had prepared me for the vastness of the building," she remembered. "The court itself didn't have the intimate environment of many of the venues we played."[35] In an effort to gain a sense of familiarity, she requested that she change in the visitor's clubhouse so she could use the locker of her brother, Randy Moffitt, a Major League Baseball player who performed in the Dome as a visiting player for the San Francisco Giants.

Surrounding the court were the best seats in the house, the courtside $100 temporary seats for celebrities and VIPs. Behind them were black-tie waiters and bartenders serving up food and plenty of drinks for the courtside crowd. Rod Steiger, Glenn Campbell, and countless other celebrities could grab a drink and a plate, smoke a cigarette, and watch the unique tennis extravaganza unfold only a few yards away. Meanwhile, the rest of the fans sat far away in the stands. Those in the upper decks could not have seen a whole lot of tennis from their vantage points. But poor visibility did not keep them from attending this historic event, as it didn't when the baseball arena staged boxing matches, concerts, and basketball games. Being there live was just as important as being able to see the intricacies of Riggs's lobs or King's backhands. Indeed, more than thirty thousand fans came to witness the women's libber face off against the male chauvinist pig.

Just as the Astrodome left its mark on the historic event, so did another influential technology of the day: television. And the medium created an archive that allows the sport historian to come close to experiencing the event as the audience did in 1973.[36] Revisiting the King-Riggs match reveals how understandings of womanhood and manhood were changing in sport and in the broader American society during the 1970s and in subsequent years. The telecast also vividly illustrated the novelty of the event itself, showing the commercial possibilities of tennis on television. And King's performance dramatically exemplified the capabilities of women as athletes. And the television broadcast especially illuminates the workings of sexism in a moment when it was directly challenged by a woman athlete who was determined to win.

Jerry Perenchio's promotional flair and boxing-style braggadocio blended perfectly with the narrative storytelling drama sold to America by Roone Arledge's ABC Sports, which paid $750,000 to televise the match. The Battle of the Sexes was tailor made for Rooney Pinckney Arledge's narrative genius. Born in Forest Hills in 1931 and raised in Long Island, Arledge revolutionized television sports and news coverage. During his long tenure as president of ABC Sports and ABC News, he turned both from second-rate operations to profitable and innovative television divisions. The key to his success was his commitment to storytelling, something he learned during his time as a student at Columbia University in the early 1950s. In a story that would make any liberal arts educator proud, Arledge repeatedly attributed his success in television to the lasting impression his literature professors made upon him at Columbia. "My God, Mark Van Doren was teaching in humanities then," Arledge recalled to Ron Powers in his 1984 book, *Supertube*. He was also a student of Lionel Trilling, the renowned literary critic and prominent New York intellectual. As he and his biographers have frequently highlighted, it was Trilling who taught young Roone the "art of narrative." From Trilling, he learned that the "wisps and fragments of narrative drama lay beneath the surface of the most random behavior, and that it was the task of the artist to sift and isolate this drama, and heighten it, and render it in such a compressed and ordered way that the reader could respond."[37] Arledge took these ideas and applied them to television coverage in an unprecedented manner.

Under Arledge's leadership in the 1960s, ABC Sports converted sport into a drama that foregrounded what became known in the business as storylines. "The thrill of victory, and the agony of defeat," that memorable phrase from ABC's *Wide World of Sports* weekly television program, perfectly encapsulated the distinctive approach of the network's sports division. By 1969 or 1970, when Arledge was fully in charge of the sports division, his ideas were fully incorporated into the network's sports programming, both in his weekly NCAA college football telecasts and in *Monday Night Football*, ABC's wildly popular prime-time football series. For the Battle of the Sexes, ABC's coverage featured Arledge's best men, a mixture of the *Monday Night Football* and NCAA College Football teams, with star commentators Howard Cosell and Frank Gifford in front of the cameras and Chuck Howard and Chet Forte directing from the truck.

The Battle of the Sexes theme was perfect for the Arledge broadcast team. Though the event featured a star woman athlete, Howard and Forte ensured that viewers would pay as much attention to attractive women celebrities in the stands. Arledge's cameraman and his team of reporters made sure everyone in the audience would appreciate women for their looks all night long, even as King provided a wider conception of womanhood with every one of her touch volleys and zinging backhands. ABC Sports paid a lot of money to broadcast the Battle of the Sexes, but it viewed the match as more of a profitable comedic spectacle than a real sporting event.

Arledge's indifference to the social impact of the match was clear in his initial decision to ask Jack Kramer to commentate the match with Howard Cosell and Rosie Casals. In addition to his promotional work, Kramer was a regular commentator on CBS's coverage of the US Open. Clearly, the ABC Sports boss was operating under the same formula that he used in his *Monday Night Football* telecasts, which pitted Howard Cosell against Don Meredith, two diametrically opposed personalities, to stir up controversy that would further stimulate ratings. But Billie Jean and Larry King were opposed to Kramer's presence on the broadcast. In a meeting they had with Arledge and his team the day before the match, King threatened to pull out of the match if Kramer was given yet another platform to air his hostile views of the women's game. Though Arledge was incredulous, he finally relented to their demands, but not before he gave Kramer a chance to whine to America about his exclusion from the match. At the opening of the telecast, ABC gave the aggrieved Kramer the chance to air both his side of the controversy and his views on King and the match:

> [King] feels that I am completely opposed to what she is try-ing to do in tennis, and I have to say Billie Jean is right. I don't believe that a champion should walk off the court with a full house as she did in Los Angeles years ago; I don't think she should have defaulted to Julie Heldman at Forest Hills. I want to make one thing clear: when I realized that when I thought I would be a problem for Billie Jean, I thought she would use me as an excuse for losing to Bobby Riggs. . . . I am withdrawing voluntarily and I'm wishing 100 percent good luck to my pal Bobby Riggs.[38]

Right there in front of a national television audience, the gen-tleman tennis star of yesteryear proved himself to be the "ass" Gladys Heldman had said he was. Even if his statement was de-signed to simply juice up the hype of the match, his firing of in-sults to King's character showed how he still took the low road even as he was positioned by ABC's crew as the one taking the high road.

After Kramer's performance, the telecast switched to a pre-match interview with Riggs, who offered one more soliloquy on behalf of the country's male supremacist movement: "I'm gonna try to win for all the guys all over the world, who feel as I do that the male is king; the male is supreme. I've said it over and over again: girls play a nice game of tennis, but for girls, when they get out there on the court with a man, even a tired old man of 55, they're gonna be in trouble."

After Riggs's outburst, ABC cut to Frank Gifford, himself a gentlemen athletic star from yesteryear, interviewing King in the visitor's locker room. After asking her about the match, Gifford floated a friendly but revealing query to the tennis star: "The fem-inist thing, how important is that, Billie?" To that question, King replied: "The women's movement is important to me, as long as it stays practical, and I think that the women's movement is making a better life for more people other than just women, and I feel very strongly about that." Earlier that year, King had offered a more developed articulation of her conception of feminism and its relationship to sports. "I'm interested in the women's movement, but from an action point of view, not an intellectual one," she told Grace Lichtenstein at Wimbledon. "Tennis helps the women's movement just by *doing*. We're *there*, we're visual, like blacks in sports who helped their movement. If people see us out there every day, that changes people's minds, not *talking* about it."[39] Gifford was unsure about the "feminist thing," but whether he knew it or not, the former football star turned television broadcaster got a good taste of King's vision of feminism that night in the Astrodome.

ABC Sports' coverage of the Battle of the Sexes shows how exclusion and sexism occurred—and occurs—not merely in the articulation of blatant sexist language but in the subtle ways that men occupy spaces, are granted positions of authority, and are allowed to articulate nonsensical claims in the guise of objectivity and expertise. All types were on full display that evening. In the pre-match hoopla, as King was carried out to the tennis court by muscle-bound hunks on a feathered litter, Cosell infamously remarked: "Billie Jean King is calm and poised. She is wearing a new gown, not a gown of course, a skirt," as if somehow he didn't quite know how to describe women's apparel in an athletic contest such as this one. Cosell then told the audience, groping for words, "And looking like Billie Jean King always looks, a very attractive young lady, and sometimes you get the feeling that if she ever let her hair grow down to her shoulders, take off her glasses, you'd have someone vying for a Hollywood screen test."

The Arledge formula of playful tension between broadcasters ensured that the Battle of the Sexes would happen both on the court and in the television booth, even without Jack Kramer. After the interviews with Riggs and King, Cosell introduced fellow members of that night's broadcast team, starting with "little

Rosie Casals." The six-foot-one Cosell came on camera with his arm draped around the shoulder of the diminutive Casals, who was wearing a yellow T-shirt with King's face and "Billie Jean is #1" plastered in the middle. When Cosell asked Casals for her prediction, without hesitation she called the match 6–3, 6–4, 6–3 in favor of King, almost the exact score of the eventual outcome. Cosell egged her on some more, encouraging the opinionated Rosebud to express her honest opinion of Bobby Riggs, to which she bluntly replied, "He's a duck-footed man; he's just bad news, really bad news."

Casals was cast as the emotional and blatantly partial Billie Jean King rooter, while her counterpart in the booth, Eugene Scott, was introduced by Cosell as the broadcast's other "resident expert." Scott was indeed an expert, having been a top-ranked player in the men's tour during the 1960s. Notably, Cosell did not put his arm around Scott, and instead, unlike his comportment with Casals, maintained a respectful distance from him. True to his role as the Riggs rooter in the telecast, Scott predicted a win for the "old man." His prediction was based on Riggs's performance against Court, as well as his claim that King, "as all women, may be a little bit slower than the men." With the battle lines clearly drawn on the court and in the booth, the Battle of the Sexes was now officially on.

*   *   *

During the first few games of the match, both players were clearly nervous. Riggs found that he was already breaking a sweat, due in part to the canary yellow Sugar Daddy jacket he wore to pick up a few bucks advertising Nabisco's candy product. Each player was tentative and made many unforced errors. The adrenaline flowing through King was made evident by the many groundstrokes and volleys that she hit long. Both players held serve during the first four games of the match, but an adrenaline-induced shot from King skipped long in the fifth game and enabled the "old man" to break her serve and put him up three games to two.

Now the experts who predicted Riggs would win saw their moment at hand. The nerves that undid Margaret Court would now surely overwhelm the emotionally fragile bespectacled "girl" from Southern California. Though most histories of the match rightly underscore King's dominance over Riggs throughout, some overlook the key sixth game in the first set, after Riggs broke King to go up 3–2. "This was the most critical moment of the entire match for me," she recalled years later. King regained her focus and seized command of the very next game, and it was Riggs who wilted under the pressure. Down 15–30, he double faulted to give King a double break point opportunity. In the television booth, Casals saw exactly what was unfolding; she poked fun at Riggs's nerves and softball serve, wisecracking, "How can you ever double fault with that kind of a serve?" On the very next point, King broke right back, tying the set at 3–3. Cosell, looking to say something positive about Riggs and perhaps contributing to his own gentleman myth-making, told viewers, "I say this for Bobby, he told her 'good shot' in a very sportsman-like way." The quick-witted Casals would not tolerate Cosell's attempt to recast Riggs as a sporting gentleman and sarcastically replied, "I think he's a gentleman, really."

* * *

During the very next game, King consolidated the break and was buoyed by one of the most memorable points of the match a few games later. With King serving at 15–0, Riggs hit a weak backhand return. She jumped on Riggs's weak shot with a backhand approach shot deep into the ad corner. He then hit one of his patented lob shots to try to send the ball over King's head. But she caught it with a backhand volley to the deuce side of the court. Now King had the "old man" running around the court. After Riggs tried to trick her with a backhand flip at a sharp angle, King tracked it down and hit another backhand into the empty deuce court. The supposedly fragile "girl" outsmarted the "old man," compelling him to take a seat to catch his breath as King fans roared their approval. The dramatic point showed that King was decisively taking control of the match.

Normally, sports commentators and directors used instant replay to analyze such impressive exhibitions of athletic skill as King had exemplified for millions of viewers. But ABC's team refused to see the athletic and social revolution happening before their very eyes. It was a classic exhibition of strategic blindness. Rather than linger on King's excellent game, ABC decided to send Frank Gifford to interview one of the many women spectators that transfixed the boys in the truck. After a commercial, Gifford spoke with Claudine Longet, the French actress. "The Houston Astrodome is a beautiful scene and speaking of beautiful things, this is Natlaine Nitschke," he joked to the presumed male audience because Longet was wearing the #66 jersey of Green Bay Packer linebacker Ray Nitschke. The sight of the conventionally attractive Longet in a football jersey must have caught Gifford's eyes, but her replies to his questions showed her clear analysis of the action on the court. She pointed out that King "was playing so well, so hard, she's the aggressor." Meanwhile she mocked Riggs by saying "he looks like a rabbit and all that, but it is fun to see a lady with a lot of dignity playing so well."[40]

With Riggs now down 4–5 and desperately serving to stay in the first set, he shocked the experts who predicted him to win by double faulting to hand the game and the set to King 6–4. The crowd unleashed a thunderous roar, and Cosell declared to the national television audience in his typical hyperbolic style, "And the women in this arena are standing and cheering for Billie Jean King!" With comments like these, ABC peddled the myth that all the women cheered for King and all the men for Riggs, even though their pre-match interviews showed that to be an inaccurate interpretation of the rooting interests of fans. A few games later, a revealing exchange between Cosell and Scott revealed the broadcasters' own growing awareness of the situation. "There are more 'I Love Billie Jean King' buttons around here, even a lot of men wearing them," Cosell noted in wonderment.

With one set in her favor, King was much more confident at

the beginning of the second set. She smiled occasionally and tried riskier shots. But a Riggs ploy caused her to lose her concentration. During a break between games, he placed a bet on himself to win and challenged her to place a bet as well. She refused, but the gall of the "old man" to place bets in the middle of the match distracted King as she lost the first game of the second set. During the next game, Scott grudgingly admitted that King forced Riggs to change his tactics by making him serve and volley, "which is certainly not his strong point." Almost on cue, Riggs missed a volley and whipped his racket in disgust. The error allowed King to break back in the very next game with another backhand winner after a long rally. "A brilliant rally, and a brilliant placement by Billie Jean King," Cosell exclaimed. The cameras cut to Billie Jean Campbell, the wife of music star Glen Campbell, jumping up and down with glee. After a commercial break, the magnitude of the moment—a woman beating a man in an athletic contest in a large stadium on national television—was finally setting in on Cosell. He breathlessly told the audience in typical Cosellian terms:

> Again the scene at the Houston Astrodome and it's really one of the most extraordinary scenes I've witnessed in my lifetime on the sports beat. That is not an extreme statement, to see this kind of crowd for a tennis match unique, a fifty-five-year-old man who walks like a duck, who's made all kinds of noise over the recent weeks and months, who disposed of such dispatch of Margaret Court, going against a twenty-nine-year-old woman, the number-one women's player, certainly in this country . . . and it is $100,000 winner take all, but it's more than that really.

But the match still had to be won, and occasional errors by King kept Riggs in the second set. He fruitlessly tried to hit harder serves, but he did not possess the strength to overpower her. Neither could he get his first serve to work. Except to those who were blinded by their sexism, it was clear that the male chauvinist pig had nothing left: no go-to shots, no tricky tactics, nothing. Casals

The lobber serving to the libber. AP photo.

stated the obvious when she told Cosell, "He cannot hurt her because he can't hit over the ball with topspin. He can't hit with any kind of speed." The best he could do was hit off-speed slice shots with the hope that King would somehow misjudge them and hit them out. During the eighth game of the second set, King jumped on his weak second serve with a hard slice backhand return that Riggs couldn't even touch. On the next point, King broke his spirit by chasing down one of his weak lobs before rocketing a topspin forehand passing shot that he could not reach. During the next point, he foolishly served to her backhand side, and she flung a backhand slice return at his feet that he once again was unable to touch. The point gave her another break of service to put her up 5–3 and serving to take the second set. The emotional fragility that undid Margaret Court was not going to derail the tennis champion from Southern California. With the second set within reach, King poured it on. She smashed one of Riggs's weak lobs to put her up 15–0. Then he missed a lob to fall behind further. Finally, at 40–0, King hit a serve right down the middle of the T that divides the service boxes. All he could manage in response was a weak return into the bottom of the net. King dominated the game at love, taking the second set 6–3. "Looks like I'm gonna make some money on this match," crowed Casals.

This sequence and much of the match show that one of the major storylines of the Battle of the Sexes was not Bobby Riggs's outlandish behavior. Neither was it the sequined blue dress designed by Ted Tinling or the trademark blue Adidas sneakers that King donned that night. Nor was it the pomp and circumstance of the promotional operation that compelled America to tune in to watch a tennis match. For the tennis fan, the real story of the Riggs-King battle was King's backhand. Time and time again, she whistled backhand winners past her befuddled opponent. Her dominant shot became more and more evident as the match moved through the second and third sets.

After a commercial break, Gifford once again interviewed King between the second and third sets. He asked her if the match had been easier than she anticipated. King, struggling to find words in the midst of an intense competition, replied formulaically, "I don't know . . . just play my game. . . . I never think I've won until it's over." The football commentator was paying attention to the match enough to ask her about her backhand. King rightly observed, "He seems to keep hitting it to my backhand, and that's my best shot." Gifford, impressed with the determined athlete, closed the interview by saying, "Good luck, you're a helluva gal."

Before the third set began, the exhausted Riggs managed to change the only thing he could at that point in the match: his shirt. He discarded his soaked blue polo shirt for a bright yellow one, which only showed his perspiration all the more and did little to change the momentum of the match. King broke his serve again with yet another backhand winning return. Seeing the match slip away, a male fan yelled in desperation, loud enough for everyone to hear, "Come on Bobby, baby!" His plea reflected the growing realization among the male chauvinists that the libber was going to take down the lobber on this night. Casals crowed some more after King took another point from Riggs, saying, "I wonder what Bobby Riggs will do next; he can't play all of the women."

Although the Riggs supporters in the Astrodome could do little more than rally their hero, at least those watching on television could be entertained by ABC. Arledge's cameramen tried to keep their attention by continually showing all the lovely ladies attending that night in the Astrodome. After another commercial break, Gifford told the audience, "Well, there's a bevy of beauties here in Houston" as he interviewed Jo Ann Pflug, the then-popular film and television actress. As Gifford, Cosell, and the ABC team continued to salivate over the "beauties" in the arena like frat boys, the woman on the court was continuing to dominate her male chauvinist opponent. Soon after the Pflug interview, Gifford interviewed the notorious misogynist Leroy Neiman, who was sketching the athletes and spectators that night. "Leroy has been concentrating on the ladies here tonight," Gifford assured the audience as the camera zeroed in on yet another pretty lady. Neiman applied his artistic skills to a sketch of a photographer on the sidelines, accentuating her derriere. "This is Jessica, a girl photographer . . . a real beauty," he told an approving Gifford. "And here we got the lineswoman, another beauty; this is an angle I've had all night and it's been a little distracting to me." Gifford chuckled, admitting that the young woman was "a little distracting."

What was plainly evident, if not that night, certainly to the viewer decades later, were the ways that the action on the court could not be comprehended by the men on the broadcast team or by the many men who predicted a Riggs victory. Every backhand winner and volley from King challenged the sexist ideologies that convinced many that a fifty-five-year-old man could defeat a woman athlete almost half his age. The cultural revolution that took place at the Battle of the Sexes wasn't just King beating Riggs; it was also the ways the event challenged gender conventions on the telecast all night long, even as they were disregarded by the men who worked the broadcast.

After King won another game, Cosell, doing his best to mimic the gender conventions of the tennis world, reported, "Game to Mrs. King." After King easily held serve a few games later to go up 5–3, Scott was finally ready to acknowledge that his prediction of a Riggs triumph was dead wrong. "I'm looking mighty bad, Howard; so does Bobby," he admitted. But the nerves that occasionally creeped into King's game returned in the next game, when she lost multiple match points on unforced errors. Riggs helped her cause by missing easy shots himself. Scott, in an attempt to offer objective analysis, claimed Riggs had "nonchalanted a forehand." Cosell, now ready to disregard Scott's expertise, disagreed: "I don't think he's nonchalanting anything, Gene. I think he's tired." Indeed, fatigue and nerves were affecting both players. After another exchange of errors, Riggs double faulted to create a third match point for King. He summoned whatever energy he had left to will one last serve over the net. King responded with a forehand chip shot, to which he replied with a weak backhand that softly hit the net for a final unforced error. Game. Set. Match. The victor threw her racket in the air, releasing the enormous pressure she felt that night. Riggs, like many gentleman tennis players of his generation, managed to jump over the net congratulate his opponent.

"It is over!" Cosell declared as the Astrodome crowd roared.

Cosell, having begun the telecast by describing Billie Jean King as a woman who could screen for a Hollywood audition with a little makeover, became convinced of her athletic greatness by the end of her memorable performance.

It was Billie Jean who fought for equal pay for women at the US Open tennis tournament, and she got it. All of the women of America, or at least most of them, seemed to be caught up in this match. Billie Jean went into virtual seclusion. There was talk before the match about her health, whether or not she'd be able to go ahead with the match as scheduled or postpone it. It turned out, instead, that Billie Jean King was perfectly ready, not only ready, but willing and able. . . . Billie Jean King reigns supreme.

*   *   *

And the women pro players of the 1970s were also ready, willing, and able. The Women's Tennis Association formed to unify the women's pro tour in one organization. The renegade quality of the Virginia Slims Tour remained, though it was tempered by Heldman's departure and the USLTA's management. Still, the emergence of the women's professional tennis tour was a major victory for the second-wave feminist movement, even if many of the players did not identify as feminists, and even if many feminists tended to ignore the sporting world. Younger stars such as Martina Navratilova and Chris Evert, among others, built upon the pioneering activism of King, Casals, Richey, and the other members of the Original Nine. The 1970s alliance of commercial capitalism and insurgent women tennis players produced a profitable and entertaining sport, even though many gender and racial inequities remained.

*   *   *

Billie Jean King's victory capped off the first three years of the sports revolution in tennis that started in that Forest Hills locker room, took shape at the Houston Racquet Club, and came to fruition in the Houston Astrodome. Tobacco money from Philip Morris, like Lamar Hunt's oil fortune, also helped, as did Gladys Heldman's promotional wizardry. The sport that was confined to the country club set suddenly became a profitable business and a force for social transformation. Years later, King summarized the importance of these years and of the fact that much of it took shape in the hot and muggy capital of the Gulf South:

> The symmetry of those years was impossible to escape. We began our quest in Houston in 1970, rebels with a cause and an uncertain future. And we came back to Houston in 1973 after proving that we could make it on our own. We began our quest in Houston in 1970 because a man, Jack Kramer, under-

estimated our value as athletes and entertainers. And we came back to Houston in 1973 because another man, Bobby Riggs, dared to make the same mistake. "You've come a long way, baby," was our slogan in 1970. Three years later, when I shook hands with a defeated and tired-looking man, we had come a very long way, indeed.[41]

One year later, in MacGregor Park a few miles away from the Astrodome, the revolution would continue. Following in the footsteps of Billie Jean King and Rosie Casals, more young women from the Sunbelt learned their games on the public courts rather than in the country club. John Wilkerson, a park and recreation tennis instructor, began working with Zina Garrison and Lori McNeil, two talented young black girls, on the public courts of Houston. On those courts lay the future of women's tennis in the United States as Garrison and McNeil broke more barriers and became top professionals in the 1980s. And as they were winding down their careers in the 1990s, two other young black girls from Southern California, Venus and Serena Williams, under the tutelage of their father, Richard, emerged from the public courts of Compton to make more tennis history.[42]

CHAPTER 5

Labor and Lawlessness in Rangerland

O
N THE NIGHT OF APRIL 22, 1972, SPORTS FANS IN THE DALLAS-FORT WORTH
Metroplex witnessed a noteworthy event in Texas athletic history. The region's new Major League Baseball franchise, formerly known as the Washington Senators and now called the
Texas Rangers, began their existence in a game against the California Angels. Robert E. Short, the team's owner, moved his franchise from Washington, DC, to the fast-growing North Texas
metropolitan area in search of riches and higher attendance figures. The move crushed the hearts of baseball fans in DC while
delighting sports fans in Texas. But on opening night, a less-than-
sellout crowd of 20,105 fans, many of them arriving in Arlington
late because of a traffic jam on the Dallas–Fort Worth Turnpike,
came through the turnstiles at Arlington Stadium, the former minor league ballpark that was refurbished for the Rangers. The new
team was given a Texas-style welcome. During the pregame ceremonies, their manager, the legendary Ted Williams, was given
cowboy boots with baseball spikes on the bottom, and each of his
players was given cowboy hats. Arlington's mayor, Tom Vandergriff, the man largely responsible for bringing Major League
Baseball to the region, threw the ceremonial first pitch.

Texas's new professional sports team started with a bang in the
bottom of the first inning when Frank Howard, previously a Senator fan favorite, delighted the Texan crowd by slugging one of his

prodigious home runs over the center field fence. Later, two of the team's younger talents, shortstop Lenny Randle and second baseman Toby Harrah, collected three hits each. Third baseman Dave Nelson also homered for the home team. The team now known as the Rangers jumped out to a 6–1 lead before holding off an Angels rally in the late innings to win 7–6.[1]

This auspicious start turned out to be the high point of the season for the Texas Rangers. The opening night victory was a mirage. As the season unfolded, Rangers fans quickly learned what Washington Senators fans already knew: that the group of ballplayers that took the field in Arlington that night was not a good baseball team, because it was owned by a man who ran a shell operation in the guise of a sports franchise. On the field and at the box office, the Rangers inaugural season in North Texas turned out to be a colossal flop. The team finished with fifty-four wins and one hundred losses, good for last place in their division. During the last month of the season, the hapless Rangers lost fifteen games in a row, echoing a similarly futile run during their penultimate season in Washington, when they lost fourteen games in a row under the same manager. By September 1, Frank Howard, the first-game hero and beloved franchise player, was gone—traded to the Detroit Tigers. And Bob Short did not come close to achieving his goal of attracting a million fans to the ballpark. Only 662,974 fans attended Rangers games in 1972, an average of 8,610 fans per game, which were virtually the same attendance figures from their last season in Washington. Short's visions of a financially profitable team with new fans in a rapidly growing Sunbelt city were eclipsed by a perpetually empty stadium and poor results on the field during that first disastrous season in Texas.

The 1972 campaign was the first in a number of unremarkable seasons for Major League Baseball in the Dallas–Fort Worth region. On one level, Short's decision to move the team to Texas made sense. He was simply trying to do what the owners of the Dallas Cowboys, the Houston Oilers, and the Houston Astros had already done: build a professional sports team in state with a rap-

Opening night for the Texas Rangers, 1972. Courtesy Fort Worth Star-Telegram *Collection, Special Collections, the University of Texas at Arlington Libraries.*

idly growing population and a dynamic economy that seemed to be on a perpetual upward trajectory. Sports franchises in the Sunbelt were following the national trend of population growth. In addition to the teams in Texas, during the late 1960s and early 1970s, professional sports franchises popped up in New Orleans, Atlanta, Phoenix, and San Diego. Yet their success, both financially and on the field of play, was not inevitable, and many franchises, particularly those in basketball and baseball, struggled to make it at the box office in the 1960s and '70s. On another level, Bob Short's decision to move to the Metroplex was a gamble, for the region remained dominated by college football and the Dallas Cowboys, and even the latter had to work hard to attract a following and turn a profit in North Texas. In this period, North Texans were largely indifferent to non-football professional sports teams.

While the late 1960s and early '70s saw the NFL's rising popularity, they also signaled an impending crisis for Major League Baseball. The AFL-NFL merger hatched by Lamar Hunt, Tex

Schramm, and Pete Rozelle had strengthened the league's monopoly on professional football and catapulted it to the status of America's most popular spectating sport. The advent of the Super Bowl championship game and the NFL's expanding television package, which included the wildly successful *Monday Night Football*, made football a national obsession. Meanwhile, baseball seemed to be floundering. Attendance at games was dropping, and team owners explored, or threatened to explore, franchise relocation as a strategy to keep their teams afloat.

But the story of Major League Baseball's decline in this period is a bit mythical. What was really happening in the 1970s was that big league baseball was in transition. A new game and a new spectating culture were emerging, and the baseball establishment and old-school baseball men struggled to corral this unwieldy process. Owners were losing their decades-long control of players' labor power as the Major League Baseball Players' Association fought for and won unprecedented victories: higher salaries and, remarkably, free agency. The ol' ball game was also getting blacker and browner and more exciting on the field, while owners were scrambling for more revenue. And yet even with owners in retreat, they still managed to make some money. And the Texas Rangers, the team that the Texas Sunbelt stole from the nation's capital, exemplifies this transformation better than any other.

* * *

Sam Blair, a *Dallas Morning News* columnist, had warned DFW sports fans about Bob Short. The day after the announcement of the Senators' move to Texas, Blair wrote a column detailing the owner's sordid dealings in Washington and his questionable business practices while he owned the Lakers. "Let's face it," he wrote, "Short is receiving a great deal in being allowed to set up shop at Turnpike Stadium. Until he proves he will shape up and give this area a good organization and a sound program for building a contending team, no one should rush out and strew roses in his path."[2] Blair's warning highlighted the fact that success in the

Dallas–Fort Worth market required the creative labors of team management, and he was rightly skeptical of Bob Short's interest in facing the challenge.

Blair's rendering of Short's previous ownership history indicated that the Rangers owner was much more interested in turning a quick profit from his sports franchise. The Minneapolis trucking magnate first got into the sports business when he bought the National Basketball Association's Minneapolis Lakers in 1957. Claiming financial losses in his home city, he made a shrewd move by taking his franchise to Los Angeles in 1960. It was in this period that Southern California was establishing itself as a national sporting capital with successful college football programs, the National Football League's Rams, and the recently arrived Brooklyn Dodgers. Plus, Los Angeles had the fourteen-thousand-seat Sports Arena, a spanking new facility that had hosted the 1960 Democratic National Convention and was perfectly suited to house a professional basketball franchise. And in the 1960s, the Lakers made a significant impact on the LA sporting scene and on the growth of the league itself, led by the transcendent play of Hall of Fame talents Elgin Baylor and Jerry West. Short's Lakers were annual contenders for league titles during his reign as Laker owner, though they frequently lost to their perennial tormenters, the Boston Celtics. Still, Short managed to turn a business that was $300,000 in debt into a popular and profitable franchise. After five seasons, Short sold the Lakers to wealthy Canadian sports enthusiast Jack Kent Cooke in September 1965 for $5.175 million, a then unheard of figure for a professional basketball franchise.[3]

Aside from his activities as a sports entrepreneur, Short also had an ill-fated career in politics. He twice ran for office and lost, most recently during his campaign for Minnesota lieutenant governor in 1966. He eventually became the treasurer of the Democratic National Committee during the 1968 presidential campaign of fellow Minnesotan and close friend Hubert Humphrey. But he yearned to get back into the sport business, and his DC political connections put him in a position to buy the Washington Senators baseball club. The Senators of the 1960s were actually the second incarnation as a big league franchise after Calvin Griffith moved the original Senators, nicknamed the "Nats," out of Washington, DC, to Minnesota in 1960. Determined to keep a team in the historically significant baseball town, and eager to stave off competition from the recently formed Continental Baseball League, the American League allowed the creation of an expansion team in DC, which took the name (and the nickname) of the Senators in 1961.

With a new facility, DC Stadium, and new enthusiasm, the Senators seemed to be poised for success in the 1960s. But success on the field or at the box office never happened. Like their predecessors, the new Senators produced the same old results: routinely finishing in or near last place throughout their short existence. By 1968, franchise owner Jim Lemon was looking to unload his woeful ball club. At first, the Hollywood celebrity Bob Hope seemed to be in good position to buy the team. But he was ultimately outbid by Short in December 1968, who bought the team for $9.4 million even though he only put down $1,000 cash out of his own pocket, raising the rest through a shrewd orchestration of loans from multiple banks.[4] Bob Short represented the new pro sports owner of the 1960s and '70s: the already established businessmen with real or imagined wealth who invested in sports for the tax breaks and for the profits it could produce.

During his second go-round as head of a pro sports team, Bob Short's management philosophy was based on the principle "If your name is in lights, we'll take you," artfully described by his former broadcaster Shelby Whitfield.[5] In other words, the embattled owner aimed to generate quick publicity rather than create a system that might facilitate long-term success on the field. Short felt that big-name players and managers would generate headlines and interest, which would increase the value of his franchise. The first big name Short brought to his team was the legendary Ted Williams, whom he coaxed out of retirement in Florida to be the team's manager in early 1969. The new owner hired the iconoclastic Williams, touted by baseball historians as the greatest hitter in the history of the game, to create a splash with the baseball media—and he did. The move seemed to be a stroke of genius. The beloved "Teddy Ballgame" occupied hero-like status in the US public, not only for his exploits on the field but also for his service as a fighter pilot in World War II and the Korean War. Widely seen as a student of the game who knew more about the science of hitting a baseball than anyone, Williams led the team to their best season in decades, finishing with an 86–76 record and drawing a record season attendance of 918,106. Even though they finished a distant fourth place, twenty-three and a half games behind the dominant first-place Baltimore Orioles, for the Nats, this was a successful season, their best since 1945. Williams was named the American League's manager of the year.

Yet Short was less than satisfied. He complained about the condition of the turf at DC Stadium (renamed Robert F. Kennedy, or RFK, Stadium that summer), and he moaned and groaned to the press about not reaching his stated goal of attracting one million fans. In September, he claimed he was standing to lose $250,000 if the press didn't help him achieve his attendance goals.[6] Such complaints did little to endear him to local sportswriters and fans. Short's critic Shelby Whitfield and others saw these complaints as evidence of the disgruntled owner's underlying agenda, which was, contrary to his public position, to move the team.[7]

The Nats' success of 1969 was short lived. During the next two seasons, Short embarked on a course of franchise destruction that revealed his true intentions of moving his team away from the nation's capital. In 1970, Williams's squad lost as many games as they won in the first few months of the season, before slipping into last place in their division and finishing the year by ignominiously dropping their final fourteen games. Short disregarded the advice of his appointed baseball men and made ill-advised trades of some of his better players for big-name players whose best days on the field were behind them. The most mind-boggling transaction was Short's trading of young, promising players for second-rate players and Denny McLain, the washed-up former All-Star pitcher. McLain had an epic 1968 season by winning thirty-one games, and he came back with twenty-four more wins the next year. By 1971, however, he was a shell of what he once was. The deal was a total disaster for the Senators, who had a miserable 10–22 record in 1971, and McLain was a constant source of dissension on the team.

The rest of the 1971 campaign was an utter failure for the Senators, and Short's complaints about attendance, his finances, and his lease arrangement with the DC Armory Board, the body that managed RFK Stadium, grew louder and louder. Meanwhile, he found a group of Texan sports enthusiasts in Arlington, Texas, of all places, who were promising him a solution to his problems. By the late summer, the prospect of Major League Baseball leaving the nation's capital again suddenly seemed possible, though most baseball observers felt confident that the team would stay. On September 21, 1971, an American League meeting was held in Boston, where team owners would decide the fate of Short's franchise. A motivated delegation from Arlington, Texas, led by the energetic mayor Tom Vandergriff, made its case for the region's readiness for baseball. A group of DC investors, led by Giant Supermarket chain head Joe Danzansky, came up with a bid to buy the Senators from Short. After hours of politicking and maneuvering by Short and other owners, ten out of the twelve team owners voted to let him move his team to Texas. Even Commissioner Bowie Kuhn, a DC native, was disappointed at the outcome of the owner vote, claiming that "the difficulty was to find a buyer with enough working capital; our efforts were unavailing."[8]

Washington fans and sportswriters were stunned. "The Washington Senators died at age 71 tonight," wrote the *Post, Times-Herald* sportswriter George Minot Jr.[9] Frustrated Washington baseball fans pinned the blame for the Senators' demise on a variety of sources. The Letters to the Editor pages of the *Post, Times-Herald* provide examples of the kinds of explanations offered by fans and sportswriters. One put it squarely on the shoulders of politicians for not taking the concerns of white fans seriously and pandering to black political interests. According to this writer, the move was a "jolt" that was "deserved retribution for the failure to maintain law and order in a city that is driving residents away. Washington will doubtless receive many more jolts of equal severity as long as politicians have no higher aim than to buy minority votes." Another claimed that the "city of Arlington is getting a team that personifies the charge that baseball is a boring national pastime." Another bitter fan suggested that the team be renamed the "Fort Worthless Senators." Still another saw the departure of Short's team as part of the broader structural changes enveloping US society, namely, the moving of capital and people from the cities to the suburbs and the impact of television. This person opined, "So you can see the loss of the Senators is another tacit admission of changes in America. The trolley car tracks are now the beltways, and the city in the region. King TV rules the region. In this transition we have all lost something. Today it was the Senators."[10]

During the team's final weeks in DC, fans were not shy about expressing their opinion of Short at the ballpark. First, they stayed away from the team's remaining games of the season, as no more than four thousand fans attended each of the next four contests at the fifty-five-thousand-seat RFK Stadium. Then, during the final game of the season, they made their feelings known in a much more disruptive fashion. On September 30, 1971, 14,460 spectators, a "big crowd" according to the team's radio broadcaster Ron Menchine, turned out for the final home game of the Washington Senators, against the New York Yankees.[11] The fans came ready to display their loyalty to the players and their disdain for Short. Banners with "Send Short to Texas, Keep the Senators" and "Short Stinks," among other messages, were displayed by fans all night long as security tried in vain to take them down. The crowd, which was in a jovial mood at the outset, watched as the Yankees jumped out to a 5–1 lead after five and a half innings. The ball club seemed to be on course for yet another loss, a feat they had accomplished ninety-five other times during the 162-game season. But in the bottom of the sixth, fan-favorite slugger Frank "Hondo" Howard ignited the team and the crowd with a prodigious home run to cut the score to 5–2. The Senator faithful went wild as Hondo rounded the bases. Swooped up in the moment, he uncharacteristically tossed his cap into the crowd and took two curtain calls in response to nonstop cheers from the fans. "I just wish the owners of the American League could see this. The ones who voted 10–2 to move this club out of Washington," Menchine bitterly told his radio audience.[12] Hondo's blast set off a four-run rally in the sixth, which tied the score at 5–5.

After the Senators went ahead 7–5 in the next inning, the mood of the crowd turned angry as the realization of the end of big league baseball in the nation's capital settled in. Cries of "We want Short!" echoed through the stadium. Fireworks could be heard ringing in the stands. Menchine told his listeners that the field seemed to be "covered with snow," which was actually confetti made from torn game programs that was tossed on the field by the fans. During the broadcast, Menchine could not contain his anger at Short and the American League owners for the team's impending move to Texas. "I think sooner or later, baseball is going to discover that they're going to have to promote and build up, not run out of town. You can't keep running forever. You've got to build this great game up," he cried. "There's no finer sport than baseball and there are no finer fans than those in Washington. The American League club owners took the coward's way out. And now there's no baseball team for the time being, but maybe someday soon there will be." Baseball failed in Washington, DC, not because the fans stayed away but because the league's unimaginative owners did not actively cultivate new fans. Short, listening from his home in Minneapolis, called the radio station to try to get Menchine off the air. The producers refused. Now the broadcasters and the radio station joined what was becoming a public uprising against the hated Senators owner that evening.

The revolt exploded in the top of the ninth inning. After Washington pitcher Joe Grzenda quickly retired the first two Yankee batters, groups of fans ran onto the field. They had run onto the diamond the previous inning, but security had successfully cleared the field and the game had resumed. But in the ninth, fans were determined to experience the final minutes of Major League

Baseball in Washington as active participants on the field, not as passive spectators in the stands. They streamed onto the diamond and immediately started scrounging for souvenirs, collecting dirt and stealing the bases. Soon thereafter, they took off for the right field scoreboard "like an army of ants," according to broadcaster Tony Roberts, taking it apart and making it nonoperational. Eventually, the umpires determined that the game could not continue, and they awarded the official victory to the Yankees. For one of the rare times in Major League Baseball history, the actual outcome of a contest was irrelevant. Why send Short to Texas with one final victory? Menchine declared to his listeners, "It's a strange way to lose a ball game. It's a strange way to wind up baseball in the nation's capital. . . . No one believed that there would not be baseball in the nation's capital, but it is sad to report, it no longer is."

Menchine's unabashed criticism of his employer revealed a growing realization among the city's baseball fan base. "Washington is not the capital of the United States. Washington is the capital of the world, and can you imagine, the capital of the world not having major league baseball?" Menchine wondered in disbelief. Washingtonian baseball enthusiasts were forced to confront their own investments in US imperial mentalities. The departure of the Senators showed that affiliating with the nation's capital was no longer able to shield DC baseball fans from the harsh realities overtaking big-time professional sports. In his column the day after the uprising, Shirley Povich claimed to speak for the fans, but he might as well have been describing his own feelings about "Arlington as some jerk town with the single boast that it is equidistant between Dallas and Fort Worth." "The Senators were finished," he ruefully wrote, "even if the ball game wasn't."[13]

Ten years before, Washington had seemed poised to embark on a new era in the city's sports history. A new stadium was built on the banks of the Anacostia River. Civil rights activists had forced the Kennedy administration to compel the Washington Redskins, the city's NFL franchise owned by arch segregationist George Preston Marshall, to integrate. Although the team was the last NFL franchise to integrate, during the 1960s and especially the '70s, the team came to resemble its fan base in terms of racial and ethnic diversity, even though it remained marred by its racist Native American mascot. And though Calvin Griffith took his Senators from the predominantly black city to the "good hard working white people" of Minnesota in 1960, the American League quickly responded by granting the city a new baseball team.[14] In those eleven years, Senator games resumed their symbolic national importance as theaters for presidential statecraft. The new Senators attracted the attentions of President John F. Kennedy, who continued the tradition of presidents throwing out the first ball on opening day and again at the 1962 All-Star game. On Short's first opening day in April 1969, Richard Nixon also threw out the first ball, and he also attended the All-Star game at RFK Stadium a few months later. But Nixon's commitment to baseball paled in comparison to his fanatical investment in football. Now, just two years later, Nixon looked on as the local baseball team left the nation's capital for the imagined greener pastures of Texas. The team's move to Arlington mirrored Nixon's own shift of focus to the South when he quickly jumped on the Texas-Arkansas college football bandwagon in December 1969. A few months after throwing out the first ball in Washington, he was found in front of Roone Arledge's ABC Sports television cameras handing a championship trophy to Darrell Royal, proclaiming a Texas team "national champions," milking the moment for all of the political capital he could muster. Short's move to Arlington symbolized Major League Baseball's own "southern strategy," or rather "Sunbelt strategy," where support and profits could revitalize a sport that was losing the interest of the white American public.

A place called Arlington, Texas—not nearby Arlington, Virginia—had inexplicably stolen the nation's capital's team. When the Arlington delegation returned victorious from the owners' meetings in Boston, a press conference was held at Dallas Love Field airport. "I think this is significant," roared a Major League Baseball booster in Texas to supporters. The man held up a Washington, DC, newspaper and read the headline with glee: "It says 'Nation's Capitol'[sic] loses to Arlington, Texas."[15] That man was the visionary mayor of Arlington, Tom Vandergriff, who had labored to bring a Major League Baseball team to the Metroplex area for more than a decade. Many outsiders must have wondered, Where is Arlington, Texas? Arlington was a rural area with a population of seven thousand in 1950. After Vandergriff was elected mayor in 1951, he helped set the town on a course from a bedroom community to a "post-suburb" by attracting industries like General Motors, the Great Southwest Industrial Park, and amusement parks such as Seven Seas and Six Flags over Texas. In 1958, the DFW Turnpike opened, facilitating automobile access to the town. When Vandergriff won the Rangers, Arlington became part of a metropolitan area that boosters were branding as the "Metroplex." DFW International Airport opened in 1974. Industries, amusement parks, and now Major League Baseball were literally putting Arlington on the map as the center of the "Metroplex." Arlington now joined the ranks of other suburbs or post-suburbs such as Anaheim, California; Bloomington, Minnesota; East Rutherford, New Jersey; Pontiac, Michigan; and of course Irving, Texas: previous no-towns that became notable in the national landscape due to the arrival of big-time sports. The little rural town off Highway 80 was remaking itself into a big league city.

How did Vandergriff pull this off? He did what pro-growth politicians were getting very good at doing in this period: perfecting the formula of offering publicly funded sports facilities for the benefit of private sports interests, which produced enormous political capital. Even as evidence of baseball's declining popularity continued to mount, scoring a big league franchise counted as a feather in the cap of an aspiring politician. Following in the footsteps of Roy Hofheinz, Vandergriff convinced voters to finance the building of a stadium. But unlike the Judge, the Arlington mayor did not have a magical state-of-the-art stadium to attract potential clubs. However, he did manage to build what became known as Turnpike Stadium in 1961, a small, ten-thousand-seat minor league facility that Vandergriff cited as evidence of the region's commitment to eventually attracting a big league baseball team. But throughout the 1960s, Vandergriff confronted the obstacle of Judge Hofheinz, who wasn't interested in cultivating competition in the Texas sport market and used his power among the owners to block an expansion team from coming to Dallas–Fort Worth.

Undaunted, the mayor sought out current franchises that were looking elsewhere, and it was then that he found a fellow traveler in the embattled owner in Washington, DC. In 1970, Vandergriff raised $10 million to renovate Turnpike Stadium to expand the capacity to twenty-one thousand. After Short agreed to move his ragtag outfit to Arlington, Vandergriff summoned another $2.75 million in construction bonds to add eighteen thousand bleacher seats in the outfield. In addition, he borrowed $7.5 million to pay Short $750,000 per year for ten years for the rights to broadcast the club's games on radio and television. Short no longer had to worry about high stadium rental fees, as Vandergriff cooked up a deal in which he would only be obligated to pay a one-dollar rental fee for the first million fans who attended games. By the end of 1972, the mayor had gotten his constituents to invest $44 million in the endeavor, and that would not be the end of it.[16] More public dollars would be needed to ensure that the Rangers would stay in Arlington.

Maybe it was the questionable decision to remake a team named after lawmakers (Senators) into one named after lawmen (Rangers), especially when the latter, who are often celebrated as heroic figures in Texas lore, were actually *lawless* men who terrorized Texas's black and brown populations for decades. Maybe this attempt to reimagine a baseball team in this legacy conjured some bad mojo that resulted in "seasons in hell," as sportswriter Mike Shropshire hilariously described his time covering the Rangers in their early years.[17] During their first two seasons, the change of scenery from Washington, DC, to Arlington, Texas, did not change the team's performance. In fact, Short's team was more pitiful. The Rangers were a minor league team play-

Arlington Stadium under construction, 1972. Courtesy Fort Worth Star-Telegram *Collection, Special Collections, the University of Texas at Arlington Libraries.*

ing in a minor league ballpark. Vandergriff's refurbished Arlington Stadium had none of the bells and whistles of the Astrodome in Houston. Whereas Houstonians sat in air-conditioned comfort, Rangers fans in Arlington had to suffer through the brutal Texas heat, though boosters minimized this fact in the early reporting on the stadium. Merle Heryford, a *Dallas Morning News* sportswriter, got a bit carried away with the idea of covering a Major League Baseball franchise when he promised Rangers fans that the ballpark would be "5 to 10 degrees cooler in the stands."[18] Even if that was true, five to ten degrees wasn't much of a difference on hot summer Texas days, when temperatures could soar to well over one hundred degrees. Scheduling night games didn't help much. As any Texan knows, nightfall takes very little edge off the notorious Texas heat.

In the months after Short's announcement, engineers and construction workers hustled to make Turnpike Stadium into a major league facility for the opening day of the 1972 season. Additional seating, mostly in the form of eighteen thousand uncovered bleachers in the outfield, were added. Clubhouses were upgraded, an air-conditioned press box was built for the brethren of the DFW sports media, lighting was improved, the field was resodded, and a gigantic rectangular scoreboard with the outlines of a map of Texas was erected high above the left field stands, though it was unfinished on opening day.[19] Vandergriff promised a major league facility for the Rangers, but the fact was that the ballpark, renamed Arlington Stadium, still had the feel of a minor league facility, though that turned out to be one of its charms. The mayor had promised to expand the seating capacity in 1973, but that wouldn't happen until 1978, when he hustled more public funds to expand the stadium to more than forty thousand seats. The mayor needn't have worried, however, since the Rangers never sold out a single game during their first year and a half in Arlington. Why should fans endure the Texas heat and DFW Turnpike traffic to sit and watch the Rangers lose 100 out of a scheduled 154 games as they did in 1972?

The change of scenery, the new name, and the new red, white, and blue uniforms cast in the style of the Old West did nothing to alter the fortunes of Short's ball club on the field. The Rangers were by far the worst team in the league, finishing dead last in the American League Western Division, thirty-eight and a half games behind the first-place Oakland A's. Ted Williams, the "name in lights" Short hired to publicize the franchise in 1969, was fired after the season ended. Washington's sportswriters could not help but delight in the ineptitude of Texas's "wayward Senators." "One should not gloat at the rooking the Dallas Fort Worth area suffered when it inherited the Senators," George Minot Jr. sardonically wrote. "One should be sad and compassionate at a funeral."[20] Even DC fans got a measure of revenge on Short during a Ranger–Baltimore Oriole game at Memorial Stadium in May. Short underestimated the lingering anger he left behind in the Washington area. During the game, he was mocked with various iterations of "Short stinks" banners, an effigy was hung over his head, and he was forced to suffer the indignity of a beer shower from an angry female fan who was finally escorted away by ballpark security.

The Texas Rangers were losers on the field and on the financial ledgers of Short and Vandergriff. At the start of the second Rangers campaign, *Sports Illustrated* reported major losses for the Arlington Park Corporation, Vandergriff's entity that bought broadcast rights to Rangers games and managed Arlington Stadium.[21]

Covering the new Major League Baseball team in North Texas was an astute and talented cadre of sportswriters who penned stories for the region's news publications, including the *Dallas Morning News*, the *Fort Worth Star-Telegram*, the *Times Herald*, and others. Mike Shropshire was one of those writers and chronicled his experiences covering the team in his irreverent and insightful book *Seasons in Hell*. Shropshire's Jim Boutonesque rendering of baseball culture—the womanizing, the alcohol abuse, the vulgarities of locker-room and press box culture—are hilariously recounted on the pages of his book. This was an era when the growth of the sports media industry was resulting in jobs for aspiring sports writers, nearly all of whom were white men. As these men enjoyed the delights and perils of the sportswriter's life, they found themselves with the daunting task of conjuring stories from a team that produced little more than uninspired losses on the field. Still, Shropshire, Randy Galloway, Merle Heryford, and others provide informative first drafts of the team's inglorious history. Those first drafts of history, however, do not include the potential contributions of Samantha Stevenson, a woman journalist who was trying to break into the male-dominated world of sportswriting. On opening night at Arlington Stadium, a *Dallas Morning News* sportswriter crowed that "women libbers can rest easy" after Stevenson was grudgingly given full press credentials at the ballpark. Stevenson continued her sports freelance work for different publications in subsequent years.[22]

Even as these sportswriters sought to promote the new team that kept them employed, they could not help but comment on Short's crude commercialism. Toward the end of his first season in Arlington, Short revealingly admitted to Sam Blair that he hadn't "put a World Series contender on the field." Still, he felt that "with an average team and an average intelligent management you ought to be able to draw a million [fans] in Dallas–Fort Worth."[23] But the Rangers were a *below*-average team with substantially below-average management. This became clear during the 1973 season. Short tried to lure fans to his hotbox ballpark with standard baseball promotions such as Cap Night, Bat Night, and Ball Night, but he also turned to amateurish promotions such as Farm and Ranch Night, Panty Hose Night, and, following in the footsteps of Dallas Cowboys Cheerleader creator Tex Schramm, "Hot Pants Night." Few of these stunts convinced fans to come sweat it out at Arlington Stadium to watch the last-place Rangers.

Perhaps the biggest victim of Short's mismanagement was David Clyde, the Texas high school phenom from Houston. The fireballing left-handed prospect looked to be the second coming of former Dodger pitching legend Sandy Koufax. He dominated high school competition by going 18–0 with 328 strikeouts in 148 innings and an 0.18 earned run average (ERA). The Rangers made him their number-one pick in the 1973 amateur draft and signed him for $150,000 in June 1973. Rather than slowly develop the talented left-hander in the minor leagues, as most franchises would do, the Rangers front office saw Clyde as an immediate box office hit. Ignoring the concerns expressed by his manager, Whitey Herzog, Short insisted that Clyde be brought straight to the major leagues. In the weeks after his signing, the club orchestrated a robust publicity campaign to promote the eighteen-year-old southpaw. "Clydemania" took hold, with advertisers jumping in at every turn. On June 27, 1973, only two weeks after his signing, the young pitcher made his major league debut against the Minnesota Twins. The event was dubbed David Clyde Night before the first-ever sellout crowd at Arlington Stadium. "From now on," said Arlington mayor Vandergriff, "time here shall be marked from June 27, 1973."[24] The stadium came alive for the first time, as 35,698 fans slowly made their way through another Turnpike traffic jam to sit in the sweltering ninety-degree evening heat and watch a star being born, or so it seemed. Fans were treated to pre-game ceremonies of customary Shortesque gimmicks of Polynesian dancers and circus-like tricks from animals at the nearby Seven Seas and Lion Country Safari amusement parks. Ron Mercer, a Rangers radio broadcaster, assured listeners that Clyde was "a very mature young man at 18[,] . . . a fine gentleman and as perfect a person in this situation as you can have."[25]

Fighting off nerves, the talented young pitcher pulled off an exemplary first start. He received a standing ovation from the fans as he walked on the field donning number thirty-two, the same number as Sandy Koufax, who had sent him a congratulatory note before the game. After walking the first two Twins hitters, he struck out the next three batters, drawing wild cheers from the standing-room-only crowd. He labored a bit with his control: throwing 112 pitches over five innings, he gave up one hit, walked seven batters, but struck out eight. The Rangers went on to win the game 4–3. Short got himself a rare win and, more importantly, the short-term cash flow he needed, raking in $75,000 that night just from ticket sales.[26] The self-styled luckless owner addressed those who rightly criticized him as an exploiter: "Sure, Bob Short can be accused of exploiting, but all I'm doing is giving this kid a chance he's earned. I guarantee you that if he had been signed by any one of the other clubs, he'd be a starter today. Look, I've got a big investment here. I'm not going to risk losing it by ruining Clyde's career for the sake of one big box-office appearance," Short insisted.[27]

During the rest of the summer, Clydemania continued to draw attention to Arlington Stadium. Advertisers used him to sell their products. The press played up his conventional good looks, his "curly brown hair, wide eyes and bashful smile," and it highlighted his many young women admirers. On other evenings, attendance slumped back to the usual paltry numbers. The night after Clyde's start, the Rangers drew little more than three thousand spectators. But Clyde's success was short lived, and he began to craft his more lasting legacy as the poster child of big league flameouts. He never fulfilled his promise as a pitcher, and most observers blame Short's greed for burning out the talented young pitcher. He was demoted to the minors two years later. Eventually he was traded, and by 1979 he was out of the major leagues for good at the age of twenty-four with a career record of 18–33 and a 4.63 ERA. Looking back on that period forty years later, Clyde accurately concluded, "Bob Short, God rest his soul, was in it for the quick turn rather than the long-term investment."[28]

In the summer of 1973, David Clyde gave Short the "quick turn" he needed: an injection of cash flow and name recognition that would make his fledgling franchise attractive to potential buyers. The plan, according to Shelby Whitfield, the former Senator broadcaster, was proceeding on schedule. Whitfield, who was one of Short's staunchest critics, accurately predicted that the polarizing owner would sell the Rangers in 1973, the year the depreciation claim for tax purposes was due to expire. "He'll probably ask for a $13 to $14 million for a handsome capital gain," he wrote in his 1973 book, *Kiss It Goodbye*, "and likely, he'll get it from rich and provincial Texans."[29] Whitfield was indeed prophetic, though Short's sale of the Rangers didn't transpire until March 1974. True to his plan, he found a rich Texan to buy his sorry outfit, and it was yet another figure who profited from oil who took up the challenge. At last, Short got his wish. Though he played the part of the regretful owner who couldn't build a winner for the press, the wizard performed his last magic act in professional sports by walking away from the sale with a nice profit.

*   *   *

Brad Corbett, a nouveau riche businessman, bought Short's team, and he was determined to make it competitive. A native of New York City, Corbett arrived in Dallas in 1967 looking to make some money. He capitalized on a loan from the Small Business Administration to create a company that profited handsomely from the sale of polyvinyl chloride (PVC) pipe. Corbett's company, eventually known as Robintech, earned $55 million in sales of Corbett's products, turning him into a self-made millionaire before the age of thirty. By 1974, the enterprising Corbett was eager to transfer some of his profits into another business. Like Bob Short, he wanted to benefit from the tax advantages of owning a professional sports franchise. More importantly, he was looking to fulfill a boyhood dream of owning a baseball team. In April 1974, the sale was announced for $10 million. "I grew up right there at Yankee Stadium, baseball has always been an important thing to me," he told the congregation of Metroplex sportswriters.[30] The reference to Yankee Stadium unintentionally placed the new Rangers owner on the same platform as the new owner of the New York Yankee franchise, George Steinbrenner. Like Steinbrenner, Corbett pledged ignorance of the baseball business and a hands-off style of management when he first took over his baseball franchise, only to become an impulsive, volatile, and meddling owner who liked the public attention that baseball ownership could bring to rich and restless men such as himself.

As the team was turning over to a new ownership group in 1974, a miraculous thing happened in Arlington: the Rangers became a winning team. Corbett was fortunate enough to inherit two of the smartest decisions Short had made before he left town. One was allowing Whitey Herzog to convince him to trade for Ferguson "Fergie" Jenkins, the six-time twenty-game winner, who arrived in Arlington determined to reignite his career after a frustrating 1973 season with the Chicago Cubs. Short then turned around and fired the capable but then-unproven Herzog and replaced him with Billy Martin, the ambitious, swashbuckling manager who instilled some feistiness in the feeble team and helped them to become winners. Martin had succeeded in previous stints as manager of the Minnesota Twins and Detroit Tigers, but he was fired in both cases due to his hair-trigger temper and his penchant for becoming embroiled in alcohol-induced incidents off the field. Martin came to spring training in 1974 predicting a winning season, and he delivered.

But the Rangers revival had less to do with Short's business acumen or the genius of the new Corbett regime in town than it did the team itself. Increases in Rangers victories and fans in the stands were largely due to the talents and skills of the players who donned the team's red, white, and blue colors that summer. They turned things around because Major League Baseball was in the midst of an unprecedented talent boom as the full ramifications of racial integration of the game came to fruition in this precise moment. The revolution inaugurated by Jackie Robinson's signing with the Brooklyn Dodgers in 1947 was at its peak in the mid-1970s with the influx of gifted black and Latino athletes in Major League Baseball. This generation of ballplayers was ambitious and eager to benefit from the growing profits produced by television revenue. Under the skillful leadership of MLB Player's Association chief Marvin Miller, major league ballplayers successfully won higher salaries from team owners, salary arbitration, and then perhaps the most extraordinary victory: the abolition of the reserve clause and the inauguration of free agency in 1975. Now big league baseball players were like workers in other industries insofar as they could sell their labor power to the highest bidder.[31]

Moreover, the ballplayer of the 1970s changed the aesthetics of the game. Speed, fashionable uniform adornment, and stylized play were hallmarks of player self-expression. Artificial turf may have been a nightmare for football players, but in baseball it facilitated the need for faster, more athletic players. Frequently these roles were played by black and Latino ballplayers, who were arriving on major league rosters in substantial numbers. They symbolized the new player of the 1970s: the line-drive hitter who could run the bases and track down fly balls in the outfield or ground balls skittering on Astroturf infields. Aesthetically, players rejected the model of the white American baseball hero à la DiMaggio, Williams, and Mantle—a model exposed as fraudulent by Jim Bouton's *Ball Four*—and embraced the cultural aesthetics of the antihero, the performer who didn't necessarily play nice for the fans and sportswriters. This transformation was particularly evident among the black and Latino players of the 1970s.[32] The political revolution of the civil rights movement had major cultural and social ramifications in Major League Baseball. Building upon the struggles of Robinson's generation, black ballplayers of the 1970s, like black professional athletes in basketball and even football, shed performances of gratitude for projections of entitlement. Black ballplayers argued that they were entitled to higher salaries, to comport themselves as they pleased on the field and off, and to wear facial hair and Afros. And perhaps most surprising, they were not afraid to admit that they were playing the game because it was a job rather than some sort of honor, as the disgruntled Rangers outfielder Alex Johnson did when he plainly told Mike Shropshire in 1973, "Work is work. It don't matter where."[33]

* * *

"An overwhelming amount of baseball storytelling," writes baseball historian Dan Gilbert, "involves two complex and intertwined themes: labor and place."[34] In 1974, labor and place came together to make the hapless Rangers into a winning team. It wasn't Short's shrewd dealings or Corbett's millions that transformed the Rangers. It was the athletic talent of the team's roster and the efforts of the managers and coaches on the field who brought the fans out to the ballpark on the DFW Turnpike in the summer of 1974. The long-awaited attendance boom in Arlington finally happened that summer. Fans didn't come to milk cows on Farm and Ranch Night or to see sexualized women in hot pants. They came, in part, to see their new ace pitcher, Ferguson Jenkins, mow down opposing batters. Jenkins, the Hall of Fame right-handed pitcher, is one of the all-time greats in MLB history.

Jenkins's racial identity as "black" oversimplifies the hemispheric character of his experience, one that is defined by struggle and migration across borders. Born in Chatham, Ontario, in 1942, Jenkins grew up in a small town where he starred in all the sports he played. His mother, Delores, was a descendant of runaway slaves who escaped to Canada through the Underground Railroad. Jenkins and his biographers liked to tell stories of his mother's commitment to ensuring that his uniforms were meticulously clean and his spikes spotlessly shined before all of his games. These tales of her domesticity might lead one to overlook her own athletic talents, which were hindered not only by sexism and patriarchy but also by her own personal health challenges. Delores was athletic herself, growing to six feet, one inch tall, but she lost her eyesight while Ferguson was growing up. Still, she was a powerful force in his life before she passed away in 1971. His father, Ferguson Sr., grew up in Windsor, Ontario, a child of immigrants from the Bahamas who played semipro and Negro League baseball and eventually became a chef.

Jenkins was a natural athlete, playing hockey and basketball, but he eventually settled on baseball. He grew to be six feet five, and he was signed by the Philadelphia Phillies, who traded him to the Chicago Cubs in 1966. The Cubs were a perennial loser that hadn't won a pennant in two decades at that point, but by the time Jenkins arrived in Chicago, the team's fortunes were turning under Leo "the Lip" Durocher, the legendary manager who had led the New York Giants to championship glory in the 1950s. After Durocher made him a full-time starting pitcher in 1967, Jenkins began a remarkable string of six straight twenty-game winning seasons to become the ace of the pitching staff. In 1971, he won the Cy Young Award as the National League's best pitcher. The Cubs, too, underwent a renaissance, becoming a pennant contender during this period, only to come up short every season. As artfully illustrated by *King of the Hill*, an insightful, Canadian-produced documentary on Jenkins and the Cubs of the early '70s, the pitcher and the team saw their fortunes change for the worse in 1972–1973.[35] Durocher was fired in 1972, and Jenkins proceeded to have his worst season as a pro in 1973, when he finished the season with a 14–16 record and a 3.89 ERA. The Cubs inexplicably gave up on their perennial ace, claiming he had a "dead arm," and traded him to the Rangers.[36]

Jenkins came into the '74 season with something to prove after being cast aside as damaged goods by his former team. He began his comeback trail on the second night of the regular season against the reigning world champion, the Oakland A's. The A's were exactly what the Rangers were not: a talented club of young veterans who were in the midst of a run of three consecutive World Series championships. They had style—with green, gold, and white uniforms, mustaches and long hair—and talent, led by slugger Reggie Jackson, Sal Bando, Joe Rudi, and the speedy Dagoberto "Bert" Campaneris. Like all winning teams, they had a stellar pitching staff led by Jim "Catfish" Hunter, Ken Holtzman, Vida Blue, and reliever Rollie Fingers. On opening night 1974, the A's conducted business as usual with a 7–2 easy victory over Texas. But the next night would be different. A crowd of 16,965 turned out on a warm night in Arlington to see if the Rangers' new acquisition could rediscover his Cy Young Award–winning form. Wearing his characteristic long-sleeved undershirt, Jenkins was nearly perfect, pitching a complete game, facing twenty-eight Oakland batters—one over the minimum—and walking one and striking out ten. The only blemish was a fourth-inning bunt single by Campaneris. The A's hit only two balls out of the infield all night, and the Rangers won 2–0. It was a vintage performance that set the tone for Jenkins's season and the 1974 year for the Rangers. They pestered the defending champions throughout the season, and Jenkins, in particular, would be a thorn in their side, beating them five separate times without a loss.

*　*　*

"Jenkins was a great control pitcher," notes Donald Brittain in *King of the Hill*. "He had the full arsenal of pitches, the fastball, the slider, and the big league curve. And he could put each of them in whatever area of the strike zone suited his purpose."[37] For the first time since their arrival in the Metroplex, Rangers fans got a chance to watch a Hall of Fame–caliber talent at work for the home team. Each pitcher has a unique style of throwing a baseball, and one of the delights of the game is to observe how each player develops his own style to become effective. Brittain's film showcases the work of the pitcher as craftsman. Jenkins's windup and delivery seemed effortless. He raised both hands over his head, ball in his glove. He kicked his left leg straight out, then dropped his right arm below his waist. Unlike his contemporary Hall of Famers Nolan Ryan and Tom Seaver, who generated their velocity and effectiveness from a long stride and deep leg drive toward the plate, Jenkins took a short stride and landed almost straight legged as he whipped his right arm in a three-quarters motion. Ryan and Seaver's facial expressions and pitching motions made them look like they were working hard on the mound. Jenkins, in contrast, released the ball in a seemingly effortless fashion.

Like many pitchers from this era, Jenkins worked quickly to get himself into a rhythm with his catcher and to keep the opposing batter from getting too comfortable at the plate. When he was on the mound, Jenkins never seemed to break a sweat. Like his contemporary Vida Blue, the fireballing left-hander whose smooth delivery could lull opposing hitters to sleep before he breezily delivered his blazing fastball, Jenkins's motion was also smooth, but more compact. When the pitch left his hand, it would arrive at unpredictable speeds even as his arm motion remained unchanged. Although Jenkins threw the ball at a high velocity, his real gift as a hurler was ball placement and changing the speed of his pitches to fool the hitter. In this sense, he was just like Catfish Hunter, who made his living by "hitting the corners," shooting for the black outline of the plate, a location that made the hitter swing at pitches that were close enough to be called strikes but not ideal to hit. He used his slider to break the ball away from right handers and to bust the ball in on the fists of left-handed hitters. Relying on copious notes about each hitter's strengths and weaknesses, he would start a hitter with an off-speed curveball, then follow it up with a fastball on the outside corner of the plate. He might throw another pitch, perhaps a slider on the outside corner, then finish off the batter with a fastball on the inside corner of the plate, where a hitter could only manage a feeble swing and a weak infield groundball.

The tall right-hander was a control pitcher who rarely walked a batter. His control often resulted in him giving up a lot of home

Ferguson Jenkins, 1974. Photo by Herb Scharfman/ Sports Imagery.

runs, but more often than not, his extraordinary command of the baseball led him to pitch a lot of innings and strike out hitters. He also tended to finish what he started. "When Durocher was managing the Cubs," he recalled to the local press, "he would hand me the ball and tell me to go out there and pitch nine innings and forget about getting any help."[38] Jenkins routinely finished among the leaders in games started, complete games, and innings pitched. In his first season in Arlington, he led the league with twenty-nine complete games, a figure that is unthinkable in baseball today. In an era when specialized relief pitching was just becoming a regular part of team strategies, Fergie Jenkins was a holdover from previous eras when starting pitchers regularly pitched all nine innings of baseball games.

After a fast start when he won six of his seven decisions, the new Rangers ace had a prolonged slump in May and June, when he lost eight of eleven decisions and looked like the pitcher the Cubs traded away. Then, suddenly he caught fire and won fourteen of his final sixteen decisions. His most impressive performances were once again against division rival Oakland. On August 6, Jenkins delighted Rangers fans by beating the A's with another shutout, 1–0. This time he gave up just two hits, walked three batters, and struck out eight. One month later, he pitched another masterpiece when he stifled the Eastern Division power Baltimore Orioles 2–1 before an impressive crowd of 29,699 at Arlington Stadium. He spun another stellar performance: a complete game, five-hit, one-walk, ten-strikeout performance. Even more important, the turnout gave the surprising Rangers over a million fans for the season. On September 13, Jenkins won his nineteenth game of the season with another win over the A's on a rare chilly evening in Arlington Stadium. This time he outdueled Oakland ace pitcher Catfish Hunter, his rival and mirror image with another incredible effort: a complete game victory giving up seven hits and walking one batter, while striking out ten.

Jenkins was the catalyst of the team's surprising season. But the Rangers also got remarkable efforts from some of their younger talents, such as slugger Jeff Burroughs. A holdover from Short's Senators, the young outfielder had a great season, hitting .301 with twenty-five home runs and 118 runs batted in. Other key contributors were rookie catcher Jim Sundberg, who, like Burroughs, made the All-Star team and who began his ascendance as one of the best defensive catchers in the American League. Another key member from the Senator era was Lenny Randle, the team's third baseman, who hustled his way to a fine season, hitting .302 and stealing twenty-six bases. Randle was a prototypical Billy Martin–style player, a versatile athlete who played multiple positions and who slapped line drives and ran the bases with abandon. For most of the year, Alex Johnson made solid contributions before he landed in Martin's doghouse and was traded away in September.

The Rangers never did catch the A's, but they shocked baseball observers by finishing in second place in their division with a record of eighty-four wins and seventy-six losses, five games behind the eventual champion Oakland. But many individual awards went to the upstart team from Arlington, as many Rangers swept nearly all of the major awards given in the American League. Burroughs won the league's most valuable player award, Billy Martin was voted manager of the year, and first baseman Mike Hargrove won the rookie of the year trophy. Jenkins narrowly lost the Cy Young Award to Catfish Hunter, but he did win the Comeback Player of the Year award. He finished that magical summer with a career-high twenty-five wins, while he lost twelve games and delivered an ERA of 2.82, 225 strikeouts, and six shutouts while averaging a little over one walk per nine innings. It was a remarkable season that revitalized Jenkins's career. Though he was traded after a subpar 1975 season, he returned to the Rangers and had more effective seasons before retiring with the Cubs in 1983 after winning a total of 284 games.

The performance of Jenkins and his teammates in 1974 finally brought the fans out to Arlington Stadium. Sometimes they didn't mind tussling with opposing players, such as the rowdy night of May 29, when a Rangers fan slung beers at a Cleveland Indians player. Cleveland fans retaliated by waging their own attack on Ranger players in an alcohol-induced fan uprising during the infamous Ten Cent Beer Night promotion on June 4, 1974. Fans were in a rebellious mood in the 1970s. Still, a season that is most often remembered for the Rangers' involvement in the riot in Cleveland was also the year that probably helped establish the viability of Major League Baseball in the Dallas–Fort Worth region. Attendance figures would continue to rise as the team regularly drew over one million fans during the rest of the 1970s. Brad Corbett's purchase of Bob Short's baseball team seemed to be a stroke of genius, but Corbett, like the team's previous owner, couldn't help but mess with a good thing.

On September 7, 1976, Brad Corbett called a press conference to announce the hiring of Eddie Robinson as the team's new executive vice-president. The announcement was noteworthy because of the owner's surprising pledge to "retire" from the day-to-day operation of the club. Corbett had been notoriously hands-on in his management style since he bought the team from Bob Short. Robinson, a native of Paris, Texas, was a longtime baseball man: a former player whose most recent job was running the Atlanta Braves. With his current general manager, Dan O'Brien, quizzically looking on, Corbett claimed he was putting Robinson in charge of his operation, except he offered up two disclaimers. "There's only two things I'd like to be involved with," Corbett clarified to the press. "One would be the signing of free agent players this winter . . . and the other would be if there's a trade working for any one of about five players on the team."[39] This left Corbett in line to still play a significant role in the ball club's decision-making. The unbelieving Randy Galloway wrote in the *Dallas Morning News*, "If Robinson actually thinks he'll be allowed to do the job for which he was hired then it's obvious he's not familiar with the ways of the Ranger owner."[40]

Owners of professional sports franchises like to see themselves—and often are seen by others—as shrewd businessmen. A closer look at the history of sports management illustrates that sports team owners are not as shrewd as one would think. "If a pro franchise is really such a high-risk, low-yield venture," Ray Kennedy asked readers of *Sports Illustrated* in 1977, "then why do so many supposedly astute businessmen get involved?" For the sports entrepreneur of the 1970s, the answer to that question was often simply that it was entertaining. "It's so much more fun than almost any business that I know," Jack Kent Cooke, the owner of the NBA's Los Angeles Lakers, said in the same article. "I'd much rather watch Kareem [Abdul-Jabbar] than see a bunch of Chevy Novas come off the production line."[41] Having top-flight athletes perform for them, being able to control their labor, and enjoying

President Gerald Ford, Jim Sundberg, and Brad Corbett, April 9, 1976. MLB Photos.

cigars and booze while entertaining friends and guests, like Corbett did when he hosted then president Gerald Ford on opening night in 1976, were reasons enough to shell out millions of dollars for the privilege of owning a baseball team.

In the 1970s, the management of Major League Baseball clubs had varying degrees of professionalization. Compared to today, ball clubs had fairly small front offices: general managers, scouts, coaches, and managers as well as front office staff. Few if any were trained with sports management degrees, and the most influential were former players who were seen as "baseball men," like Eddie Robinson, and who got their jobs because of their accomplishments on the field and/or their good ol' boy connections. Baseball team owners were transitioning from the old-time boss whose primary business was sports, in the mold of Bill Veeck and Calvin Griffith, to the rich businessman who dabbled in sports as a secondary business venture. Still, the new owners of the 1960s and 1970s—the George Steinbrenners, Charlie Finleys, and Ted

Turners—ran their teams like personalist dictatorships. While baseball historians have written at length about these owners, few recall the equally wacky six years that Brad Corbett owned the Texas Rangers.

The "Plastic Man" executive must have been excited about his new investment coming into the 1975 season. He had a winning team, a star pitcher, and a charismatic manager with a winning track record. But the next two seasons turned out to be disappointments on the field. Though he hired knowledgeable baseball men, he couldn't help but overrule or influence the supposed decision-makers running his franchise. "It's no longer possible for someone to buy a team, delegate everything to other people and treat it like a hobby," he told *Sports Illustrated* in 1977. "Handled this way it can be an expensive hobby, and it's ultimately counterproductive, because the players feel the remoteness of an owner they never see and they react against it."[42]

Corbett's first victim was Billy Martin, whom he fired in July 1975 after a fight the manager had with another team executive. On the day of his firing, the temperamental Martin chirped to the press, "He knows as much about baseball as I know about pipe."[43] When the season ended, Corbett and Dan O'Brien, his then general manager, started their pattern of almost compulsively trading players. Fergie Jenkins was dealt after a disappointing 1975 season and replaced with an aging Gaylord Perry. In 1976, Bert Blyleven, seen by many baseball observers as an All-Star pitcher, arrived in another trade. But both acquisitions underachieved during their brief time in Arlington. Jeff Burroughs was traded after the 1976 season. By 1979, only four players left from the 1974 roster remained on the team. Over the next six years, Arlington Stadium had a revolving door through which players came and went every season.

Corbett symbolized the new brash owner of the 1970s who sought to throw his weight around, grab some headlines in the newspaper, and tussle with an increasingly assertive and peripatetic cadre of players. He even tried to lead a campaign among the owners to fire MLB Commissioner Bowie Kuhn. He pursued a winner at all costs, trading for players and signing free agents every year. Though they frequently spoke of the financial constraints of their ball clubs, rich men like Corbett considered professional sports franchises more like toys than solid financial investments. And thanks to Peter Seitz, the arbitrator who legalized free agency for players, owners like Corbett had more "toys" to play with. During his ownership tenure, the Rangers were among the most active teams in the free agent draft. In addition to the free-spending Steinbrenner, who inked Reggie Jackson and other big-name free agents at this time, Corbett was trying to compete with Gene Autry, the man of "singing cowboy" fame who owned the division rival California Angels. Though free agency enabled some players to choose to work for Corbett of their own volition, most who wore the Rangers uniform during these years arrived in trades from other teams.

Corbett changed managers with almost the same frequency. Frank Lucchesi, the manager who replaced Martin in 1975, had led the team through a subpar 1976 and an equally mediocre first half of the 1977 season. The Dallas sports media was speculating that Lucchesi's days were numbered. It was clear that the team's listless performance was getting to Lucchesi's boss. In a June game in Cleveland's Municipal Stadium, the same site of the infamous Ten Cent Beer Night Riot, the owner challenged a fan to a fight a few rows behind the Rangers dugout. Finally on June 22, with the team saddled with a 31–31 record, he fired Lucchesi and replaced him with Eddie Stanky, who had been a star second baseman during the 1940s and '50s and was then coaching college baseball at the University of South Alabama. Stanky arrived in Arlington, managed Corbett's team for one game, and then promptly changed his mind and returned to Alabama. Stanky was eventually replaced by another longtime baseball man, Billy Hunter.

Meanwhile, Corbett was losing his grip. On July 8, he abruptly announced that he was putting the Rangers up for sale. The boss who fashioned himself as a "players' owner" now was trashing his employees in the media: "I've got players who I've put complete confidence and faith in," he told the press, "and I've found that those players don't give a damn. They don't care about anything except drawing a paycheck. They are dogs on the field and off the field."[44] But soon thereafter, the owner went back on his decision and retained his majority ownership share—but not before he got a better stadium, concessions, and television deal from the City of Arlington. His tantrum had produced at least some positive results.[45] Corbett's rant also seemed to help the Rangers on the field. New manager Billy Hunter led the Rangers to a 94–68 record, an impressive feat but still a distant second place behind the division champion Kansas City Royals.

Brad Corbett realized that managing a baseball franchise was more challenging than running his pipe operation. "The business world is different. I know exactly what to do there," he told the press. "The problems are tangible. The problem with the Rangers is ego—as in 25 different ones. I'll tell you it's pretty frustrating trying to deal with something like that."[46] He forgot to include a twenty-sixth ego—his own. In 1978, Corbett once again flew off the handle in reaction to a Rangers loss in the middle of the season. After a crushing 2–1 defeat to the Milwaukee Brewers, the owner who had once again pledged to "retire" from the day-to-day operations of his club stormed into the clubhouse and kicked out the sportswriters who were interviewing Billy Hunter at the time. He harangued his players and his manager for the team's subpar performance. "It's incredible to me that this team—with all its talent—has scored 153 runs less than Kansas City," he shrieked to the press. "We've got to start playing with some pride. We're going to have a winner here in Texas—if not this year, then next, though I haven't written off this year."[47] The hyperemotional owner was learning that his meddling and his compulsive wheeling and dealing of players and managers like Monopoly game pieces were not enough to make his team a championship ball club. But there was more drama and chaos in store for the team named after Texas lawmen before the decade came to a close.

At the start of spring training in 1977, infielder Lenny Randle did not think he was being treated well by Rangers management. The veteran Rangers utility player entered camp in competition with rookie Bump Wills for the starting second base job. He expressed his unhappiness with the situation, but his manager was unwilling to hear his complaints. In fact, Frank Lucchesi was outright hostile to Randle's concerns. "Anyone who makes $80,000 a year and gripes and moans all spring is not going to get a tear out of me," the manager crowed to the press. Lucchesi wasn't finished ripping his second baseman. "I'm tired of these punks saying play me or trade me," he continued. "If they don't like it they can get out of baseball."[48] The manager's reference to "punks" suggested that he was not simply referring to Randle, but to the typical ballplayer of the 1970s who was making unprecedented amounts of money in comparison to previous generations. Lucchesi, a career minor league player who had briefly managed the Philadelphia Phillies in 1970–1971, was like a number of managers and coaches who began to resent the players of the early free agency era for earning higher salaries and acting more assertively with management.

Lucchesi didn't care for Randle's concerns, but neither did Randle care about the resentments the manager had toward him. The situation exploded on March 28, 1977, when Randle began to talk to his manager outside the dugout before a spring training game. After the two quietly exchanged words, the powerfully built Randle drew upon his martial arts training to beat his manager unconscious with a series of blows to his face and head.[49] The incident shocked everyone; it was completely out of character for the veteran second baseman. But the episode marked the end of his career with the Rangers. He was promptly suspended and then traded a few weeks later. Meanwhile, Lucchesi managed to hold on to his job for three more months before the temperamental Corbett fired him in June.

Randle was sharply criticized by the press and some of his

teammates. But they could not grasp the profound disrespect Lucchesi had conveyed with his characterization of Randle as a "punk." The veteran utility player was well respected by teammates and even the press and the fans. But fans and sportswriters liked players when they stayed subservient to ownership, and the ballplayers of the 1970s, including many members of the Texas Rangers, were not always willing to follow dictates from management. And Brad Corbett's volatile leadership style did not inspire confidence.

Even with the drama produced by the Randle incident and Corbett's outbursts, in 1977 the team miraculously won ninety-four games, including an impressive 60–33 record under Billy Hunter. The strong finish could have led the Rangers to simply make a few minor changes to the roster of a contending team. Yet Corbett and Robinson proceeded to virtually turn over the entire roster by bringing in a host of new players. They traded for hard-hitting outfielder Al Oliver. They sent away Gaylord Perry and Bert Blyleven and replaced them with Fergie Jenkins, who they brought back in a deal with the Red Sox, and Jon Matlack, a talented left-handed starting pitcher who arrived with Oliver in a Rangeresque four-team swapping of players. The big catch of the off-season was All-Star outfielder Richie Zisk, who Texas signed to a ten-year, $2.7 million contract. After the season started, the Rangers added Bobby Bonds, the former All-Star outfielder whose arrival in Arlington marked the fifth team he had played for over the course of the previous five seasons. Despite all the turnover, many experts predicted that the 1978 Rangers would dethrone the two-time reigning champion Kansas City Royals for the division title.

On opening night, more than forty thousand Texan baseball fans packed the newly expanded Arlington Stadium to see the home team face Steinbrenner's Yankees. Corbett's club was even able to grab the attention of New York's baseball scribes. Murray Chass, a *New York Times* columnist, wrote about the formidable roster put together by Corbett. "This year Corbett and the people who work for him believe," Chass wrote, "that the Rangers can end the two-year reign of the Kansas City Royals as champions of half the American League then supplant the Yankees as champions of all the American League."[50] The Rangers got off to a great start by beating the defending champions 2–1. The stars of the evening were the new acquisitions: Matlack, who pitched a complete game five-hitter, and Zisk, who won the game with a dramatic home run in the bottom of the ninth inning.

But the players who Corbett and Robinson threw together to perform for North Texas's Major League Baseball franchise never achieved consistent success on the field. Billy Hunter touched on a key factor when he acknowledged the lack of chemistry among the roster of players who wore Ranger red, white, and blue. "The club is kind of a conglomeration of people from various organizations," he admitted to the producers of the weekly television program *This Week in Baseball*, "and they really haven't had a whole lot of time to work on fundamentals as a team."[51] They lingered around the .500 mark for most of the season and again finished in second place behind the Royals with a disappointing 87–75 record.

They were also chafing under Billy Hunter's management style. Hunter, like his predecessor, was an old-school baseball man who could not handle the ballplayer of the free agency era. Some, like Rogelio "Roger" Moret, literally broke down under the pressure. Moret was a talented Puerto Rican pitcher who arrived from Atlanta in the Jeff Burroughs trade. He was a hard-throwing left-hander who had flashes of brilliance during his five seasons with the Boston Red Sox before his brief stint with the Braves. But he injured his shoulder in his first season with the Rangers, and he pitched in only eighteen games. At the start of the next season, Moret suddenly announced he wanted to leave the Rangers. A week later, during a game against the Detroit Tigers at Arlington Stadium, he stood frozen in a "catatonic state" in the Rangers clubhouse with a blank stare and his right arm extended holding a shower shoe for almost ninety minutes. He did not acknowledge anyone who tried to talk to him. He was eventually sedated with multiple injections and taken to the Arlington Neuro-Psychiatric Center.[52]

The Moret affair befuddled his teammates and the press, yet his breakdown in the Texas clubhouse was a manifestation not merely of his mental illness but also of the many challenges Latino ballplayers confronted during these years. Even if they were making higher salaries in the free agency era, playing Major League Baseball remained an isolating existence for many Latino ballplayers thirty years after Jackie Robinson broke the color line in 1947. In the summer of 1979, the *Los Angeles Times* ran a story highlighting their ongoing struggles. Many of the players interviewed in the article revealed experiences of isolation, racism, cultural and language barriers, and hostility and mockery from the press. The Latino players of the 1970s were experiencing many of the same obstacles that the first generation of integration pioneers, such as Roberto Clemente, Juan Marichal, Vic Power, and others, had faced in the 1950s and '60s. Moret's personal struggles with mental illness were exacerbated by the broader challenges facing his generation of players. Moret attempted a number of comebacks, but he was never able to resume his major league career.

Meanwhile, black players on the Rangers team were often portrayed by management and the press as overpaid stars who were ungrateful for their chance to play Major League Baseball. And the poster child for this image was the mercurial starting pitcher Dock Ellis. Throughout his career, Ellis epitomized the voluble black athlete of the 1970s. He fashioned himself as a Muhammad Ali–like figure. The former All Star who had pitched a no-hitter on LSD in 1970 was quick to speak out against racism in baseball. He arrived in Arlington seemingly washed up in 1977, but he pitched surprisingly well for Corbett's Rangers. But as is now known in retrospect, he, like others in the peripatetic world of Major League Baseball, was struggling with alcoholism and other forms of substance abuse. Billy Hunter's rules against drinking in hotel bars did not fly with the pitcher, who liked to drink his Chivas Regal in the morning and his vodka in the afternoon. On the team bus during a road trip in Minneapolis in May 1978, Ellis started railing against his manager. After Hunter told him to sit down and shut up, Ellis went on a tirade to the beat writers traveling with the team, who willingly jotted down gems such as "[Hunter is] Hitler, but he's not going to make a lampshade out of me!" A lampshade he was not. "It's the ethics of it all," he complained to reporters. "I'm 33 years old. I'm as grown as he. If he can drink gin, so can I."[53] Ellis's revolt continued throughout the summer, though curiously, he seemed to have a good relationship with Corbett. Despite rampant trade speculation, he somehow survived the season in Arlington while much of the rest of the roster was turned over through more trades and free agent signings.

As another chaotic summer was coming to a close, Corbett decided he wouldn't let Billy Hunter finish the 1978 campaign. He inexplicably fired him with only one game left in the season. Ironically, it was the less publicized transactions that produced the best outcomes for the Rangers. As in 1974, catcher Jim Sundberg put in another All-Star effort. He led the team with 144 base hits, but his main contributions, as usual, occurred behind the plate. He was emerging as one of the American League's best defensive catchers. One of his most memorable moments was in an August 24 game in Minnesota. As the Rangers were desperately trying to stay in the pennant race, they were tied with the Twins 1–1 until Sundberg slugged a three-run homer to beat the Twins in the tenth inning. The pitcher who benefitted from Sundberg's clout was the thirty-four-year-old veteran Ferguson Jenkins, who set down the Twins in order to conclude a masterful ten-inning, four-hit, one-run complete-game victory.[54] After two injury-riddled seasons with the Red Sox, Jenkins returned to Arlington and resumed his position as the team's best starter. Pitching with his usual pinpoint control, Jenkins finished the year with an 18–8 record and a 3.04 ERA.

Corbett's wheeling and dealing and big spending on his franchise finally caught up with him the next season, when he suddenly found himself short on cash and unable to meet the payroll.

With his pipe business also in disarray, and with Rangers finances supposedly in the red, the Rangers boss needed another investor to keep the team afloat. His other big problem was his building war with the local sport press. In the late 1970s, the Dallas–Fort Worth sports media landscape was changing as newspapermen and TV journalists became more aggressive and more critical of home teams. Skip Bayless, Randy Galloway, and others frequently criticized the Rangers owner and unfavorably compared his team to the Cowboys, the model franchise that was firmly under the control of Tex Schramm and Tom Landry. The press liked to ridicule Corbett's "portly" appearance and his volatile personality. By February 1980, the Rangers owner was finally done with his baseball adventure. That spring, he sold his majority share of the club to Eddie Chiles, still another oilman who had a fondness for conservative political causes, which would help him when it was his turn to sell the team years later. The Corbett era—an era of quality baseball performances, excitement, and mismanagement—had ended. During the 1980s, the Rangers settled into a pattern of dull mediocrity, mirroring the fates of many Texas professional and collegiate sports teams.

Yet for all the drama and wackiness that took place in Rangerland, the team still managed to build up a fan base in the DFW region. Despite Corbett's frequent cries to the press about the team running in red ink, the Rangers turned out to be a winner at the gate during his tenure as the team's owner. Season attendance rose every year: from 1,250,472 fans in 1977, to 1,447,963 in 1978, to 1,519,671 in 1979. Compared to the high ticket prices of the beloved Dallas Cowboys, the cost of going to games at steamy Arlington Stadium was relatively low. Seven dollars for field box seats and two dollars for general admission seats was a pretty good bargain for baseball fans in the late 1970s.[55] The affordability of Rangers games, and the talent on the field, helped boost attendance and grow the team's fan base. Tom Vandergriff's gamble on Bob Short's franchise in 1972 in some ways had paid off, if not in an economic sense then perhaps in a cultural one. Steve Pate summed up the team's impact in the *Dallas Morning News* at the end of the decade: "Now they are Texas's team, and five million fans have attended home games in the past four years. They can still be frustrating. Perhaps they promised too much and deliver too little. But summers would not be the same without them."[56]

* * *

The baseball franchise that abandoned Washington, DC, for the Dallas–Fort Worth Metroplex in 1971 reflected the conflicting currents running through Major League Baseball in the 1970s. As the nation's center of gravity continued to shift toward the Sunbelt, sports entrepreneurs looked to places like DFW for new sources of revenue and influence. In the years after the Dodgers and Giants moved to the West Coast in 1958, owners realized they could find new markets and public officials, like Tom Vandergriff, who were willing to enhance their political careers by attracting sports teams to their cities. Some, like Bob Short, made a nice profit from their dalliances with sports team ownership. Others, like Brad Corbett, were in over their heads and mismanaged their teams.

All were reliant on the athletic talents and skills of the ballplayers who emerged in the generation after the integration of Major League Baseball. The rising number of black and Latino major leaguers changed the performance and the aesthetics of America's national pastime. They encountered new fans in places like Arlington, Texas, but they also continued to experience new forms of racism that came in the guise of resentment for their newfound socioeconomic status. Indeed, the impact of the integration of Major League Baseball teams was bolstered by the labor rights won by the Major League Baseball Players' Association. The 1970s was the decade when previously underpaid male athletes, including the black and Latino men who played in the big leagues, were able to make a livelihood in the sporting world. Others, like the women who signed up to dance in halter tops, hot pants, and go-go boots on the sidelines of Texas Stadium, would find their options much more limited.

CHAPTER 6

Sexual Revolution on the Sidelines

WASHINGTON AND DALLAS WERE INTERTWINED IN MORE WAYS THAN ONE might imagine in 1972. In addition to Bob Short's move to the Metroplex, in December 1972, the NFL franchise known as the Washington Redskins dethroned the Dallas Cowboys, their bitter rivals, to win the conference championship and a trip to the Super Bowl. Meanwhile, two more occurrences, one in Washington and the other in Dallas, would dramatically alter the experiences of people defined as women in the world of sports for years to come. On June 23, 1972, in Washington, President Richard Nixon signed the Education Amendments Act. The omnibus bill not only provided unprecedented amounts of federal aid for college students but also contained a clause that outlawed gender discrimination in education, thirty-seven words that changed everything: "No person in the United States shall, on the basis of sex, be excluded from participation in, be denied the benefits of, or be subjected to discrimination under any education program or activity receiving federal financial assistance."[1] The clause would be referred to simply as Title IX, and it would inspire advocates for women's equality in athletics and drive male athletic directors batty for decades to come.

In his remarks during the bill signing, Nixon said nothing about gender equality. In fact, he criticized at length what he saw as the law's inadequate response to federally mandated busing programs to ensure racial integration of schooling, one of the hot button issues of that year and that decade. Many whites were reacting to the legislative measures designed to address historical racial inequalities in the United States. Still, though he may not have realized it, the law Nixon signed would radically transform the educational experiences of the nation's girls and women, and some of those changes were most visible in the sporting realm.[2]

A few weeks later, the Dallas Cowboys NFL franchise decided to refashion its cheerleading squad into a professionalized group of young women entertainers who would dance in provocatively designed outfits to provide sex appeal to cheerleading. It would take a few years for the full ramifications of this decision to become apparent, but it would dramatically change the world of sport. Both Title IX and the formation of the Dallas Cowboys Cheerleaders had a profound impact on the feminist movement of the 1970s. While the Houston Astrodome was a scene of triumph for Billie Jean King and the US feminist movement, Texas Stadium became another historically significant scene where the impact of feminism and the sexual revolution was much more ambiguous. In some ways, both scenes represented two distinct and overlapping currents that shaped gender understandings in the United States during these years. Or maybe, in hindsight, they weren't so distinct, since sports and cheerleading were—and still remain—significant arenas where women have articulated their understanding of themselves as athletes, performers, and sexual beings. The sexualization of cheerleading brought the sexual revolution to the world of sports. In turn, sports exposed some of the contradictions of the sexual revolution.

*　*　*

Once upon a time, cheerleading embodied male vigor and strength. When cheerleading originated in the elite college campuses of the Northeast, it was the practice of college-age, athletic white men. The art of stirring up spectators for athletic competitions took a variety of forms. Yelling and tumbling were the primary skills of the prized college cheerleader. Male cheerleaders donned slacks and sweaters in school colors and performed all sorts of acrobatics and yells to arouse the crowd and intimidate the opposition. The megaphone enabled them to project chants and cheers to the crowd. Sometime in the 1920s, women became a greater presence in the cheerleading world. By the middle of the century, though men still performed, the cheerleader figure was becoming more feminized and more derided by the public. In Texas and elsewhere, cheerleading and sideline performance remained major aspects of high school and collegiate curriculums. The drill team, the cheerleader, and the band were all integral components of scholastic athletic culture. As the practice moved more fully into the hands of young women, the cheerleader figure became synonymous with the young Texas beauty queen. For conventionally attractive women who were also athletic, cheerleading was one of the few sanctioned spaces where girls could receive some form of physical education and notoriety.[3]

But the revitalized feminist movement in the late 1960s raised questions about the role of seemingly innocuous cultural practices that they came to see as oppressive to women. Cheerleading, like beauty pageants, drew the ire of many of the more radical segments of the movement. To Robin Morgan, a feminist leader and the editor of *Ms.* magazine, cheerleading was "asinine, stupid, sexist and totally absurd."[4] Cheerleaders personified the gender inequalities young women were compelled to endure, cheering the achievements of men rather than their own accomplishments. Such critiques became even more pronounced as feminist sports activism emerged in the years after Title IX was passed. As the 1970s unfolded, especially after Billie Jean King's triumph over Bobby Riggs, women activists were successfully struggling for increased opportunities for girls and women in athletics. The successful launching of the Virginia Slims professional tennis tour and King's ascendance as a star tennis player began to show that it was possible for women to imagine themselves as athletes. In this context, cheerleading appeared to be a relic of the pre–Title IX order that existed precisely because women had been discouraged from competing in athletics. Yet it was in this moment of transition—the 1970s—when cheerleading was revitalized by a professional football franchise in the state of Texas.

*   *   *

In a crammed, jubilant locker room in Tulane Stadium in New Orleans on January 16, 1972, NFL commissioner Pete Rozelle handed the Vince Lombardi trophy to Dallas Cowboys head coach Tom Landry. The occasion was the team's Super Bowl victory—a convincing 24–3 triumph over the Miami Dolphins. The victory was the "successful end to our twelve-year plan," Clint Murchison Jr. quipped to announcer Tom Brookshire in front of the CBS television cameras.[5] It was a remarkable achievement for the Dallas Cowboys franchise. It marked the end of a glorious 1971 season that saw the Cowboys move into Texas Stadium, their state-of-the-art facility, and climb to the top of the league by winning the championship. It also marked the end of a period when they were branded as "next year's champions" due to their recent history of painful playoff defeats. Clint Murchison had lobbied his way into the NFL and fought off the competition for Dallas's football fans by chasing Lamar Hunt's AFL team out of town, and now his franchise was the best in the league. Next year's champions were on their way to becoming America's Team.[6]

Cowboys fans and football historians rightly give a lot of credit for this success story to Texas E. Schramm Jr., whom Murchison hired to run his team in 1959. Born in 1920, Schramm grew up in San Gabriel, California, but his father, Texas Sr., was a native Texan. Tex Jr. went back to his roots by attending college at the University of Texas, where he began his longtime career in the sports world. During his years at Austin, he did some sports writing for the *Austin American-Statesman* before he jumped at the chance to go back to California to work in the front office of the Los Angeles Rams NFL franchise. With the Rams, he learned the ins and outs of running a football franchise, such as scouting players, working with the media, and attracting fans. But

Schramm was at the core a public relations man, and his background in media would greatly enhance his success as a football executive throughout his career. He eventually left the Rams for a three-year stint at CBS Sports, where he worked on television contracts with NFL teams. From there, he was hired by Murchison to be the president of the new Dallas NFL franchise. Schramm lured Tom Landry, the former Longhorn football star from Mission who was then a talented assistant coach on the New York Giants, back to Texas to be the team's head coach.

During the 1960s, Schramm's leadership turned the Cowboys from a fledgling, money-losing operation into a preeminent professional football franchise. His relationship with Pete Rozelle, forged during his days with the Rams, would serve him—and his franchise—very well for years to come. More importantly, the security provided by Murchison's deep pockets enabled Schramm to oversee the creation of a professionalized sports operation that made the Cowboys arguably the most influential football franchise in the game. One of his first orders of business was to create an innovative program of player scouting and development. He hired Gil Brandt, a former infant photographer who scouted players as a hobby, as the team's chief scout. Schramm also hired Salam Qureishi, a South Asian employee of IBM, to develop computer-based models to assess football players' talents. Qureishi's computer wizardry allowed the team to evaluate players according to objective criteria. The Cowboys were doing what is now called advanced analytics long before the practice became popular.

Murchison was a dream owner to work for: a hands-off boss who delegated authority to his team president. Schramm, in turn, delegated the coaching of the team to Tom Landry, the brilliant tactician from South Texas who was lured away from his assistant coach position with the New York Giants. For ambitious football men like Landry, opportunities were arising in Texas, not New York. Taking the Cowboys job turned out to be a wise decision. Landry went on to become one of the greatest coaches in NFL history. As the Cowboys became title contenders in the late 1960s, the team was seen by many in the sports world as a model franchise. Much of this image was carefully constructed by Schramm, who used his contacts with the league leadership and the media to cultivate this polished perception. The team even attracted interest from scholars who documented the team's innovative management strategies for the reading public.[7]

Computerized scouting and the detailed evaluation of players was consistent with the franchise's corporate orientation. Unlike other franchises, which were managed by owners who ruled their teams in a paternalistic manner, the Cowboys were not a family affair. They were a business first and foremost. Team headquarters in the Expressway Tower at 6116 North Central Expressway in North Dallas exuded the ambience of the team's cold, computerized image. So did Tom Landry's fashion sense on the sidelines. Even in an era when coach attire was not hypercommodified with team colors, corporate-branded headsets, and the like, Landry's sideline dress stood out. His impeccable suits and ties and trademark fedora perfectly reflected the team's cool corporate image. Landry looked more like a corporate executive than a head football coach. In the 1973 team highlight film, for example, executives from Southland Insurance Company got a thrill from chatting about the Cowboys' season with Landry and middle linebacker Lee Roy Jordan attired in suits and ties in a corporate office setting. Landry's notoriously distant and unemotional personality allowed him to make the hard decisions of cutting players who didn't make the roster. In contrast, Schramm's persona combined cantankerousness and charm to cultivate relationships with the media. In this sense, they were perfectly matched.

Schramm's commitment to building a profitable winning franchise influenced his approach to player recruitment. He, like his boss Murchison and like Lamar Hunt, understood that rigid Jim Crow segregation interfered with the development of a successful sports enterprise. He was what one might call a "corporate racial liberal" who was the perfect fit for the Dallas way of managing racial dynamics: desegregation should be a carefully controlled process that would solicit black support without alienating whites historically invested in segregation. To some degree, the approach worked both for the franchise and for the black football players who donned the Cowboys' silver, blue, and white colors. In the 1960s, the Cowboys signed black players and even quietly responded to their desires for adequate housing in the city's segregated housing market. When *Dallas Times Herald* beat writer Steve Perkins asked Schramm about the team's responsiveness to the needs of black players in 1968, he defensively growled, "Who integrated the Dallas hotels? We did. Who started integrated seating in Dallas? We did in the Cotton Bowl." Schramm continued, "Can anybody name another line of work, another profession, where skin color doesn't mean a damn? Where all that counts is how good a hitter you are, how fast you are, and whether you're a better man than the next man? The sports world is run by the win-loss column."[8]

Schramm was exaggerating the inherent meritocratic quality of sports, but his argument had some justification. The Cowboys quietly helped desegregate aspects of Dallas social and cultural life, and they also fielded a team with black players who weren't simply grateful employees of white men's generosity. Indeed, the team drafted an assortment of black players with varied educational and political backgrounds. One of its first players was Don Perkins, a tough fullback from New Mexico who was highly respected around the league. Mel Renfro, the All-American defensive back from Oregon and future Hall of Famer, starred for the Cowboys for many years. In 1969, the club did not prevent him from filing a fair housing lawsuit against racist real estate agents. Calvin Hill was a talented, erudite running back from Yale University who was the team's first round draft pick that same year. The Hill signing, like many others, reflected the team's commitment to finding talent anywhere, even from Ivy League schools that were not known for producing NFL-caliber players, and even if it meant signing a black player who had the educational credentials to do other things with his life. Then there was Duane Thomas, the mercurial running back from West Texas State who presented the most difficult challenge to team management. Thomas supplanted Hill as the team's best running back during his brief two-year stint with the Cowboys. He was one of the key players on their 1971 Super Bowl team even though he refused to talk to teammates and the media, and even though he publically referred to Landry as a "plastic man" and to Schramm as "sick, demented and completely dishonest."[9] Although he was eventually traded, the team showed that it was not afraid to rely on the talents of players, even those who caused trouble for team management, at least for a little while.

But as the Cowboys were generating more and more profits, the team remained tight fisted with its players. The team was notorious for underpaying all of its players, including the team's stars. Bob Lilly, their perennial All-Pro defensive tackle and eventual Hall of Famer, made far less money than players of lesser ability on other teams. In those days, leverage in the NFL rested with the owners, who managed to keep salaries low due to the lack of free agency and the league's ability to crush any competition from other leagues after the AFL-NFL merger. Players had little choice but to take the salaries owners were willing to offer. While the team's roster of male players was underpaid, so were the women who worked for the Cowboys.

* * *

As part of Schramm's constant effort to enhance the Cowboys' image, he turned his attention to the team's cheerleading squad after the team's Super Bowl win over the Dolphins. Such a project, however, had to be done on the cheap. In the 1960s, Schramm asked Dee Brock, a local model and dance instructor at El Centro Community College, to organize the team's cheerleader group. Brock convinced him to hold cheerleading competitions to find the most athletically talented performers. Their repertoire would be traditional cheers, yells, and stunts. This was consistent with the practice of other NFL teams at this time. In exchange for their services, the teenagers would receive free tickets to Cowboys games. Billed as "Belles and Beaux," the team's coed cheerleading group wore standard uniforms. Girls wore sweaters, skirts, and bobby socks, while the boys wore pants and sweaters. Cheers were conducted by yellers who used bullhorns and gimmicky stunts to try to stir up Cowboys fans. It is significant that the team used black cheerleaders on the squad, both male and female, at a time when the practice, like the broader system of Jim Crow education, was racially segregated. The Cowboys cheerleaders looked more representative of Texas's population than the Apache Belles and the Kilgore Rangerettes did.

But traditional high school and college cheerleaders struggled to get the attention of the rowdy regulars at Cowboys games in the Cotton Bowl. "Sis boom bah" were discordant notes in the serious atmosphere of professional football. In 1970, the team dumped the young men cheerers and opted for an all-girl group modeled a bit more on the Apache Belles. The young women donned new uniforms: long-sleeved, collared blue satin cowboy-style tops with stars embroidered near the shoulders, short white box pleated skirts, and white knee-high boots. On the 1970 squad, a number of the black women sported afro hairstyles. In a sense, the team was going along with the fashions of the times, following in the footsteps of the sexualized "Spacettes" who worked as ushers in Judge Hofheinz's Astrodome or go-go dancers in their eponymous boots. Still, the squad's repertoire remained pretty much in the tradition of school cheerleading: "We really did high school type cheers in those days," Vanessa Baker recalled years later.[10] Vanessa and her sister Vonciel were African American women who would be among the longest-serving members of the cheerleading squad.

When the Cowboys made their first Super Bowl in 1971, the tight-fisted Schramm refused to pay for the cheerleaders' travel to the game in Miami. Dee Brock raised the money to take the young women on the trip. She did the same thing once again the next year, when the team played in the Super Bowl in New Orleans. This practice would continue even after the team's cheerleading squad became national celebrities a few years later.

The Cowboy general manager's desire for a new cheerleading

The Dallas Cowboys cheerleading squad, 1970. Photo by Neil Leifer.

squad was clearly informed by the entertainment he witnessed during the years when his team played at the Cotton Bowl. Nell Davis's Kilgore Junior College Rangerettes and the Tyler Junior College's Apache Belles had strutted their stuff at Cowboys games during the 1960s. Both exuded "wholesome" sexiness when they performed their precision drill team routines. As influential to his thinking were the appearances of Bubbles Cash in the stands of the Cotton Bowl during Cowboys games in the 1960s. Fans turned their heads when Cash, a local exotic dancer, appeared during a game with bleach blonde hair, wearing a leopard print mini skirt, high heels, and a top that accentuated her breasts.[11] Her appearance, which was duly noted by the press, must have influenced Schramm's thinking of the possibilities for sideline entertainment. Sexiness was part of the scene at Cowboys games long before the team decided to sexualize its cheerleaders in the early '70s. And after the Cowboys moved away from the proletarian, collegiate football atmosphere of the Cotton Bowl for the sterile professional environment of Texas Stadium, the team's cheerleading squad needed a new look, one that presented whole-someness and sexiness in a whole new package.

Brock and Schramm put their heads together to revamp the team's cheerleading group. Schramm wanted models, to attract the attention of the team's male fan base, while Brock wanted cheerleaders who actually had performative skills. She also saw the need for cheerleaders who were college age or older after she experienced the challenges of chaperoning high school students during the Super Bowl trips. One model they clearly drew from was that of the Niner Nuggets, a group of women who operated more as "ambassadors" of the San Francisco 49er NFL franchise than actual cheerleaders. The Nuggets, wearing all-red jumpsuits, top hats, and white go-go boots, entertained fans at the stadium and represented them in the community.[12] The new Cowboys cheerleaders had to be at least eighteen years of age, and they had to be either in school or gainfully employed. They were recruited to be, as Schramm later put it, "atmosphere producers."[13] Brock saw that a group that focused on dancing, rather than on leading cheers, might provide the kind of atmosphere Schramm was look-ing for at Texas Stadium.

She found Texie Waterman, then a veteran dancer and chore-ographer, to serve as a judge for the 1972 auditions. Waterman had already managed to put together a career in dance as a per-former in New York and other parts of the country. Over the years, she managed to juggle her career aspirations with the demands of domesticity to perform at state fairs and teach at her own stu-dio in East Dallas, where aspiring dancers obeyed the commands from the woman with a deep voice and the tightly wound, thin dancer's body. She was a smoker who was notorious for leading classes with a cigarette in her hand, waving her arms and moving her body as ashes flew all over the place.

At the 1972 auditions, Waterman assessed the one hundred young women who tried out for the squad. Afterward, Brock con-vinced Schramm to hire Waterman to be the squad's permanent choreographer. Schramm paid her the puny sum of $300 for her efforts that first year. Waterman, like so many of Schramm's em-

The Dallas Cowboys Cheerleaders high-kick routine. AP photo.

ployees, accepted the subpar compensation in exchange for an affiliation with the Cowboys franchise. "I thought it was a fun thing for me to dabble around with. It afforded me good publicity," she recalled years later.[14] Still Waterman wondered, "How in the world can you get dancers on a football field? There's no stage, no lights, no illusion."[15] She decided to draw upon and modify the repertoire of New York–style jazz dance. She instructed her dancers to use big, exaggerated movements such as long steps and overhead arm movements so that their bodies could be seen on the mammoth stage of the stadium environment rather than in the more intimate theater setting. Over time, she figured out how to bring jazz-style dance into the repertoire of sideline cheerleading. Big steps, big movements, and big kicks became standard practice among professional cheerleaders after Waterman made them part of the Dallas cheerleader repertoire. Perhaps this is why some former cheerleaders argue that it was Waterman, not Schramm, who was a major part of the genius behind the Dallas Cowboys Cheerleaders.[16]

While Waterman went to work on the new team's choreography, Brock and Schramm figured out how to redesign the squad's uniforms. The general manager's contacts put him in touch with Paula Van Wagoner, a local designer. Schramm's directions were simple: he wanted something different than the typical pleated skirt cheerleader look. "I had four things in mind when I designed the uniform," Van Wagoner told the press ten years later. "It had to be western because of the Cowboys. It had to be something they could move in, it had to be sexy. And, in keeping with the image of the Cowboys players and coaches, it had to be in good taste."[17] Harmonizing good taste with sexiness was hard to pull off, but Van Wagoner's uniform seemingly brought them together. Van Wagoner came up with two designs. She replaced the conventional pleated skirt with white polyester hot pants. Above the waist, the cheerleader would wear a blue halter blouse under a white fringed bolero vest to go with white go-go boots. An alternate uniform, which was used often in the first few years of the revamped cheerleaders, was a blue body suit, sometimes a blue turtle neck with a white fringed skirt. The uniform would attract the attention of admirers and critics for years to come. It would also compel the women who performed in them to frantically keep their weight low enough to squeeze into the hot pants and halter tops, a practice that would have long-standing psychological consequences years after their cheerleading days were over.

In the summer of 1972, Brock and Waterman picked seven women for the refashioned cheerleading group: Anna Carpenter, Carrie O'Brien, Deanovoy Nichols, Dixie Smith, Dolores McAda, Rosemary Hall, and Vonciel Baker. Some of them had previous dancing or cheerleader experience in high school or college. Smith had been on the drill team in her high school. Baker, the sister of Vanessa Baker, couldn't make the cheerleading squad at her all-black Dallas Lincoln High School but managed to become the first black cheerleader at Texas Lutheran College in Seguin. Meanwhile, O'Brien had been with the Apache Belles squad that performed on the field during the Cowboys victory in Super Bowl VI. What seemed to be an inauspicious group turned out to

The Dallas Cowboys Cheerleaders working on the sideline, 1974. Photo by Heinz Kluetmeier, Sports Illustrated.

be a paradigm-shifting collection of young women, though they did not know it at the time.[18]

The life and labor of being a cheerleader for Schramm's Cowboys was not as glamorous as it would become a few years later. Like Schramm's players, the women who danced and kicked at every home game were underpaid, but sexism ensured that they were especially undercompensated. The team paid them only fifteen dollars per home game ($14.12 after taxes). They were not compensated for any of their rehearsals, and they were expected to maintain their uniforms themselves. And from the beginning, their rehearsal schedule was rigorous. Auditions were held in July, and practice began in August every night at Texie Waterman's dance studio in East Dallas. During the football season, they rehearsed one night a week and on game day at Texas Stadium hours before kickoff. Still, the number of cheerleaders on the squad increased from seven in 1972 to fifteen in 1974 to twenty-one in 1975. Cheerleaders, even those who had made the squad previously, were required to try out every year. They were minor local celebrities, but they were hardly the national sensation they would become after the 1975 season. It wasn't simply the sexy uniform, the choreography, or the attractiveness of the group that eventually made them "America's sweethearts." For that to occur, they needed help from the technological medium that drove so many aspects of the sports revolution of the 1960s and '70s.

* * *

The story has been told before. During a break in the Super Bowl action an astute television cameraman let his lens wander over to the sidelines, catching a row of lovely young women clad in blue and white. One of the Cheerleaders caught his gaze and winked. It probably never occurred to her that she was on national television. But 75 million viewers—fully one-third of the nation— were watching. And they didn't take their eyes off what they saw.
MARY CANDACE EVANS, *A DECADE OF DREAMS*

It supposedly happened during Super Bowl X on January 18, 1976, when the Dallas Cowboys faced the Pittsburgh Steelers in the Orange Bowl on a bright and sunny day in Miami, Florida. The tale has been narrated so many times it is hard not to regurgitate it again. It is the epic moment when a Dallas Cowboys Cheerleader spontaneously winked at a television cameraman during a break in the action. Some accounts provide the name of the cheerleader who made the famous wink: Gwenda Swearingen. As the story goes, this wink unleashed the ensuing tidal wave of interest in the scantily clad cheerleaders of the Dallas Cowboys. Though they had been caught on camera before, this Super Bowl X moment made the cheerleaders into celebrities, according to Cowboys team histories. Soon thereafter, the team was overwhelmed with interest from women who wanted to become a cheerleader for the Cowboys and from the media, especially the television networks, which could not keep their camera lenses off the sexy women who danced on the sidelines. All of it was set off by a cheerleader's wink on national television.

Except that the story has been a bit of a minor myth spun by the Cowboys to make the ascendance of the cheerleaders seem like a natural response to their beauty and talent rather than to careful planning and orchestration by the team itself. No visual evidence of the wink moment at Super Bowl X has survived. The recordings of the telecast that exist on YouTube do not contain the wink moment. In fact, a close viewing of the telecast reveals that CBS director Sandy Grossman seemed relatively uninterested in the women dancing and cheerleading on the Orange Bowl's threadbare Polyturf that day. Grossman, like most sports television directors at the time, was more interested in showing the head knocking that was occurring among the men on the gridiron. While it is possible that those brief moments were enough to propel the cheerleaders to a national sensation, it was not because of the CBS telecast of the Super Bowl on that sunny January day in Miami.[19]

One Texan woman who certainly *did* appear many times in front of the CBS cameras that day was Phyllis George, the former Miss America who was one of the co-hosts on *The NFL Today*, the network's paradigm-shifting pregame show. The Denton, Texas, native was, in many ways, the 1970s version of the Texas beauty queen of decades before. The former cheerleader and pageant contestant was famous for being crowned Miss America in 1971. In 1974, Robert Wussler, then vice-president of CBS Sports, hired her even though she had no experience in sports journalism. George wasn't the first woman network sportscaster—Jane Chastain was—but she was the first to break through with sustained success in the male-dominated world of sports television. She, along with Irv Cross, the African American former football player turned astute football analyst, joined Brent Musburger to form a historic trio in network sports television, making the pregame show a staple of football TV coverage.

George's signing with CBS Sports elicited many snickers from the sportswriting brethren. But most men who were hired to broadcast games didn't have much experience in the booth either. Indeed, ABC's *Monday Night Football* helped inaugurate the phenomenon of sports "personalities," celebrities who were valued for their ability to entertain as much as inform. Though she struggled to find her way as a sportscaster, a task made more difficult by sexism from colleagues, fans, and players, George doggedly produced some groundbreaking journalism. Her specialty became the interviews that prompted players to discuss their personal lives, not just Xs and Os. Her most famous interview moment was when she managed to get straight-arrow quarterback Roger Staubach to discuss the pleasures of his monogamous sex life.

Wussler's hiring of George was motivated, in part, by his desire to compete with Roone Arledge's ABC Sports. By the mid-1970s, ABC was the leading sports television network, leaving behind NBC and CBS, the previous lords of sports on TV. ABC's ascendance in the 1970s compelled NBC and CBS to scramble to compete. In 1974, NBC hired Don Meredith away from Arledge's *Monday Night Football* announcing team and made him the lead color analyst on its Sunday football package. That same year, Wussler took a page out of the Arledge book by hiring George. Sports television executives could not fathom hiring a woman who did not have sex appeal, and George's conventional, pageant-style good looks fit the bill. CBS's hiring of George was part of a larger pattern of New York–based television networks hiring Texas-based broadcasters, which would continue in the years to come.

George's arrival in 1974 happened at the precise moment that college athletic programs and the NCAA were in the midst of launching a campaign against Title IX's implementation. The implications of equality in collegiate sports was setting in for male athletic directors and football coaches across the country, and they reacted with vigorous opposition. In May 1974, Texan Republican senator John Tower introduced an amendment to exempt revenue-generating sports from Title IX legislation. The amendment failed, but male opposition to the law persisted. The pressure to include women in sports undoubtedly figured into the thinking of CBS. Predictably, their vision of inclusion centered on women who were valued for their attractiveness to men, not for their knowledge of sports. During the famous Super Bowl X telecast, George smiled prettily for the cameras and did her best to squeeze in some insights in the limited time allotted to her by the show's director.

Though Gwenda Swearingen's wink during Super Bowl X has not survived in the archives, another wink moment, one that perhaps is often confused with Super Bowl X, happened three months before—not under the sunny skies of a Miami Sunday in January 1976 but under the bright lights of a *Monday Night Football* game on November 10, 1975, between the Cowboys and the Kansas City Chiefs. The game was memorable for a variety of reasons. It brought the past and present of Texas football together. The game's marquee might have read "Dallas vs. Kansas City," but both teams were actually Texas creations. The Chiefs were originally Lamar Hunt's Dallas Texans when they began as an AFL franchise in 1960. A few years after Hunt's team left for Kansas City, the Cowboys began more than a decade of franchise excellence on the field with two Super Bowl berths and multiple playoff appearances. Conversely, after years of success, including their own Super Bowl victory in 1970, the Chiefs' fortunes on the field declined and would continue to do so for years to come. Still, their starting quarterback that night was Mike Livingston, the former SMU star quarterback during the Jerry LeVias years who was coming back home to play in Dallas.

By 1975, ABC's *Monday Night Football* had become one of the most popular shows on television. Under Arledge and his pioneering directing and announcing team, the show became a runaway success. It produced record television ratings and commanded hundreds of thousands—eventually, millions—of dollars from advertisers, which made network executives happy and the owners of National Football League teams ecstatic. The *Monday Night* team's Arledge-inspired storytelling skills and its creative usage of cameras, close-up shots, and paradigm-shifting announcers helped make the NFL into a national phenomenon.

The story ABC Sports liked to tell was tailored to men. Its research department found that the majority of football viewers were males, and many were middle- to upper-middle-class professionals.[20] But the male-centered character of ABC Sports was not built simply on market research but on Arledge's own distinctive vision. Arledge's programs had always been centered on men—from the urbane, sophisticated pipe smoker to the proletarian, beer-guzzling sports fan. One of his first projects was a program entitled *For Men Only*, a pilot show modeled on Hugh Hefner's *Playboy* magazine. The renegade swashbuckling character of the network's sports coverage traded heavily in misogyny and sexism.

One of the chief exponents of this brand of television broadcasting was Andy Sidaris, the director of the network's college football telecasts. The Shreveport, Louisiana, native was yet another influential figure in sports who graduated from SMU in 1955. After years working at WFAA, a TV station in Dallas, he was hired by ABC to be a director of *Wide World of Sports* and of the network's coverage of the Olympics. Decades later, Sidaris eventually became a Hollywood producer of fleshy and violent Hollywood B movies, appropriately dubbed "Bullets, Bombs, and Babes," but he made his reputation—and his money—as director of ABC's football telecasts, often working with longtime producer Chuck Howard. And if there was one through line in his career, it was his fanatical obsession with subjecting conventionally defined pretty girls to his filmic gaze. During his tenure at ABC, Sidaris became best known for creating the "honey shot," shooting cheerleaders and women in the stands in his football broadcasts. Sidaris made his attraction to young college women abundantly clear in interviews he did with the press over the years. "After seventeen years of directing college football telecasts, I have come to appreciate the face of a beautiful girl—spectator or cheerleader—at a game," Sidaris said in 1971. "In fact, during our weekly telecast, I assign one of our 10 cameras to do nothing but focus on what we call 'honey shots.'"[21]

His appreciation for the college coed came from his days as a college student at SMU, where he saw "the most beautiful women in the world. All in cashmere little skirts, penny loafers." "It was fantastic; I loved them!" he crowed to the makers of *Seconds to Play*, the fascinating 1976 behind-the-scenes profile of ABC college football telecasts.[22] Over the years, Sidaris regularly espoused his views on the prettiest cheerleaders in college football. He and his team liked to churn out school cheerleader rankings for the amusement of male sportswriters and readers. He had a particular fondness for the cheerleaders from USC, UCLA, and of course his alma mater, SMU.[23] Though Arledge's men often claimed to focus on women to attract them as viewers, it is clear that the honey shot was designed for heterosexual men who could enjoy such eye candy as they watched the male football players tackle each other on the gridiron. The "beauties" that the team went out of their way to put in front of their cameras during the Battle of the Sexes tennis match could also be found on Monday nights, and on Saturday afternoons during NCAA college telecasts. The conclusion of *Seconds to Play* underscores the enormous impact of directors and producers of sports network television: "This is how Americans consume football, choreographed by fifty men for an audience of thirty-one million. Sidaris and Howard decide what we [see] and how we [see] it. Television gave them an elaborate power over the events on the field, shaping and transforming a college football game into a commercial television show."[24]

It was the power of the sports television producer and director that nationalized the sports revolution of the 1970s. And it was the power of the sports television producer and director that brought the sexual revolution to the realm of sports.

Sidaris's honey shot bore a rather striking resemblance to another filmic technique that was becoming prevalent in movies in the United States at that time: the "money shot," which became popular in pornographic films after the release of *Deep Throat* in 1972. Rather than zero in on the moment of male ejaculation, Sidaris's cameras aimed to stimulate male pleasure by focusing on an attractive woman's face or body, especially when they moved in a sexy, provocative gesture. The honey shot became part of a repertoire of camera angles and cuts designed to provoke reactions from the announcers in the booth. They especially liked to goad Frank Gifford, Don Meredith, and Howard Cosell, all of whom had legendary egos. All of these techniques were part of the fraternity house atmosphere that spilled over into the telecasts.[25]

By the mid-1970s, Sidaris's honey shot was a standard technique used by other directors in the ABC sports division, including Chet Forte, the longtime director of *Monday Night Football*. Forte, the former Columbia University basketball star, fashioned himself, like Sidaris, as a cigarette-smoking, foul-mouthed boss who relished his job as director of *Monday Night Football* telecasts. As the show gained more and more notoriety, Forte and his producer Don Ohlmeyer liked to woo women into their truck during telecasts. "Like so much else about *Monday Night Football* at its height, the locker-room mentality was taken to extremes," Marc Gunther and Bill Carter have written. "The cast and crew amounted to an exclusive male club. Women were rarely hired as anything but gofers. Some younger, low-echelon crew members were taken aback by the brazenly macho atmosphere."[26] The bosses of football telecasts, Howard, Sidaris, Ohlmeyer, and Forte presided over a crew of men who thought of themselves as celebrity king makers. The producers and directors loved to wield their power over their underlings, barking out profanity-laced commandments to the production team from the truck outside the stadium: "Get me some broads," "Give me the blimp," and "Cut to commercial" were common commandments uttered by Arledge's chieftains on-site.[27] Field coordinators issued instructions to cheerleaders to coordinate movements and poses for the television cameras.

The cocksure men who ran ABC Sports' football telecasts relished the fact that they worked for the leading network in sports television. And when they arrived in Irving, Texas, for the Chiefs-Cowboys Monday night game on November 10, 1975, they were eager to find new material on the field to fuel their distinctive creative vision—and they found them on the sidelines of Texas Stadium.

On what turned out to be a historic night in Texas Stadium, ABC's crew was ready to bring the drama of football to the nation.[28] The *Monday Night Football* announcing team now included Alex Karras, the former Detroit Lion defensive lineman who had replaced Don Meredith after he was hired away by NBC. All night long, the sideline cameramen fixated on the cheerleaders in their white pants, blue halter tops, white fringe vests, and white go-go boots. The directors seemed to be particularly keen on using the shots of the cheerleaders to elicit responses from Gifford, who tried to ignore the brief cuts to them throughout the first half. In the second quarter, the screen cut to two cheerleaders holding a plastic cup sipping on a drink, prompting Karras to ask Gifford: "Did you like that pop, little girl?" In the third quarter, the cameras cut to Gwenda Swearingen raising her arms, shaking her pompoms, and looking askance. Then, probably cued by a cameraman, she looked straight at the camera and provocatively winked, letting the audience know that she knew she was being watched by millions of viewers. This was a moment that Gifford could not possibly ignore. When Swearingen winked, he immediately responded by yelping, "Ooh!" But Swearingen wasn't finished. She turned her back to the camera and looked over her shoulder while shimmying her body. Cosell jumped in on the game being played by the *Monday Night* crew, telling Gifford, "I think she was doing that for you, Frank." Gifford replied with feigned objectivity, "I don't know; she was very effective." After chuckles from the announcers and an awkward silence, Karras would not let up, asking Gifford, "Did you like that, Frank?" to which Gifford replied, "I *did* like that . . . little wink!"

Ohlmeyer and his director were not finished pestering Gifford with their little games. Later in the telecast, the screen cut to Swearingen once again, doing the same exact move—looking at the camera, holding her arms up, and shaking the pompoms. Gifford pleaded with his director and producer, "Would you please get her off of our screen? . . . She hasn't looked at the game; she has found every camera we have in the stadium!" In reality, it was the cameraman who had found her and made sure the national television audience watched her perform on the sidelines. Far from being a simple, spontaneous moment between cheerleader and cameraman, the "wink" episode was carefully hatched between ABC crewmembers and the Dallas Cowboys Cheerleaders. At that moment, the cheerleaders transformed from ornamental and incidental actors in football telecasts to active participants in the televising of football contests.

ABC Sports had done its job. The honey shot gave the Cowboys cheerleaders fifteen minutes of fame. Now the group needed a leader who would convert the cheerleaders' Monday night notoriety into a sustained marketing campaign that would make the women who danced at Texas Stadium national celebrities.

* * *

Suzanne Mitchell was looking for a job. Like Dee Brock and Texie Waterman, she was an upwardly mobile white woman seeking opportunities for material advancement and some level of personal satisfaction. She was a college graduate looking to make her way in Dallas after working on the East Coast. But in the 1970s, even for a white woman with a college degree, job prospects were limited. She took one of the few positions available in the white-collar world, that of the boss's secretary. The story goes that she applied for a job to be Tex Schramm's secretary. When Schramm asked her in the interview where she wanted to be in five years, she replied, "Your chair looks pretty comfortable!" The answer delighted the Cowboys president, who admired Mitchell's gumption and ambition. He hired her on the spot. Later, when Dee Brock, who had led the cheerleaders for little to no pay, left the Cowboys, Schramm needed a replacement. Mitchell had by that point helped Schramm with all sorts of daily administrative tasks, and the Cowboys executive now asked her to add managing the team's cheerleading squad to her list of responsibilities. Interest in the cheerleaders swelled after the 1975 season, and the Cowboys boss needed someone to manage the rapidly expanding cheerleading operation. Mitchell took on the task in 1976, and she never looked back.[29]

In Suzanne Mitchell, Tex Schramm found a kindred spirit: an ambitious visionary who was loyal to the Cowboys organization to a fault. Born in 1943, Mitchell was a Fort Worth native who grew up in Dallas. She went to college at the University of Oklahoma, got married, and moved to New York with her husband, where she worked for Ziff-Davis publishing house. Her previous experience in the sports world had occurred when she did public relations work for the United States Olympic Ski Team. Like Texie Waterman, however, she divorced and returned to Texas. After Schramm put her in charge of the team's cheerleading squad, she made directing the cheerleaders her life's work, working fourteen to sixteen hours a day, seven days a week, for thirteen years.[30]

Under Mitchell, they became Dallas Cowboys Cheerleaders, Inc. (DCC), a subsidiary of the Dallas Cowboys Football Club. Like her boss, Mitchell was a public relations master, and it was her tireless efforts, and her fierce advocacy for the cheerleaders, that led to their sudden emergence in US popular culture in the late 1970s. America didn't simply fall in love with the women who danced in the hot pants and halter top blouses. They were put in front of the country through Mitchell's relentless public relations work, which became evident soon after she took over for Dee Brock. In previous years, news of the cheerleader auditions had been spread by word of mouth. That spring, Mitchell solicited the participation of KVIL, a popular Dallas radio station, to promote the auditions. The station ran advertisements, and veteran cheerleaders came on the air to discuss the wonders of dancing for the Cowboys. That summer, 250 women applied for the job. The numbers of applicants increased dramatically each year thereafter. Mitchell had made the audition an annual event that Cowboys fans, including aspiring young women, eagerly awaited.

Mitchell became the Tex Schramm figure of the DCC while Waterman operated like Tom Landry, coordinating the strategies and dance steps of the team. They became a parallel management structure, and the cheerleaders, like the team's male players, were the workers. Except that Roger Staubach, Randy White, Drew Pearson, and the rest of the roster got paid much more than the women who labored in the go-go boots and hot pants. And while the Cowboys management was notorious for micromanaging their players on the field, the players enjoyed more freedom than the women who cheered them on from the sidelines.

One only needed to read the pages of rules and regulations that were handed out to the cheerleaders to appreciate the policing of the young women who worked for Mitchell. The rules were designed not only to protect the young women from real and imagined dangers, but, like Nell Davis's Rangerette operation, to make girls into respectable ladies—to prevent them from being agents of self-destruction. The rules were meant to give them, in Cowboys parlance, "a touch of class," which presumed, of course, that they needed to be taught to be classy. They were required to enroll in an eight-week Dale Carnegie course designed to teach them "personal development" and how to handle themselves in front of people. Cheerleaders were not to fraternize with players, chew gum, be seen in public barefoot or with rollers in the hair, wear their uniform without Mitchell's permission, or be caught in bars excessively drinking. A warning would be issued after the first rule violation, and expulsion would occur if a rule was broken the second time. Following the rules was particularly challenging for women who were juggling multiple responsibilities, such as working another job, attending school, or managing domestic responsibilities. It was not uncommon for Mitchell's women to drive all over the Dallas Metroplex area to make practices and games. A labor regime governed by patriarchy and sexism relies on multitasking survival skills employed by generations of working-class women. Working for Schramm and Mitchell's Cowboys felt like a 24/7/365 job, even if the position only paid fifteen dollars per game for fourteen to eighteen times a year.[31]

Part of being ladylike was also to be thin, which took some work, even for college-age women. No jelly rolls or bellies were allowed. The cheerleaders had to fit into the tight uniforms, or else. They had to be strong and athletic but also thin, and they needed to possess some cleavage. Mitchell routinely demanded that her cheerleaders lose weight. Such were—and still are—the prevailing body images of the world of show business, but Mitchell went to extreme measures to terrorize her troops to keep their weights down. The cheerleaders' bodies were carefully scrutinized by Waterman and Mitchell. Cheerleaders had to weigh in at the beginning of the season. If exercise and long practices didn't keep the pounds off, starvation diets, diet pills, diuretics, and vomiting would do the trick. Diet soda, sugar, and sometimes cocaine were necessary stimulants to keep the young women energetic and ready to go.

Like the Apache Belles and the Rangerettes, and probably like all cheerleaders across the state, the Cowboys dancers rehearsed in the inhumane conditions of Texas heat, not just outdoors on the hot Tartan Turf of Texas Stadium but also in the sweaty, sauna-like conditions of Texie Waterman's dance studio. Cowboys cheerleader literature advertised with pride the extreme lengths they went to ensure that the roster was "in shape": "During the summer, the Cheerleaders rehearse four hours every night for more than six weeks, not only to master their routines, but also to get in shape for 100-degree heat in Texas Stadium. As if it isn't hot enough in Texie's studio, many of the girls wear rubber sweat pants to help them lose weight."[32]

Like football coaches who ran oppressive two-a-days during training camp, Mitchell deprived the cheerleaders of air conditioning and water during rehearsals to coerce them to master Waterman's routines. The extreme heat was meant to build up the stamina of the cheerleaders to work during hot summer and fall seasons in Texas Stadium, but it was also meant to get dancers to drop pounds as fast as possible. The knots of their halter tops were carefully tied to ensure that the push-up bras worked to protrude their breasts. Mitchell could treat her chargers in this way because she believed herself to be a parental figure. "I am their surrogate mother in a lot of respects," she told a skeptical Sarah Purcell, the journalist who interviewed Mitchell in a feature for the show *Real People* in 1979.[33]

Such talk was part of the language of social control employed by the Cowboys over their female workers on the sideline. Mitchell played the role of mother to her "girls" while remaining fanatically invested in maintaining the Cowboys' pristine image. In some ways, her authoritarian control over the dancers was based on long-standing practices of social control over young women who were perceived to be defenseless by their elders and by the society at large. But they were also based on the genuine desire to protect the young women from the forces of sexism, violence, and patriarchy, which were particularly pernicious for women in the public eye. "I felt so deeply about them, that they became totally and completely why god had put me here," Mitchell recalled decades later.[34] Sexual harassment, stalking, lewd letters, everyday microaggressions, and the specter of violence were part of the life of the Dallas Cowboys Cheerleader in an era before the #MeToo movement brought the toxic quality of these actions to public attention. Marketing young, attractive women to men who presumed to have privileged access to their bodies was a hazardous exercise. Mitchell did her best to ward off men who would threaten her cheerleaders, using any means necessary—from calling upon police to enacting other forms of law enforcement to protect her merchandise. "It is amazing that one woman could do what she did," recalled Dana Presley, a former cheerleader from the early 1980s. "She protected us."[35] Still, Suzanne Mitchell ran a tight ship. Many of the young women who danced for the Cowboys stayed on board. Others did not. Those who abandoned ship insisted on pursuing a different understanding of women's freedom and self-fulfillment.

* * *

The United Nations declared 1975 International Women's Year. Over the next two years, a grassroots movement with support from President Gerald Ford sought to put together a platform advocating for the rights of women. The campaign, carried out by an extraordinary coalition of activists, intellectuals, and politicians from various racial and ethnic backgrounds, culminated in a historic conference in Houston, Texas. In November 1977, twenty thousand women descended upon Houston for the National Women's Conference. Houston had hosted the monumental Battle of the Sexes tennis match in 1973, and four years later, it was the scene of a major national conference that demonstrated the impact of the second-wave feminist movement. The event was kicked off by a 2,600-mile torch relay that began in Seneca Falls, New York, the site of the famous women's rights convention of 1848. During the final phase of the run, leaders Bella Abzug, Betty Friedan, and Susan B. Anthony II were joined by Billie Jean King. The relay showed the symbolic role of sports, and sports figures like King, in the aspirations of the second-wave feminist movement of the 1970s. Still, the convention paid little attention to the concrete struggles of women and girls in sports, which were largely overshadowed by seemingly more pressing concerns, including the Equal Rights Amendment, the rights of women of color and lesbians, and reproductive rights.[36]

Another consequential event that had major repercussions on the fates of women and sports had happened up the road in Dallas, Texas, seven months earlier. In April 1977, hundreds of women converged on Texas Stadium in Irving to try out for the Dallas Cowboys Cheerleaders. Suzanne Mitchell and Tex Schramm's promotional efforts were paying off. Hordes of women—estimates varied from four hundred to more than a thousand—drove into the parking lot of Clint Murchison's football palace to pursue their dreams of fame and self-fulfillment. Many arrived from other parts of the state, while others came from all over the country. They were competing for thirty-six positions on the 1977 squad. They showed up in short shorts, in specially designed outfits, in heels, or in go-go boots ready to impress. They would be evaluated by a panel of judges including Mitchell; Waterman; Ron Chapman; Bert Rose, the general manager of Texas Stadium;

and W. W. Mitchell, a prominent Dallas attorney who also happened to be Suzanne Mitchell's brother. The judging criteria was capacious enough to allow even those who had little to no performance expertise to judge the contestants. "There is no emphasis on anything except sparkle," Suzanne Mitchell explained to the *New York Times* that year. "These girls are all different—even to their bodies. We're not looking for the same thing in every person."[37] With her characteristic frankness, Texie Waterman told the press, "I would say we are looking for 35 Farrah Fawcetts, but even that would get boring."[38] The 1977 auditions were an event itself, helping the DCC to grow into a nationally recognized brand. KVIL would once again promote the auditions, but now ABC television was added to the mix to televise the semifinals of the auditions that year. Returning cheerleaders were exempt from the preliminary and semifinal rounds of the auditions and were not required to compete until the finals. Competition among the women was fierce, too intense to allow men to compete. One male aspirant was turned away at the door. The brave new world of sexualized professional cheerleading was no place for male performers, no matter how kinesthetically talented or attractive they might have been.[39]

When the Stadium Club was installed in Texas Stadium, it was envisioned as a banquet room for the affluent fans Murchison wanted to attract to his football palace. During tryout season, however, it was reconfigured into an audition space with a dance floor and seats for the judges and contestants. In the background was a glass window that enabled applicants to look out on the empty stadium and fantasize about dancing for the Cowboys. Rows of contestants introduced themselves and their occupations to the judges. Then, they were asked to dance for ninety seconds on the makeshift dance floor in the Stadium Club. From there, the judges narrowed down the list of applicants to approximately two hundred to return to audition for the semifinal round one month later. Tensions increased during the semifinal round as the judges scrutinized the group to see if they could pick up a dance routine from Waterman. Those who passed the semifinals were invited back to compete with veteran cheerleaders in the final round.

In the 1977 auditions, ninety-five women made it to the finals to compete for the thirty-six spots on that year's roster. They were asked to perform their own talent show. One by one, they performed routines that resembled competitions for a variety show. Some women sang, others danced, and some did both. Afterward, the finalists took an exam that assessed their knowledge of football and the Cowboys organization. Finally, the tryouts ended with interviews conducted by Mitchell and the judges, who sought to gauge the applicants' commitment to the "Cowboy way." On June 19, the team announced the winners, nineteen of which were new faces. Because the finals were televised by ABC's *Wide World of Sports*, everyone in the nation would know who the 1977 cheerleaders were. Some of the veterans who did not make the final cut would subsequently strike out on their own to capitalize on their talents and experiences as Dallas Cowboys Cheerleaders, much to Mitchell's dismay.[40]

Mitchell and the team had big plans for the thirty-six women who danced on the sidelines for the team that year. The first was a photo shoot for *Esquire* magazine. The second was a poster produced by ProArts, the same Ohio-based poster producers that published the legendary Farrah Fawcett poster that featured the Texas-native actress and model in a swimsuit looking sexily at the camera. The Fawcett poster became the hottest-selling cultural item of the 1970s, a fact that was not lost on Cowboys management. One didn't have to look at the Cowboys cheerleaders poster too long to notice the team's explicit attempts to market the group as sex objects. Five cheerleaders stand in a sultry pose looking provocatively at the camera of Bob Shaw, the Dallas-based photographer who was fond of shooting the cheerleaders. Smoke rises from their feet, conveying the impression they were in a disco club, or a strip joint, ready to entertain. The poster enabled the group to join the ranks of pin-up girls. It sold like hotcakes at stores throughout the country.

The *Esquire* shoot also made a splash. On the cover of the October 1977 issue was a similarly posed Debbie Wagener, one of the cheerleaders who worked at the check-out counter of Tom Thumb grocery store. The cover story headline boldly proclaimed, "The Dallas Cowgirls (the Best Thing about the Dallas Cowboys)." The pictorial, entitled "Cowgirls," had short descriptions of eight of the cheerleaders. Yet the descriptions were not exactly taken from the Mitchell-Schramm public relations script. Of Wagener, the magazine wrote, "She is the leasing agent for an apartment complex. Cheerleading pays fifteen dollars a game and a girl has got to eat." Of Dawn Stansell, the profile explained, "Twice a week during the summer, she drives to Dallas for evening practice that lasts over two hours. You've got to hang tough." Accompanying the photos of Vanessa and Vonciel Baker, two of the squad's black cheerleaders, the magazine asked, "Will they have the stuff next year? They'd better." Of Rhonda Sellers, the magazine quipped, "She has it every bit as tough as the players. On game days, she has to get to the stadium an hour before them, and after half time, she has to be back on the field before they are. . . . No-cut contracts are not even mentioned."[41]

The pictorial conveyed a story of women who "work hard for the money," in the words of disco singer Donna Summer—except that their employer did not treat them right. Even as the story was promoting the team's cheerleaders and seeking to showcase their attractiveness for its readership, the not-so-subtle jabs at Cowboys management show that the magazine was highlighting their exploitation.[42] *Esquire*'s gentle criticisms were not inaccurate, for even as the Dallas Cowboys Cheerleaders became a national sensation, their pay scale remained the same, a mere fifteen dollars per game.

Still, the team's promotional efforts paid off as the DCC attracted more and more media attention during the 1977 football season, which also turned out to be a major success for the male sector of the Cowboys labor force. The Cowboys handily won their division with a 12–2 record. They steamrolled their playoff opponents, the Chicago Bears and the Minnesota Vikings, to earn their fourth Super Bowl bid of the decade. In Super Bowl XII on January 15, 1978, in New Orleans, the site of their first Super Bowl victory seven years earlier, the Cowboys beat the Denver Broncos 27–10 to win their second league title.

But during the game telecast, the men on the gridiron were almost a sideshow to the main attraction on the sidelines. It may not be clear whether CBS Sports actually helped launch the Dallas Cowboys Cheerleaders phenomenon during the 1976 Super Bowl, but it is quite clear that the network helped bolster their popularity during the network's 1978 Super Bowl telecast. For all of the attention Super Bowl X has gotten in Dallas Cowboys Cheerleader lore, it was really Super Bowl XII in which the dancers from Dallas grabbed the attention of the cameramen directed by veteran television man Tony Verna. They were unquestionably part of the show right from the opening moments, when each team's cheerleading squad was prominently displayed during the announcement of the starting lineups. During nearly every break in the action, Verna clearly showed he had assimilated the Arledge/Sidaris/Forte mode of broadcast by featuring both the Cowboys cheerleaders and the Pony Express, the women clad in sparkling silver uniforms and cowgirl hats who worked the sidelines of the Denver Broncos. "We got bouncing cheerleaders, smiling cheerleaders, prancing cheerleaders, wiggling cheerleaders and even cheering cheerleaders," wrote TV critic Howard Smith in his article reviewing the telecast for the Associated Press.[43] Part of the storyline of the game spun by CBS was the "competition" between both teams' cheerleading squads. Close-ups, zoom-outs, and frequent commentary from the announcers ensured that objectifying the ladies on the sidelines was part and parcel of television sports coverage. Unlike the men who earned game checks for their participation in Super Bowl XII, the cheerleaders did not earn one cent for their efforts. In fact, Mitchell's squad did not even get the chance to spend a night in New Orleans, as they were ushered in and out of town on the day of the game.

Over the next few seasons, the Dallas Cowboys Cheerleaders were making appearances everywhere, it seemed. And once again, ABC television was a willing partner. The cheerleaders were fea-

The Dallas Cowboys Cheerleaders getting ready to perform. Photo by Shelly Katz.

tured on an Osmond Brothers Special. Later that year, in advance of the *Monday Night Football* season opener, they were the subject of a one-hour television special entitled *The 36 Most Beautiful Girls in Texas,* co-hosted by actors Hal Linden, Joey Travolta, and Charles Nelson Reilly. And of course, the network also televised a made-for-TV movie called *Dallas Cowboys Cheerleaders.* The film, whose script was approved by Mitchell and the Cowboys, was part fictional, part documentary, and total propaganda piece for the Cowboys organization. Actress Jane Seymour, who was known for playing a Bond girl in James Bond movies, plays a New York–based reporter who tries out for the squad in an effort to find the "real story" behind the DCC's all-American image. The idea was pitched to her by her unscrupulous editor (played by Bert Convy), who wants her to find dirt on the squad by any means necessary. What she finds instead is that there is no "real story" after all. As she endures the intense tryouts and wins a spot on the team, she meets a group of young women who have the burning desire to make it—including a housewife from Tyler who commutes to Dallas for the auditions because she wants to please her husband and herself, and a struggling working-class woman who escapes her shady boyfriend and her past as a wayward youth and makes the squad—and the team managers who desire nothing more than to help these women fulfill their dreams. The film featured Texie Waterman, Bill Chapman, and many of the real cheerleaders, which gives the film a sense that the viewer is getting an inside look at the Dallas Cowboys Cheerleaders organization. The corny film was a ratings hit, becoming the second highest rated made-for-TV film in television history.

Mitchell's crew also appeared on ABC's *The Love Boat*, the hit TV series produced by Dallas-native and SMU graduate Aaron Spelling. It was fitting that they appeared on the show. Lauren Tewes, who starred in the *Dallas Cowboys Cheerleaders* movie, was also one of the stars of *The Love Boat*. And Spelling, a pioneer in "jiggle TV" with his role in the creation of *Charlie's Angels*, naturally found the cheerleaders appealing for his television show. But Mitchell had the young women performing all over the country, not just with celebrities such as Bob Hope and the Oak Ridge Boys, but also as drawing cards for car shows, boutique openings, hotels, and banks in places like Amarillo, Texas; Columbia, South Carolina; Frederick, Oklahoma; and other small towns throughout the country. The fees for these appearances were negotiated by Mitchell, who made sure the team got its cut of the money earned by the women before the rest would supposedly be divided up among the cheerleaders. The real compensation for the cheerleaders was fame, potential attention from powerful men, and the privilege of dancing for the Cowboys. Indeed, by 1978, the thirty-six women who wore the blue-and-white Cowboys uniform were genuine national celebrities.[44]

The explosion of the Dallas Cowboys Cheerleaders was represented by the franchise as one more innovation that propelled its ascendance to the status of "America's team," a label conveniently applied to them by NFL Films for the team's 1978 highlight film. And the slogan wasn't mere propaganda. Cowboys merchandise was the highest selling in the league. The team appeared on national television more than any other team in the league. The highest rated Super Bowl, Thanksgiving, and *Monday Night Football* games were contests featuring the Cowboys. The team had the largest radio network (225 stations) than any team in all of sports, including sixteen Spanish language outlets in the United States and Mexico. And, of course, the poster featuring the cheerleaders had sold over a million copies by 1979. Even the new nighttime soap opera *Dallas* tied itself to the Cowboys brand, featuring shots of the seemingly ubiquitous Texas Stadium in the show's opening. All of it was promoting the team and the city as symbols of Sunbelt affluence, style, and conspicuous consumption.[45]

* * *

The Dallas Cowboys had unleashed a national craze, and now other NFL teams were looking to copy their formula. Texie Waterman, who knew that success was fleeting in show business, could see the competition coming. "Success is wonderful," she told the *Dallas Morning News* during the 1977 season, "but when everyone starts copying you, you've got to give them something new or you're not going to be special anymore."[46] Super Bowl XII was also a boon to the Denver Broncos' Pony Express, whose fame skyrocketed in subsequent months. The Baltimore Colts and the Chicago Bears were among the first teams to dump their college-style cheerleading troupes and replace them with sexy dancing women. The Bears launched their own widely publicized cheerleading group known as the Honey Bears in the spring of 1977.

But it was the "Great Cheerleader War of 1978" that would upend the league and raise the question of the exploitation of cheerleaders by the NFL. In March, the Miami Dolphins replaced their high-school-age group with an older, sexualized group of college-age women called the Super Brites. The San Diego Chargers unveiled new uniforms and a new group of dancers for their Chargettes. Perhaps the raunchiest display of all was orchestrated by the Los Angeles Rams, who hired a Hollywood agent to summon as many aspiring models and celebrities as he could to create the Southern Californian version of the Dallas Cowboys Cheerleaders. The team held a widely publicized audition in the sun-drenched Los Angeles Coliseum. Eight hundred women turned out in their sexiest outfits to audition for twenty-four slots on the new squad to be called the Embraceable Ewes. It was described by one critic as a "cattle call" in which the "top-heavy, beefed up zombies looked like bad Xeroxed copies of the clods from Dallas." Most sports journalists treated the phenomenon with derision laced with misogyny, either because they hated the blatant sexualization or because they feared football was threatened by the presence of women taking attention away from the men on the gridiron. Brent Musburger described the showcasing of the cheerleaders as a "tacky peep show," overlooking the role of his own network in the spreading of the trend. By the fall, twenty-two of the league's twenty-six franchises had refashioned their cheerleading squad into sexualized dance groups. Cheerleaders were expected to work hard, rehearse, and perform while enduring the same strict guidelines that Mitchell's women endured in Dallas for little to no compensation.[47]

The sexual revolution initiated by the Cowboys was spreading throughout the NFL. Despite the criticism coming from sportswriters, the league office seemed perfectly fine with their own version of Jiggle TV. But some of the cheerleaders who were dissatisfied with the arrangements they had with the teams they danced for decided to expand their earnings beyond the pennies they were receiving from their employers. Some of the first to go wayward were ex-employees of Dallas Cowboys Cheerleaders, Inc. The seeds of their rebellion can be seen in an 1977 *Esquire* pictorial. Deborah Kepley, one of the cheerleaders featured in the article, made her feelings about Mitchell's micromanagement abundantly clear. "You've got to keep the uniform clean and neat yourself, and if you lose it you've got to replace it. Miss one practice and you can be kept out of the next game. Miss two and they can kick you off the team," she told *Esquire*. And there was more:

"They're always telling you about your weight or your makeup. They keep trying to make me look like a little girl. But I'll tell you, when I go out on that field, I'm going to go out looking like the woman I am."[48]

In the summer of 1978, Kepley became part of a group of former Cowboys cheerleaders who set out to create their own rival organization. Their leader, Tina Jimenez, wanted to take the Cowboys model to greater heights. Jimenez was on the 1976 Cowboys cheerleading squad, but she did not make the cut during the auditions the following spring. Her time with the Cowboys came to an end, but as far as she was concerned, her career in entertainment was just getting started. She and former DCC dancers Kepley, Linda Kellum, Charyl Russell, Dawn Stansell, Janice Garner, Meg Rossi, and others decided to strike out on their own to form the Texas Cowgirls, Inc. "After we were cut, we thought, 'Why go back to a nine-to-five job?,'" she told the press. "I figured since we did all that work for the Cowboys for nothing we should try to get something for ourselves."[49]

If the entertainment world wanted an alternative version of sexy cheerleaders and entertainers, then they were ready to give it to them. The Texas Cowgirls fashioned themselves as a talent and modeling agency, with Jimenez operating as president and mother hen. Though they claimed to be interested only in gigs in "good taste," they dispatched with Mitchell's stringent "archaic rules" of performing only in alcohol-free spaces.[50] Free from the constraints imposed by the Cowboys, the gigs started coming: store openings, charity softball games, a birthday party for a Dallas millionaire, and a job as the opening act for Gabe Kaplan in Las Vegas. But the biggest one came along in the form of a *Playboy* pictorial. Eager to cash in on the NFL's newfound fondness for women on the field, the magazine contacted various teams throughout the league to convince them to have their young women pose for them. Some clubs gave permission, while others, including the Cowboys, did not. Still other clubs waffled but eventually gave into the magazine's persistent efforts. Jimenez's Cowgirls accepted the offer from *Playboy* on the spot. "The Cowboys turned them down and I just grabbed it. I figured it would be good for us, and it sure was," she recalled.[51]

The *Playboy* pictorial was clearly modeled on the *Esquire* issue from the previous year. It featured sultry shots of various NFL cheerleaders, which goaded readers into indulging in male fantasy. But it also included a lengthy essay about the NFL's hypocrisy and the precariousness of the women's financial situations. Some cheerleaders posed nude, while others did not. The centerpiece of the fourteen-page photo spread and essay was a feature on Jimenez's Texas Cowgirls. The photograph, soon to be a poster, by Arny Freytag was a brilliant parody of the iconic poster that was released the year before. Ex-Cowboys cheerleaders Deborah Kepley, Charyl Russell, Linda Kellum, Janice Garner, and Meg Rossi posed in a uniform that looked just like the DCC uniform, looking seductively at the camera as smoke rose from the floor. They stood in front of nightclub lights that were arranged as an outline of a map of Texas. The poster version of Freytag's photo included an inscription, also in cursive, that read, "The Ex-Dallas Cowboys Cheerleaders."

Throughout the article, Jimenez reported her liberation from Suzanne Mitchell's authoritarian regime. "Suzanne Mitchell has stated publicly that she didn't want the girls to use the Cowboys as a 'steppingstone to stardom,'" she was quoted as saying. "Well, we want to become somebody. And without the organization holding us back, we think we can." The point was unambiguous. The Cowboys sell sex appeal, but they do not compensate the women who provide it. Now, a rogue group of ex-employees were sticking it to their former bosses and looking to get paid.[52]

Only a few weeks into the 1978 football season, all hell broke loose when news of the *Playboy* photo shoot was leaked to the press. Blinded by their own sexism and their inability to grasp the contradictions in their efforts to play the skin game, the league's office and team owners were ill prepared for the stir the *Playboy* shoot would cause. Even though the franchises had consented to the photo shoots, they unceremoniously fired the women who posed for *Playboy*. The San Diego Chargers didn't just fire the women who posed; they disbanded their entire cheerleading squad. Dressing in tight-fitting body suits and go-go boots was acceptable on the sidelines, but striking similar poses nude or seminude for *Playboy* was not, even though the team had helped arrange the photographing of their cheerleaders. Charger owner Gene Klein sent Tank Younger, the team's assistant general manager, to face the music from the press and their former employees. In his playing days during the 1950s, Younger had been among the first African Americans to play in the NFL. Now, he was operating as a lackey of sorts for the team ownership. Meanwhile, Diahann "Dee" Miller, one of the members of the Broncos' Pony Express and the only African American to appear in the *Playboy* pictorial, was reportedly arrested for supposedly trying to pick the pocket of an undercover police officer, though charges against her were dropped. She, too, was fired by her employers.

Many of the fired cheerleaders rightly decried the hypocrisy and sexism behind the actions of the league. Jackie Rohrs, one of the Chicago Honey Bears who was dismissed for posing for *Playboy*, pointedly asked, "We were never told, 'No, you can't pose for *Playboy*' . . . and what do they think *Playboy* is, *Good Housekeeping*?" Rhonda Bosworth, the director of the Chargettes, felt the disbanding of her squad was actually because they had agreed to unauthorized paid appearances rather than the *Playboy* pictorial itself. "We feel we should be getting a little bit of glory and side benefits outside of just being on the field," she told the press. Though many fans and journalists criticized the firing of the cheerleaders, in the end none of them found enough public sympathy to force the teams to hire them back. Their careers as NFL entertainers were over. During the league meetings in October 1978, NFL commissioner Pete Rozelle cheekily raised questions about the league's "hands off" policy vis-à-vis team cheerleaders. He urged teams to do a better job screening prospective cheerleaders to ensure that they would not pose nude or commit other sorts of tasteless acts. Then the meetings moved on to other pressing matters.[53]

Meanwhile, the Cowboys went to war against Jimenez's agency and the company that produced the "Ex–Dallas Cowboys Cheerleaders" poster. The team filed a lawsuit against the maker of the poster for copyright infringement and to protect the image of the club's cheerleaders. "It's a poster done in bad taste," Tex Schramm insisted. Jimenez, well acquainted with the ways of the image-conscious Cowboys, was unsurprised. "When you're a big corporation and you see a little guy more popular than you are, you get worried," she told the *Washington Post*. "You can see why the Cowboys wanted it stopped." The lawyer representing Scoreboard Posters attacked Schramm's argument. "I think the poster's making a valid social statement, a valid first amendment criticism: Are the Cowboys selling football, or are they selling sex?"[54]

While the propaganda and legal battles prompted by the *Playboy* shoot raged, the Cowboys were presented with another problem when *Debbie Does Dallas* was shown in the Pussycat Theater in November 1978. The film would go on to be considered part of the so-called golden age of pornographic films of the 1970s. It centered on the story of Bambi Woods, a young woman who, along with a group of her friends, sought to make enough money to travel to Dallas to try out for the "Texas Cowgirls," a fictitious cheerleading group clearly modeled on the DCC. In the film's final scene, Debbie performs sex acts dressed in a blue-and-white uniform that is virtually identical to that of the Dallas Cowboys Cheerleaders. Images of Bambi Woods in uniform were used widely to market the film.

The team once again went to court, successfully arguing that the filmmakers' unauthorized usage of a virtually identical uniform was a case of trademark infringement. Though they eventually won their legal case, they were unable to stop the proliferation of sequels and other imitation pornographic films in the years to come. The legal victory became further evidence of Suzanne Mitchell's steely resolve. The gutsy, reed-thin woman who managed Schramm's dancers faced off against the Mafia-controlled pornography industry and won. For all the damage the team claimed the film made to the Cowboys trademark, in the end, the episode only created more publicity for the Dallas Cowboys Cheerleaders, Inc.

In their efforts to distinguish themselves from their competitors, Cowboys managers endlessly claimed that their cheerleaders stood for a tasteful, polite, wholesome sexiness. "People want a clean American apple pie image," Mitchell insisted. They want someone to look up to, someone who's up-front and first class."[55] Yet their own publications contradicted their claims—not just the 1977 poster, but also the centerfolds the team published in *Cowboys Weekly* magazine. The Scholz sisters—Suzette, Stephanie, and Sheri—who were once the golden girls of the DCC in the late 1970s and early 1980s brilliantly articulated the central contradiction in the DCC enterprise years later in their tell-all memoir:

> How do you tap into the paradox of the sexy, wholesome girl? Well, take Miss America and dress her in hot pants and a halter top. Then put her out on a football field grinding out a lot of provocative dances, but the whole time keep telling the fans that these are good girls, wholesome girls. Barrage the fans with the girl-next-door rhetoric while you tease, tease, tease. Tell them they're not seeing what they're seeing. Make them feel like they got caught in the spin cycle of some giant brainwashing machine. Get them hot over these girls, then tell the fans they can't have them. They're sweet and untouchable.[56]

What was at stake in the Great Cheerleading War of 1978 was not decency or wholesomeness, but rather who could legitimately profit from the athletic labor of these women and who could not. What the Texas Cowgirls and, to some extent, the women who posed for *Playboy* sought to do was to benefit more fully from the products of their sexualized labor. They were trying to operate by the rules of supply and demand. But neither the Cowboys nor the editors of *Playboy* were really invested in letting the market determine the value of these women.

*   *   *

*I like to express myself through dance. I like to see people
feel what I feel when they watch my movements. My
message is mostly love.*
DALLAS COWBOYS CHEERLEADER VONCIEL BAKER

Dallas Cowboys Inc. and the NFL were the winners of the Great
Cheerleading War of 1978. They endured the negative publicity and toned down their cheerleading acts for a while. Eventually they returned to the Schramm-Mitchell formula, and many
of these cheerleading squads remain firmly entrenched on NFL
sidelines. Yet, all the fierce debates and hand wringing about
exploitation and objectification tend to overlook the fact that
for many of the young women who labored for the NFL and for
other professional leagues, cheerleading was never about making money or about gratifying men. For some, joining the Dallas
Cowboys Cheerleaders was certainly driven by dreams of glamour, fame, and maybe even fortune. But, especially for many of
the women who were working class and socially marginalized, it
was also about self-fulfillment and self-expression. In this sense,
the sexual revolution on the sidelines gave them something that
allowed them to dance even as they were grossly underpaid by
their cheap employers.

Many sports television directors and male fans imagined all the
Dallas Cowboys Cheerleaders as buxom blondes. But the women
who danced on the sidelines at Texas Stadium were more varied
than the blonde stereotype suggested. Some of the ethnic and racial diversity of the squad was based on Mitchell's plan to con-
struct a team that could attract fans from all backgrounds. But
the consistent presence of nonwhite women on the squad pre-
dated Mitchell's arrival. In fact, though the Cowboys tended to
foreground their white cheerleaders, the real poster children of
the team's dancing squad were their black dancers, especially Vanessa and Vonciel Baker, both of whom were the longest-tenured

members of the group during the 1970s. While SMU and the Cowboys profited from the athletic talents of black football players from local predominantly black high schools like Dallas Lincoln and South Oak Cliff, so, too, did the Cowboys cheerleaders profit from the athletic talents of young black women from the same schools.

Vanessa Baker began her tenure with the cheerleaders as a high school senior in 1970, when the group was directed by Dee Brock. She was a cheerleader at Dallas's Lincoln High School when her teacher encouraged her to try out for the Cowboys. Aside from the one year she did not make the team, 1972, Vanessa performed on the sidelines every season during the 1970s. She became one of the leaders of the squad, and in many ways she exemplified what cheerleading could do for young women. Throughout her time dancing for the Cowboys, she attended college and became an educator, working as a special education teacher and eventually as a school principal. Still, her commitment to her cheerleading job was total, even though it meant missing her graduation. When the team discovered this, they arranged a special graduation ceremony for her during halftime of a game in 1977. Allowing a black woman to graduate at Texas Stadium generated good publicity for the Cowboys, but it was also a powerful moment for Vanessa Baker.

Vanessa's tenure as a Dallas Cowboys Cheerleader was part of a longer life of bigger and better things. Such was also the case for Vonciel, her sister. Unlike her sister, who was outgoing, as a youth Vonciel was shy. She sought to follow in her sister's footsteps by trying out for the cheerleading team at Lincoln. But she did not make the team. Encouraged by her sister, she tried out for the cheerleading team in college at the predominantly white Texas Lutheran College, and she made the squad. Like her sister, she went on to be one of the longest-tenured cheerleaders with the Cowboys, missing one season to have her son. And like all the women who danced for the Cowboys, she juggled various domestic and work responsibilities to keep her cheerleading career going. The Baker sisters are now recognized as black cheerleading pioneers, not merely by the team when they want to showcase the club's racial diversity, but also by subsequent black cheerleading groups.[57]

Dancing for the Dallas Cowboys was particularly appealing to young women from small towns, even those who self-identified as tomboys. Carrie O'Brien was a former Apache Belle who made the 1972 squad. As a girl, she dreamed of playing quarterback for a football team, but gender conventions necessitated that she had to settle for being a cheerleader. Tami Barber, who was cast by Mitchell as the cute blonde with pigtails when she performed for the Cowboys in the late 1970s, found herself as a Dallas Cowboys Cheerleader. Like other cheerleaders who came from small towns, she found the cheerleading life exhilarating. "I was a twenty-year-old who was experiencing fame, and I was from a small town," she recalled in the film *Daughters of the Sexual Revolution*. "And my parents were proud of me. I was somebody, and that was really all that mattered."

A similar story emerges in Sherrie McCorkle's recollections of her cheerleading days. McCorkle was from rural Collinsville, a small town north of Dallas. Like Nell Davis, she was drawn to dancing as a form of resistance to the strict gender conventions of the Bible Belt. In her hometown, dancing in school was strictly prohibited. When she decided to try out for the Cowboys in 1976, she did not tell her family. Ironically, as much as the Cowboys cheerleaders might have reinforced women's sexual objectification, for many of the women, dancing was a form of rebellion against the male-dominated, patriarchal world. In this sense, the young women who danced for the Cowboys were similar to the young men who embarked on careers as athletes. Athletic labor meant more than material advancement. It meant respect and self-fulfillment.

Cheerleading for the Cowboys could also be a ticket to a good time, and good times could be had in late-1970s Dallas. This was the era of disco, which, even with its simplistic arrangements and seemingly vacuous culture, provided important outlets for young women, as it did for gay men, during the 1970s. Mitchell's rules did not stop DCC women from dancing in clubs in the off hours. The tales of partying cheerleaders that were revealed by the team's critics who were eager to debunk the "America's sweethearts" image belie the simple fact that the disco scene was a channel of self-expression and desire for young women. Even second-wave feminist critics of cheerleading overlooked the possibility that unapologetically inhabiting one's sexuality was more than simply succumbing to male objectification. "It was during the seventies that the sexual revolution burrowed deeply into American culture, with disco operating as both cause and effect," Alice Echols has astutely written.[58] Some converted their celebrity into fun times with other men and women, throwing Cowboys propaganda to the wind. Others used their time with the Cowboys to forge bonds with other women in a sorority-like sisterhood whose demanding schedule and training regimen allowed them to push themselves as far as they could go individually and collectively.

Becoming further entrenched in professional sports during the 1980s, the Dallas Cowboys Cheerleaders served as a source of inspiration, even as opportunities to participate in sports were increasing for girls and young women. For aspiring young women who had dancing ability, the Dallas Cowboys Cheerleaders were role models. Their presence on the sideline suggested that for women spectators, football games at Texas Stadium could be re-envisioned as "ladies night" at the club rather than as a simple dude-dominated affair on the gridiron. In an era when the Title IX revolution was just getting started, cheerleading provided—and still provides—a space for female sisterhood and individual self-expression for athletically inclined young women.

*   *   *

Tex Schramm's reign as Cowboys team president came to an abrupt end in 1989 after Jerry Jones, yet another rich oilman, bought the team. Jones fired the legendary Tom Landry, and Schramm left the team soon thereafter. Tex Schramm's front office had finally succumbed to the forces that it helped unleash on the sports world. Clint Murchison's oil fortune enabled Schramm and Landry to profit handsomely from the cold calculations they had made for decades, while the men and women who worked for them on the field were undercompensated for their labor. Now a new owner seized the Cowboys brand, made his own calculations, and concluded that the services of Landry and Schramm were no longer needed.

Suzanne Mitchell followed Schramm out the door soon thereafter. It was not surprising that the man who sought to remake the Cowboys in his own image was not going to be able to work with such a tough and ambitious woman as the longtime leader of the team's cheerleading squad. The regime change provoked not only Mitchell's departure but also the departure of fourteen Dallas Cowboys Cheerleaders after Jones insisted they perform for his business associates, wear skimpier uniforms, fraternize with players, and appear in beer commercials. "It appeared to me that we were being treated as bimbos," former cheerleader Cindy Villarreal recalled years later, "and I wasn't a bimbo."[59] Since the heyday of the DCC, NFL cheerleaders have remained a grossly underpaid class of laborers, even though an increasing number of them have sued their former employers for wage theft, substandard working conditions, sexual harassment, and other forms of abuse and exploitation. The persistence of the underpaid NFL cheerleader is one of the legacies of the sexual revolution that occurred on the sidelines during the 1970s.

* * *

Texas was the site of some of the fiercest battles prompted by the feminist movement and the sexual revolution. The National Women's Conference in Houston, the resistance to the implementation of Title IX, and the debates prompted by the Dallas Cowboys Cheerleaders made the state a key battleground for what womanhood and sexuality was supposed to mean in the United States during the 1970s. The Dallas Cowboys football franchise—the team that played a decisive role in the professionalization of sports marketing and sports management—found itself in the midst of these struggles. These conflicts exposed the contradictory tendencies of the sexual revolution. Women's sexuality was commodified, celebrated, and/or vilified in a context where they struggled—and continue to struggle—for equal rights and access.

As the sexual revolution and the feminist movement were raging on the sidelines of Texas Stadium, another monumental change was unfolding in the world of Texas basketball—not in Dallas or Houston, but in an often overlooked city in South Texas.

CHAPTER 7

The Greek, the Iceman, and the Bums

THE BEER WAS FLOWING IN SECTION 20 OF CONVENTION CENTER ARENA IN downtown San Antonio on February 28, 1976, and apparently so was the guacamole. This section of the arena was controlled by the Baseline Bums, the official fan club of the San Antonio Spurs, the new professional basketball team in the city. Since their creation in 1973, the Spurs, of the upstart American Basketball Association (ABA), took San Antonio by storm by playing compelling basketball and by cultivating a rabid fan base among the city's working-class population, including its Mexican American majority. Dime beer night promotions also helped bring the fans to the arena. Unlike today, when beer is sold from the draft and served in plastic cups, in the '70s the cold stuff was sold in aluminum cans, which could be used as weapons to be tossed at opposing players or officials. On this night, the target of the Baseline Bums' ire was the Denver Nuggets, one of the Spurs arch rivals.

In February 1976, the Spurs were in the midst of a set of fiercely competitive games against the league-leading Nuggets. The rivalry spilled over onto the sports pages, where media members dutifully reported on the salvos fired by both clubs. Spurs coach Bob Bass threatened Larry Brown, his counterpart with the Nuggets, to stop razzing the Spurs' best player, George Gervin. In turn, Brown declared to the press that the Spurs were a "dirty team." But he didn't leave it there. "The fans always get on me during the 10-cent Pearl nights or whatever it is," he whined to the press. Then he uttered a taunt that would come back to haunt him and live on in Spurs lore: "The only thing I like about San Antonio is the guacamole salad."[1]

When the Nuggets came to town a little more than a week later, the fans in San Antonio were ready. Before the game, members of the Baseline Bums gave the coach a dose of Texas hospitality by presenting him with ingredients to make a guacamole salad. During the game, which the Spurs won in a typical ABA high-scoring shootout 134–122, Gervin scored thirty-three points and his backcourt mate, James Silas, added thirty-five points. But the real story of the evening was the activities of the Baseline Bums in the stands. The Bums taunted Larry Brown by hanging him in effigy in section 20. It is impossible to separate fact from fiction in the last part of the story. Some remember Brown being doused with a bowl of guacamole by the Bums as he walked into the tunnel under their section. Years later, Brown seemed to give credence to the guacamole bath story when he recalled people hitting him with avocados and throwing dip on him. Others omit the dip and simply remember the flying avocados. Each story shows that opponents messed with Spurs fans at their peril. And the fact that the subtext was the guacamole, a staple in the diets of Mexican-origin peoples, indirectly revealed the stamp of Latino culture in the Spurs fan base.

The foundation of professional basketball in Texas was laid in San Antonio. Today, the San Antonio Spurs are known for their extraordinary run of winning seasons and championships during the early 2000s, led by Hall of Fame stars Tim Duncan, David Robinson, Tony Parker, Manu Ginobli, and of course their legendary coach, Gregg Popovich. Since 1999, the Spurs have been perennial championship contenders and have won four NBA titles and well-deserved acclaim for their sustained excellence. They are easily the most successful of the four ABA franchises that merged into the NBA and are one of the great teams in pro basketball history. Yet despite their remarkable success, the Spurs remain largely overlooked in US sport history and even in histories of sport in Texas. Aside from Terry Pluto's classic history of the ABA, virtually nothing has been written about the history of one of the most successful Texas professional sports franchises.[2]

The roots of this success on the court, and—as important— off the court, date back to the 1970s, when the team emerged as a franchise in the American Basketball Association. The Spurs, like the upstart league itself, creatively showcased the game with style and finesse while creating a space for marginalized fans in a city that has often been characterized as second class by the national and state media punditry. Unlike many NBA arenas today, which all seem to be cut from the same cloth, the AT&T Center in San Antonio still illustrates the impact of that era on the franchise, even if it is largely straightjacketed by contemporary corporate design and marketing. As you walk past such heavily corporatized concession areas such as the Bud Light Pavilion, the Taco Cabana food stand, and the HEB Fan Zone, you'll find hints of the team's renegade past. An installation with images of the team's early years can be found near one of the main entrances to the arena. And the Baseline Bums are still around, though they've been tamed by their new role as part of the team's official hospitality operation. The team's survival in a city defined as a "small market" was due to a unique combination of far-sighted management, a risk-taking professional league, talented athletes, and an eager fan base that made San Antonio one of the most unique sports cities in Texas and the United States. It helped that they were the only pro team in town, but nevertheless the Spurs helped remake San Antonio, once known as a high school football town, into a big league city with national visibility.

It was the San Antonio Spurs, not the Houston Rockets or the Dallas Mavericks, that first demonstrated that pro basketball can flourish in a region dominated by football. The fact that this revolution was ushered in by a franchise in a city often overlooked because of its predominantly Mexican American, blue-collar fan base is not insignificant. And it is significant that it was a sports team in the Texas-Mexico borderlands, like the legendary Texas

Western NCAA men's team in El Paso, that helped usher in more inclusive sporting cultures that foregrounded the talents and aspiration of the region's Mexican American and black populations. Much of this can be pinned on the Spurs' roots in the American Basketball Association.

* * *

No professional sports entity epitomized the rebellious and innovative spirit of the late 1960s and early 1970s than the ABA. While Major League Baseball, the National Football League, and the National Basketball Association (NBA) sought to micromanage the integration of black athletes into their leagues, the ABA, by contrast, eager to attract the best talent to compete with the established NBA, embraced black players and black athletic aesthetics. In 1967, the league was launched with eleven franchises. Following in the footsteps of Lamar Hunt and the AFL, the owners—pulled together by Dennis Murphy, a Southern Californian sports entrepreneur—sought to crack open the establishment league's stranglehold on professional basketball. They calculated that the NBA was vulnerable to competition and more willing to accommodate new franchises. They were correct on the league's vulnerability, but they misjudged the NBA's willingness to welcome new investors.

Like all upstart professional sports leagues, the ABA was in financial turmoil throughout its existence. But it was a revolutionary sporting enterprise whose legacy lives on in professional basketball today. The ABA pioneered the three-point shot, up-tempo styles of play, and of course its iconic red, white, and blue basketball that was widely derided by the "brown ball" NBA but turned out to be a stroke of marketing genius. The league pushed professional basketball into untapped areas of the Midwest, South, and Southwest. Aside from New York and Los Angeles, the league tried to establish teams in smaller cities that did not have professional basketball franchises, many of them in the Sunbelt. Franchises came and went throughout its nine-year history, but the league stubbornly hung around, thanks to innovative marketing and a willingness to spend money on talented basketball players. The league engaged in a war for basketball talent, and it convinced players and even referees to come over from the NBA. The league revolutionized professional basketball by creating more job opportunities for players, which drove up salaries and gave basketball players unprecedented bargaining power vis-à-vis the NBA. As in baseball, the arc of history was bending toward the bargaining power of players.

The ABA story is also a Texas story, because two of the original ABA franchises were in the Lone Star State: the Houston Mavericks and the Dallas Chaparrals. The Mavericks floundered through two forgettable seasons and were sold and moved to North Carolina. Meanwhile, the Dallas Chaparrals stumbled through six inauspicious seasons in North Texas. The Chaps, as they were nicknamed by the press, never became more than a nondescript basketball franchise in football-crazy Dallas. The Chaparrals seldom drew more than a few hundred fans while they played their home games in Memorial Auditorium in downtown Dallas. In their first few years, they built their team around Cliff Hagan, an aging but still effective white Hall of Famer basketball star who was the Chaps' player-coach. In 1970, desperate for fans, they tried to rebrand themselves as the Texas Chaparrals in an attempt to regionalize their fan base by playing home games in Fort Worth and Lubbock in addition to Dallas. This plan also backfired.

Fans continued to stay away, and the team ownership somehow concluded that the paltry attendance figures were due to the preponderance of black players on the team. Unlike many of their fellow owners, Chaps managers were oblivious to the black freedom struggle's impact on the sporting world. In the summer of 1972, they traded two of their best players, Donnie Freeman and John Brisker, to the Indiana Pacers for one white player, Bob Netolicky, a serviceable forward who was not as talented as the players traded for him. Joe Geary, the Chaps' managing partner, made no bones about his rationale for the trade: "Last year Dallas had only two white players . . . compared to 10 black players and we drew less than 100 fans a game who were colored," Geary explained. "A bunch of people want white faces, someone they can identify with."[3] Geary's usage of the term "colored" in a period when the preferred and widely used term of the time was "black" illustrates the backward-looking mentality of the team's ownership group.

Geary's argument that white fans would cheer only for white players overlooked the fact that all pro basketball teams by the early 1970s featured black frontline players, including those in other ABA franchises in cities with sordid racial histories, such as Indianapolis. Not surprisingly, the Chaps' black players, led by Steve "Snapper" Jones, the future longtime basketball television personality, were not happy with the ownership's statements and threatened to boycott games. Though the team's owners retracted their statements, the damage was done. The 1972–1973 season turned out to be the worst in franchise history as the Chaparrals finished in last place with a 28–56 record. By the spring of 1973, the club's owners were ready to throw in the towel and sell the team.

They were lucky to find willing investors in San Antonio, which was often positioned as the sleepy stepchild of Houston and Dallas. Unlike those cities, San Antonio was not based on the region's energy economy and instead was based on tourism and its deeply rooted military industrial complex. It was—and is—a predominantly Mexican American, working-class urban center, and most sports entrepreneurs did not see it as a viable market for professional sports, despite its long history of minor league baseball. But Angelo Drossos felt an investment in an Alamo City sports franchise was worth the risk, and he turned out to be the right person to undertake the task of helping establish a professional sports team there.

The San Antonian of Greek descent was a classic self-made man. A former boxer and boxing promoter, he attended Central Catholic High School and St. Mary's University. In the early 1960s, he started working as a car salesman for Billy Joe "Red"

McCombs, the auto dealer magnate who eventually earned fortunes through his network of car dealerships. Drossos later became a stockbroker at Dean Witter, and his background in sales, banking, and boxing prepared him to be a tough negotiator. His business savvy was written all over the deal that brought the Chaps to San Antonio. He worked out an imaginative arrangement in which he, McCombs, and thirty-six other investors would lease, rather than buy, the team from the Dallas group and move it to San Antonio if they could prove they had $800,000 of working capital to run the franchise. The Drossos group then had the option to buy the team within two years. The desperate Chaps owners had little choice but to agree to these terms, and the team relocated to the Alamo City and was renamed the San Antonio Spurs in April 1973.[4] The new nickname, entered in a team-sponsored contest by Mike Vavala, finished first ahead of the perhaps more San Antonio–appropriate name of Aztecs. Vavala won two season tickets and a trip to an ABA playoff game in the upcoming season. He had no idea how fortunate he turned out to be. "San Antonio Spurs. It does seem to have a nice ring," opined the *Express*.[5]

As was the case with urban elites throughout the country, San Antonian boosters sought to put their city on the map through urban revitalization projects. Spurred by their contacts with President Lyndon Johnson, they staged the 1968 World's Fair, which, like most mega events, turned out to be a financial failure for San Antonio, though it did help to promote the city to visitors from throughout the Americas. Like so many urban renewal projects of the post–World War II era, HemisFair '68 also resulted in the displacement of residents who lived in the neighborhoods south of downtown. But one of the buildings that turned out to have a substantial afterlife once the fair was torn down was Hemis-Fair Arena (a.k.a. Convention Center Arena), a ten-thousand-seat arena that gave San Antonio something Dallas did not have: a suitable facility for basketball. The 1960s and '70s were also the period when the city's Mexican American and black populations were starting to enjoy the promises of full citizenship. The complex tripartite racial system, in which local whites dominated a city with a Latino demographic majority and a smaller African American minority, gave segregation a different dynamic in this South Texas city.[6]

Like so many sports entrepreneurs of the period, Angelo Drossos had virtually no background in sports management. But he knew how to negotiate, and he knew he had to hire the right people to help him run his team, even though he remained the ultimate decision maker in the Spurs operation and let everyone know it. As team broadcaster and executive Terry Stembridge recalled to Terry Pluto, Drossos "fell in love with running a basketball team."[7]

Unlike the ownership group of the Chaps, the Spurs management team actively cultivated fans among the local black and Latino population. Right from their first season in San Antonio, the Spurs broadcast their games in Spanish on KCOR radio, the pioneering US Spanish-language radio station that had been on the air since the 1940s.[8] Moreover, a little-known fact about the Spurs ownership group is that it included four African American investors: Joseph A. Pierce; Jim Hadnott and his sister-in-law, Janis Hadnott; and Robert Hilliard. The Hadnotts and Pierces were all physicians who represented the upwardly mobile class of black Texans of the civil rights era. Pierce, along with his energetic wife, Aaronetta, became major promoters of black art in the city and were active in the community's cultural arts scene. Their initial modest investments turned out to be a pretty good deal for the Pierces and the Hadnotts when the Drossos group sold the team in the late 1980s. More than just a simple footnote in the history of the Spurs, the Pierces and the Hadnotts illustrate the inclusionary spirit of the franchise in that period.[9]

* * *

A modest crowd of 5,879 spectators came to Convention Center Arena to watch the Spurs play their first game against the San Diego Conquistadors on October 10, 1973. Coaching the Conquistadors that night was NBA legend Wilt Chamberlain, who had signed with the team after retiring from the Los Angeles Lakers. Throughout the first few months of the season, Spurs attendance figures averaged around three thousand, the average size of most ABA crowds. Over time, however, the fans started coming in larger numbers after Drossos and his general manager went to work on acquiring talent. In a few months, they traded for Swen Nater, a six-foot, eleven-inch young center who had been a backup center to All-American Bill Walton at UCLA but was coming into his own as the starting center for the Virginia Squires. The owner of the Squires, Earl Foreman, had a knack for signing talented players, but he struggled to keep them on his payroll. Drossos zeroed in on Foreman and worked out a deal for Nater in exchange for badly needed cash.

But the biggest deal came in January 1974, when Drossos once again convinced the vulnerable Squires owner to sell a budding star named George Gervin for $225,000. The transaction was originally made as an under-the-table agreement between the two owners during the ABA All-Star break because Foreman did not want negative publicity for a franchise that had already lost All-Stars Charlie Scott, Julius Erving, and Nater. When news of the Gervin deal was leaked to the media, Foreman changed his mind and fought to keep the now bewildered young star. ABA commissioner Mike Storen tried to file a legal injunction to keep Gervin with the Squires, using his powers as commissioner to argue that it was in the league's best interest for the star forward to remain in Virginia. But Storen lost his battle in court and Gervin wound up in San Antonio, where he would star for the franchise for the next ten years.[10]

The Spurs turned out to be successful on the court in their first season in San Antonio. As the team started winning, led by its new frontline players Gervin and Nater, the fans in this high school football and baseball town demonstrated that they were willing to come out to watch pro basketball. In their first season, the team finished with a 45–39 record. They made the ABA playoffs, but they lost a tough seven-game series to the defending league champion, the Indiana Pacers. But Drossos wasn't satisfied, and his next big move was firing the well-liked head coach Tom Nissalke twenty-seven games into the 1974–1975 season and replacing him with Bob Bass. The move was initially poorly received by the press and the fans, since the team had a winning record of 17–10 at the time of Nissalke's firing for the nebulous reason of "conduct detrimental to the franchise."[11] But hiring Bass turned out to be a pivotal move, for it gave the team a coach who could better maximize the talents of its roster. John Trowbridge, the *San Antonio Light*'s sports editor, described Bass as a "short, stocky, bespectacled man from west Texas who, if he had been wearing a collar and touting a bible, could have passed for your friendly down-home preacher."[12] To be sure, his short stature and West Texas drawl made him seem to be an unlikely basketball coach.

But Bob Bass was actually a basketball visionary. Like other successful white coaches in the civil rights era, Bass figured out that adhering to Jim Crow segregation would not help him advance in his career. Bass had many of his formative experiences playing and coaching at the small Oklahoma Baptist College, where he recruited Buddy Hudson, who went on to break the color line at Bass's school and again at the University of Oklahoma, where he transferred one year later. Indeed, Bass became a pioneer in signing black players during his college coaching days at Oklahoma Baptist and Texas Tech. His decision to recruit Hudson was based on the fact that he saw the game changing from set plays orchestrated by coaches to more improvisation based on the quickness and athleticism of players. "When I played I'd walk the ball up the court, move it around, a guy would be open for a 15-foot shot and 25 passes later, we'd wind up taking that same 15-foot shot," he told the *Light* soon after he was hired by the Spurs. "Gradually we got more talent, the black athlete came in, we started moving, pressing more, running more, playing faster. The black player had a lot to do with the changes because he brought individualism into the game," Bass insisted.[13] With players like Hudson and Al Tucker, another African American recruit, Bass went on to a successful 275–146 record in fifteen seasons at Oklahoma Baptist, winning the NAIA title in 1965. In 1969, while coaching at Texas Tech in Lubbock, he signed Ron Douglas, the school's first black varsity player.[14]

Given this background, it is not surprising that Bass coached a style of play that emphasized speed and athleticism. Still, his resume as ABA coach and executive for the Dallas Chaparrals, Miami Floridians, and Memphis Tams was unimpressive. But the West Texas native understood how to reach the ballplayer of the 1970s by implementing a free-flowing, fast-paced style of play with the Spurs. "The main thing I wanted to do was get the guys to feel loose and just play to their talents," Bass recalled to Terry Pluto. "I let them loose, and by the end of the season we were averaging 116 points [per game], second-best in the ABA."[15] After Bass took over in December 1974, the team, which had been stifled by Nissalke's patterned offense, remade itself into a freelancing, fast-breaking group that lit up the scoreboard. Gervin, the team's new star, proved the worth of Bass's run-and-gun philosophy when he torched the lowly Memphis Sounds for fifty-one points in the middle of a seven-game winning streak in February 1975. After a rough extended road trip, the Spurs hit their stride and finished another strong regular season with a 51–31 record. Bass's coaching philosophy made the team exciting to watch, but he was helped by the unique talents of a pencil-thin shooter from Detroit, Michigan.

* * *

George Gervin was to San Antonio what Babe Ruth was to New York. Babe Ruth was baseball in New York City, he was the New York Yankees. Well, Gervin was the San Antonio Spurs and he was the symbol of basketball in this town.
ANGELO DROSSOS, QUOTED IN TERRY PLUTO, *LOOSE BALLS*

George "Iceman" Gervin was a quintessential ABA player. Like so many of the league's stars, he seemingly came from nowhere.

In the early 1970s, scouting in professional basketball was not nearly as robust as it was in Major League Baseball or the National Football League. Gervin was among the first wave of ballplayers who turned professional without playing four years of college ball. Spencer Haywood's signing with the ABA's Denver Rockets as an underclassman in 1969, and his subsequent successful lawsuit against the NBA, ushered in a new era of freedom for young players who wanted to play basketball for a living.[16] The ABA facilitated the first challenge to the NCAA's domination of young basketball talent. And like many black players during the 1970s, sports enabled Gervin to achieve a rags-to-riches story. Born in inner-city Detroit, Michigan, in 1952, Gervin was raised by his mother in a family of seven. Though he, like many black athletes of this period, played up his "ghetto" background for white sportswriters and fans, he was raised solidly working class in a city where black workers had achieved a degree of stability before it was undone by the decline of the region's auto industry. White sportswriters learned to spin the "up from the ghetto" narrative when writing about black athletes, whether they came from the ghetto or not. James Solomon, a longtime educator in Detroit and Gervin's high school coach, scoffed at the stories of Gervin's ghetto background, telling the *New York Times* in 1979 that he "lived in a relatively modest neighborhood. No big, fancy homes or big, fancy cars. It wasn't the epitome of what a ghetto would be."[17]

The young Gervin was pencil thin, and his slender stature became more pronounced as he shot up from five feet seven to six feet six while starring in basketball at Martin Luther King High School in the late 1960s. His fame led him to be recruited by Long Beach State to play for legendary coach Jerry Tarkanian. He quickly found out that he did not like the West Coast and he returned home to Michigan, where he played college ball for Eastern Michigan University in Ypsilanti. He was eventually discovered by former NBA great Johnny "Red" Kerr, who was then a scout for the ABA's Virginia Squires. Kerr was astonished by the razor-thin Gervin's ability to shoot and score with ease. However, his tenure playing at Eastern Michigan abruptly ended when he was kicked off the team for punching an opposing player. After a pit stop with a sandlot team in Pontiac, Michigan, Kerr convinced the Squires to sign him in 1972. At Virginia, the then nineteen-year-old found himself playing alongside the young Julius Erving, then a rising superstar who was developing his reputation as "Dr. J." But Earl Foreman couldn't afford them, and both went on to star for other teams.

Gervin's game was the essence of 1970s basketball creativity. He was first and foremost a scorer. NBA historians often celebrate his patented shot: the finger roll. The shot, first popularized by Wilt Chamberlain, is a difficult maneuver to master. It is usually taken while the player is rising toward the basket. As the player jumps, he lifts the ball with his shooting hand and rolls it into the basket. But Gervin could roll it with enough force to bounce the ball off the glass and into the net, a truly difficult task to accomplish. Yet the finger roll was hardly a go-to shot for Gervin. Unlike many scorers in pro basketball today whose points come off fairly predictable isolation plays or three-point shots created by ball movement, Gervin, like Dr. J, got his points in a variety of ways: jumpers, shots off the glass from different angles, reverse layups, and hook shots. Improvisation was his method.

At six feet seven, he was an ideal height to play small forward, but he flourished after his coaches realized he was most effective when he played the guard position, where he could regularly shoot over shorter opponents. His leaping ability enabled him to hang in the air and make reverse layups and shoot over defenders who could not jump as high as he could. Even his jump shot had an irregular quality to it. At times, it could look flat with very little arc. At other times, he could hang in the air and arch the ball over shorter (or taller) opponents contesting his shot. He could also shoot off the dribble. His arms formed a diamond shape as he shot the ball. It almost looked like he pushed the ball to the hoop. Yet he rightly insisted that his style wasn't unorthodox at all. "My style isn't unusual," he said. "Anywhere you go in Detroit they shoot like I do."[18] That Detroit style propelled him to be one of the most accurate shooting guards in pro basketball history.

He made 50 percent of his shots for his entire career, which is a high percentage for a scoring guard. Paul Attner of the *Washington Post* aptly described Gervin's game this way: "George Gervin has created a Motown sound even the Supremes couldn't duplicate. His instruments are sweet jump shots and driving layups that flow with a slow, ice-cool rhythm. And his tunes almost always end with the same refrain: swish, swish, swish."[19]

The term *flow* perfectly encapsulates Gervin's movements on the basketball court. His "Iceman" nickname was given to him by Fatty Taylor, his former teammate with the Squires, because he was smooth and cool and never seemed to sweat. While other players of the 1970s sported mile-high afros and adorned themselves with wrist bands and knee pads, Gervin was quite vanilla in his style. He came on the court with his black, silver, and white Spurs uniform, knee-high tube socks, and not much else. The most outlandish aspect of his adornment was the word "Ice," which appeared on the back of his Spurs warm-up jacket. His hair was short by 1970s standards. He would sport a thin mustache and a goatee some years, giving the effect of a cool gangster without a menacing look on his face. "I'm conservative. I got the short hair, the pencil 'stache, the simple clothes,' he told Curry Kirkpatrick of *Sports Illustrated* in 1978, "I just do my thing and stay consistent."[20]

The Iceman's demeanor was consistently cool on the court. He seldom expressed emotion while he played. There were few fist pumps, celebratory gestures, or expressions of anger. Yet his unique style of play conveyed an enormous charisma. Still, his game, like everyone's, had weaknesses. He was not known for his play on defense, opting to exert most of his energy on the offensive end. He was quick, but not fast. He wasn't a great ball handler or a great passer. Some criticized him for not being a "clutch" shooter and for sometimes disappearing late in games. Terry Stembridge perceptively noted that "Ice would have 20-point first quarters, 30-point first halves, but he could be shut down for a while down the stretch because he was vulnerable to a good double-team."[21]

The Spurs in the Gervin era, like the ABA itself, seemed to

make pro basketball about playing for pleasure as much as for the purpose of winning basketball games. Gervin told the filmmakers of *Longshots: The Life and Times of the American Basketball Association*, an HBO documentary on the history of the ABA,

> We had to establish ourselves any way we can, but the only way we really could have done it is to be able to fill that basket up, and that's what the fans really admired about the ABA. You know, it was our fast-pace style; you really had a chance to show your skills and make some great moves and stuff because you stayed in the flow of the game, you know. That's the way I feel basketball is supposed to be played.[22]

Thus Gervin's competitive drive was less about wins and losses, and more about mastering the art of playing with flair and creativity. "I played basketball to entertain our fans," he has said. "I wanted our fans to go home and say, wow! Did you see that move that Ice laid down today?"[23] From the time he arrived in San Antonio until he was traded away in 1985, the Iceman left many basketball fans talking about the moves he laid down in arenas across the country. And in San Antonio, he was one of the key ingredients that made the Spurs a treasure in South Texas.

The Iceman was the team's star, but the Spurs of the mid- to late 1970s had an array of talented ballers on their roster. Drossos and Bass constructed an exciting and likable cross-racial roster of players that showcased much of the grassroots playground style of basketball that spurred the game's popularity during these years. The captain of the team was the underrated James Silas, one of the few holdovers from the franchise's days in Dallas. Born in Tallulah, Louisiana, Silas was another player who was largely disregarded by NBA clubs. He played his college ball at Stephen F. Austin, an NAIA school in Nacogdoches, Texas, where he averaged 30.7 points per game and led the school to a 29–1 record in his senior year. After he failed to hold a spot with the NBA Houston Rockets, he was picked up by the Chaparrals and then eventually became the lead guard of the Spurs. He was more of a scor-

George Gervin shooting his finger roll. Photo by Manny Millan.

ing point guard who complemented Gervin well by doing the bulk of the ball handling and passing, and taking many shots when the game was on the line. His signature shot was the fifteen-footer, which he could shoot off the dribble. Silas came into his own during the 1975–1976 season, the team's last in the ABA, when he averaged 23.8 points per game, 5.4 assists, 4 rebounds and 1.8 steals per game while shooting 52 percent from the field. Though his career was seriously curtailed by ankle and knee injuries, Silas was one of the best backcourt men in the league during the team's ascendance in the mid-1970s.

No one play epitomizes Silas's skills and clutch play, and the Spurs approach to basketball, in this period more than a game-on-the-line sequence toward the end of the memorable game seven playoff against the Washington Bullets in 1979. The Bullets, who had trailed most of the game, went ahead by two points on two free throws by Greg Ballard. Whereas today's coach would have attempted to micromanage the game by calling a time out to call a set play, then Spurs coach Doug Moe simply clapped his hands and let Silas take the team down the court for another score. "The Late Mr. Silas," as Stembridge loved to call him on the radio, did not need any instruction on what to do. Silas took the ball and dribbled across the half court line. As he approached the free throw line, he went into one of his patented moves. He did a quick

James Silas driving to the hoop against the Denver Nuggets during the 1974–1975 season. Photo by John Iacono.

crossover dribble, turned away from an oncoming double-team, and shot—and made—a clutch fifteen-footer to tie the game.

Silas and Gervin were the centerpieces of the new run-and-gun Spurs, but another first-round loss to the Pacers in the 1975 playoffs led Drossos to once again make some trades. In the summer of 1975, the "Ice Age" Spurs would form its core when Larry Kenon and Billy Paultz arrived in trades with the New York Nets. To Bob Bass, the trade for Kenon was particularly important: "After the Gervin deal, it's the most important trade this franchise ever made. I really think we became a winning team for the next eight years because of that deal."[24] The Kenon trade was particularly polarizing among fans and sportswriters, because it involved sending away the popular Swen Nater and longtime Spur/Chaparral Rich Jones. But Kenon's exceptional skill set was an upgrade over Nater's, especially for a team committed to an up-tempo style of play. "The ABA games were always fun to watch," John López recalled, "but the Spurs, playing that run-and-gun offense, were like a circus." He went on to say, "Here were these graceful athletes dashing up and down the floor as no athletes ever had done in San Antonio." To López, Kenon was a key to the fast break, the art of scoring baskets quickly before the opposing team could set up to defend their basket. "Larry Kenon is the best I've ever seen as a forward on the wing during a fast break," he insisted. "He could outrun anybody and finish the play."[25]

Kenon was born in Birmingham, Alabama, a city where the civil rights struggle encountered some of its most violent resistance. Though he said little about his background growing up in a town that was so violently racist that it was called "Bombingham," Kenon's court affect exuded a steely confidence, a refusal of black Alabamans to be crushed by the virulent racism of segregationist commissioner of public safety Eugene "Bull" Connor and Governor George Wallace. As a basketball player, Kenon was a proto–Kevin Durant, a long, lean, supremely athletic man who could dribble, shoot, and pass. Whereas Durant is the prototype of today's big man who shoots long-range three-point shots, Kenon preferred shots ten to fifteen feet from the basket, the cus-

Larry Kenon flying in the air during the 1976 ABA Dunk Contest. Photo by Carl Iwasaki.

tomary range for perimeter-oriented big men in the 1970s. But his favorite maneuver was to grab a rebound, take off down the length of the court, and slam dunk the ball. He was a six-foot, nine-inch forward who acted very much like a guard, by pushing the ball up the court and making a jump pass to a teammate for a layup. Sometimes his fondness for jumping left him caught out of position and vulnerable to turning the ball over. And sometimes he could be streaky by scoring in one game and disappearing the next. Still, he was one of the most exciting players in the league, and he made the Spurs nearly impossible to defend.

Then there was "the Whopper," Billy Paultz. If Silas, Gervin, and Kenon epitomized 1970s basketball athleticism, Paultz embodied the underdog status of the ABA and its team from San Antonio. The six-foot-eleven, 240-pound center out of St. John's University in New York City was a deceptively skilled big man whose talents were obscured by his rather unathletic appearance. Like Gervin and other ABA players, he left college ball before graduation to sign with the New York Nets, where he teamed with Dr. J and his rookie teammate Larry Kenon to lead the team to the 1974 ABA championship. Though his tall but awkward and unmuscular body made him seem almost cartoonish, he managed to compete with more talented players throughout an exemplary seventeen-year career in professional basketball.

Paultz's graceless appearance masked his basketball skills. He was a savvy inside player who knew how to position himself to snatch rebounds, set picks, and get himself open for short, ten- to fifteen-foot jump shots. Paultz used his remarkable shooting touch to score points. He could also shoot an old-school 1950s-era rolling hook shot. He was also a good shot blocker, leading the ABA with three blocks per game in his first season with the Spurs. He possessed all of the skills that got him to average fifteen to sixteen points and seven to ten rebounds per game during his four and a half years in San Antonio. Though he was a fixture in the New York basketball scene—he participated in the playground scene with Dr. J—Paultz smoothly transitioned to life in San Antonio. If Gervin represented the influence of Detroit basketball on the Spurs, then Paultz, in his own way with his East Coast background, embodied the influence of New York basketball.

* * *

At the start of the 1975–1976 season, the pieces were in place for a championship run. But as the Spurs were coming together, the league they belonged to was teetering on the verge of collapse. The Baltimore Claws, formerly the Memphis Sounds, folded before the season began, and the San Diego Sails, formerly the Conquistadors, also closed operations shortly thereafter. By early December, the Utah Stars, previously a model franchise with a loyal fan base, also folded. The league that started the season with ten teams was now down to seven, and it seemed that the end was near. Yet the ABA held on, spurred by the talents of its top three teams: the Spurs, the Denver Nuggets, and the New York Nets. Gervin, Silas, Kenon, and Paultz all made the All-Star team, a memorable event that featured the historic slam dunk contest, which was won by Julius Erving. While Dr. J's dunks stole the show, few recall that Gervin and Kenon were also among the league's stars who threw down some memorable dunks of their own that day.

The Spurs enjoyed another fifty-win regular season, finishing with a 52–32 record in third place behind the first-place Nuggets and second-place Nets. In the first round of the playoffs, San Antonio faced off against Dr. J's Nets in what turned out to be a fiercely contested series. The recent trades between the two teams added some tension to the series, but the Spurs suffered a devastating blow during the first game when James Silas broke his ankle and was out for the rest of the series. Indeed, the injury would have lasting consequence, as he would never return to the level of play he had before the injury. Still, the Spurs pulled out a game two win on the Nets' home court in Long Island, and they went up 2–1 after winning game three in front of a stoked-up crowd in San Antonio. In the fourth game of the series, they were on the verge of going up 3–1 when Dr. J made a last-second dunk after a controversial steal to give the Nets a narrow 110–108 win to tie the series in front of ten thousand outraged Spurs partisans. Meanwhile, Rich Jones, the former Spur who was now with the Nets, was at war with his former team and their fans. In the second quarter, he was in the middle of a brawl with the voluble Spurs guard George Karl that led to a riot-like atmosphere in the arena. Fans expressed their displeasure by flinging all sorts of projectiles onto the court. In the end, Jones and the Nets had the last laugh as they eliminated San Antonio in a decisive game seven victory.[26] The Nets went on to win the last ABA championship. Yet the bit-

Dr. J going for a rebound with Billy Paultz (5) and Larry Kenon (35) looking on. Photo by John D. Hanlon.

terly contested series showed how close the upstart Spurs came to taking a bit of the luster off the Dr. J legend by nearly denying him his second championship.

But wins and losses on the court were only part of the Spurs impact on the national sporting scene. In fact, the disappointment of another first round playoff loss subsided once the news of the merger of the ABA and NBA broke in the summer of 1976. This had been the desired outcome for many of the ABA's owners since the league's inception. In 1971–1972, ownership in both leagues seemed to be on the verge of an agreement, but their efforts were blocked by opposition in Congress and a lawsuit filed by the legendary NBA player Oscar Robertson, who successfully argued that a merger would be detrimental to the interests of professional basketball players. In the interim, players enjoyed the benefit of negotiating between the two leagues for the highest bidder for their services. After years of servitude to owners, NBA players, like those in Major League Baseball, had been able to gain a measure of leverage against professional basketball team owners. The Robertson suit successfully blocked the merger until 1976, when NBA commissioner Larry O'Brien came to an agreement with Robertson by insuring that the reserve clause would be abolished. With the suit resolved, an end of the nine-year ABA-NBA conflict was now possible if the will could be summoned among team owners.

Angelo Drossos, along with owners of the Nets and Nuggets, represented the interests of the ABA in the negotiations with the NBA, which was skillfully represented by league commissioner Larry O'Brien. With only six viable franchises left (the Virginia Squires had finally come to an inglorious end) and two more barely hanging on, the ABA owners were forced to negotiate with very little leverage except for the talent they had on their rosters. Finally, in June 1976, after weeks of intense negotiations, the Spurs, along with the New York Nets, the Indiana Pacers, and the Denver Nuggets joined the NBA.[27] But these teams paid a steep price to become part of the establishment league; they were each forced to pay a $3.2 million indemnity to join the NBA.

San Antonians were ecstatic that their city was now "big league." Mayor Lila Cockrell immediately began to lobby the public to support the expansion of the ten-thousand-seat HemisFair Arena to meet the NBA's twelve thousand minimum capacity requirement. Riding the wave of excitement of the team's admission to the NBA, Cockrell argued that shelling out $3.6 million to enlarge the arena "made good economic sense" because the "NBA franchise is the thing that will help our city achieve a national image."[28] During the next two and a half years, six thousand seats were installed by literally raising the roof to accommodate a second tier of seating. Much to the surprise of outsiders, the team that had failed in oil-rich Dallas was somehow succeeding in supposedly second-rate San Antonio. The Spurs franchise succeeded because of skilled leadership by Drossos, gifted athletes like George Gervin, and thousands of fans who regularly filled up HemisFair Arena and gave the team and the league a fan base and a basketball scene unlike any other.

* * *

If we have learned anything at all in the past few seasons about the San Antonio Spurs, it is that they are not a normal everyday pro basketball team. What they are fairly faithfully reflects their city, which is about as American as enchiladas and about as laid back as bedlam.

JOHN PAPANEK, "MUY LOCO DOWN IN SAN ANTONE," *SPORTS ILLUSTRATED*

Professional sports franchises like to portray themselves as representatives of their home city's identity. Owners frequently spin stories about their concern for the fans, particularly supposedly authentic blue-collar fans whose loyalties they manipulate to further their financial interests. These are fables often designed to legitimate their claim on civic identity. But in San Antonio, such tales, even if they can be exaggerated by nostalgia, come close to accurately reflecting the Spurs' relationship to the city's self-perception. Arguably no professional basketball team has had a fan base like those who claimed to be adherents of the Spurs, and no team has had a fan club quite like the Baseline Bums. When then general manager John Begzos organized the Bums in 1975, he probably had little inkling of the forces he was about to unleash. In his previous job as ticket manager for the San Antonio Brewers, the city's minor league baseball franchise, Begzos convinced David Doyle and Larry Braun, two local high school seniors, to head up a semiofficial fan club. After Begzos started working for the Spurs, he convinced Doyle and Braun to switch their allegiance to the city's new professional basketball team. Daunted by the prospect of rows of empty seats in Convention Center Arena, Begzos told Doyle and Braun that they could have the entire section of four-dollar seats for the discounted rate of one dollar per seat. Hence the Baseline Bums were born, a unique fan club whose rise to prominence in the stands paralleled the success of the team on the court. By the middle of the team's first season in San Antonio, the Bums were up and running and attracting members. "There's no prerequisite for admission to the club," the *San Antonio Light* sports editor John Trowbridge reported in February 1974. "Only that members attend as many games as possible, root like the devil for the home team, have a healthy set of lungs, an artistic flair (if you want to get into banner making), and a sound elbow to hoist a can or two of brews."[29]

One of the more memorable Bums who hoisted more than his share of brews was Ernest Muñoz Jr. The story, which seems to have some basis in fact, was that Muñoz, a shy truck driver, delighted the Convention Center Arena crowd by dancing during a Spurs game after downing a few beers. Seeing his impact on the crowd, Begzos sent over a few bucks to encourage Muñoz to drink a few more beers, and the truck driver turned dancer once again stirred up the crowd with his gyrations on the sidelines. Muñoz eventually became a local celebrity known as "Dancing Harry" in San Antonio; he was the face of the Baseline Bums and a fixture at Spurs games in their early years.

However, he was not the first Dancing Harry to stir up crowds at a pro basketball game. The original Dancing Harry was Marvin Cooper, an African American man who danced on the sidelines of Baltimore Bullets NBA games in the late 1960s and early 1970s. His appearances were inspired by then Bullets star Earl "the Pearl" Monroe, whose playground style of basketball made him a cult figure among basketball fans on the East Coast. When Monroe was traded to the New York Knicks in late 1971, Cooper followed him to New York, where he transferred his act to Madison Square Garden.[30] Cooper would don a hat and a cape, dance, and cast spells on opposing teams. But the conservative Knicks management was never fond of Cooper's performances on the sidelines. Undaunted, he made himself available to other teams who were interested in his services. Fittingly, it was an ABA franchise, the Indiana Pacers, who hired him during the 1975 playoffs. Later, Muñoz added his own contributions to the Dancing Harry phenomenon. He wore a black hat and a long mustache, and he gyrated to tunes on the sidelines during time-outs. Muñoz even married Deborah Lynn Smith, a fellow Baseline Bum, at halftime of a Spurs game in December 1975 before an overflowing crowd of 11,717.[31]

As years went by, the Bums became the heart of the team's fan base and were as much a part of the show at the Arena as the team itself. John Lopez, former journalist for the *San Antonio Light*, recalled to Terry Pluto that the Bums were "mostly Mexican guys who would go straight from work to the Lone Star Pavilion, where they sold pitchers of beer for a buck. They were just wasted and they'd yell and give the other team hell."[32] Perhaps López was remembering George Valle, a rotund Spurs fan who hung out at the Lone Star Pavilion and was a regular in section 20 for decades. Valle was one of the ringleaders of the Bums whose own act involved waving a large Texas flag that hung from the railing in front of the Bums' section. Valle loved to taunt opponents during the games and then commiserate with them afterward at the nearby Lone Star Pavilion. In the early 1980s, in a period when the Bums were supposedly toning down their act, Ronnie Jackson told *Washington Post* reporters that he was among the more modest beer drinkers of the group, claiming that he only "drank about 2 or 2½ six packs a game."[33]

Buoyed by attention from the press and from reactions by visiting teams, the Bums grew increasingly outrageous. The group grew to a membership of 120 strong. They were expected to pay their yearly fifteen-dollar season membership dues, buy season tickets, and root hard for the home team. They wore an assortment of T-shirts, pajamas, costumes, and uniforms that were mass-produced not by a sporting apparel conglomerate but by their own semiofficial fan club. Sports apparel production was often a grassroots phenomenon in the 1970s. They sported mega-phones and danced, sang, and cheered. They relished taunting and tormenting the opposition with various stunts and jeers, and numerous incidents between the Bums and Spurs opponents in-dicate they succeeded. "Where do you draw the line between en-thusiastically supporting your hometown team and harassing the visiting club?," the *Light* sports editor Bob Ostrom asked Spurs fans in 1976.[34] To many Spurs fans in this period, no such line ex-isted. They staged their indifference to their opponents by whip-ping out newspapers and pretending to read them while the oppo-sition's starting lineup was announced. During the 1975 playoffs, they antagonized Pacer stars Mel Daniels and George McGinnis to the point of provoking them to charge into the stands. Larry Brown endured their wrath with the avocado/guacamole shower after his dismissive comments about San Antonio.

After the merger with the ABA, NBA teams were forced to en-dure the wrath of San Antonio's faithful. Dave Cowens, the Bos-ton Celtics star center, had violent altercations with Spurs fans on more than one occasion. Some of their taunts crossed the line into the realm of the tasteless. The Bums once mocked nemesis Kareem Abdul-Jabbar of the rival Los Angeles Lakers by wear-ing goggles en masse to ridicule the star center for the goggles he wore to protect his eyes. On another occasion, they held up warped records after the star center lost his large record col-lection in a house fire in 1983. On yet another occasion, Bums mocked Chicago Bulls forward Quintin Dailey by staging a fake domestic altercation after the Bulls forward had been charged with sexual assault. Beer cans, beer cups, cigars, and other projec-tiles were known to fly out of the stands in the vicinity of section 20 and other parts of the arena during these years.[35] To journal-ists, particularly those outside San Antonio, the Bums epitomized the city's lack of sophistication and class. But to Spurs fans at the time, unbridled enthusiasm was the only way during those many nights at HemisFair Arena during the 1970s and 1980s. In an era when there were many unruly fan bases, the Bums stood out.

Today, the Baseline Bums are still going strong, holding down

The Baseline Bums, HemisFair Arena, San Antonio, 1975. Photo by John Iacono, Sports Illustrated.

three sections behind the basket on the eastern end of the plaza level of the AT&T Center. Gone are the days of Big George Valle, longtime Bums member, leading cheers with his gigantic Texas flag loaded up on cheap beers at pregame gatherings at the Lone Star Pavilion. Gone are the days when Begzos wondered how he could get the Bums to stop swearing so much. When I sat with the Bums during games in San Antonio in January 2014, it was clear that they had somewhat grudgingly left their rowdy reputation behind and become a kinder, gentler fan club that foregrounds their community service work as much as their unabashed loyalty to the Spurs. As then Bums president Bonnie Keammerer conceded to me, "We had to clean up our act."

The Bums were a big part of the show at the venue known as

HemisFair Arena, Convention Center Arena, or simply "the arena" by locals. Opened in 1968 as part of the complex of structures built for the World's Fair of 1968, the arena was designed as a facility that could house events after the fair was done. The building was a small and intimate, single-tier structure. But the building was largely underused aside from local sporting events and occasional NBA games played by the Houston Rockets, who were attempting to build up a fan base in San Antonio to make up for the lack of interest in the unremarkable team in their home city.

The arrival of the Spurs in 1973 breathed new life into the arena, converting it from an underutilized monument to urban renewal to a happening destination for the city's sports fans. By the team's second season in San Antonio, the crowds were regularly filling up the ten-thousand-seat facility, a perfect capacity for ABA crowds. The savvy Drossos scored a great deal for his team when city officials dubiously agreed to let the Spurs take all of the revenue from concessions sold at the games. Still, the arena was one of the best facilities in the league. It hosted the 1975 ABA All-Star game, a memorable affair put on by the Spurs front office that included Willie Nelson performing the National Anthem. The move to the NBA and the addition of a second tier of seating did not take away the intimate feel of the arena, though it did add pillars that created obstructions for some seats.

"This is maybe the hardest place in the league to play," Kevin Grevey of the Washington Bullets told the *Washington Post* in 1978. "I know none of us loves coming here; it's loud and they really root for their team, and they're right on top of you."[36]

Another unique feature of Spurs games in San Antonio was the arena's soundscape, which made players and fans feel like they were in the northern reaches of Mexico, though they were actually in the southern borderlands of the United States. Al Sturchio and the "sound of the Spurs" added to the South Texas atmosphere at the arena. Though a recording of the song "Cotton-Eyed Joe," an eerie reminder of the region's minstrel traditions, was often played at the beginning of games, the rest of the music was mostly played live by the musicians in Sturchio's band. Sturchio

The arena after the expansion. Note the pillars in the background. Photo by Manny Millan.

and his Mexican American bandmates played "Yellow Rose of Texas," "San Antonio Rose," Tejano conjunto tunes, and the Mexican ranchera "Volver, Volver," among other South Texas favorites. "That was on purpose," Wayne Witt, former director of communications for the Spurs, said. "We wanted that identity. That was all part of the aura, of opponents saying, 'Oh, geez, we got to go to San Antonio and play in that place, where all they do is play that loud Mexican music.'"[37]

Informed in part by their anti-ABA bias, mainstream basketball writers frequently belittled the Spurs and their fans, often portraying them as quaint and backward purveyors of the Old West peppered with stereotypical portrayals of Mexicans. *Sports Illustrated* columnist Curry Kirkpatrick was particularly fond of deriding the Spurs and their fans. Kirkpatrick's portrayals of the Spurs and San Antonio are a curious mix of admiration and patronizing East Coast media snobbery tinged with good old-fashioned racism in the guise of "colorful" prose. A passage from a 1978 profile of the team during its second season in the NBA is a representative example: "Besides being the surprising runaway leader in the NBA's Central Division and the not so surprising quintessential representative of the old ABA, if the San Antonio Spurs are not the most outlandish, disorganized, laid-back and down-to-the-rootsiest fun team to watch in the whole wide universe, then Speedy Gonzales will eat his sombrero right there in the middle of the Baseline Bums cheering section."[38]

In general, Kirkpatrick's *Sports Illustrated* columns on the NBA during these years frequently mocked the predominantly black league for his imagined white male readership. Kirkpatrick's clouded vision illustrated his inability to imagine how a cross-racial ball club with a visible Mexican fan base could exist and be successful in a professional league. Yet another passage is indicative of Kirkpatrick's patronizing portrait of the team and its fans:

When this fascinating conglomeration of heads-down operators is running and gunning, which it usually is; when the Spurs are leading the league in scoring as well as shooting from both the field and the foul line, which they usually are; when they are scattering around like illegal aliens on a jalapeño hunt and filling the nets and the seats and stunning everybody with their passing and ball movement and irrepressible, Remember-the-Alamo-by-damn hustle, there is no team in basketball more dangerous to play against.[39]

Sportswriters from the *Dallas Morning News*, still smarting from the franchise's failures in the Metroplex, also had a penchant for masking their envy by ridiculing the predominantly Mexican neighbors to the south. "There is a gigantic Latin population here," Bob St. John wrote in 1977, "and if you have ever been to a bullfight or sporting event in Mexico, then you have a clearer indication for the San Antonio Spurs' crowd."[40]

The point was clear, even if it was camouflaged in colorful sportswriter-style language. The Spurs and San Antonio were

Mexican, foreign "illegal aliens," not Americans. Their presence in professional sports was a quaint anomaly, not representative of America in the Texas-Mexico borderlands.

Blue collar in most sports towns is associated with male, masculinized white ethnic fans, such as those who are imagined to be the primary fan bases in cities like Pittsburgh and Philadelphia. But *blue collar* in San Antonio translates as Mexican American. The Spurs franchise smartly kept ticket prices among the lowest in the league. While other NBA teams, such as the Knicks and Lakers, prided themselves on bringing celebrities and politicians to their games, the Spurs created an identity based on their working-class-majority fan base. While the Knicks ushered their Dancing Harry off the stage, the Spurs routinely encouraged Muñoz and many others to dance and lead cheers on the sidelines during time-outs. This approach to fan base cultivation came straight from the top: "Coming to a Spurs game should be the thing to do socially in all segments of the city," Drossos told the *San Antonio Light* after the Spurs joined the NBA. "The blue collar worker and the country club set come together at the Arena during basketball season to share in the excitement that a winning season can provide."[41] While Tex Schramm's Dallas Cowboys sought to draw fans with eye candy in the form of sexualized cheerleaders, the Spurs front office allowed fans with a wide variety of body types take center stage at the arena.

As early as the first season in San Antonio, Spurs management signaled to locals that all fans were welcome at Spurs games. This welcome extended to women fans. "Memo to San Antonio husbands: if you think the San Antonio Spurs basketball games will be perfect excuses for a 'boys' night out,' forget it," wrote O'Lene Stone of the *San Antonio Light*.[42] These claims might be pure journalistic boosterism, but existing narratives of Spurs fans, particularly among the Baseline Bums, indicate that women could feel comfortable in the rowdy crowds that packed the arena during these years. In a region that remained haunted by its colonial legacies, a South Texas city had somehow created a raucous yet novel sports spectating culture, even if those who covered the league at the time didn't quite understand what they were witnessing at Spurs games in San Antonio.

* * *

The arrival of the Spurs and players from the ABA transformed the NBA, though much of that transformation has been overshadowed by the prevailing histories of the league during the late 1970s. This was the era when the league was thought to be "too black," when many of its stars were hooked on drugs, and when white fans stayed away until visionary league commissioner David Stern brought them back and made the league likable again in the 1980s.[43] Such tales neglect the stylistic innovations and marketing techniques the Spurs imported into the league, while also neglecting the extraordinary talent influx caused by the merger. In NBA cities like San Antonio, basketball was very much on the upswing. Revisiting those seasons in San Antonio reveals how the team and its players made their mark on pro basketball in the United States.

Leading the Spurs on the sidelines during its first four seasons in the NBA was Doug Moe, a former ABA player and close friend of fellow Brooklynite and coaching legend Larry Brown. In fact, Moe had been Brown's assistant during the guacamole salad episode a few months earlier. "I like San Antonio a lot better now than I did last year," he told local columnist Bob Ostrom. "I'm glad to have the fans with me and not against me."[44] The impatient Drossos relieved Bob Bass of his coaching duties after the bitter 1976 playoff loss to the Nets, but he kept him on the payroll in many capacities in subsequent years. In fact, Bass served as Doug Moe's assistant coach during his tenure with the Spurs. Moe was a player's coach who, like Bass, coached an up-tempo style of basketball in which ball movement and passing were preferred over set plays orchestrated from the sideline. In this regard, he was "a coach from Brooklyn with a laid-back Texas temperament" who encouraged a style that was inspired by the New York City playgrounds.[45] During his four seasons in San Antonio and in subsequent years, Moe's teams ranked either first or second in the league in points scored, though they also ranked high in points allowed, a fact noted by his critics. But the sloppily dressed, wild-haired, unkempt coach from Brooklyn turned out to be a good hire who helped the Spurs make an immediate impact on the NBA.

The ABA was vindicated after the merger as many of its players continued to star in the NBA. But the team that performed— and has continued to perform—the best was the San Antonio Spurs. The Spurs underwent a smooth transition to the NBA under Moe. In their first season, they were a bit inconsistent, but they still earned a playoff berth with a 44–38 record. The team hit their stride the following year, when they finished first in their division with a 52–30 record. Gervin actually became a more prolific scorer after the merger. In 1977–1978, he averaged 27.2 points per game while shooting an amazing 53 percent from the field. His most memorable moment from the year was the last game of the regular season, when he won the league scoring title over fellow ABA alum David Thompson. Thompson, nicknamed "Skywalker" because of his extraordinary leaping ability, was then an All-Star guard in his third year playing for the Denver Nuggets. Going into the last regular season game against the woeful Pistons in Gervin's native Detroit, Thompson was only percentage points behind the Iceman in the scoring race. On Sunday afternoon, April 9, 1978, Thompson lit up the Pistons for seventy-three points, the third most points scored by a player in an NBA game up to that point, a remarkable feat given the fact that he was a six-foot-four guard. The Skywalker's extraordinary effort put him a few points ahead of Gervin, who needed fifty-three points to overtake Thompson for the league lead.

In the Spurs' last game of the season against the New Orleans Jazz later that evening, Moe gave his star guard the green light to go for the scoring title. After a shaky beginning in which he missed his first five shots, Ice got hot and scored fifty-three points in the first half, thirty-three of them in the second quarter. In the end, he wound up making twenty-three of forty-nine field goals and seventeen of twenty free throws, for sixty-three points to win the scoring title by a few percentage points (27.2 points per game over Thompson's 27.15 points per game).[46] As was often the case with professional basketball games in the 1970s, neither game was televised. Yet these performances on the last day of that regular season secured the legendary statuses of both players, especially Gervin, who went on to win three more scoring titles in the next four years.

The Spurs did not win an NBA title during the Gervin era because they ran into teams in the playoffs that were either more experienced or a bit more talented than they were. Though the Spurs routinely made the playoffs in the years after the merger, they struggled to make up for the loss of James Silas, who was frequently injured and never regained the level of play he had before he got hurt in the 1976 ABA playoffs. In the Moe era, their main nemesis was the Washington Bullets. The Bullets, led by Hall of Famer and former University of Houston legend Elvin Hayes, one of the greatest power forwards in basketball history, and Wes Unseld, the burly and resourceful Hall of Fame center, whose rebounds, solid picks, and outlet passes bedeviled opponents for years. Both were talented veterans who formed one of the best frontlines in basketball. Though Hayes and Unseld were a formidable duo, the real key to Washington's success during these years was the underrated Bobby Dandridge, the small, versatile forward who could shoot and drive and make shots when the game hung in the balance.

At the end of the 1977–1978 regular season, the Spurs finished eight games in front of the second-place Bullets. But in the playoffs, the more experienced Bullets beat the Spurs four games to two.[47] The Bullets continued their run in the playoffs all the way to their first NBA title a few weeks later. Still, fans in San Antonio expressed gratitude for their division-winning season by greeting players at the airport when they returned from the game six defeat. Moe was proud of his team, insisting to the press, "Winning

52 games like we did this year shows we really don't need anything to improve the team." He summed up, "Let's face it, 52 wins means we had a hell of a year."[48]

Hopes were high in the Alamo City for the Spurs at the beginning of the 1978–1979 season. The feelings of satisfaction for being a big league NBA city were giving way to expectations for a championship. The city's renovation of its arena was now complete with an expanded capacity of sixteen thousand seats. During the regular season, the team was a bit more inconsistent than the previous year, but they still won their division for the second year in a row with a 48–34 record. Gervin once again led the league in scoring with a 29.6 scoring average, Kenon continued his high-flying act with another All-Star season, and James Silas seemed to make it all the way back from his injuries with a solid campaign. For the Spurs point guard and captain, the past two years had been little more than a seemingly never-ending struggle to overcome his knee injury. After a long rehabilitation process, he was able to get back on the court. Early in the 1978–1979 season, Moe put Silas in the starting lineup, and the player performed admirably and helped the team win their division.[49] The addition of the team's captain seemed to make the Spurs favorites to win an NBA title. While Billy Paultz struggled with injuries, his backup, Mike Green, another tall and slender six-foot, ten-inch, two-hundred-pound frontcourt player, turned out to be a significant contributor off the bench throughout the season, especially in the postseason.

San Antonio opened the playoffs by facing an old adversary from the ABA: Julius Erving, the former Nets legend who was starring for the Philadelphia 76ers. Although they almost blew a three games to one lead, they rebounded to shed their budding reputation as playoff losers by defeating Dr. J and the Sixers 111–108. Mike Green started for the injured Paultz and scored twenty points and pulled down eight rebounds. Kenon, who was confidently calling himself the best all-around forward in the game, lived up to his words with a twenty-seven-point, eight-rebound effort. The Iceman did his thing by scoring thirty-three points, including two key free throws with only eleven seconds remaining to clinch the win. When the final buzzer sounded, pandemonium broke out in the arena. The Spurs and their fans rejoiced as if the team had won the NBA championship. Champagne and Lone Star beer flowed in the locker room, and the fans flooded the court and celebrated. Around town, flags waved, horns honked, and bars overflowed as the Spurs had finally won a postseason series.[50]

The Spurs' next opponents were once again the Washington Bullets, the defending NBA champions. Although Washington finished with the league's best record, as they entered the Spurs series, they appeared old and vulnerable. In Washington's first playoff series, a young and unproven Atlanta Hawks gave them all they could handle before the veterans pulled out a victory in game seven. The Spurs, on the other hand, were younger, and hungry and eager to avenge their loss to the Bullets the previous year. "I predict we will beat Washington and it will go seven games," proclaimed a confident Silas. They're a great team, but so are we."[51]

Silas's words seemed prophetic as the Spurs roared to a great start by routing Washington in game one 118–97 at the Capital Centre, the Bullets' state-of-the art arena in Landover, Maryland, yet another suburban no-town that had become a place on the map when the facility opened in 1973. After the Bullets won game two, the series switched to HemisFair Arena, where San Antonio took game three with a narrow 116–114 victory. In game four, Ice put on one of his epic performances by shooting nineteen for thirty-one from the field and four of six from the foul line, to tally forty-two points and lead the Spurs to a 118–102 victory in front of the Baseline Bums and the rest of their raucous hometown fans. Gervin used his height advantage and shot-making skills to score at will over Washington's smaller guards, prompting Elvin Hayes to beg his coach to assign the taller Dandridge to guard him. "He's going crazy out there, shooting with too much confidence" Hayes told the press. "We've gotta change, make some other move."[52] The win once again gave the Spurs a commanding three games to one advantage. But as was the case against the 76ers, the Spurs let their opponents back into the series. The defending champions rallied to win game five at home, and then they shocked the Spurs faithful by winning game six in San Antonio to set up a climactic game seven in the Capital Centre.

On May 18, 1979, the normally indifferent Bullets crowd came out in full force for what turned out to be one of the greatest contests in NBA history. The game is memorable not only because it was a closely contested affair with a dramatic finish, but also because it exemplifies the beauty and aesthetics of playing the game, as Gervin liked to say, in "the flow." The few surviving clips of the game show that the Iceman played some of his best Motown tunes that night in Landover.[53] The first half was closely contested, and Washington led 50–49 at halftime. Dandridge scored twenty points in the first half, while Gervin came to life in the second period with eighteen points of his own. After halftime, the Iceman continued his torrid shooting by scoring sixteen points in the third quarter and hitting shots from all over the floor, as he had done in game four. Late in the third quarter, Gervin took a pass from Kenon on a fast break, cut from the left side of the court into the lane, and hit a running hook shot to put the Spurs up 75–68 with 1:55 left in the quarter. After a Bullets basket by Dandridge, Kenon again immediately pushed the ball up court. Quick ball movement between Paultz, Coby Dietrick, and then Gervin put the Iceman in a good position to post up the shorter Charles Johnson. He quickly turned and shot a turnaround jumper over Johnson, who fouled him as the ball swished through the basket. Gervin's subsequent free throw put San Antonio up by eight points, 78–70, toward the end of the third quarter. A few moments later, Kenon pushed the ball up the court and tried to hit Gervin on a nice alley-oop pass. Ice missed the layup, but he quickly grabbed the rebound and converted a short jumper to keep the Spurs up by a comfortable margin. As he had done all series, Gervin scored at will against the much shorter Charles Johnson.

The Spurs continued to hold on to the lead because the Iceman could not be stopped. Watching Gervin effortlessly score in the flow of the Spurs offense is reminiscent of watching waves coming in on the shore of a beach. Early in the fourth quarter, he scored a beautiful bucket early when he took a handoff from Silas at the right of the circle, dribbled toward the baseline, and jumped up to hit a soft banker high off the glass over the helpless Johnson to put San Antonio up 92–83. Soon thereafter, Bullets coach Dick Motta took Johnson out of the game and moved Dandridge to the guard spot to cover Gervin. The move didn't pay immediate dividends; Ice continued to score at a blistering pace. On the very next sequence, Paultz rebounded a missed Bullets shot and then threw a quick outlet pass to Silas, who passed it ahead to Gervin on another fast break. Seeing the taller Elvin Hayes approach him from under the basket, Ice stopped on a dime and smoothly sank a fifteen-foot jumper before Hayes could block it.

The only people in the Capital Centre who managed to stop the music that Gervin and the Spurs were playing that night were the referees. The Spurs were ahead 100–93 with three minutes left in the game. But in those final minutes, the officials made a number of questionable foul calls against the Spurs. After Kenon missed one of his patented in-the-paint jumpers, the referees called a loose ball foul on Paultz for jumping over Unseld even though replays showed that no foul actually occurred. Unseld, who was not a good free throw shooter, made both shots to make it 103–101 with 1:36 left. On the very next possession, referee John Vanak made perhaps his most egregious call of the night when he whistled Paultz for an offensive foul for setting an illegal pick on Bullets guard Tom Henderson. As Paultz was handing the ball to Silas, he tried to set a pick on Henderson, who grazed Paultz's body and flopped on the floor, prompting Vanak's whistle. It was a great acting job by Henderson.

A game that had a constant flow and tempo was clogged up by the referees' whistles. Another questionable foul call on Gervin allowed Bullets forward Greg Ballard to convert two free throws and put Washington in the lead by 105–103. After James Silas calmly came down the court and shot a contested turnaround jumper to tie the game once again, the stage was set for Bobby

Dandridge's heroics. Ironically, it was Dandridge's own improvisation that allowed him to make the game-winning shot. Dick Motta, a coach who was known for his patterned offenses, told Dandridge to "go out there and win the damn game."[54] And that is what the small forward proceeded to do. Dandridge brought the ball up the court, then gave it to guard Tom Henderson, who proceeded to give it right back to Dandridge. With the game squarely in his hands, the Bullet forward calmly drove to the baseline and shot the game winner over Kenon, Silas, and Gervin to put Washington up 107–105 with eight seconds left. A last-second shot by Silas was blocked by Elvin Hayes. Though Kenon retrieved it, Dandridge, the MVP of the game, batted it away as time expired. The Bullets withstood an extraordinary performance from Gervin and the Spurs and won the game 107–105.

The Spurs' devastating defeat that night in Landover marked the end of the ABA era with the team. The core of Gervin, Kenon, Silas, and Paultz did not recover from the fallout of the loss to the Bullets. The next season, the team never got above .500, and Drossos had finally had enough of Doug Moe; he fired him in the middle of the next season. The Spurs finished a listless season with a 41–41 record. They made the playoffs, but they lost in the first round to the emerging Houston Rockets. After the season ended, both Dietrick and Kenon departed from San Antonio. Gervin, however, continued to excel with another scoring title and the MVP trophy in that year's All-Star game, which took place in Landover, the scene of the painful defeat from the season before.

* * *

The early 1980s was the dawn of a new era of NBA basketball, in which college stars Earvin "Magic" Johnson and Larry Bird came into the NBA and helped the league achieve unprecedented popularity with fans and the television networks. But the "Bird/Magic" story overshadows other fascinating storylines from those years. It was also a time when Texas's pro basketball scene further developed and emerged in nationally impactful ways. Houston and Dallas, which had been largely indifferent to basketball, finally caught up with San Antonio. New Texas pro basketball rivalries emerged in the 1980s. Since his arrival from the ABA in 1976, Moses Malone had spearheaded a resurgence in Houston basketball. For the first time, the Rockets became a relevant basketball team in the city and in the NBA. Led by the perimeter shooting of the five-foot-nine Calvin Murphy and by Malone's prodigious rebounding, the Rockets became a playoff team. Meanwhile, Dallas, which failed as an ABA city, got a second chance at pro basketball in 1980 when the NBA awarded them a new expansion franchise called the Dallas Mavericks. Metroplex sportswriters, who had looked at the rise of the San Antonio Spurs with envy and condescension, finally got themselves a pro basketball team to cover again.

Meanwhile, the Spurs remained one of the top teams of the NBA. Gervin continued to put up All-Star seasons, and the team won the Midwest Division title each of the next three seasons. Though the Spurs kept much of the run-and-gun spirit of the ABA, they were gradually domesticated into an NBA franchise, as the team's roster increasingly comprised young and seasoned NBA players. But playoff defeats continued to haunt the team and disappoint its fans. Part of the reason Gervin and the Spurs tend to be overlooked is because they played in the same conference as the Los Angeles Lakers, who in the early 1980s were an emerging juggernaut of multiple Hall of Fame and All-Star talents, led by veteran Kareem Abdul-Jabbar and the young and irrepressible Magic Johnson. In 1982, San Antonio was unceremoniously swept by the Lakers in four straight games in the Western Conference finals. The very next year, they defeated the Spurs again in a more competitive series, four games to two.

In many ways, the loss to the Lakers in the 1983 playoffs signaled the end of the Gervin era in San Antonio. As his skills declined, he found himself on a team that had slipped behind the competition. In 1985, he was traded to the Chicago Bulls, and he retired from the NBA the next season. Three years later, the Drossos era also came to an end in San Antonio when he sold controlling interest in the franchise to his old friend Red McCombs. Spurs fortunes on the court declined as the team eventually tumbled down to last place by the 1987 season. Paralleling the trajectories of so many Texas professional and collegiate teams, the Spurs were mired in mediocrity after a remarkable ten-year run of consistency.

In the end, the Spurs did not need to win an NBA championship to make an impact on the state and the nation's sporting scene. The championships would arrive decades later. But in the 1970s, the Spurs showed that pro basketball could work in Texas, even in a city with a majority working-class Mexican American population. Their emergence showed that there could be a delicate balance between sports entrepreneurship, player compensation and creativity, and a fan culture that came close to representing the city's varied communities. The franchise and its fans had an undeniable impact on the recreational life of San Antonio. Drossos, the Iceman, and the Bums gave San Antonio entertaining basketball and fan cultures that the city possesses to this day. The Spurs helped spawn a unique sporting culture that is organically linked to the area's working-class communities, even though tickets to Spurs games are a lot more expensive today than they were in the Gervin era.

Still, the legacy of that era remains. In June 2013, eleven-year-old Sebastien de la Cruz sang the national anthem before game three of that season's NBA finals between the Spurs and the Miami Heat. De la Cruz sang the anthem decked in a Spurs-colored mariachi outfit. The performance elicited a host of racist responses on social media from observers who were befuddled at the sight of a young Latino singing the national anthem. Spurs fans and many others, including representatives of the franchise itself, pushed back against the reactionary forces who couldn't stand the sight of a brown boy singing "The Star-Spangled Banner." The strong pushback against the racist tweeters by the team and a host of basketball fans shows why the Spurs were unique: their deep roots in the city's working-class Tejano fan base were established not by professionalized sports marketers digging up facile "Latino" marketing schemes but by a confluence of organic factors including smart management, inclusive fan cultures, and talented players who emerged out of the black freedom struggles of the 1960s and '70s. The echoes of that history, even in today's corporatized and sanitized NBA, remains in San Antonio to this day.

CHAPTER 8

Slammin' and Jammin' in Houston

IN OCTOBER 1980, A TALL AND ATHLETIC YOUNG MAN FROM LAGOS, NIGERIA, arrived in New York City. Unlike the Africans who had arrived on the shores of the United States on ships and in chains centuries before, this young African landed in an airplane at John F. Kennedy Airport in search of a scholarship to play basketball for a major American university. The first stop on his scheduled itinerary was St. John's University in New York, a school at the forefront of a northeast college basketball renaissance as part of the newly formed Big East Conference. But as he stepped out of the airport, he immediately took a disliking to the autumn air. "It was cold!" he later recalled. "I had never felt cold like that." At that moment, he decided New York was not for him.[1]

The next stop on his itinerary was supposed to be Houston, Texas, which he was scheduled to visit two days later. But he managed to change his flight and leave the cold of New York later that day. Not only would the young man, Hakeem Olajuwon, go on to change national sports history, but he would also become the face of a new Houston, a new transnational Texas. His decision to abandon his plans to visit St. John's in New York and go directly to Houston paralleled the larger population movement to the rapidly growing urban centers of the South and Southwest. The African immigrant was, like many others at this time, Houston bound.[2]

San Antonio put pro basketball on the map in Texas in the 1970s. Houston inaugurated its own basketball revival in the early 1980s. It was the University of Houston Cougars who took the game to unprecedented heights, in more ways than one. Long-time head coach Guy V. Lewis led the team to the final round of the NCAA men's basketball tournament, colloquially known as the "Final Four," three years in a row (1982–1984). His team is better known for its crushing loss in the 1983 national championship game to the heavy underdog North Carolina State Wolfpack in one of the great upsets in college basketball history. The defeat was the second of three straight losses at the Final Four for Houston, and it tarnished the legacy of the program. Perhaps this is why no one has written extensively about the history of this remarkable college basketball team, while others, such as Jerry Tarkanian's UNLV Rebels, the University of Michigan's "Fab 5" teams of the early 1990s, and even the rather uninteresting Duke Blue Devils of the Christian Laettner era have gotten more historical recognition. Still, the unforgettable victory by NC State need not diminish the remarkable achievements of the team that became known as "Phi Slama Jama." Sports fans are often seduced by the narrative of losers, which elicits pity for those who don't win "the big one," the final championship game. But the impact of Houston basketball outlasted the loss and even the legacy of NC State's win in Albuquerque in April 1983.

The University of Houston's athletic program was at the forefront of the changes in college football and on the cutting edge of college basketball. Guy Lewis, like Bill Yeoman, showed he was more committed to winning games than to maintaining white supremacy when he recruited black players to his program in the 1960s. By the 1980s, he had assembled a group of talented black athletes that took the game to new heights. The ascendance of Cougars basketball from the 1960s through the early 1980s also mirrored the emergence of the sport as a popular and potentially profitable enterprise. Spurred by the historic 1968 game against the UCLA Bruins in the Astrodome, the program helped bring television money and domed stadium venues into the world of college basketball. The program's revival during the Phi Slama Jama era of the early 1980s facilitated the creation of marketable college basketball teams, which helped transform the annual NCAA tournament into a television-orchestrated national spectacle known as "March Madness." Cougars basketball rode the wave of commercialization until the program could not keep up with the increasingly competitive world of college basketball.

*   *   *

Guy V. Lewis was a visionary. In many ways, he was the heart and soul of University of Houston basketball for almost forty years. Born in the East Texas town of Arp, he was an all-sport athlete in high school, and after serving in the US Army Air Forces during World War II, he wound up at UH in 1946. He starred on the school's basketball team during the program's first few years before Harry Fouke, the school's director of athletics, hired him to be head basketball coach in 1956. His teams were competitive in the early 1960s, but they didn't become a nationally ranked program until after he broke with the state's Jim Crow traditions by recruiting talented black players.[3] His first star recruits were black Louisianans Elvin Hayes and Don Chaney in 1964. Like Texas Western's Don Haskins, the competitive and ambitious Lewis understood that he could not be successful as a basketball coach without the talents of black players. Unlike Haskins and Bill Yeoman, who were not from Texas, Lewis was a native Texan raised in the ideologies of the Jim Crow South. The fact that he decided to break with Jim Crow's hold on the world of college basketball illustrates that he was a forward-thinking individual. To some extent, so was Harry Fouke and the university's administration, who gave Lewis the green light to recruit Hayes and Chaney. Lewis personally recruited Chaney, convincing his mother to send him to UH from his native Baton Rouge. He sent Harvey Pate, his assistant coach, to sign Hayes in Rayville, a small town in Northeast Louisiana. Though Lewis had Chaney and Hayes room with white teammates, like many black integration pioneers, they lived isolated from the campus scene, relying instead on Houston's black community. Yet Hayes and Chaney referred to the years at Houston in positive terms years after they left the campus.

In addition to being a catalyst of the racial integration of college basketball in the South, Lewis also played a significant role in the commercialization of the sport when he helped engineer the greatest college basketball spectacle in history in 1968. Seeing that he had the talent to compete with nationally ranked programs, Lewis set his sights on John Wooden's UCLA Bruins, the dominant program in the country led by its seven-foot-two superstar center, Lew Alcindor (later known as Kareem Abdul-Jabbar). In 1966, Lewis started to pester Fouke to schedule a game with the Bruins. Fouke thought he was mad and rebuffed him multiple times. Why would the top-ranked Bruins play the unknown Cougars in a basketball game in football-crazy Texas? But then the Cougars made a surprising trip to the 1967 Final Four, where Alcindor's Bruins handily defeated the Cougars 73–58 in the national semifinals. But Lewis was insistent. "Damnit, we could have a good crowd and I'm telling you we can beat them," Lewis recalled telling his athletic director years later.[4] Eventually, Fouke gave in to his determined coach. A few weeks later, a rematch to be held during the next season was announced. Lewis and Fouke persuaded a skeptical Roy Hofheinz to host the game at the Astrodome. The idea of staging a basketball game in a giant arena made for baseball and football seemed preposterous.[5]

The "Game of the Century," as it became known, was a revolutionary event in college basketball history. A record crowd of 52,693, the largest to ever see a basketball game in the United States up to that point, filled the Astrodome to see if the Cougars could upset the Bruins. The contest was the first ever college basketball game televised in prime time. The game was brought to the country by TVS, the small television network created by Eddie Einhorn. TVS would go on to broadcast many college basketball games during the 1970s before Einhorn sold his network and moved on to CBS, and later to owning the Chicago White Sox. Einhorn, like so many white men during the 1960s and '70s, found a lucrative career in sports media. The UH-UCLA contest signaled to many that the game could draw a substantial crowd and television audience. It helped that Elvin Hayes pulled off a truly epic performance. He outplayed Alcindor, who had been slowed by a preexisting eye injury, by scoring thirty-nine points, twenty-nine of those during a torrid shooting run in the first half, and led the Cougars to a 71–69 upset victory. The game ended UCLA's forty-seven-game winning streak, and it made Hayes a national star.

The game also foreshadowed the movement of college basketball championship games to dome settings. The NCAA returned to the Astrodome for the Final Four in 1971, and what had seemed to be an absurd idea in 1968 became standard procedure in the 1990s, when the revenue-hungry NCAA permanently staged its men's basketball championship in front of huge crowds in domed stadiums. Meanwhile, Einhorn's vision of televised college basketball came to full fruition in the 1980s, as the newly created cable sports network ESPN televised games nearly every day during the regular season and the NCAA tournament. March Madness became a gigantic cash cow for television networks, the NCAA, and universities. Recalling the significance of the Game of the Century in 1968, Lewis said years later, "A lot of people say the game did great things for college basketball and some folks made a lot of money from it too. . . . I only made $30,000 up until the eighties, when they finally gave me a contract for $60,000 and then $75,000."[6]

The Game of the Century turned out to be even more than what Guy Lewis bargained for. The win over the powerful Bruins gave Houston Cougars basketball greater regional and national visibility, even though UCLA trounced them 101–69 in a rematch at the NCAA semifinals later that spring. Like the football program, which played its home games in the Astrodome, the men's basketball program regularly used the Game of the Century in the Astrodome to market their program to prospective players. "Space Age Basketball" was how the athletic department liked to promote UH basketball in the many publications turned

*Cecile Rose on the game program, January 12, 1975. Courtesy Special
Collections Division of the M. D. Anderson Library, University of
Houston.*

out by the Sports Information Office. The shift in the racial rep-
resentation of the basketball program in these publications is telling. Whereas program covers from 1968 had silhouetted images
of white players, the covers from the 1970s onward—the "Space
Age"—featured the team's black stars. To be forward thinking
was to be a program that promoted the team's black stars, like
Cecile Rose.

The Game of the Century also helped the program get its long sought-after on-campus arena. In December 1969, the school opened a new facility fittingly named after Roy Hofheinz. The "plush Hofheinz Pavilion," as it was frequently described in the program's promotional materials, was a spanking new facility for basketball and other indoor events. The program that never had a consistent home gym now had a new place to play, one that could have been named "the House that Hayes and Chaney Built." The intimate eight-thousand-seat arena would be the home to Cougars basketball for the next forty-eight seasons.

After the departure of Hayes and Chaney, Lewis continued his remarkable run of winning seasons. His sideline demeanor added to his notoriety. He always seemed to be a nervous wreck, holding and waving, and sometimes throwing, his trademark red and white checkered towel. He gulped down at least twenty cups of water and chomped on ice during games. He also had the undeserved reputation of simply rolling out balls to his players and giving little instruction. Whereas most men's college basketball coaches relied on set plays on offense, Lewis demanded that his teams regularly run a fast break. Fast-break basketball looks undisciplined, but basketball players and coaches understand that it requires constant practicing and excellent conditioning. Lewis's former players almost uniformly describe Cougars practices as demanding. "Practices were tough, hard, and competitive," Hakeem Olajuwon would recall of his time with the Cougars. He remembered warming up with fierce two-on-one and three-on-two fast breaks with players finishing with dunks.[7]

Lewis, unlike many college coaches of his generation, loved for his players to dunk the basketball. The dunk, a shot in which players jump up and stuff the ball into the basket in a variety of ways, was outlawed by the NCAA from 1967 to 1976, supposedly to equalize play between the defense and offense. In reality, it was a futile attempt to blunt the impact of black players on the game, such as Lew Alcindor and Elvin Hayes, who were dominating the sport. Conversely, Lewis was a proponent of the shot, and he made it a central part of the Cougars offensive attack:

Guy Lewis barking instructions to his team on the sideline. Photo by Peter Read Miller.

The dunk was an important part of our game, and we worked on it. It's a high-percentage shot, and I think when a big man gets around the basket he ought to just explode up there and stick it in the hole. We practiced it over and over—a four-step movement where you catch the ball, check the defense, step to the basket, and then dunk. It wasn't for show. I would tell coaches who didn't like it, "You can't dunk without hustling."[8]

During the 1970s, he also continued to recruit gifted black players, mostly from Southeast Texas and the nearby Southwestern Louisiana areas. Dwight Davis was the first local black player he brought to the program. The Worthing High School product starred for the Cougars and made the 1972 Olympic team. Other Cougar stars from the '70s were Dwight Jones, who starred at Houston Wheatley High School before going on to play in the NBA; Otis Birdsong from Winter Haven, Florida, who was a four-time All Star in the NBA; and Louis Dunbar, who went on to

Harlem Globetrotter fame. From the Bahamas came Cecile Rose, a sharp-shooting guard and brother of Lynden Rose, who was one of the original members of Lewis's Phi Slama Jama team.

Guy Lewis helped usher men's college basketball into the future in the 1960s. He continued to field exciting teams throughout the 1970s, though he was often criticized by sportswriters for not winning any championships. As he entered his sixties in the early 1980s, he would help orchestrate another revolution in the game of basketball by fielding a college team unlike any other in the game's history. He did it by once again finding players from the Houston area, but he was also extremely fortunate to have another one unexpectedly arrive from a faraway continent.

* * *

The Fonde Recreation Center is one of the meccas of pickup basketball in Texas (and the nation). But that might not be apparent when visitors first approach the single-story red brick building at 110 Sabine Street near downtown Houston. Drivers who pull up to the building might be confused by the presence of a large mural displaying George H. W. Bush and the achievements of his presidency on the front of the building. The mural reflects the wealthy Connecticut family's co-optation of Houston and Texas, for the career of the Yale-educated sportsman miscasts the identity of an institution that is more defined by the achievements of Houston-area athletes than by the leisurely life of a patrician from the Northeast. An image of Bush in his Yale baseball uniform from his college days hardly strikes the right note after one sees the ethnic and racial backgrounds of the ballplayers inside the gym. The homage to the Bush family on the outside of the building gives way to a host of monuments and display cases on the inside that more accurately reflect Fonde's legacy. There are modest displays to Fonde and NBA greats such as Moses Malone, Clyde Drexler, Otto Moore, and many others. Fonde has housed summer league basketball since it opened its doors in 1960, and in the late 1970s and early 1980s, it spawned a renaissance in Houston hoops by attracting talented players at all levels.

Today, Fonde is an intimate, seemingly well-managed facility with a few rows of bleacher seats for spectators. It is rightly known as the "Rucker of the South," as it formed one of pickup basketball's great theaters along with Harlem's Rucker Tournament and Philadelphia's Baker League. As in these summer league basketball scenes, professional and collegiate players competed with high schoolers and semipro players at Fonde. To be sure, one had to be good to get on the court at Fonde. As Hakeem Olajuwon remembered it, "Fonde had two courts separated by a blue plastic screen. One of them always had two half-court games going on between street players, and the other was for the Cougars and the pros."[9] The players, whether they were pros or not, didn't wear uniforms in those days. They distinguished their teams in the old-school way of shirts versus skins. Today, the players are adorned in baggy, corporate-sponsored uniforms, but one can still feel the sweat coming off of their glistening bodies as they skillfully make their way up and down the court.

As visitors make their own way from the entrance into the gym, they come upon the Fonde Hall of Fame, which is simply adorned with plaques to some of the famous figures in the gym's history. One of those names is Angelo Cascio, who ran the gym for more than two decades after it opened its doors in 1960. In the late 1960s, the rec center allowed Guy Lewis's Cougars to practice in the facility at a time when the school gym was unavailable. The biggest name that graces the walls of the old gym is that of NBA legend Moses Malone, who, along with other local NBA All Stars such as Calvin Murphy, began to make Fonde his summer home in the late 1970s. In those days, pro ballplayers Dwight Jones, Tom Henderson, Robert Reid, and Allen Leavell faced off against the young Cougars in epic battles in the gym. Malone was the biggest professional star to play at the gym at this time. It was fitting that it was yet another ABA alum who helped spearhead the revival of the local basketball scene. As a high school basketball star in the

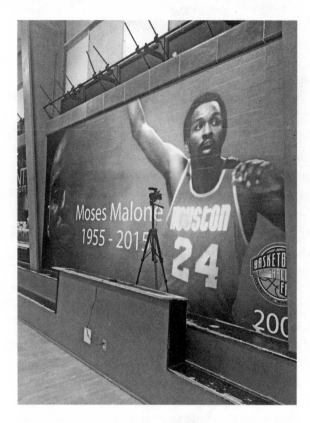

Moses Malone,
Fonde legend.
Author photo.

small town of Petersburg, Virginia, Moses was highly sought after by colleges across the country. When Malone rejected an athletic scholarship from Lefty Driesell's Maryland Terrapins for a
contract with the ABA's Utah Stars in 1974, he became the first
player to sign a professional basketball contract right out of high
school. After the ABA-NBA merger, Malone was passed over by
the Buffalo Braves and the Portland Trailblazers, two NBA franchises that found little use for his services. Moses often mumbled
when he spoke, and pro coaches and scouts mistakenly assumed
his mumbling and creative use of the English language was evidence of a lack of intelligence. The Houston Rockets snatched
him up in a trade, and he quickly helped revitalize a formerly dor-

mant franchise. He was known for his inside scoring, shooting touch, quickness, and, most importantly, peerless ability to grab offensive rebounds. In an era when seven-foot centers dominated the sport, Moses stood out as one of the best in the game.

While Malone led the Rockets to prominence in the NBA during the winter and spring months, in the summer, he plied his craft at the gym and became the "King of Fonde," which also made him King of Houston as far as the city's ballplayers were concerned. He was a down-to-earth celebrity who drove around in his Maserati, hung out at Frenchy's Fried Chicken in South Houston, and mentored younger players by competing against them hard at the gym. While the mainstream press tended to portray Malone as a sullen and inarticulate figure, at the Fonde, he was an affable, exuberant personality who was the center of attention and a crowd favorite. In the summer of 1981, when Moses was at the peak of his powers, he came across a raw but supremely gifted seven-foot African immigrant who eventually competed with him for his title of King of Fonde.

*   *   *

Maybe Ọlọrun, the Yoruba god of the heavens, decided for some reason to drop a gift on Guy Lewis's lap when Hakeem Olajuwon arrived on the UH campus in the fall of 1980. Olajuwon was born and raised in Nigeria, the West African nation that achieved its political independence from British colonial rule in 1960. The most populous and linguistically diverse country in sub-Saharan Africa, it was the center of the old British West African empire. During the time of the Atlantic slave trade, four million Africans were forcibly captured and sold into slavery from an area of West Africa that today lies mostly within the nation of Nigeria. In the twentieth century, the divide-and-conquer system of British colonial rule revived and reconfigured the ethnic tensions that had facilitated the slave trade and catalyzed ethnic-based violence in the Nigerian Civil War of 1967 to 1970. Olajuwon's family seems to have evaded the violence of the period. He was Yoruba, one of the major ethnic groups in the country, and his parents were practicing Muslims.

The child of cement makers in the cosmopolitan capital city of Lagos, the athletically gifted Olajuwon played soccer and team handball. However, Ganiyu Otenigbade, a basketball coach for Lagos State, saw the tall young man's extraordinary talent and encouraged him to take up basketball. Otenigbade taught Olajuwon the fundamentals of the game. The player's height and superior leaping ability and timing allowed him to block shots and dunk the basketball with ease, which shocked his Nigerian coaches and teammates. While he was playing in African continental basketball competitions, Olajuwon came to the attention of Christopher Pond, an American who was coaching the rival Central African Republic's team. Pond was convinced that Hakeem was talented enough to play at the college level in the United States. After his fateful decision to abandon his plan to visit St. John's, Olajuwon flew to Houston, where he showed up on campus to a pleasantly surprised Guy Lewis, who was taken by the young Nigerian's height and coordination. Lewis offered him a scholarship, and the young Nigerian easily established his academic and athletic credentials. He was mentored by Terence Kirkpatrick, Lewis's African American assistant coach. Olajuwon's arrival in Houston foreshadowed the emergence of a generation of Nigerian American athletes who became increasingly numerous in subsequent decades.

Hakeem Olajuwon had a lot to learn, but he proved to be a quick study. Kirkpatrick, who became Hakeem's legal guardian so that the player could accept UH's scholarship as a seventeen-year-old, helped him manage his transition to American (and Texan) culture. He took him in, taught him the delicacies of Texas cuisine such as chicken-fried steak, and watched him like a hawk so as to keep his talents under guard by the basketball program. But Olajuwon didn't simply have to learn how to be an American; he also had to learn how to be a *black* American in his early years with the Cougars. He picked up phrases like "What's up, man?"

He learned how to detect the subtle racism of the post–civil rights era from his teammate Lynden Rose, who showed the unknowing Nigerian how to detect racist put-downs. As important, he learned the ways of African American pickup basketball in Houston. Those lessons were imparted through the fierce competitions he experienced at the Fonde Recreation Center, and his mentor was Moses Malone.

Malone didn't tutor the young basketball-player-in-the-making. He just played hard against him and dominated Olajuwon until the young center figured out how to compete with him. "He showed me the respect of playing hard against me," Olajuwon recalled in his memoir. Moses threw his entire arsenal of skills at Olajuwon, using his power to back him in when he had the ball or push the lighter center away from the hoop when he was on defense. Malone used his quickness to spin off of him, shoot his jump shot, or go straight to the "rack," as he liked to call the boards. "He never instructed me—not once did he tell me how to do something—but I watched the way he played and it was all-out," Olajuwon wrote. Basketball at Fonde, as in many playground scenes, was serious business. "There were no weaknesses allowed," he recalled. "You did not call a ticktack foul at Fonde. You're going to the basket and someone slashes at your arm, you don't call a foul—you go in and dunk on him."[10] The young center eventually was able to compete with Malone. "Moses couldn't take a day off against him anymore," McCoy McLemore told *Sports Illustrated*'s Curry Kirkpatrick in November 1983. "They were two titans. The beauty of it was both were laughing—Moses was so proud and tickled. They recognized they could stop each other while nobody else could. It was a dead standoff."[11]

During the summers, Olajuwon worked diligently on his game. He worked on his shot-blocking and defense to make the seasoned Malone work for his points. He also began to draw from his extraordinary balance and footwork to develop a range of offensive moves to score. His leaping ability and height enabled him to develop a turnaround jumper and, when all else failed, to jump and dunk on his opponents. Hakeem's game was made in those spirited battles with Malone at that sweaty gym in downtown Houston as much as it was in the practices and games at UH's Hofheinz Pavilion. Recreation centers and gyms were akin to the jazz clubs and community centers where black jazz musicians and other artists learned their craft in the pre-professionalization age. Like black male basketball players across the country, Olajuwon received a basketball education in the pickup scene. There were no coaches; no parasitic experts and agents who made the seven-footer fit into some sort of "advanced analytic" scheme; no sneaker companies to commodify the athletic labor of a black basketball player. Those forces were on the horizon, spurred in part by the success of college teams like the Houston Cougars.

At Fonde, Olajuwon learned how to be a basketball player and how to perform black manhood on the court. "'Be a Man!' That was the phrase at Fonde. You heard it all the time," he recalled. "Moses would back into me, I would grunt, and he would back in again. And each time he hit me he would say, *'Be a man! Be a man!'*"[12]

*   *   *

Olajuwon might have been living the American dream as a young African immigrant, and he certainly turned out to be a dream come true for the Houston Cougars basketball program. Apprenticing with Malone at Fonde and learning the team game in Lewis's practices enabled the gifted center to accelerate his learning of the sport. He sat out the 1980–1981 season, but he began getting minutes the next season.

Olajuwon wasn't the only talented player who was working to hone his craft at Fonde. He was joined by a host of local players assembled by Lewis and Kirkpatrick. As they had done since the late 1960s, Lewis's staff tapped into the rich talent pools in and around the Houston area. Lewis said, "I made a commitment several years ago that if I was gonna find a Houston guy as good as a guy from New York, I was going to opt for the Houston guy."[13] Unlike college football recruiting in the 1970s, which was a fiercely competitive endeavor, college basketball talent was a little easier to find, since the forces of commercialization had not yet fully descended on the sport. Some players, like Rob Williams, came from recently integrated schools like Houston Milby. Williams was a slick shooting guard who was the team's leading scorer and the first star of the Phi Slama Jama era. From Ross Sterling High School came Clyde Drexler, the then-underrated, smooth-gliding small forward who eventually became a Hall of Famer.

Other Cougars were recruited from some of the same high schools that had produced talented black athletes during the Jim Crow era. From Houston Worthing came Larry Micheaux, the sleek and powerful frontcourt player nicknamed "Mr. Mean." Micheaux also had great hands, which enabled him to catch tough passes, rebound, and shoot soft shots off the glass. From Houston Yates, a stone's throw away from UH, came the highly recruited Michael Young, the six-foot, seven-inch, left-handed sharp-shooting guard/forward, who was among the most highly sought-after players in the state in 1980. Young became one of the team's noteworthy dunkers, but he was also one of the team's better outside shooters. One of his favorite shots was his jumper from the baseline.

In 1982, freshman point guard Alvin Franklin arrived from La Marque, Texas, thirty-three miles southeast of Houston. Even their less talented players were from the Houston area, like six-foot-seven guard Reid Gettys and Dan and David Bunce, all from Conroe, Texas. Others, like the superbly gifted Benny Anders, the six-foot-five forward whose leaping ability and long arms terrorized opponents, came from Louisiana. Anders came from an athletic family: he was a cousin of New York Knicks Hall of Famer Willis Reed and of Orlando Woolridge, the talented basketball player who enjoyed a productive college and professional career. His Jheri curl hairdo and flashy clothes made him one of the more iconoclastic Cougars, and his comet-like career symbolized the Cougars' meteoric rise and fall in the early 1980s.

Of all the Houston-area talents on the 1980s Cougars team, the most compelling was arguably Clyde Drexler, who arrived as an afterthought with his friend Michael Young. Like generations of black Houstonians, the Drexler family had Louisiana roots. His mother, Eunice Drexler Scott, left Clyde's father and moved to Houston, where she remarried and made a new life in a city that seemed to have more opportunities for black people. She and her brother managed Green's Barbecue, a part of a small family business in that part of town, and Clyde worked there as a teenager. Eventually, his interests veered to the basketball court.[14]

Drexler developed his basketball skills later than most of his peers. When he was in high school, he was viewed by basketball observers as a scrawny kid who had leaping ability but not much else. He could barely get in a game at the highly competitive Fonde. But the slights and disregard fueled his competitive drive. He played pickup ball with Michael Young at Macgregor Park, where Zina Garrison and Lori McNeil had learned tennis from John Wilkerson. But over time, Drexler developed into a complete ballplayer. He had the ability to score, and many of his points came off of steals and rebounds. He was also the Cougars' flashiest dunker. He loved his tomahawk-style dunk in which he took the ball and curled it under his arm as he leaped into the air and slammed it through the basket. He was also a skilled defensive player who regularly led the Cougars in steals. He learned to use his quickness and anticipation to jump in the passing lanes and steal passes. His experience playing center in high school enabled him to learn how to be a skilled rebounder, even though at six feet six he was shorter than most of his peers on the frontline. In the end, the lowly regarded Drexler became the team's best all-around player.

"Clyde the Glide," as he was dubbed by Jim Nantz, then a UH student and announcer, patterned his game and his public persona after Julius Erving. In the early 1980s, Erving was arguably the most beloved black sports celebrity among black and white fans. During the same basketball season as Phi Slama Jama's emergence, the Doctor was in the midst of his long-awaited NBA championship run. Erving's charm, affable nature, availability to the press and fans, and seemingly genuine class contrasted with the more contrived nature of O. J. Simpson's public persona. The public nature of his family life, especially his marriage to Turquoise Erving, made him the head of the "first family" of black America. Drexler, like so many young black athletes of this era, patterned himself after Dr. J. Like Erving, he was often described as "classy," and he was a well-spoken leader of Phi Slama Jama who carried himself in a calm and regal manner. His good looks and easygoing nature also enhanced his popularity. And like Dr. J, his awesome dunks revealed the competitive energy that was masked by his seemingly detached demeanor on the court.

During the 1980–1981 season, the nucleus of the Phi Slama Jama era began to come together. With Williams leading the way, the Cougars had a solid regular season and then won the Southwest Conference tournament by blowing out the Texas Longhorns 84–59 in the championship game. But the Cougars crashed back to earth with a loss to the Villanova Wildcats in the first round of the NCAA tournament. Villanova was from the Big East Conference, a group of eight schools in the Northeast that were emerging on the national college basketball scene.

Expectations were high for Guy Lewis's team for the 1981–1982 year. Olajuwon began his first season of eligibility with Micheaux, Young, and Drexler on the team's frontline and with Lynden Rose and Rob Williams in the backcourt. The season was a roller coaster ride. Williams's star text and his ego began to expand as he set his sights on a future career in the NBA. Williams openly defied Lewis's authority, and the coach tolerated his behavior because he produced on the court. In the middle of January, the team lost four in a row in the Southwest Conference, and they seemed to be floundering. But the Cougars reeled off fourteen wins in their next sixteen games, which took them all the way to the Final Four in New Orleans. While Williams had scored his points, Drexler had developed his all-around game and Olajuwon had come off the bench and started to provide glimpses of his extraordinary talents on the defensive end. The young center excelled at blocking shots and intimidating players who tried to go to the hoop. Suddenly, the unranked Cougars arrived at the

Final Four, where they faced off against the North Carolina Tar Heels at the cavernous Louisiana Superdome. Guy Lewis's team had made a name for itself in the Astrodome fourteen years earlier. Now, the coach saw the game rising to heights he had helped set in motion. The NCAA tournament was becoming March Madness, and the Houston Cougars would again become part of the next phase of its evolution.

*   *   *

On the evening of March 29, 1982, CBS cameras scanned down on the Superdome, the monstrous, spaceship-like edifice in downtown New Orleans that was inspired by the Houston Astrodome. The trumpets of New Orleans jazz blared as broadcaster Brent Musburger introduced the national semifinals of the NCAA tournament to millions of television viewers. College basketball was becoming big time, which meant that its signature event needed to be housed in a giant, seventy-thousand-seat domed stadium rather than a traditional fifteen- to twenty-thousand-seat basketball arena. During the week leading up to the national semifinals, Guy Lewis was frequently asked about the 1968 Game of the Century in the Houston Astrodome fourteen years earlier. What seemed like an insane idea at that time was now seen as a catalyst of the game's growth. In the early 1980s, men's college basketball was soaring to unprecedented levels of popularity. It was joining football as the top so-called revenue-generating intercollegiate sports. The key to the transformation, as was the case with all big-time sports, was television. After the historic 1968 Game of the Century, Eddie Einhorn's TVS network broadcast many games, often featuring Wooden's dynastic UCLA Bruins throughout the 1970s. Meanwhile, NBC Sports began to televise the NCAA tournament in 1969. They covered more college basketball games over time, though the amount of college basketball coverage was not on par with televised college football. But it was the 1979 championship game featuring Magic Johnson's Michigan State Spartans against Larry Bird's Indiana State Sycamores that made the tournament a major prime-time event. The game, which achieved the highest rating of any televised basketball game in history, initiated the Bird versus Magic rivalry and increased the popularity of men's college basketball.[15]

Just as NBC Sports started to benefit from the popularity generated by the Magic-Bird 1979 final, the tournament coverage was snatched away by CBS, who paid the NCAA a then-astronomical $48 million to take over the coverage of the tournament. The network televised its first NCAA tournament in 1982. CBS, and the new upstart cable network based in Bristol, Connecticut, called ESPN, paid big money to the NCAA to broadcast college basketball games for national television audiences. These historic television contracts brought universities unforeseen amounts of revenue. Since then, the cost of broadcasting the NCAA tournament has risen over 4,000 percent. In 1985, CBS paid double what it had in 1979—$96 million—to broadcast the NCAA tournament for three more years. By 2011, the investment in the tournament was so great that CBS partnered with Turner Broadcasting to pay $10.8 billion dollars to televise the tournament for fourteen years, and the rights fees keep going up.[16] Meanwhile, in the mid-1980s, shoe companies started to get into the act of commodifying the labor of "amateur" athletes, which brought dollars not only to the schools but also to the coaches, who were becoming celebrities in their own right. In fact, one could argue that college coaches benefitted the most from the money generated by their players and television contracts. The image of coaches changed from largely obscure physical educator figures to national celebrities with their own brand and public personas. And when they weren't coaching on the sidelines, they could find jobs behind the microphone as television commentators.

The seemingly endless possibilities presented by television prompted another revolutionary transformation in college athletics: the creation of the Big East Conference in 1979. The brainchild of the visionary Dave Gavitt, the league comprised nine schools in the historic hotbed of Northeast basketball. The league revived college basketball in a region that had declined after the point-shaving scandals of the 1950s and '60s. Filled with talented players, charismatic coaches, and regular television coverage, the Big East quickly rose to the top of the college basketball world and challenged historic conferences and programs in the Atlantic Coast Conference and the Big Ten for national supremacy. The Big East not only commanded coverage on ESPN but eventually created its own television network, which further popularized its programs. Gavitt was widely seen as a genius because the conference produced national powerhouse programs that made deep runs into the NCAA tournament. By 1989, multiple teams had made the Final Four (Georgetown, Villanova, St. Johns, Syracuse, Providence, and Seton Hall) and two of them, Georgetown and Villanova, won national championships.

Thus, the revolution that began in Houston's Astrodome in 1968 came full circle when the Cougars took the court to face Dean Smith's powerful North Carolina Tar Heels on Final Four Saturday in March 1982. But while Elvin Hayes had been ready for prime time in 1968, the Cougars' star of 1982, Rob Williams, was not. More than sixty thousand fans packed the Superdome to watch the Cougars quickly fall behind the Tar Heels 14–0. Williams tried to take control of the game, but he could not hit a basket all night long. He finished with only two points—both free throws—while missing all eight of his field goal attempts. With their star player in an ill-timed shooting slump, the Cougars were carried by Lynden Rose, the senior point guard and eventual lawyer and school trustee, who had one of the best games of his career. Meanwhile, Drexler provided glimpses of the form he would fully unveil in subsequent years with his rebounding, defense, and hang-in-the-air shots. And Houston's African center made his presence felt with shot-blocking and interior defense. These efforts enabled the Cougars to fight back from the large deficit, but they could not overtake the Tar Heels. They lost by only five points, 68–63, even though their best scorer did not score a basket during the entire game.

Though they played under the patterned system of legendary coach Dean Smith, the Tar Heels possessed stars who played in a style that the Cougars would build upon the following season. In addition to Michael Jordan's memorable game-winning jump shot in the NCAA final victory over Georgetown, some of the more lasting images of the 1982 Final Four were James Worthy's otherworldly quickness and his soaring dunks. Olajuwon recalled Worthy's deep impression on him: "Every time I looked he was waving the ball with one hand and on his way to dunking on the other end—with no one around him."[17] The other player who would have a lasting influence on the young Nigerian was Patrick Ewing, his contemporary and future rival. The similarities between them are striking: both were foreign-born seven-footers (Ewing was from Jamaica), and they had similar skill sets. At that stage of their careers, Ewing's game was more developed than Olajuwon's, though both displayed their extraordinary shot-blocking skills during that memorable weekend in New Orleans. The young Jamaican started as a freshman and was one of Georgetown's impact players. It is striking that these black players from the diaspora would change the way the center position would be played in the 1980s. Ewing and Olajuwon would cross paths many times in the coming years.

The disappointing loss to North Carolina did not dim the Cougars' outlook for the 1982–1983 season. In fact, prognosticators expected them to be better, and they were right. Williams left the Cougars for the NBA draft, and Clyde Drexler became the de facto leader of the team. Whatever outside shooting they lost with Williams's departure was made up for by Michael Young's development as the primary perimeter player, Drexler's continual rise as the team's best all-around player, and Olajuwon's astonishing development as a force in the middle. In the early part of the season, they played well, but they ran into a mini-losing streak against strong non-conference opponents. In December, the Cougars played poorly in a televised contest against Big East power Syracuse, losing 92–87, and then against the Virginia Cavaliers, without their All-American center Ralph Sampson, in Japan, losing 72–63. The performance against the undermanned Cavaliers prompted Lewis to apologize for the team's subpar performance.

"I didn't even recognize our team out there," Lewis moaned to the press. "It was not a typical Houston basketball game and for our poor showing I apologize to the Japanese fans."[18] The next night, they handily beat the University of Utah. They would not lose again until a fateful night in Albuquerque, New Mexico, three months later.

* * *

The Phi Slama Jama nickname was not created by a smart guy in an advertising firm on Madison Avenue in Midtown Manhattan. It was coined by a sports columnist who was trying to figure out how to write a column about a 112–58 blowout victory by the Cougars over a school called the University of the Pacific on January 2, 1983. The Houston sports scene was depressing that winter. At the Astrodome, the "Luv Ya Blue" era of the Oilers had long passed, for the team had just finished a woeful 1–8 strike-shortened season. At the Summit, the NBA Rockets were trudging through their first season without Moses Malone, who had been inexplicably traded to the Philadelphia 76ers the previous fall. In early January, they were in the midst of an eight-game losing streak on their way to a dreadful 14–68 season. Thomas Bonk had to come up with something catchy. He noticed the team had ten dunks during the game, and there lay the inspiration for what became a legendary sports column. "As members of the college roundball fraternity Phi Slama Jama, the Houston chapter has learned proper parliamentary procedure," he began his column. The key criteria for joining this fraternity was your ability to dunk the basketball. "If you are a Phi Slama Jama, you see how many balls you can stuff into a basket." Bonk highlighted the particular skills of Drexler, who Bonk quoted as saying, "Sure, 15-foot jumpers are fine, but *I* like to dunk."[19]

Sports journalists always have the ambivalent position of being boosters and critics of local sports teams, but Bonk's column inadvertently raised journalistic boosterism to a whole new level. Soon thereafter, the UH Athletic Department read the

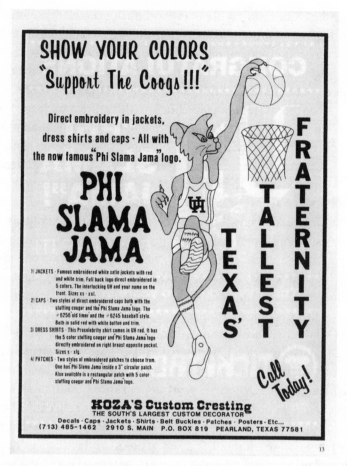

Phi Slama Jama for sale. Courtesy Special Collections Division of the M. D. Anderson Library, University of Houston.

column and asked him if they could use it to market the team. Bonk agreed, and a cultural phenomenon was unleashed soon after. The school quickly put together a whole line of school paraphernalia. T-shirts, dress shirts, caps, patches, buttons, and other items with the Phi Slama Jama logo were suddenly hot items on the market. This was home-grown sports marketing at an embryonic stage before sports apparel passed into the hands of Nike and other athletic corporations.

The Phi Slama Jama phenomenon built up steam because the team kept on winning. They rolled through the Southwest Conference regular season schedule, usually winning in a decisive and compelling fashion. The Cougars rolled into the gyms of the conference teams and beat them handily. In the early 1980s, most college basketball teams played in small facilities with ten thousand seats or fewer. They were more like field houses than arenas (though Hofheinz Pavilion felt a bit more like an arena than Arkansas's Barnhill Arena in Fayetteville). As the season rolled on, the Cougars packed the small gyms of the conference and drew large crowds eager to see them slam and jam.

The Cougars' biggest conference rival were the Arkansas Razorbacks, who, along with the Cougars, were the class of the conference. In the 1970s, the Razorbacks athletic program was shedding its Jim Crow heritage under its formerly segregationist football coach and men's athletic director Frank Broyles. In 1974, Broyles hired Eddie Sutton to coach the men's basketball team. The Oklahoma native was a disciple of the controlled style of play of coaching legend Henry Iba. Sutton would eventually lead the team to multiple Southwest Conference championships and nine straight NCAA tournament appearances. In 1978, the Razorbacks made it to the Final Four led by the "Triplets," Marvin Delph, Ron Brewer, and the multitalented Sidney Moncrief. Sutton's teams were among the most athletic and skilled in the region and were on par with the Cougars. Moncrief became a prototype of the type of guard Sutton recruited to the Razorbacks: six feet four to six feet six, long and lean, defensive-minded guards who also were scoring threats. In the early 1980s, Darrell Walker and Alvin Robertson fit this mold of the Sutton player. Sutton's arrival in Fayetteville happened at the same time the Cougars joined Southwest Conference play, and they formed the fiercest basketball rivalry in the region.

The Phi Slama Jama show rolled into Barnhill Arena in Fayetteville for a late-season showdown against Arkansas on March 3, 1983, hoping to win its first conference championship. But Lewis's team had never won in the wild and crazy Barnhill environment. The game turned out to be a typical Houston-Arkansas hard-fought contest. Led by Benny Anders's scoring off the bench, Houston led 34–27 at halftime. In the second half, key shooting by Michael Young and thunderous jams by Drexler demoralized the Razorbacks and their fans. After one of Drexler's patented tomahawk dunks, the crowd tossed trash onto the court in dismay and frustration. In the end, Houston escaped Fayetteville with a 74–66 victory. The win was their nineteenth in a row since the loss to Virginia in Japan, and it was the highlight of their undefeated SWC season.[20]

Next was the SWC tournament in Dallas, where the Cougars defeated SMU and Texas Christian to head into the NCAA tournament as the number-one seed in the Midwest Regional. Whereas the previous year they had been underdogs, this year they were heavy favorites to win the NCAA title. In the tournament, the number-one ranked Cougars beat their next three opponents relatively easily. In the regional final, they got their revenge against Villanova from the Big East by handily beating them 89–71. Olajuwon emerged as both a scoring and a defensive force. During the tournament run, with the television cameras on every game, the national media discovered what Thomas Bonk had seen firsthand all season long: a dominant team that seemed destined to win it all. Phi Slama Jama was one of the lead stories heading to the national semifinals in Albuquerque, New Mexico.

* * *

In 1982, the NCAA held the Final Four at the cavernous Superdome. The next year, it was held at a traditional basketball arena known as "the Pit" on the campus of the University of New Mexico. The arena opened in 1966, and it resembled other indoor facilities that were built at the time. Yet the Pit had its own charms that would endear it to basketball fans for decades. It was a tough place to play basketball for home and visiting teams alike. The nickname came from the fact that the arena was built into a thirty-seven-foot hole carved into the ground. The small top tier was at street level with seats running down to the floor below. The compact style and the closeness of the stands gave it a claustrophobic feel and made it a loud and intimidating place to play. But the real challenge was the altitude, which was 5,108 feet above sea level and imposed serious challenges for players.

The Final Four arrived in Albuquerque due to the efforts of the University of New Mexico's athletic program. During the 1970s, athletic director Lavon McDonald and his flamboyant head coach, Norm Ellenberger, were determined to take the UNM Lobos basketball team to the big time. Ellenberger made himself into a local legend by recruiting talented players and churning out winning and exciting teams that generated greater fan interest. Meanwhile, McDonald politicked his way to the NCAA basketball committee and got them to award the tournament's main event to UNM in 1978. But the renaissance in New Mexico basketball was halted by "Lobogate." The scandal, which revealed creating fake vouchers for recruiting trips, forging transcripts for student-athletes who would have been academically ineligible to play, and betting on games, got both men fired in 1979. The program was put on probation for three years by the NCAA. Ellenberger and McDonald's reign yet again illuminated the contradictions in the NCAA's "amateur" enterprise. Jerry Kirschenbaum's warning in *Sports Illustrated* in 1980 would be written again and again in subsequent years: "Somebody had better do something. As the New Mexico situation suggests, the pressures on college coaches to win are so enormous that they are encouraged to recruit academically deficient athletes, then go to disturbing lengths to make them eligible."[21]

The suspension stopped the UNM basketball renaissance in its tracks and threatened to derail the agreement to stage the NCAA's showcase event at UNM. But the suspension and the basketball program's rebuilding demonstrated to the NCAA that the Lobos had paid for their sins. The university made the Pit more "TV ready" by adding more lights and rows for the national press. The pomp and circumstance of the Final Four obscured the real structural flaws in the world of big-time "amateur" athletics. CBS and hundreds of members of the national media descended on Albuquerque. The show went on during that memorable weekend in April 1983. It turned out to be quite a show.

* * *

Houston's opponents in the national semifinals on Saturday afternoon, April 2, 1983, were the vaunted Louisville Cardinals, who were among the preeminent college basketball programs in the country. The Louisville and Houston programs mirrored each other in some ways. Both were schools in the South that were among the first to break with Jim Crow and recruit black players. They were upstart programs looking to compete with segregationist flagship state institutions. For Houston, it was the University of Texas and the Southwest Conference powers. For the Cardinals, it was their in-state rivals, the establishment Kentucky Wildcats, who were coached by Adolph Rupp. Rupp, of course, led the all-white team that was defeated by Texas Western in the 1966 NCAA finals.

At Louisville, following the lead of the football program, which had signed Lenny Lyles in the 1950s, head basketball coach Peck Hickman recruited Wade Houston (father of future pro Allan Houston), Eddie Whitehead, and Sam Smith to be the first black players on the university's basketball team. Wes Unseld and Butch Beard, two future NBA players, arrived in the mid-1960s.[22] In 1971, Denny Crum, a John Wooden protégé at UCLA, was hired as Louisville's head coach. Crum, who had been a skillful recruiter as Wooden's assistant, signed more black players than his predecessors. Within a few years, his roster had more black players than most Division 1 college basketball programs. He prioritized athletes from the South, but he faced the challenge of competing for players with the establishment Kentucky Wildcats. As a result, he was able to sign players from all over the country, including the talent-rich Northeast.

Under the energetic Crum, the Cardinals became a national title contender. They made the Final Four in Crum's first season in 1972 and again in 1975, but both times they lost to Wooden's UCLA Bruins. In 1980, they made it back to the championship round and won the NCAA championship with a 59–54 win over UCLA, then coached by Larry Brown. They were nicknamed the "Doctors of Dunk," mostly because the star of their 1980 championship team was Louisville native Darrell Griffith. Griffith, nicknamed "Dr. Dunkenstein," was a six-foot-four guard who was a prolific shooter and an extraordinary leaper known for his impressive dunks. After Griffith's departure, they revamped their team around the talents of Scooter and Rodney McCray, two brothers from Mount Vernon, New York, a predominantly black suburb of the Bronx. They followed in the footsteps of Gus and Ray Williams, two other star players who came out of Mount Vernon. The McCrays were versatile forwards who could score and defend. Like the Cougars, the Cardinals made the 1982 Final Four only to lose a close game to Georgetown in the national semifinals.

The 1982–1983 Cardinals were even better. In addition to the McCrays, they had two talented starters from Mississippi: Charles Jones, who at six-feet-eight was an undersized center who made up for his shorter size with his scoring, passing, and shot-blocking ability. He was joined by fellow Mississippian Lancaster Gordon, a junior guard from Jackson, who was a skilled shooter. Moreover, Crum recruited two other East Coasters from Camden, New Jersey, sophomore point guard Milt Wagner and a raw freshman forward named Billy Thompson. Wagner and Thompson would eventually star on the 1986 national championship team, but in 1982–1983 they were up-and-coming underclassmen who played big minutes for Crum's Cardinals. The team's only real weakness was its lack of depth, as Thompson and freshman sharp shooter Jeff Hall were the only players who got regular minutes among their reserves.

Still, the Cardinals were one of the favorites entering the NCAA tournament. In the NCAA tournament, Louisville beat Tennessee 70–57, then came from behind to beat Eddie Sutton's tough Arkansas Razorbacks 65–63, and finally bested their hated in-state rivals, the Kentucky Wildcats, 80–68 in an exciting overtime victory in the regional final. The win over Kentucky was especially sweet for the Cardinals, since the pompous Wildcats had refused to play their upstart in-state rivals up to that point. With their win over Kentucky, the Cardinals had a 32–3 record, including fifteen wins in a row.

In the first semifinal game in Albuquerque, the North Carolina State Wolfpack took the court against the Georgia Bulldogs. Both underdog teams had unexpectedly made the trip to Albuquerque. They battled it out before the Wolfpack pulled out a fairly comfortable 67–60 win. The other national semifinal, however, turned out to be a truly historic basketball game, one that is worthy of a lengthy revisit.

*　　*　　*

"Good afternoon, Ladies and Gentlemen," Frank Fallon said in his characteristically smooth voice. "Welcome to University Arena, for game two of today's national semifinal doubleheader between the Cardinals of the University of Louisville and the Cougars of the University of Houston."[23] Fallon, the longtime announcer of the Baylor Bears, Southwest Conference basketball, and other sports, was in the midst of his eighteen-year run as the regular public address announcer at the Final Four. Fallon's presence added another small bit of Texas influence at the NCAA's men's basketball tournament. Like Jim Nantz, who eventually called all of CBS's big-time sporting events, and Verne Lundquist, who also worked for CBS for decades, Fallon was yet another Texas-based sports announcer who became a fixture at nationally televised sporting events. As Fallon announced the starting lineups, astute observers of the Cougars noted their new warm-up shirts, which had "Phi Slama Jama" written on the front in script. The warm-ups were provided by Larry Micheaux's father, not by Nike, as would be the case in subsequent decades. Grassroots entrepreneurship and marketing characterized the selling of Phi Slama Jama. Even Phi Slama Jama's swag was homegrown.

Experts saw the Louisville-Houston semifinal as the "real" national championship. It was billed as a matchup between the Doctors of Dunk versus Phi Slama Jama. After a few minutes of play, it was clear that the pregame hype was warranted. The contest that Saturday afternoon in Albuquerque became one of the most historic games in NCAA history because it showcased the dunk at a skill level previously unseen by college basketball observers. The game was a hyper-competitive affair between two superbly talented teams, but it also became a forum of self-expression for the predominantly black players on the floor. It was in the 1980s when the creative playground style of basketball finally made its way to the mainstream Division 1 level. Both teams spent the entire afternoon running up and down the floor and dunking whenever possible. Patterned plays and set offensive sets, which typically dominated college basketball games, were put into the background. Olajuwon remembered that it was "like a game at Fonde" because "everyone felt free and comfortable to create." The pace was lightning fast as "everyone was running down the floor—pass the ball, pass the ball dunk. Up tempo all the way."[24]

But Scooter McCray astutely recalled years later, "What really stands out were the skills, not the dunks. The passing, the ability to feed the post and defend. The fundamentals on display. You had me, my brother, Drexler, Young—tall people for that era being able to handle the ball."[25]

The energy in the building was pulsating as the game began. Houston freshman point guard Alvin Franklin began his impressive performance with a short jump shot in the lane, which was followed by a corner jump shot by Milt Wagner over the Houston 2–3 zone defense. Wagner would hit many jumpers over the Cougars zone from the corner and elsewhere all afternoon. With the score tied 4–4, CBS analyst Billy Packer, who was broadcasting the game, prematurely told the national television audience that the game was a "little mild right now" even though the teams were firing shots as if they were compelled by a shot clock. In the NBA, teams had twenty-four seconds to get off a shot each possession. But no shot clock existed in college basketball until

*Hakeem Olaju-
won battles Rod-
ney McCray for a
rebound. NCAA
Photos.*

1987. In the era before the shot clock, teams often held the ball to
slow down the action, a strategy used by lesser teams when they
wanted to minimize the time more talented teams had the ball.
Louisville would occasionally hold on to the ball to reboot their
energies, but for the most part, both teams fired away at a furious
pace all afternoon.

It was as if the players were egged on by Packer's premature
statement. Minutes later, Louisville's Charles Jones blocked a shot
by Olajuwon. Lancaster Gordon recovered the ball and quickly
flung it up-court to Wagner, who chased it down before it could
bounce out of bounds and, with tremendous court awareness,

tapped it backward to the trailing Rodney McCray, who stuffed it through the hoop. The dunk was the first of eighteen of the night, thirteen executed by the Cougars.

The McCray breakaway slam kick-started the furious tempo that the play sustained most of the afternoon. Yet the loquacious Packer couldn't quite grasp what he was seeing. Perhaps he was waiting for a slow-down half-court game to develop. Perhaps he couldn't help but overanalyze the action, which he had a penchant for doing during his long career on television. He continued to insist to Gary Bender, his partner on the telecast that day, that the teams "hadn't gotten into a flow yet." He did perceptively point out that the players were already exhausted. The first apparent victim of the altitude was Louisville's Charles Jones, an allergy sufferer who had to contend with playing at a breakneck pace in an arena one mile above sea level. With the score tied 14–14, the Cardinals slowed things down to allow Jones to catch his breath. He stood at the foul line bending over with his hands on his shorts. Immediately thereafter, he literally sucked it up by rolling to the basket on a beautiful pick and roll for a dunk.

In his summation of the historic game, Robert Weintraub wrote, "Houston and Louisville brought Rucker Park to the Final Four and changed the college game forever."[26] The legacy of Rucker was present in a general sense, but the Cougars actually represented the impact of Fonde on the game of basketball. In effect, it was Rucker and Fonde all rolled up into one. The Fonde connection was revealed in the ways Drexler and Young teamed up with many memorable plays. In one sequence, Young recovered a blocked shot by Olajuwon and led a fast break with Drexler running alongside him, "on the wing" in basketball parlance. As Young dribbled into the lane, he suddenly dished the ball to Drexler, who jammed it over Scooter McCray trailing behind trying to contest the dunk. The Cougars supporters in the Pit roared their approval.

Drexler's first slam of the afternoon ignited an even faster-paced game over the next several minutes. Wagner continued to hit from the outside, and Jones played heroically even as he struggled with his breathing in the high altitude. Young and Drexler teamed up for a number of two-man games to score layups. Packer once again mischaracterized the action, saying that there weren't a lot of "x's and o's" out there. "These are just athletes going after each other," he said in awe. But the "natural" athleticism masked the fact that there were two well-coached teams executing everything they had worked on in practice. These teams had taken John Wooden's notion of preparation through practice, rather than relying on in-game "x and o" interventionism by a "genius" coach. The lack of a trend that Packer and Bender were looking for was hiding in plain sight: two teams going at each other at a back-and-forth pace in which each would immediately retaliate with a basket or a great defensive play. Olajuwon was gaining the edge over Jones with his shot blocking, which occasionally fooled the referees who mistook his legitimate blocks for goaltending. With the Cardinals up 34–32, Franklin recovered an Olajuwon block and began to dribble downcourt. Keeping his head up, like point guards are coached to do, he threw a great chest pass down to Drexler on the wing. Clyde the Glide soared to the basket with a tomahawk dunk over Thompson, who somehow managed to deflect the dunk attempt. Unbelievably, the ball rolled around the rim and bounced through the hoop. Houston and Louisville were tied, 34–34.

Yet again, Louisville came right back at the Cougars. Wagner followed with another jumper, and Jones hit two free throws to put the Cardinals up 38–34. The Cougars tried to apply a more aggressive "press" defense to try to force turnovers, but Louisville passed right over the Houston defenders. Gordon passed to McCray in the middle of the court, who tossed a long crosscourt pass to Wagner in the corner, where he had been firing jump shots at will all game. Rather than fire another jumper, however, he decided to pass the ball to a wide-open Scooter McCray coming down the lane for another dunk. This was one of the prettiest plays the Cardinals executed all night.

The Cardinals score made Guy Lewis livid, setting the scene for another memorable moment. After a steal by Scooter Mc-Cray, the coach completely lost his cool and tossed his trademark checkered towel onto the floor. The referees issued him a technical foul, and minutes later the first half ended with the Cardinals leading 41–36.

The seesaw nature of play continued in the opening minutes of the second half. Houston mounted a little 7–0 run to go up 43–41. But their senior leader, Larry Micheaux, who had two personal fouls, suddenly collected three fouls to bring him to five, which results in a mandatory disqualification from the game. He fouled out with 13:28 left in the contest. Lewis admitted after the game that he and his staff had lost track of Micheaux's foul count. "I had a bench full of assistants and none of us noticed," he told the press after the game.[27] Micheaux's departure turned out to be the game's turning point. What seemed to be a devastating loss for the Cougars opened the door for the mercurial Anders, the player dubbed as "Instant Offense" by his teammates, to make his mark on the game. Anders provided the spark that the Cougars needed. But the next surge by the Cougars was initiated by defense and rebounding. With the Cougars trailing 57–49, Olajuwon rebounded a Scooter McCray miss and passed it to Franklin, who immediately passed the ball to Drexler, who fired a beautiful lob pass to his friend Young, who jammed it home with one hand.

The Young dunk began what would turn out to be an epic run of defense and fast-break offense by the Houston Cougars. After a Cardinals miss and an Olajuwon rebound, Franklin took an outlet pass from the Nigerian center, who fired a pass to Drexler for another dunk. Louisville's lead was cut to 57–53. Then, one of the more memorable sequences of the game took place. Jones tried to find Scooter McCray with a good bounce pass in the lane, but Benny Anders swooped in and stole the ball and took off for the basket on the opposite end of the floor. As Packer astutely pointed out, after Anders stole the ball, he veered to his right to get a forty-five-degree angle on the basket to evade a block by the trailing Jones. He raced to the hoop and emphatically jammed

Benny Anders soars to the hoop against NC State. Photo by Peter Read Miller, Sports Illustrated.

it over Jones. It was the most dramatic dunk of the night. "Oh!" screamed a disbelieving Bender. Louisville's lead was now 57–55.

The Anders slam further energized the Cougars and their fans. After Wagner picked up a critical fourth foul, which forced him to the bench to keep him from fouling out, the Cougars hit two free throws to put them ahead 58–57. With a tiring Rodney McCray also on the sideline sucking up air from an oxygen tank, Anders and Drexler pulled off another extraordinary sequence. Anders picked off another Jones pass, came down the sideline, and found Drexler speeding down the opposite side. "Here's Drexler!" yelled Packer as Clyde the Glide received a pass from the alert Anders. The Glide took off for the hoop, starting his characteristic tomahawk slam, but in mid-air he changed his mind in anticipation of a block attempt by the defending Jones and slammed it home with two hands. The Cougars went on a 23–5 run, which turned a 57–49 deficit into a 73–62 lead.

Houston kept the pressure on Louisville. Cardinals fans tried to pick up their team with chants of "Defense!" but again, Franklin played like an experienced, fundamentally sound upperclassman. He took control of the offense, made crisp passes, kept his head up to look for someone to pass the ball to on the break, and shot when opportunities presented themselves. On another possession, he passed to Young in the corner, who ran a brilliantly executed two-man pick and roll play with Drexler, who took a nice pass from him off the baseline and hit a layup to extend Houston's lead to 75–64. It was solid fundamental basketball. The layup gave the Glide twenty-one points for the afternoon. After another Louisville missed shot, Drexler grabbed the rebound and started down the court. After a behind-the-back dribble while he ran at full speed, he dished a one-handed pass to the cutting Anders, who emerged from underneath the hoop to lay in yet another fast-break layup. Packer, now in awe of what he was seeing, asked Bender, "Is there any doubt he can do it all?"

Bender reminded viewers that Louisville had come back in their wins over Arkansas and Kentucky in the Mideast Regional. But there would be no Louisville turnaround on this afternoon. They literally ran out of gas, overwhelmed by the Cougars and utterly depleted by the altitude of Albuquerque. On the very next possession, Young penetrated and found Olajuwon, who dunked it. Houston led 82–74. Louisville's comeback was then dealt another blow when the young Thompson missed a breakaway slam that would have cut Houston's lead to six points.

Now it was time for Olajuwon to remind everyone of his presence in the game. Houston went into their spread offense, and Anders found Olajuwon for another dunk. Then Olajuwon blocked a Gordon shot. The ball rebounded directly to Young, who broke away with another one-handed slam. An exhausted Wagner, seeing the handwriting on the wall, let Young go right by him. All the players were completely spent. Lancaster Gordon recalled later, "The Pit is an ungodly place to play. They should never have a tourney game in there. It's so humid, and the effects of the elevation are worse when it's humid. During the timeouts, we were fighting for oxygen more than listening to the coaches." Likewise,

Louisville head coach Denny Crum said, "I always thought if we'd had played at sea level, we would have won."[28]

Houston players were also depleted. After his last dunk, Young squatted down at the center court, unable to move. Louisville could not muster any more baskets on this exhausting afternoon. But Bennie Anders had one more for the national television audience. He rebounded another miss and went all the way in for a reverse dunk to cap off his career-defining game. Minutes later, the Cougars polished off their historic performance with one more block from Olajuwon—his eighth of the night—and Young going coast to coast with a finger roll to end this extraordinary game and extraordinarily grueling test of wills. The Cougars won 94–81.

The gassed Cougars celebrated their incredible win as the Louisville players trudged up the long tunnel that led players to the locker rooms from the court. The scoreboard indicated that the Cougars had "won," but both teams pushed each other beyond their limits as few college basketball teams have ever done. Except for the inexperienced Thompson, no one had a "bad" game. The Cougars filled up the stat sheet and everyone had top-flight performances. A pickup-style game starring two teams dominated by black rosters produced a game that even basketball purists could admire. The awesome exhibition by Guy Lewis's team led all the experts to predict that Houston would roll over North Carolina State in the NCAA final.

The memorable win over Louisville marked the high point of the Phi Slama Jama era. Two nights later, the Cougars suffered a crushing last-second loss to North Carolina State in the championship game. With only seconds left, NC State guard Dereck Whittenburg launched a desperate twenty-five-foot jump shot toward the basket. The ball was falling short when, out of nowhere, forward Lorenzo Charles grabbed it as it was reaching the cylinder and, fittingly, dunked the ball through the hoop. The Wolfpack pulled off a stunning 54–52 upset. NC State's Cinderella story and unbelievable win against Houston catapulted the NCAA tournament into the status of "March Madness." CBS and the NCAA could not have been happier. Jim Valvano's legend was launched, and Guy Lewis was viewed as a coach who blew a sure national championship. Though the young Cougars were devastated, their spirits were lifted a bit when 4,500 fans attended a welcome-back rally in Robertson Stadium.[29]

The Cougars were favored to return to the Final Four the next season, but the forces of commercialization were chipping away at their status as a nationally ranked program. Clyde Drexler decided to leave school a year before he was scheduled to graduate to enter the NBA draft. Hakeem Olajuwon almost followed him to the pros before eventually deciding to stay at Houston for another season. In the early 1980s, star basketball players were leaving the college game for the pros to sign contracts with professional teams, rather than remain unpaid laborers for universities. Big-time NCAA basketball was looking more and more like a glorified minor league system for pro basketball. To incentivize Olajuwon to stay at UH, the suddenly generous NCAA awarded the young Nigerian another season of eligibility, hoping to capitalize on the nation's top player and one of its top programs. Olajuwon decided to stay and play for the Cougars one more season.

Despite the loss of Clyde the Glide, the Cougars had another successful season in 1983–1984. They returned to the Final Four, which was held in the Kingdome in Seattle. After defeating the University of Virginia Cavaliers in the national semifinals, they lost to the tough Georgetown Hoyas in the championship game 84–75. East Coast basketball had once again defeated the best from Texas on the national stage. Weeks later, Olajuwon said goodbye to the University of Houston and declared his eligibility for the NBA draft. His departure marked the denouement of Phi Slama Jama and, in many ways, the end of UH basketball's status as a nationally ranked program. Lewis retired in 1986, and the program has never regained its stature since, overmatched by other college basketball programs with more resources. Once again, an innovative Texas sports operation succumbed to the commercializing forces that it had helped unleash.

For Hakeem Olajuwon, the Cougars years were only the beginning of his long basketball career in Houston. He was chosen as
the number-one pick in the 1984 NBA draft by the Rockets, where
he became a Hall of Famer and one of the greatest centers in the
history of the game during his eighteen seasons as a professional.
In 1994, he led the Rockets to the franchise's first NBA championship. They defeated the New York Knicks, led by Olajuwon's old
rival Patrick Ewing, in a tough seven-game series. One year later,
the Rockets won the NBA championship once again. This time
Olajuwon got help from his old college teammate Clyde Drexler,
who arrived in a mid-season trade to help the Rockets win the title for the second year in a row. The fact that Olajuwon and Drexler, an adopted Houstonian and a native one, were the stars of the
team could not have been lost on many of the city's sports fans. It
is hard to resist the story of the old Cougars finishing off their careers with the championship they were denied during their college
days. One could also view Olajuwon and Drexler as representatives of what Houston had become in the decades after desegregation. It was not by accident that this Texas team, led by an African
American and an African immigrant, cheered on by a multira-
cial, transcultural fan base, took shape in one of the most ethni-
cally diverse cities in late twentieth- to early twenty-first-century
America.[30] Though one of the legacies of the Phi Slama Jama era
was that it helped college basketball transition to an untenable
situation in which "amateur" athletes were producing seemingly
limitless amounts of profits for universities, coaches, and television networks, another is that the team helped usher in the emergence of a new Houston, one that is more representative of the
community than what had existed before the Cougars emerged as
a basketball power. This is one of the legacies of the sports revolution of the 1960s, 1970s, and early 1980s, which shaped, and was
shaped by, forward-thinking management and the athletic talent
of Texas's historically marginalized communities.

Conclusion

The Revolution Undone

DOZENS OF MEMBERS OF THE LOCAL AND NATIONAL MEDIA CRAMMED INTO THE Humphrey Lee Student Center on the campus of Southern Methodist University on a cold drizzly day on February 25, 1987. They came to report on the results of the latest NCAA investigation of the SMU football program. Even after Ron Meyer left for the NFL, the SMU Mustangs remained one of the top football programs in the nation, going 51–5–1 from 1981 to 1984. Booster money from bankers and real estate and oil magnates ensured that blue chip talent continued to arrive at SMU, but it also drew scrutiny from the NCAA's Committee on Infractions. Too much money was indiscreetly flowing into the hands of athletes. This state of affairs was sanctioned by influential members of the university's board of governors, even after the program was put on probation in 1981 and again in 1985. But now, armed with new penalties for repeat violators of their rules, the NCAA was going to drop the hammer on the Mustang program once again.

The press conference on that dreary day in Dallas turned out to be a funeral, as the NCAA levied the harshest penalty ever placed on a college football program. "The university will be prohibited from participating in any football game or scrimmage with outside competition in 1987," NCAA official David Brest somberly announced to the stunned congregation. During the 1988 season, the university was to be "limited to no more than seven games, none of which may be considered a home game." As a repeat violator of NCAA rules—for the seventh time in twenty years and for the second time in five years—the program received a modified but still severe version of the death penalty: no recruiting, no scholarships, no games. No football for a year, which SMU voluntarily extended to two years. There was nothing to be gained for playing seven away games in 1988 with a depleted roster. The era of SMU football as a top program in the country ended on that day.[1]

Texas college football had played a leading role in the commercialization of intercollegiate athletics, and now it would play a defining role in the determining of who would benefit from the profits of athletic labor and who would not in the 1980s. As soon as the "death penalty" was announced, recruiters from eighty college football programs descended on Dallas to scoop up a new supply of athletic laborers. Dismayed Mustang football supporters watched helplessly as players freed up from their commitments to SMU fled to UCLA, Oklahoma, and other universities.

The cataclysmic events that unfolded on that historic day had ripple effects throughout the regional college football landscape. SMU football may have been the most egregious violators of NCAA rules, but they were one of many Southwest Conference schools that were put on probation in the mid-1980s. TCU, the University of Texas, Texas Tech, Texas A&M, and the University of Houston all were put on probation during the 1980s. The numerous probations crippled the SWC. In 1990, the Arkansas Razorbacks left for the Southeastern Conference, effectively signaling the end of the SWC. It also marked the shifting gravity of college football power to the Southeastern Conference, which comprised schools in another region haunted by slavery and Jim Crow. A few years later, UT, Baylor, Texas A&M, and Texas Tech announced that they would leave the SWC and join the Big 8 Conference to form a new Big 12 Conference. The era of "power conferences" had now arrived, and UH, lowly Rice, TCU, and of course SMU were left out in the cold.[2] In 1995, the SWC, once the premier athletic conference in the Southwest, was no more. It would be among the first of a flurry of conference realignments that defined big-time college sports over the next two decades.

Exactly two years after the death penalty was announced on SMU's campus in North Dallas, another seismic event took place a short drive away at the Dallas Cowboys headquarters in suburban Valley Ranch. On February 25, 1989, Bum Bright, who had bought the team from Clint Murchison Jr. five years before, announced he was selling America's Team to a rich Arkansas businessman named Jerry Jones. Jones's first act as team owner was to fire legendary head coach Tom Landry and replace him with Jimmy Johnson, his longtime friend and successful coach of the University of Miami Hurricanes. The news shocked the football world, and it instantaneously ended the Schramm-Landry partnership that had run the Cowboys since the franchise was founded in 1960. Cowboys fans and the Dallas sports media, who had been calling for Landry's head regularly during the previous seasons as the team struggled, expressed outrage at the news. A few months later, Tex Schramm resigned from the Cowboys, and the reign of the NFL's most influential front office had come to an end.[3]

The SMU death penalty and the end of the Schramm-Landry regime in Dallas are usually told as separate stories, but they both reflect the larger shifts in big-time sports in Texas during the 1980s. The historic breakup of the NCAA's regulatory power over television rights of member schools' television contracts in 1984 sent universities scrambling to find as much television money as possible. This situation was further complicated by the proliferation of cable television networks, spearheaded by the ascendance of ESPN, which accelerated the scramble for television money. Over the next few decades, conferences and individual schools developed their own television networks. Maximizing television revenues, not rivalries or geographic proximity, became a primary justification in the organization of athletic conferences.[4]

Universities were scrambling for revenue because the costs of running athletic programs kept going up. And in the 1980s, coaches and athletic directors were just starting to reap the big dollars made possible by the sports revolution of the previous twenty-five years. The signing of head coach Jackie Sherrill by Texas A&M in 1982 to a then-unheard of $1.6 million six-year contract signaled that a new day had arrived for college football coaches. Debates and criticism raged about the misplaced priorities clearly evident in the historic contract, but what Sherrill's signing did was blow the roof off the limits of what college football and basketball coaches could make for their labor. Decades later, head coaches receive salaries of $7 million a year with no evidence that their earning potential will plateau any time soon. High school and college football coaches are among the highest paid employees in public institutions, while athletes remain undercompensated with athletic scholarships and pennies for expenses, not to mention that essential public services like health care and education continue to lose support. Amateurism was destroyed in professional tennis in the early 1970s, but it stubbornly persists in the world of big-time intercollegiate athletics that Texas schools helped create.[5]

The revolution in Texas professional basketball had also petered out by the mid-1980s. The San Antonio Spurs also lost their way in the mid-1980s. In the years after the painful defeat to the Lakers in the 1983 NBA playoffs, the team floundered with an aging roster. George Gervin fell out of favor with management, and the team slumped out of playoff contention. After leading the franchise for fifteen memorable years following his ownership group's "borrowing" of it from Dallas investors, Angelo Drossos decided it was time to leave sports management and sold the team in 1988. Meanwhile, the Houston Rockets began a sudden ascendance with Hakeem Olajuwon and Ralph Sampson in 1986. But the era of the "Twin Towers" fizzled out as fast as it had grown, and Houston's pro basketball team dipped over the next several years.

The fates of Texas's major college and professional teams mirrored the larger crisis in the Texas economy. After decades of seemingly perpetual growth, the oil industry suddenly entered its biggest crisis since the 1930s. After reaching record high prices of thirty-four dollars per barrel in 1981, oil prices dipped in 1982, launching a series of layoffs that led the state to lose 220,000 jobs. The downward trend continued over the next few years before it was dealt a more severe blow when prices plunged to historic lows in 1986—below ten dollars per barrel. The Texas unemployment rate shot up to 10 percent, higher than the national average. Soon the state, especially the oil-dependent areas, became a sea of unemployment, empty oil rigs, empty high-rises, and empty mansions. Migrants who were lured to the Sunbelt by tales of prosperity and good times fled as fast as they had arrived, it seemed.[6]

The oil bust inevitably affected the regional sports landscape significantly. Among the most dramatic evidence of the collapse of the house of cards that was the Texas economy was the fall of the Murchison dynasty. Clint Murchison's failing health and mounting debts were exacerbated in the context of the economic recession. Forced to sell the team in 1984, one of Texas's most influential families declared bankruptcy soon thereafter. By 1987, Clint Murchison was dead. Even Lamar Hunt's financial empire took hits during the 1980s. His family fortune, rooted in oil, real estate, cattle, sugar, and silver, was shaken by the decline of these industries in the mid-1980s. Meanwhile, attendance figures were down in all sports, but they were particularly pronounced at Cowboys games at Texas Stadium and Oilers games in the Astrodome, where thousands of seats and several luxury suites remained empty. The financing and innovation that drove the fragile alliance of capital, enlightened sports managers, and athletic labor power were gone.[7]

As men's professional and collegiate sports were cast adrift in the 1980s, women's sports in the state were on the rise. Spurred by the activism inspired by the passage of Title IX, the descendants of Babe Didrikson emerged on the national stage, and, fittingly, it was a women's basketball program that brought them to the surface. The University of Texas helped usher in a new era of women's sports when it hired Donna Lopiano to be the women's athletic director. A relentless advocate for women's sports and fueled by her own experiences of sexism, Lopiano built the women's athletic program virtually from scratch. As her colleague Darrell Royal whined about Title IX's supposed negative impact on college football, Lopiano proved doubters wrong by building one of the leading women's athletic programs in the country during the late 1970s and 1980s.[8] And under the leadership of Jody Conradt, who was hired as head coach in 1976, UT women's basketball dominated the Southwest Conference and became the top ranked women's program in the country, winning the national championship in 1986.

Furthermore, the legacy of Gladys Heldman and the Original Nine was continued by two black Texan women tennis players from Houston: Zina Garrison and Lori McNeil. Like Clyde Drexler and Michael Young, Garrison and McNeil were products of Houston's grassroots youth sports scene. They learned the game from John Wilkerson, who ran tennis clinics on the public courts of McGregor Park. In the mid-1980s, Garrison and McNeil were among the top-ranked players on the women's tennis tour, challenging the supremacy of Martina Navratilova and Chris Evert. In 1987, McNeil upset Evert at the US Open, while Garrison defeated Navratilova in an exciting three-set match in the semifinals of the US Open one year later. Garrison made another memorable run to the finals of Wimbledon in 1990, where she lost in straight sets to Navratilova. While neither Garrison nor McNeil won a grand slam title, their ascendance signaled the arrival of talented women of color at the top of the professional tennis game.[9]

Meanwhile, the sexual revolution sparked by the Dallas Cowboys Cheerleaders remains stuck in its contradictions. Even as the team's squad of dancers continued to hold the title of America's Sweethearts, they, like all NFL cheerleaders, remained exploited and objectified. The proliferation of lawsuits by former cheerleaders against NFL clubs in recent years reveals another legacy of the sports revolution. Women had greater opportunities to excel and even pursue careers in sports, but most women, including cheerleaders and sideline reporters, remain undercompensated and, as #MeToo-inspired activism has vividly shown, subject to sexual harassment and assault.[10]

But the doldrums of the 1980s gave way to a rebirth among Texas pro and college teams during the 1990s. The Jones-Johnson partnership resulted in another, shorter-lived, Cowboy dynasty. Stars Troy Aikman, Emmitt Smith, and Michael Irvin led the team to three Super Bowl titles. In Houston, Hakeem Olajuwon led the Rockets to consecutive NBA championships in 1993 and 1994, while in San Antonio, the Spurs, sparked by Tim Duncan's arrival, began their remarkable string of six titles. Even the nondescript Mavericks, with star Dirk Nowitzki, won an NBA title in 2011. After years floundering in mediocrity, the Texas Longhorns reemerged in the newly formed Big 12 Conference, culminating in the scintillating performances led by Vince Young that won them the 2005 NCAA title. Even the previously ordinary Texas Rangers became competitive in the 1990s.

These sports storylines, compelling as they were, had little social significance, however. The unique combination of entrepreneurial spirit and social change had been largely overrun by commodification and profiteering. Black male athletes continued to be a dominant presence on the rosters of football and basketball teams, but the transformative impact of racial integration had long subsided. The social dynamism that fueled the innovation of the sports revolution was replaced by a hyper-commodified world of exploitation. New hierarchies have emerged that benefit a few select athletes while the bloating white male management class in all levels of sports finds new ways to extract value from athletic labor.

The trends in Texas politics since the 1960s reveal another set of forces that lingered around and ultimately undermined the sports revolution. The political transformation of the regional ruling class was virtually complete by the 1990s. George Herbert Walker Bush successfully rode the forces that took him from the Texas-Arkansas game in 1969 all the way to the White House in the 1980s. His political playbook borrowed from Richard Nixon's handbook of sports statecraft, as he appeared at many sporting events, especially those in Texas, cultivating an image of a sportsman politician. Indeed, the Southern Strategy in the Sunbelt, used by Republican Party politicians to capitalize on and foment white reactionary grievances against desegregation, paid big dividends for the Bush family. They successfully represented a new form of conservative right wing politics of a "kinder, gentler" America that masked an aggrieved white conservativism that fueled their drive to the White House.

The governor's office and the state legislature also came under control of the Republican Party. Bill Clements—the same Bill Clements who sanctioned the continuing payments of SMU football players when he was chair of the university's board of governors—was the first Republican elected governor since Reconstruction. By the 1990s, party politics had been completely realigned. Texas Democrats had lost ground to the groundswell of white-grievance, anti-state interventionist politics catalyzed by the Republicans. Gerrymandering helped as well. Mark White and Ann Richards in the 1980s were the last Democrats to serve as governor. George W. Bush's political ascendance is instructive, as he parlayed his ownership of the Texas Rangers into the state governorship in 1994 and the White House in 2000. His initial $600,000 investment in the team turned into a $14.9 million dollar payday when the team was sold to Tom Hicks in 1998.[11]

The contradictory legacies of the sports revolution can be seen in the explosion of mega stadium projects since the 1990s, and to some extent, Texas was a trendsetter. After commodifying every inch of Texas Stadium real estate for years, Jerry Jones decided it was time to push for a more opulent stadium for America's Team. When the City of Irving wisely balked at his demands, the enterprising Cowboys owner took his team to Arlington, the suburb that Tom Vandergriff helped make into a sports and entertainment zone in the Metroplex. The city that lured the Senators away from the nation's capital was excelling at creatively finding ways to use public money to build more stadiums, building the Ballpark (later named Globe Life Park) in Arlington for the Rangers in 1995 and then the new Globe Life Field ballpark for the Rangers set to open in 2020. Joining the wave of NFL stadiums that have been built over the past two decades, Jerry Jones opened his

$1.4 billion Cowboys Stadium (later renamed AT&T Stadium) in 2009. The facility, also called "Jerry's World," is essentially Murchison's Texas Stadium on steroids. It covers three million square feet of space covering seventy-three acres (140 acres including the parking lot), with a seating capacity of one hundred thousand and a gigantic LED display television that hangs down from a retractable roof. While the Astrodome was among the first stadiums to combine accessibility with affluence, AT&T Stadium was simply an unabashed monument to those who possessed or aspired to possess affluence. With more hyper-technological sports palaces built after Jerry World's opening, and with more on the way, the revolution unleashed by Roy Hofheinz and Clint Murchison continues without end.[12]

Indeed, not even Hofheinz's "Eighth Wonder of the World" survived the sea change in stadium construction that swept the United States in the 1990s. Bud Adams, the widely disliked owner of the Houston Oilers, began agitating for improvements to the Astrodome in the middle of the economic recession of the 1980s, claiming, with some justification, that the stadium's small seating capacity was inadequate for an NFL franchise. Harris County officials caved in to his demands after Adams openly entertained offers to move his team to Jacksonville, Florida. The county agreed to take down the stadium's beloved exploding scoreboard to install ten thousand extra seats and sixty-six additional luxury suites. NFL commissioner Pete Rozelle had promised that the Dome would receive "strong consideration" as a Super Bowl site if the county agreed to expand the stadium for the Oilers. But the Super Bowl never came, and only seven years after the 1989 renovation, the Oilers would be off to greener pastures in Nashville as the rebranded Tennessee Titans.

Three years later, the Astros left the Dome, arguably the most significant aspect of the team's identity since 1965. Thirty-five years after it opened its doors, the Eighth Wonder of the World was deemed obsolete. In 2000, the team moved into a new downtown ballpark with a retractable roof, appropriately named after Enron. But the energy corporation went bankrupt in an igno-

AT&T Stadium, aka "Jerry's World." Photo by Richard Rodriguez.

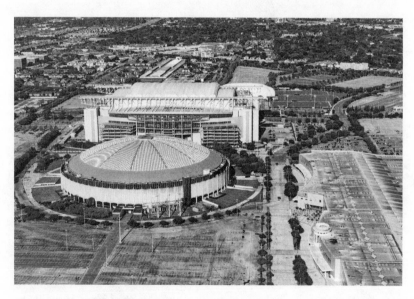

The Astrodome with the Houston Texans' home stadium in the background. Photo by Art Wager.

The Eighth Wonder of the World, 2017. Boston Globe *photo.*

minious fashion soon thereafter, and the facility's naming rights were sold to the Coca Cola subsidiary Minute Maid, with which they still lie to this day. Meanwhile, the National Football League could not leave the fourth largest television market in the country without a pro football franchise. Houston eventually found the money it would not give to Adams to build a new football-only stadium for a new expansion franchise, the Houston Texans.

In the shadow of the new football stadium, the Astrodome sits empty. What was once the Eighth Wonder of the World is now a white elephant. Yet many understandably cannot fathom a Houston without it. In 2015, twenty-five thousand people gathered in the Dome to commemorate the arena's fiftieth anniversary, desperate to convince local politicians to keep it alive as a usable facility. The emotional outpouring among those who can't bear to see the Dome demolished is evidence of the stadium's impact on the lives of Houstonians.

In 2009, before the facility officially closed its doors, I had the opportunity to tour the decaying Astrodome. The iconic Lucite paneled roof remained intact, letting in the rays of sunlight that bedeviled outfielders for thirty-five years. Looking up at the roof, I couldn't help but visualize the many significant moments that took place on the Astrodome floor, where black and white Houstonians carried Elvin Hayes off the floor after beating UCLA in 1968, where Earl Campbell made his memorable touchdown run against the Dolphins in 1978. The fading upholstered seats where integrated crowds of Houstonians watched their heroes for years were covered with layers of dust. As I walked by the abandoned locker rooms, the stench of the mildew was suffocating as I imagined where Billie Jean King told Frank Gifford about feminism and sports, where Bill Yeoman got his Cougars ready to play, where Muhammad Ali shadow-boxed before demanding Ernie Terrell say his name. The dark and dank corridors, the rolled-up rugs of Astroturf, the stench of the mildew, the chipped paint, the dust, the thousands of seats that sit empty, and the eerie silence that pervades the Houston landmark seem to be apt reminders of what has been lost from the sports revolution of the 1960s and 1970s.

Acknowledgments

BOOK PROJECTS SEEM TO FIND ME. WHEN DAVE HAMRICK, THEN THE DIRECTOR OF the University of Texas Press, unexpectedly asked me whether I was interested in writing a history of sport in Texas, I couldn't help but give his offer careful consideration. I was not trained as a Texas historian, but I had been conceiving of a project on a history of the Houston Astrodome as I was transitioning away from my earlier work on Cuban history. I was endlessly fascinated with Texas, the place I called home for ten years. Dave's invitation came at the precise moment I was leaning toward taking up the challenge of integrating my long-standing passion for sports into my work as a scholar and teacher. I decided to accept Dave's offer, and I am glad that I did.

Like all historians, I am deeply indebted to all the archivists who make it possible for us to do our work. I am grateful to Joan Gosnell at the DeGolyer Library at SMU for her timely assistance, expertise, and sense of humor. Thanks to Gerry York for sharing his infectious enthusiasm for SMU football and for sharing materials with me from Heritage Hall at SMU, especially the DVDs of Doak Walker. Thank you to Mary Manning and the rest of the staff in the Special Collections department of the University of Houston Library. I am also grateful to the staffs of the Elizabeth Huth Coates Library at Trinity University, the Dolph Briscoe Center for American History at UT-Austin, the Houston Metropolitan Research Center at the Houston Public Library, and the University of Texas at Arlington. A big thank-you goes to Roland Rainey for sharing his expertise on the history of the Cotton Bowl with me.

As I transitioned into the world of sports scholarship and sports writing, I found an extraordinary group of interlocutors who enriched my understanding of sport and society. Heartfelt gratitude goes to Jasmine Mitchell, who read and commented on many chapters of the manuscript. I am indebted to the extraordinary women of the "Burn It All Down" feminist sports podcast—Brenda Elsey, Amira Rose Davis, Jessica Luther, Shireen Ahmed, and Lindsay Gibbs—whose research, writing, and commentary on sports and feminism have profoundly enriched my intellect and life. To Noah Cohan, the visionary scholar who almost singlehandedly created the Sports Studies Caucus of the American Studies Association, which has become an unexpected space of valuable intellectual engagement for me in recent years. Academics get a bad rap these days, sometimes with good reason, but such criticisms overlook the transformative possibility of innovative scholarship and teaching that I've been blessed to experience throughout my career.

Sincere thanks to Nancy Richey for generously agreeing to let me interview her about her life and career, and to Julie Heldman, who also offered insights on her mother, Gladys, and on the tennis life as women players experienced it in the 1960s and '70s. Her memoir, *Driven*, is one of the most gripping books that I have ever read. Heartfelt thanks also go to Bonnie Keammerer for opening up the world of the Baseline Bums to me, and to Chip Rives, whose excellent documentary films on Houston sports have been a major influence on this project.

Thank you to the following colleagues and friends for the various ways they helped make this book possible: Howard Bryant, Ben Carrington, Paul Chamberlin, George Chauncey, Lee Edwards, Ellen Gambino, Robert Gooding-Williams, Ron Gregg, Farah Jasmine Griffin, Sharon Harris, Karl Jacoby, Mónica Jiménez, Daniel Alexander Jones, Matt Joseph, Rashid and Mona

Khalidi, Minkah Makalani, Stephanie Lang, Steve Marshall, Stephanie McCurry, Andrew McGregor, Shawn Mendoza, Patricia Morel, Alondra Nelson, Mae Ngai, Lien-Hang Nguyen, Aaronetta Pierce, Millery Polyne, Judy Polyne, Eli Reed, Theresa Runstedtler, Brooks Swett, Shirley Thompson, Lucia Trimbur, and Claudia Voyles. I am also profoundly grateful to the many students whom I have had the privilege of teaching in my Sport and Society in the Americas class at Columbia. Their insights and enthusiasm, as well as their feedback, have enriched my understanding of sport in the past and present.

During my time in Austin, I was also privileged enough to be surrounded by a group of scholars and students who contributed to what might be described as an "academic renaissance" at the University of Texas. From 2004 to 2015, I was extremely fortunate to be part of a large cohort of scholars that the university hired in the humanities, the social sciences, the arts, and the field of education who were exemplary scholars and teachers. In our own way, we helped transform the University of Texas from an institution that was defined by its Jim Crow legacy to one that was more representative of the state's ethnic, racial, and gender diversity. It was also at UT that I learned from Deborah Paredez, Jill Dolan, and Stacy Wolf how performance shapes our understanding of feminism and sexuality. I was also enriched by my association with sports enthusiasts who compelled me to combine my long-standing interest in sports into my work as a professional historian. It occurred to me, as it has to many others, that sport is an important arena of study where scholars interested in identity formation, sexuality, feminism, and social justice could forge new histories of the United States. When I was director of the Warfield Center for African and African American Studies, I encountered the extraordinary members of the Prairie View Interscholastic League Coaches Association (PVILCA), a group of retired educators and coaches who are dedicated to preserving and promoting the inspiring athletic history of African Americans in Texas. It was from Robert Brown, Joe Pierce, and Michael Hurd that I learned about the extraordinary impact of black Texan athletes, and it was my many conversations with them that compelled me to write about aspects of sports history that have tended to be overlooked in US and the state's history. I was profoundly enriched by the work I did with them, and many others who are too numerous to name here, on the Thursday Night Lights Symposium at UT in 2013.

At UT Press, my editor, Robert Devens, has been a pleasure to work with. I am grateful for his patience, encouragement, and expertise throughout this process. Thanks also to the rest of the press's team who helped this book come to fruition. During the review process, Amy Bass provided extremely generous and incisive feedback on the manuscript, as did Charles Martin, whose book on the integration of intercollegiate sports in the South is still the go-to text on the subject.

Coming back to New York has allowed me to be in closer proximity to my family again. This book is dedicated to my parents, Francisco and Amparo, who first introduced me to sports. I was not a star athlete, but it was on the baseball diamond, not at school, where I learned some of the most valuable lessons in life as a young boy of color coming up in the Bronx in the 1980s, when the public schools were in the process of being abandoned by the state. My brother Daniel knows more about the challenges of teaching and coaching in New York City public schools than anyone, and I am grateful to him for his support and encouragement. The Díaz, García, and Toplitsky families continue to leave their imprints on my life and on this book in innumerable ways.

I am extraordinarily grateful to my San Antonio family, because it is they who convinced me to retire my allegiance to my favorite basketball team, the Los Angeles Lakers, and join the ranks of the adherents of the San Antonio Spurs. More importantly, they showed me what Mexican American fan culture looks like. Thank you to Gilberto "Grouch" and Consuelo Villarreal, and to my brother-in-law Gilbert, a master soccer coach who has taught me many things about the game. And thanks to the rest of the Salinas, Bustillo, Lozano, Villarreal, and Rodriquez families, who have always been loving to me in that sweet San Anto' way.

Words cannot adequately convey the enormous love and gratitude I have for my beloved, the incredibly gifted writer, poet, and scholar Deborah Paredez. She did the hard work of convincing me that I should write a book about sports, and then she did the harder work of enduring my crankiness as I wrote it. She also read chapters on demand and offered her invaluable insights as only she could. And last, but not least, thank you to my daughter, Zaya Alegría, who knows how indebted she is to Billie Jean King and the Original Nine, and who lives out the legacies of the sports revolution in ways even I did not. Thank you, Zaya, for the timely writing schedule you suggested to me as I was finishing the book and for giving me the opportunity to be a better person every day.

Notes

INTRODUCTION

1. "Nov 20, 1978—Week 12—MNF-Oilers vs. Dolphins-(First Half)," YouTube video, posted June 26, 2016, by Bran Stark, https://www.youtube .com/watch?v=PfpYYmLsjjk; "Nov 20, 1978—Week 12—MNF-Oilers vs. Dolphins-(Halftime and Second Half)," YouTube video, posted June 26, 2016, by Bran Stark, https://www.youtube.com/watch?v=HKYJcH4GjpU.

2. Jane Wolfe, *The Murchisons: The Rise and Fall of a Texas Dynasty* (New York: St. Martin's, 1989); Michael Macambridge, *Lamar Hunt: A Life in Sports* (Kansas City, MO: Andrews McMeel, 2012); Joe Nick Patoski, *The Dallas Cowboys: The Outrageous History of the Biggest, Loudest, Most Hated, Best Loved Football Team in America* (New York: Little Brown, 2012); and John Pirkle, *Oiler Blues: The Story of Pro Football's Most Frustrating Team* (Houston: Sportline, 2000).

3. Benjamin D. Lisle, *Modern Coliseum: Stadiums and American Culture* (Philadelphia: University of Pennsylvania Press, 2017); Robert C. Trumpbour and Kenneth Womack, *The Eighth Wonder of the World: The Life of Houston's Iconic Astrodome* (Lincoln: University of Nebraska Press, 2016).

4. The literature on Reconstruction and the civil rights eras is too voluminous to cite here. For the purposes of this discussion, see Eric Foner, *Reconstruction: America's Unfinished Revolution, 1863–1877* (New York: Harper & Row, 1988); W. E. B. DuBois, *Black Reconstruction in America* (New York: Harcourt, Brace, 1935); C. Van Woodward, *The Strange Career of Jim Crow* (New York: Oxford University Press, 1957); and Manning Marable, *Race, Reform, and Rebellion: The Second Reconstruction in Black America, 1945– 1980*, 2nd ed. (Jackson: University Press of Mississippi, 1990).

5. Bruce J. Schulman, *From Cotton Belt to Sunbelt: Federal Policy, Economic Development and the Transformation of the South, 1938–1980* (New York: Oxford University Press, 1991).

6. Jack Scott, *The Athletic Revolution* (New York: Free Press, 1971); Harry Edwards, *The Revolt of the Black Athlete* (New York: Free Press, 1969); Billie Jean King with Cynthia Starr, *We Have Come a Long Way: The Story of Women's Tennis* (New York: Regina Ryan, 1988).

7. "Nov 20, 1978—Week 12—MNF-Oilers vs. Dolphins-(First Half)."

CHAPTER 1: SPORTS IN THE SHADOW OF SEGREGATION

1. All *Dallas Morning News* quotes are from "Old South to Live Again on Bowl Day," *Dallas Morning News*, December 17, 1950; Frank X. Tolbert, "Kilgore's Girls Leave 'Em Sighing," *Dallas Morning News*, January 3, 1951.

2. Dwonna Goldstone, *Integrating the 40 Acres: The 50-Year Struggle for Racial Equality at the University of Texas* (Athens: University of Georgia Press, 2006), 4.

3. Bill O'Neal, *The Texas League: A Century of Baseball* (Austin, TX: Eakin Press, 1987); Robert Fink, *Playing in the Shadows: Texas and Negro League Baseball* (Lubbock: Texas Tech University Press, 2010).

4. Michael Oriard, *King Football: Sport and Spectacle in the Golden Age of Radio and Newsreels, Movies and Magazines, the Weekly and the Daily Press* (Chapel Hill: University of North Carolina Press, 200), 65.

5. George White, "Mustangs Defeat Steers in Nerve Tingle, 14–13," *Dallas Morning News*, November 2, 1947.

6. Charles H. Martin, "Integrating New Year's Day: The Racial Politics of College Bowl Games in the American South," *Journal of Sport History* 24, no. 3 (Fall 1997), 365.

7. Charles K. Ross, *Outside the Lines: African Americans and the Integration of the National Football League* (New York: NYU Press, 1999), 145–146.

8. Darwin Payne, *In Honor of the Mustangs: The Centennial History of SMU Athletics, 1911–2010* (Dallas: Southern Methodist University De-Golyer Library Lettermen's Association, 2010), 82.

9. "Southern Methodist," *Life*, September 27, 1948, 79.

10. "Dallas Officially Welcomes Babe Didrikson Home Thursday," *Dallas Morning News*, August 7, 1932.

11. Susan B. Cayleff, *Babe: The Life and Legend of Babe Didrikson Zaharias* (Urbana: University of Illinois Press, 1995), 22.

12. Cayleff, *Babe*, 51–57.

13. Cayleff, *Babe*, 65.

14. All Davis quotes from Ann Atterberry, "Kicks! She's High-Stepping Down," *Dallas Morning News*, March 3, 1979.

15. Elliott Erwitt, *Beauty Knows No Pain* (Briarcliff Manor, NY: Benchmark Films, 1973), Internet Archive, accessed March 8, 2018, https://archive.org/details/beautyknowsnopain.

16. Phil Deloria, *Playing Indian* (New Haven, CT: Yale University Press, 1998).

17. Erwitt, *Beauty Knows No Pain*.

18. Sam Blair, "Rangerettes: Never a Loss," *Dallas Morning News*, September 14, 1958.

19. Erwitt, *Beauty Knows No Pain*.

20. Oriard, *King Football*, 181; "Bill Henry Says," *Los Angeles Times*, December 3, 1935.

21. Ann Draper, "Coeds Plan Cheers for Ponies," *Dallas Morning News*, September 3, 1959.

22. "Local Negro Gridmen Bid for State Crown in Thursday Go Here," *Dallas Morning News*, November 2, 1931.

23. Michael Hurd, *Thursday Night Lights: The Story of Black High School Football in Texas* (Austin: University of Texas Press, 2017).

24. Stan Wright and George Wright, *Stan Wright, Track Coach: Forty Years in the "Good Old Boy Network": The Story of an African American Pioneer* (San Francisco: Pacifica Sports Publications, 2005).

25. This memorable phrase is from historian Earl Lewis, *"In Their Own Interests": Race, Class, and Power in Twentieth Century Norfolk* (Berkeley: University of California Press, 1991).

26. Thurman W. Robins, *Requiem for a Classic: Thanksgiving Turkey Day Classic* (Bloomington, IN: Author House, 2011).

27. Hurd, *Thursday Night Lights*, 32–39.

28. Ignacio M. García, *When Mexicans Could Play Ball: Basketball, Race, and Identity in San Antonio, 1928–1945* (Austin: University of Texas Press, 2013).

29. Robert D. Jacobus, *Houston Cougars in the 1960s: Death Threats, the Veer Offense, and the Game of the Century* (College Station: Texas A&M University Press, 2015), 192–193.

30. All Landry quotes from Tom Landry with Gregg Lewis, *Tom Landry: An Autobiography* (New York: Harper Collins, 1990), 51.

31. R. Gaines Baty, *Champion of the Barrio: The Legacy of Coach Buryl Baty* (College Station: Texas A&M University Press, 2015).

32. Ty Cashion, *Pigskin Pulpit: A Social History of High School Football Coaches* (Austin: Texas State Historical Association, 1998).

33. "UT Teams Officially Integrated" *Austin Statesman*, November 19, 1963.

34. Goldstone, *Integrating the 40 Acres*, 126.

35. Terry Frei, *Horns, Hogs, and Nixon Coming: Texas vs. Arkansas in Dixie's Last Stand* (Langham, MD: Taylor Trade, 2002).

36. Ronald E. Marcello, "The Integration of Intercollegiate Athletics: North Texas State College as a Test Case, 1956," *Journal of Sport History* 14, no. 3 (Winter 1987): 286–316.

CHAPTER 2: SPACESHIPS LAND IN THE TEXAS PRAIRIE

1. Houston Sports Association, *Rain or Shine* (Houston Sports Association, 1960), Robert J. Minchew Houston Astrodome Architectural and Engineering Collection, box 94-274/19, Dolph Briscoe Center for American History, University of Texas at Austin.

2. John Eisenberg, *Ten Gallon War: The NFL's Cowboys, the AFL's Texans, and the Feud for Dallas's Pro Football Future* (New York: Houghton Mifflin Harcourt, 2012), 20.

3. Tyina L. Steptoe, *Houston Bound: Culture and Color in a Jim Crow City* (Berkeley: University of California Press, 2016), 5.

4. On the making of the Sunbelt, see Bruce J. Schulman, *From Cotton Belt to Sunbelt: Federal Policy, Economic Development and the Transformation of the South, 1938–1980* (New York: Oxford University Press, 1991). On the environmental aspects of this process, see the excellent Martin V. Melosi and Joseph A. Pratt, ed., *Energy Metropolis: An Environmental History of Houston and the Gulf Coast* (Pittsburgh, PA: University of Pittsburgh Press, 2007).

5. For an overview of the advent of racial segregation in Houston, see Howard Beech and Cary D. Wintz, eds., *Black Dixie: Afro-Texan History and Culture in Houston* (College Station: Texas A&M Press, 1992), 87–101. On the "progressive southwest" propaganda, see Houston's bid for the 1974 Super Bowl, General Rice Stadium information file, Woodson Research Center, Fondren Library, Rice University.

6. Michael Macambridge, *Lamar Hunt: A Life in Sports* (Kansas City, MO: Andrews McMeel, 2012), 92.

7. F. Kenneth Jansen, "The Houston Sit-in Movement of 1960–61," in *Black Dixie: Afro-Texan History and Culture in Houston*, ed. Howard Beech and Cary D. Wintz, 211–222; Thomas R. Cole, *No Color Is My Kind: The Life of Eldrewey Stearns and the Integration of Houston* (Austin: University of Texas Press, 1997); and Brian D. Behnken, *Fighting Their Own Battles: Mexican Americans, African Americans and the Struggle for Civil Rights in Texas* (Chapel Hill: University of North Carolina Press, 2011), 72–83.

8. See Thurman W. Robins, *Requiem for a Classic: Thanksgiving Turkey Day Classic* (Bloomington, IN: Author House, 2011); and Michael Hurd, *Thursday Night Lights: The Story of Black High School Football in Texas* (Austin: University of Texas Press, 2017).

9. Stan Wright and George Wright, *Stan Wright, Track Coach: Forty Years in the 'Good Old Boy Network': The Story of an African American Pioneer* (San Francisco: Pacifica Sports Publications, 2005).

10. "Bud's Eyeview," *Houston Forward Times*, August 27, 1960.

11. Hosea Evans to Gloster Current, 15 September 1961, and other correspondence in NAACP Selected Branch Files, 1956–1965, Houston, Texas, film 17412, series A, reel 15. On the impact of black players on the Oilers and the American Football League, see Charles K. Ross, *Mavericks, Money, and Men: The AFL, Black Players, and the Evolution of Modern Football* (Philadelphia, PA: Temple University Press, 2016). Ross's otherwise useful study of race in the AFL imprecisely argues that the Oilers policy of segregated seating "appears to have ended after the 1960 season." See Ross, *Mavericks*, 27. In fact, black sports fans and activists continued to protest segregated seating and the lack of black players on the Oilers into the 1961 and beyond.

12. "Some Scenes from Chargers Loss to Houston Oilers at Jeppesen Today," and "Special Negro Fans Support the Oilers," *Houston Informer*, December 9, 1961.

13. Lloyd C. A. Wells, "Dateline Sports," *Houston Informer*, December 2, 1961.

14. Jeff Miller, *Going Long: The Wild 10-Year Saga of the Renegade American Football League in the Words of Those Who Lived It* (Chicago: Contemporary Books, 2003), 153–154.

15. "G Kirksey Says No Baseball Bias Here," *Houston Informer*, December 30, 1961.

16. Quentin R. Mease, *On Equal Footing: A Memoir* (Austin, TX: Eakin Press, 2001), 87.

17. Edward W. Ray, *The Grand Huckster* (Memphis, TN: University of Memphis Press, 1980), 219; Mease, *On Equal Footing*, 81.

18. Cole, *No Color Is My Kind*, 59.

19. See, for example, "Houston B and P Men Endorse Stadium Bonds," *Houston Informer*, December 22, 1962; and "Astro Dome Is Giving Team Wide Significance," *Houston Informer*, February 13, 1965.

20. Mease, *On Equal Footing*, 91.

21. All of the Dome's "firsts" were documented in the detailed, lavishly illustrated promotion book published by Hofheinz's Houston Sports Association, *Inside the Astrodome* (Houston: Houston Sports Association, 1965). Ray, *Grand Huckster*; Bruce C. Webb, "Diamond in the Round: The Astrodome Turns 25," *Cite* 24 (Spring 1990): 7–10; Benjamin D. Lisle, *Modern*

Coliseum: Stadiums and American Culture (Philadelphia: University of Pennsylvania Press, 2017).

22. *The Pleasures of This Stately Dome*, directed by Geoff Winningham and Jack York (Houston: Rice University Media Center, 1975).

23. Winningham and York, *Pleasures of This Stately Dome*.

24. Lisle, *Modern Coliseum*, 172.

25. Houston Sports Association, *Inside the Astrodome*, 45.

26. Herskowitz quote from Winningham and York, *Pleasures of This Stately Dome*.

27. Daniel Rosensweig, *Retro Ball Parks: Instant History, Baseball, and the New American City* (Knoxville: University of Tennessee Press, 2005), 84–85.

28. On stadiums and suburbanization, see Lisle, *Modern Coliseum*, and Eric Avila, *Popular Culture in the Age of White Flight: Fear and Fantasy in Postwar Los Angeles* (Berkeley: University of California Press, 2006).

29. Ross, *Mavericks, Money, and Men*, 65–82.

30. On UH's pioneering role in the recruitment of black athletes in the South, see Robert D. Jacobus, *Houston Cougars in the 1960s: Death Threats, the Veer Offense, and the Game of the Century* (College Station: Texas A&M University Press, 2015); and Katherine Lopez, *Cougars of Any Color: The Integration of University of Houston Athletics, 1964–1968* (Jefferson, NC: McFarland, 2008). The emergence of Latino stars on Houston teams happened soon thereafter, in the early 1970s, with the rise of César Cedeño, the talented outfielder for the Houston Astros.

31. Ray, *Grand Huckster*, 334–335.

32. John Eisenberg, *Cotton Bowl Days: Growing up with Dallas and the Cowboys in the 1960s* (New York: Simon and Schuster, 1997), 73.

33. Roy Edwards, "The Mayor's View," *Dallas Morning News*, July 3, 1967.

34. *America's Game: The Super Bowl Champions*, season 1, episode 6, "1971 Dallas Cowboys" (NFL Productions, 2007).

35. Eisenberg, *Cotton Bowl Days*, 264.

36. Jeane Barnes, "Spectators Sport Luxury," *Dallas Morning News*, October 23, 1971.

37. Eisenberg, *Cotton Bowl Days*, 264.

38. *America's Game: The Super Bowl Champions*.

CHAPTER 3: THE OUTLAWS

1. Charles H. Martin, *Benching Jim Crow: The Rise and Fall of the Color Line in Southern College Sports, 1890–1980* (Urbana: University of Illinois Press, 2010), 211.

2. Walter Robertson, "Interception, Punt Return Nip Ags, 21–14," *Dallas Morning News*, November 6, 1966.

3. Martin, *Benching Jim Crow*.

4. Steve Pate, "Houston's Coloring Book," *Dallas Morning News*, September 24, 1975.

5. David Whitford, *A Payroll to Meet: A Story of Greed, Corruption, and Football at SMU* (Lincoln: University of Nebraska Press, 2013), 29–37.

6. Jerry LeVias interview, April 24, 2018, Southern Methodist Oral History and Digital Humanities Student Project, http://digitalcollections.smu.edu/cdm/singleitem/collection/ohdh/id/26/rec/1.

7. Hayden Fry, *Hayden Fry: A High Porch Picnic* (Champaign, IL: Sports Publishing, 1999), 67.

8. Richard Pennington, *Breaking the Ice: The Racial Integration of Southwest Conference Football* (Jefferson, NC: McFarland, 1987), 79.

9. Martin, *Benching Jim Crow*, 195–198.

10. Morton Sharnik, "Too Small to Be Overlooked," *Sports Illustrated*, November 30, 1970, 24.

11. Temple Pouncey, *Mustang Mania: Southern Methodist University* (Huntsville, AL: Strode Publishers, 1981), 210.

12. Bob St. John, "Levias—Top Student, Citizen," *Dallas Morning News*, November 21, 1966.

13. Robert Morehead, "More on Sports," *SMU Campus*, November 22, 1966, 8.

14. Pouncey, *Mustang Mania*, 218.

15. Fry, *Hayden Fry*, 82.

16. Jerry LeVias interview.

17. "Levias Excels in Spite of Abuse," *Dallas Morning News*, November 20, 1966.

18. Richard Boldt, "Boldt from the Blue," *Austin Statesman*, December 2, 1966.

19. Fry, *Hayden Fry*, 77.

20. Jerry LeVias interview.

21. The entire ABC Sports telecast of the game was posted by Virgil Moody. "1969 NCAA Football #1 Texas at #2 Arkansas," YouTube video, posted February 1, 2017, by Virgil Moody, https://www.youtube.com/watch?v=ORAFBpWrNZ8.

22. John Underwood, "The Desperate Coach," *Sports Illustrated*, August 25, 1969, 66–76.

23. Giles Tippette, *Saturday's Children* (New York: Macmillan, 1973), 118–144.

24. Lou Maysel, "UT Seeks Black Gridders," *Austin American-Statesman*, January 16, 1970.

25. "Students Want More Black Athletes," *SMU Campus*, February 4, 1969, 5.

26. Harry Edwards, *The Revolt of the Black Athlete* (New York: Free Press, 1969).

27. "Black Demands," *The Horned Frog Yearbook*, vol. 67 (Texas Christian University, 1971), 102–103.

28. John Anders, "Right on, Rodrigo Barnes," *Dallas Morning News*, September 1, 1972.

29. "Levias Eased the Way," *Dallas Morning News*, November 26, 1972.

30. Jack Scott, *The Athletic Revolution* (New York: Free Press, 1971), vi. Emphasis in original.

31. "Sauer to Retire; Assails Football," *New York Times*, April 17, 1971.

32. Gary Shaw, *Meat on the Hoof: The Hidden World of Texas Football* (New York: Dell, 1972), 280–281.

33. Shaw, *Meat on the Hoof,* 11.

34. "Money a Big Factor in Recruiting Blacks," *Daily Texan*, November 14, 1972.

35. Wann Smith, *Wishbone: Oklahoma Football, 1959–1985* (Norman: University of Oklahoma Press, 2011), 125.

36. Barry Switzer with Bud Shrake, *Bootlegger's Boy* (New York: William Morrow, 1990), 67.

37. Jimmy Banks, *The Darrell Royal Story* (Austin, TX: Shoal Creek, 1973), 150.

38. See Asher Price's excellent biography, *Earl Campbell: Yards after Contact* (Austin: University of Texas Press, 2019).

39. "Teaff Looks to Future," *Dallas Morning News*, December 8, 1974.

40. "'The Big One' Next," *Austin Statesman*, September 15, 1968.

41. "'The Big One' Next."

42. "Ponies Pack Punch; Steers in Standoff," *Dallas Morning News*, September 22, 1968; Jerry Wizig, *Eat 'Em Up Cougars: Houston Football* (Huntsville, AL: Strode Publishers, 1977), 222–224.

43. Robert D. Jacobus, *Houston Cougars in the 1960s: Death Threats, the Veer Offense, and the Game of the Century* (College Station: Texas A&M University Press, 2015), 91–114; Quentin R. Mease, *On Equal Footing: A Memoir* (Austin, TX: Eakin Press, 2001), 88–90.

44. "Setting Their Own Tradition," *Dallas Morning News*, December 10, 1979.

45. "Setting Their Own Tradition."

46. The veer offense is succinctly explained to the nonexpert in Lou Mayel, "Top O' the Mornin'," *Austin Statesman*, September 21, 1968.

47. Jack Gallagher, "Life and Times of the School That Grew Too Fast," *Dave Campbell's Texas Football* 17, no. 1 (July 1976): 34.

48. Randy Galloway, "Cougars' Win Doesn't Stop Davis' Tears," *Dallas Morning News*, January 2, 1977.

49. Galloway, "Cougars' Win."

50. Wizig, *Eat 'Em Up Cougars*, 343.

51. Wizig, *Eat 'Em Up Cougars*, 334.

52. "Setting Their Own Tradition."

53. Skip Bayless, "Nothing Black, White in Houston's Success," *Dallas Morning News*, December 27, 1979.

54. Steve Pate, "Davis Rusty but Still Full of Drive," *Dallas Morning News*, September 20, 1978.

55. "1979 Cotton Bowl—Houston vs. Notre Dame," YouTube video, posted August 28, 2013, by Stephen Bowman, https://www.youtube.com/watch?v=-05nTh80JuE.

56. Mike Jones, "Going Out in Style," *Dallas Morning News*, December 30, 1978.

57. "Dr. Danny Davis, Pastor," Jordan Grove Missionary Baptist Church, accessed June 24, 2019, http://www.jordangrove.org/about-us/pastor-davis/.

58. *Pony Excess*, directed by Thaddeus D. Matula (United States: ESPN Films, 2010).

59. Temple Pouncey, "SMU Ends Coup, Signs Eric," *Dallas Morning News*, February 17, 1979. On Dickerson's recruitment and the inducements he undoubtedly received from A&M, SMU, and other programs, see Whitford, *Payroll to Meet*, 54–57.

60. Whitford, *Payroll to Meet*, 75–85; *The Bishops' Committee Report on SMU, Friday, June 19, 1987: Report to the Board of Trustees of Southern Methodist University from the Special Committee of Bishops of the South Central Jurisdiction* (Dallas: University Methodist Reporter, 1987).

61. "Mustang Coach Ron Meyer," in *SMU Football: Mustang Mania '79* (Southern Methodist University, 1979), 9; Whitford, *Payroll to Meet*, 3–11.

62. Steve Pate, "Ponies End Search; Named Meyer Coach," *Dallas Morning News*, January 23, 1976.

63. On Meyer, see Whitford, *Payroll to Meet*, 3–11; *SMU Football*, 9.

64. Skip Bayless, "Russ Potts: Director of Athletics," *Mustang Mania Illustrated, SMU vs. Arkansas 1980* (Southern Methodist University, 1980), 16.

65. Dennis Fulton, "College Football Sells Itself to Big Business," *Dallas Morning News*, October 29, 1978.

66. Fulton, "College Football Sells Itself to Big Business."

67. Skip Bayless, "Potts: Taking the Red out of SMU Athletics," *Dallas Morning News*, July 22, 1980.

68. Mike Raubun, "Mania on a Rampage," *Dave Campbell's Texas Football* 19, no. 4 (March 1979): 5.

69. Pouncey, *Mustang Mania.*

70. Sam Blair, "Dandy Roast Earns SMU $1000 Tip," *Dallas Morning News*, April 29, 1979.

71. Bayless, "Russ Potts: Director of Athletics"; Whitford, *Payroll to Meet*, 50–51.

72. John Papanek, "What's Black and White, and Red Hot?" *Sports Illustrated*, October 26, 1981, 60–61; "SMU Placed on 2-year Probation," *Dallas Morning News*, June 11, 1981.

73. Papanek, "What's Black and White." On the "Dallas Way" model of racial integration, see Brian Behnken, "The 'Dallas Way': Protest, Response, and the Civil Rights Experience in Big D and Beyond," *Southwestern Historical Quarterly* 111, no. 1 (July 2007): ix–29.

74. Sam Blair, "Potts Takes Job with White Sox; SMU Faces Probe," *Dallas Morning News*, February 12, 1981.

75. Michael Oriard, *Bowled Over: Big-Time College Football from the Sixties to the BCS Era* (Chapel Hill: University of North Carolina Press, 2009), 2.

CHAPTER 4: WE'VE COME A LONG WAY TO HOUSTON

1. Julie Heldman, "Casals Hustles Her Way to Virginia Slims Win," *Houston Post*, September 27, 1970; Donn T. Gobbie, "Gladys Heldman and the Original Nine: The Visionaries Who Pioneered the Women's Professional Tennis Circuit" (PhD diss., Purdue University, 2015), 446.

2. *Billie Jean King*, directed by James Erskine (Arlington, VA: PBS, 2014).

3. Grace Lichtenstein, *A Long Way Baby: Behind the Scenes in Women's Pro Tennis* (New York: William and Morrow, 1974), 52–53.

4. Quoted in Kevin Jefferys, "The Triumph of Professionalism in World Tennis: The Road to 1968," *International Journal of History of Sport* 26, no. 15 (December 2009), 22–67.

5. John M. Lee, "British Tennis Body Votes to Allow Pros to Play in Wimbledon Tournament," *New York Times*, October 6, 1967.

6. Jack Kramer with Frank Deford, *The Game: My 40 Years in Tennis* (New York: GP Putnam's Sons, 1979), 80.

7. Quoted in "Women Tennis Stars Threaten Boycott over Unequal Purses," *New York Times*, September 8, 1970.

8. Kay Crosby, "Everything 'Love' at Tennis Gathering," *Dallas Morning News*, November 24, 1971.

9. "Judge G. Z. Medalie Dies in Albany at 62," *New York Times*, March 6, 1946.

10. Julie Heldman, *Driven: A Daughter's Odyssey* (self-pub., 2018), 22–27.

11. "A Revolution in Cycles," editorial, *World Tennis*, February 1971, 10.

12. "A Revolution in Cycles," 10.

13. Gobbie, "Gladys Heldman and the Original Nine," 152–156.

14. Jay Stuller, "Gladys Heldman: A Few Words with the Architect of Women's Pro Tennis," *Women's Sports*, May 1979, 29.

15. Heldman, *Driven*, 74–77.

16. "1969 US Open Tennis Chps Highlight Film," YouTube video, posted March 7, 2015, by dgobbie1, https://www.youtube.com/watch?v=tbOhDl177 i8&t=704s.

17. Gladys Heldman, "World Tennis Magazine Signs 9 Girls to Pro Contracts," *World Tennis*, November 1970, 14, 48–49.

18. Kramer and Deford, *Game*, 100; Billie Jean King with Kim Chapin, *Billie Jean* (New York: Harper and Row, 1974), 103.

19. Julie Heldman, Gladys's daughter, herself a top-ranked player, replaced Patti Hogan, who pulled out of the Houston tournament for fear of retaliation by the USLTA. Heldman was injured but played a symbolic point against Billie Jean King during the tournament. Heldman, *Driven*, 269–270.

20. Joseph F. Cullman III, *I'm a Lucky Guy* (New York: Philip Morris, 1998), 176.

21. Heldman, "World Tennis Magazine Signs," 49.

22. Cullman, *I'm a Lucky Guy*, 174.

23. "USLTA Won't Rank Contract-Signers," *Houston Post*, September 26, 1970.

24. "USLTA Won't Rank Contract-Signers"; Heldman, "Casals Hustles Her Way."

25. Heldman, "Casals Hustles Her Way."

26. Heldman, *Driven*, 271–272.

27. Lichtenstein, *Long Way Baby*, 56.

28. King and Chapin, *Billie Jean*, 32.

29. Tomás Summers Sandoval, *Latinos at the Golden Gate: Creating Community and Identity in San Francisco* (Chapel Hill: University of North Carolina Press, 2013).

30. Kim Chapin, "A Bright Future for Little Miss Bombshell," *Sports Illustrated*, October 24, 1966, 69.

31. On Casals, see Rita Liberti, "Rebel with a Racket: Rosie Casals," in *San Francisco Bay Area Sports: Golden Gate Athletics, Recreation, and Community*, ed. Rita Liberti and Maureen M. Smith (Fayetteville: University of Arkansas Press, 2017), 221–234; and Kristi Tredway and Rita Liberti, "'All Frocked Up in Purple': Rosie Casals, Virginia Slims, and the Politics of Fashion at Wimbledon, 1972," *Fashion Style and Popular Culture* 5, no. 2

(2018): 235–247. On Casals's resemblance to an "Apache brave on the war-path," see Lichtenstein, *Long Way Baby*, 52.

32. Frank Deford, "The Highest Ranking Family in Tennis," *Sports Illustrated*, July 5, 1965, 47–53.

33. Christopher Clarey, "1968 Was a Revolutionary Year for France and the French Open," *New York Times*, May 27, 2018.

34. Neil Amdur, "Young Black Players Will Join Women's Tennis Tour in 1973," *New York Times*, November 2, 1972; Bonnie Logan, "Visit to the Unknown Land," *World Tennis*, June 1972, 16–17.

35. Billie Jean King with Christine Brennan, *Pressure is a Privilege* (New York: LifeTime Media, 2008), 69.

36. "ABC Sports Special: Tennis Battle of the Sexes: Billie Jean King vs Bobby Riggs," catalog ID: T:43470, Paley Center for Media, New York, NY. See also Selena Roberts, *A Necessary Spectacle: Billie Jean King, Bobby Riggs, and the Tennis Match That Leveled the Game* (New York: Crown Publishers, 2005).

37. Ron Powers, *Supertube: The Rise of Television Sports* (New York: Coward-McCann, 1984), 134–135.

38. Kramer quote and all subsequent quotes from the telecast are drawn from "ABC Sports Special: Tennis Battle of the Sexes: Billie Jean King vs Bobby Riggs," aired September 20, 1973, on ABC.

39. Lichtenstein, *Long Way Baby*, 151.

40. Roberts, *A Necessary Spectacle*, 126.

41. Billie Jean King with Cynthia Starr, *We Have Come a Long Way: The Story of Women's Tennis* (New York: Regina Ryan, 1988), 146.

42. Sundiata Djata, *Blacks at the Net: Black Achievement in the History of Tennis*, vol. 1 (Syracuse, NY: Syracuse University Press, 2006), 88–106.

CHAPTER 5: LABOR AND LAWLESSNESS IN RANGERLAND

1. Merle Heryford, "Rangers Sound Last Harrah, 7–6," *Dallas Morning News*, April 22, 1972.

2. Sam Blair, "So, Back to Reality," *Dallas Morning News*, September 23, 1971.

3. Dan Hafner, "Cooke Buys Lakers for $5,175,000," *Los Angeles Times*, September 17, 1965, B2. Cooke would himself become a controversial owner of the Lakers and eventually the NFL franchise known as the Washington Redskins.

4. George Minot Jr., "Short Re-enters Sports World as Nats' Owner," *Washington Post, Times-Herald*, December 4, 1968; Shelby Whitfield, *Kiss It Goodbye* (New York: Abelard-Schuman, 1973), 13; Shelby Coffey III,

"Short Wheeled $1000 into Franchise Worth Millions," *Washington Post, Times-Herald*, December 19, 1971, D1.

5. Whitfield, *Kiss it Goodbye*, 165.

6. Bob Addie, "Short Again Asks the Press to Help Draw a Million Fans," *Washington Post, Times-Herald*, August 30, 1969, D2.

7. Whitfield, *Kiss It Goodbye*.

8. George Minot, Jr., "Short Takes Senators to Texas," *Washington Post, Times-Herald*, September 22, 1971, A1.

9. Minot, Jr., "Short Takes Senators to Texas."

10. "Letters to the Editor," *Washington Post, Times-Herald*, September 26, 1971, E7.

11. The entire radio broadcast is available on YouTube. See "Yankees vs Senators 090301971 RFK's Final Senators Game WWDC Radio," YouTube video, posted September 7, 2016, by ernie kyger, https://www.youtube.com /watch?v=UZi_GYMp2l0.

12. "Yankees vs Senators 090301971." All subsequent quotes from this broadcast are from this source.

13. Shirley Povich, "This Morning," *Washington Post, Times-Herald*, October 1, 1971, D1.

14. Griffith's racial calculation was offered years later in a speech he gave in 1978. Nick Coleman, "Griffith Spares Few Targets in Waseca Remarks," *Minneapolis Tribune*, October 1, 1978.

15. Randy Galloway, "A Hero's Welcome," *Dallas Morning News*, September 23, 1971.

16. On Vandergriff's efforts to promote Arlington and his dealings with Short, see Galloway, "A Hero's Welcome"; Shirley Povich, "Ayes for Texas Leave Chisox' Allyn at Sea," *Washington Post, Times-Herald*, September 24, 1971; Mark S. Rosentraub and Samuel R. Nunn, "Suburban City Investment in Professional Sports," *American Behaviorial Scientist* 21 (January/February 1978), 393–414; and David Lynn Cannon, "Arlington's Path to Post-suburbia" (PhD diss., University of Texas at Arlington, 2000).

17. Mike Shropshire, *Seasons in Hell: With Billy Martin, Whitey Herzog and "The Worst Baseball Team in History"—the 1973–1975 Texas Rangers* (Lincoln: University of Nebraska Press, 2005).

18. Merle Heryford, "New-Old Ranger Home Rises," *Dallas Morning News*, January 9, 1972.

19. Simon W. Freese and D. L. Sizemore, *A Century in the Works: Freese and Nichols Consulting Engineers, 1894–1994* (College Station: Texas A&M Press), 207–208.

20. "Wayward Senators Still Falling Short," *Washington Post, Times-Herald*, October 2, 1972, D1.

21. "Baseball Down," *Sports Illustrated*, April 30, 1973, 10.

22. "Traffic Tie Ups, Kudos to Stadium," *Dallas Morning News*, April 22, 1972. Stevenson became better known for her relationship with "Dr. J," Julius Erving, a few years later, while she covered him as a sportswriter. They had a daughter, and, by mutual agreement, Erving stayed out of her life due to the scandal it would create for Erving and his then wife, Turquoise. The fact that Dr. J was black and Stevenson was white only added to the "scandalous" nature of their relationship. In 1999, their relationship became public when their daughter, Alexandra Stevenson, a tennis player, made an unexpected run at Wimbledon and the press exposed Stevenson's relationship with Erving.

23. Sam Blair, "The Days Dwindle Down," *Dallas Morning News*, September 12, 1972.

24. Ron Firmite, "Bonny Debut for David Clyde," *Sports Illustrated*, July 9, 1973, 16–19.

25. Firmite, "Bonny Debut for David Clyde"; "David Clyde Debut Texas Rangers 1973: Original Radio Broadcast Bill Mercer and Dick Risenhoover," YouTube video, posted October 11, 2013, by Bill Mercer, https://www.youtube.com/watch?v=yJTkgVhh7A8.

26. "He Won't Come Up Short," *Dallas Morning News*, June 28, 1973.

27. Firmite, "Bonny Debut."

28. Brad Townsend, "Townsend: 40 Years after Memorable Debut, Ex-Ranger David Clyde Reflects on a Career Cut Short," *Dallas Morning News*, June 22, 2013, https://sportsday.dallasnews.com/texas-rangers/rangers headlines/2013/06/22/townsend-40-years-after-memorable-debut-ex-ranger-david-clyde-reflects-on-a-career-cut-short.

29. Whitfield, *Kiss It Goodbye*, 255.

30. Randy Galloway, "Short Sells Rangers for $10 Million," *Dallas Morning News*, April 3, 1974.

31. Daniel A. Gilbert, *Expanding the Strike Zone: Baseball in the Era of Free Agency* (Urbana: University of Illinois Press, 2013).

32. Dan Epstein, *Big Hair and Plastic Grass: A Funky Ride through Baseball and America in the Swinging '70s* (New York: Thomas Dunne Books, 2010).

33. Shropshire, *Seasons in Hell*, 23.

34. Gilbert, *Expanding the Strike Zone*, 2.

35. *King of the Hill*, directed by William Canning and Donald Brittain (National Film Board of Canada, 1974).

36. Randy Galloway, "Jenkins Trade Official," *Dallas Morning News*, October 23, 1973.

37. *King of the Hill*.

38. Randy Galloway, "Jenkins Seeks Third Win," *Dallas Morning News*, April 19, 1974.

39. Randy Galloway, "Corbett 'Retires,'" *Dallas Morning News*, September 8, 1976.

40. Randy Galloway, "Robinson No Puppet?," *Dallas Morning News*, September 11, 1976.

41. Ray Kennedy, "Who Are These Guys?," *Sports Illustrated*, January 31, 1977, 50–60.

42. Kennedy, "Who Are These Guys?," 53.

43. Randy Galloway, "Martin Ousted by Rangers," *Dallas Morning News*, July 25, 1975.

44. Steve Pate, "Get Too Close and You're Smothered," *Dallas Morning News*, July 6, 1977.

45. Carl Freund and Susan Yoachum, "Corbett Offers to Drop Rangers 'For Sale' Sign," *Dallas Morning News*, August 13, 1977.

46. Kent Hannon, "Huffing and Puffing in Texas," *Sports Illustrated*, August 7, 1978, 41–42.

47. Hannon, "Huffing and Puffing," 41.

48. Randy Galloway, "A Furor at Second," *Dallas Morning News*, March 25, 1977.

49. Randy Galloway, "Ranger Manager Lucchesi Attacked by Unhappy Player," *Dallas Morning News*, March 29, 1977.

50. Murray Chass, "The Building Up of the Texas Rangers," *New York Times*, April 16, 1978.

51. "1977 08 30 This Week in Baseball," YouTube video, posted August 29, 2019, by Classic MLB1, https://www.youtube.com/watch?v=G4FgCvDk8gE.

52. Randy Galloway, "Mystery Shrouds Actions of Moret," *Dallas Morning News*, April 13, 1978.

53. Steve Pate, "Ellis' Antics, No Party Joke," *Dallas Morning News*, May 26, 1978.

54. Randy Galloway, "Die-Hard Battery Fires Texas by Twins," *Dallas Morning News*, August 24, 1978.

55. Randy Galloway, "Ranger Bleacher Seat Prices Up, but Still Relatively Cheap," *Dallas Morning News*, December 14, 1979.

56. Steve Pate, "Home, Home for the Rangers," *Dallas Morning News*, November 25, 1979.

CHAPTER 6: SEXUAL REVOLUTION ON THE SIDELINES

1. *An Act to Amend and Extend the Higher Education Act of 1965, the Vocational Education Act of 1963, the General Education Provisions Act (creating a National Foundation for Postsecondary Education and a National*

Institute of Education), the Elementary and Secondary Education Act of 1965, Public Law 874, Eighty-first Congress, and related Acts, and for other purposes (Washington, DC: US GPO, 1972).

2. "Statement on Signing the Education Amendments of 1972, June 23, 1972," in *Public Papers of the Presidents of the United States: Richard Nixon, Containing Public Messages, Speeches, and Statements of the President*, vol. 4 (Washington: Federal Register, 1972), 701.

3. Mary Ellen Hanson, *Go! Fight! Win! Cheerleading in American Culture* (Bowling Green, OH: Bowling Green State University Press, 1995), 9–27; John Hawkins, *Texas Cheerleaders: The Spirit of America* (New York: St. Martin's, 1991), 13–30.

4. John Jeansonne, "Leading Cheers Isn't What It's About," *Newsday*, April 4, 1978.

5. Sam Blair, "Cowboy Dressing Room Wet and Wild," *Dallas Morning News*, January 17, 1972.

6. The breezy yet encyclopedic *Dallas Cowboys* is the most comprehensive history of the franchise. Joe Nick Patoski, *The Dallas Cowboys: The Outrageous History of the Biggest, Loudest, Most Hated, Best Loved Football Team in America* (New York: Little Brown, 2012).

7. Ronald Chipman, Randolph Campbell, and Robert Calvert, *The Dallas Cowboys and the NFL* (Norman: University of Oklahoma Press, 1970).

8. Steve Perkins, *Next Year's Champions: The Story of the Dallas Cowboys* (New York: World Publishing, 1969), 135.

9. Bob St. John, "Maybe Thomas has Outrun his Blockers," *Dallas Morning News*, July 22, 1971.

10. Mary Candace Evans, *A Decade of Dreams: Dallas Cowboys Cheerleaders* (Dallas: Taylor Publishing, 1982), 13.

11. Patoski, *Dallas Cowboys*, 171–176.

12. On the Niner Nuggets as "ambassadors," see Stephanie Salter, "There's Gold in Them Nuggets," *Sports Illustrated*, September 23, 1974, 38–42.

13. Robert Blair Kaiser, "Pro Football's Main Attractions," *Playboy*, December 1978, 155.

14. Diane Justice, "Texie Waterman," *Dallas Morning News*, November 20, 1983.

15. Evans, *Decade of Dreams*, 17.

16. Suzette Scholz, Stephanie Scholz, and Sheri Scholz, *Deep in the Heart of Texas: Reflections of Former Dallas Cowboys Cheerleaders* (New York: St. Martin's Press, 1991), 71–72.

17. Keith Anderson, "How the Cheerleaders Got Their Hot Pants," *Dallas Morning News*, January 10, 1979.

18. Joe Nick Patoski, "The Original Dallas Cowboys Cheerleaders,"

Texas Monthly, September 2001; Kristin Green Morse, "Dallas Cowboys Cheerleaders," *Sports Illustrated*, July 2, 2001, 87.

19. "Super Bowl 10 Full Game Dallas Cowboys vs. Pittsburgh Steelers," YouTube video, posted March 24, 2020, by NFL, https://www.youtube.com/watch?v=ukjvHFzVp48.

20. "The Game Plan of the Networks," *Los Angeles Times*, September 29, 1974.

21. John Hall, "Talk of the Town," *Los Angeles Times*, August 20, 1971.

22. *Seconds to Play*, directed by Patrick Crowley (Wilmette, IL: Films Inc., 1976).

23. Sam Blair, "Stare Way to the Stars," *Dallas Morning News*, September 19, 1969; "Talk of the Town," *Los Angeles Times*, August 2, 1971.

24. *Seconds to Play*.

25. The fraternity house culture of the *Monday Night Football* crew is described in Marc Gunther and Bill Carter, *Monday Night Mayhem: The Inside Story of ABC's Monday Night Football* (New York: Beech Tree Books, 1988).

26. Gunther and Carter, *Monday Night Mayhem*, 132.

27. *Seconds to Play*.

28. Once again, thanks to the labors of football aficionados on the internet, the entire telecast of the game has been posted on YouTube. See "1975 Dallas vs. Kansas City," YouTube video, posted January 7, 2017, by Wade Randy, https://www.youtube.com/watch?v=-tMU8IUxojM&t=605s.

29. On Mitchell's hiring, see Patoski, *Dallas Cowboys*, 360; and *Daughters of the Sexual Revolution: The Untold Story of the Dallas Cowboys Cheerleaders*, directed by Dana Adam Shapiro (El Segundo, CA: Gravitas Ventures, 2019).

30. Evans, *Decade of Dreams*, 38–39; "Suzanne Mitchell, 73, Dies," *New York Times*, September 30, 2016.

31. *Dallas Cowboys Cheerleaders: A Touch of Class* (Dallas: Jordan and Company, 1979).

32. *Dallas Cowboys Cheerleaders*, 10.

33. *Real People*, season 2, episode 1, directed by Dave Campbell, aired September 5, 1979, on NBC, streamed on Amazon Prime.

34. *Daughters of the Sexual Revolution*.

35. *Daughters of the Sexual Revolution*.

36. Susan Ware, *Game, Set, Match: Billie Jean King and the Revolution in Women's Sports* (Chapel Hill: University of North Carolina Press, 2009), 147–149.

37. Neil Amdur, "Cowboy Cheerleaders: Sexist or Just Sparkling," *New York Times*, December 26, 1977.

38. Douglas Martin, "Dallas Cheerleaders Don't Really Cheer, but Do Get Cheered," *Wall Street Journal*, May 12, 1977.

39. "A Nice Figure Doesn't Bring Cheer to a Hopeful," *Dallas Morning News*, May 8, 1977; Katherine Ellison, "Three Men Seek to Lead Cheers for the Rams," *Los Angeles Times*, July 14, 1978.

40. "36 Cheerleaders Chosen for the '77 Season," *Dallas Morning News*, June 19, 1977; "Saturday's Sports Thrills Are on ABC!," *Dallas Morning News*, June 24, 1977.

41. "Cowgirls," *Esquire*, October 1977, 82.

42. "Cowgirls."

43. Howard Smith, "CBS' Saturation: Was It Necessary?," *Los Angeles Times*, January 16, 1978.

44. "Cowgirl Cheerleaders Hit Celebrity Circuit," *Newsday*, April 4, 1978.

45. Thomas Boswell, "America's Team: The Nation Is Sold on Tex's Club," *Washington Post*, December 14, 1979.

46. Maryln Schwartz, "Texie Looking for New . . . Material," *Dallas Morning News*, November 26, 1977.

47. Dorothy Collin, "NFL Cheerleaders Play Skin Game," *Chicago Tribune*, September 26, 1978; Elizabeth Wheeler, "Sexy Ram Squad Takes Shape," *Los Angeles Times*, April 23, 1978; "Cattle Call," *Los Angeles Times*, April 29, 1978.

48. "Cowgirls," *Esquire*, October 1977, 82.

49. "And Now for Something Completely Different: Texas Cowgirls, Inc.," *Playboy*, December 1978, 162; Jack Mathews, "Cash Cheers Them Up," *Baltimore Sun*, December 18, 1978.

50. "And Now for Something Completely Different," 162.

51. Mathews, "Cash Cheers Them Up."

52. "And Now for Something Completely Different."

53. "'Chauvinism' Is Charged by Dismissed Chargettes," *Newsday*, September 23, 1978; "Cheerleaders Boo the NFL," *Baltimore Sun*, November 2, 1978.

54. All quotes in paragraph from Bill Curry, "Something Else to Cheer about in Dallas," *Washington Post*, January 17, 1979.

55. *Dallas Cowboys Cheerleaders: A Touch of Class.*

56. Scholz, Scholz, and Scholz, *Deep in the Heart of Texas.*

57. Evans, *Decade of Dreams*, 106–112; Maryln Schwartz, "The Oldest Living Cheerleader," *Dallas Morning News*, May 12, 1980.

58. Alice Echols, *Hot Stuff: Disco and the Remaking of American Culture* (New York: W.W. Norton, 2010), 81.

59. *Daughters of the Sexual Revolution.*

CHAPTER 7: THE GREEK, THE ICEMAN, AND THE BUMS

1. John Trowbridge, "Nuggets Clean, 'Dirty' Spurs, 142–111," *San Antonio Light*, February 19, 1976.

2. Terry Pluto, *Loose Balls: The Short, Wild Life of the American Basketball Association* (New York: Simon & Schuster, 2007).

3. "Chaparrals Drop Two Black Players in Order to Get More White Players," *New York Times*, September 1, 1972.

4. Pluto, *Loose Balls*, 290–291; "We're the Spurs," *San Antonio Express*, May 20, 1973.

5. "We're the Spurs."

6. Lisa Song, "Last Words: The Ghosts of HemisFair Park," *San Antonio Current*, April 9, 2003. On race and the freedom struggles in San Antonio, see Brian D. Behnken, *Fighting Their Own Battles: Mexican Americans, African Americans and the Struggle for Civil Rights in Texas* (Chapel Hill: University of North Carolina Press, 2011).

7. Pluto, *Loose Balls*, 295.

8. See "San Antonio Spurs" KCOR Radio advertisement, *San Antonio Light*, October 31, 1973.

9. See Bob Ostrom, "Thursday to Be NBA Day for Spurs," *San Antonio Light*, July 14, 1976; and Mike Monroe, "Black Owners Played Vital Role in Spurs' Early History," *Rivard Report*, January 16, 2017, https://therivard report.com/black-owners-played-vital-role-in-spurs-early-history/.

10. Pluto, *Loose Balls*, 298–301; "S.A. Court Rules against Storen," *San Antonio Light*, February 12, 1974.

11. "Bass to Make Changes as New Spur Coach," *San Antonio Light*, December 14, 1974.

12. John Trowbridge, "Spurs' Coach Takes Challenge in Stride," *San Antonio Light*, March 30, 1975.

13. John Trowbridge, "Bass: 'A Different Game Now,'" *San Antonio Light*, March 31, 1975.

14. "Tulsa Prep Star Becomes 1st Negro Cager at Texas Tech," *Dallas Morning News*, May 29, 1969.

15. Pluto, *Loose Balls*.

16. Billy Libby and Spencer Haywood, *Stand Up for Something: The Spencer Haywood Story* (New York: Grosset and Dunlap, 1975); Sarah K. Fields, "Odd Bedfellows: Spencer Haywood and Justice William O. Douglas," in *Sport and the Law*, ed. Samuel Regalado and Sarah K. Fields (Fayetteville: University of Arkansas Press, 2014), 18–31.

17. Malcolm Moran, "Gervin, No. 1 in Both Polls: 'I've Seen a Lot,'" *New York Times*, January 29, 1979.

18. Paul Attner, "Gervin Advances to Center Ring," *Washington Post*, May 15, 1979.

19. Paul Attner, "Gervin Has Perfect Pitch," *Washington Post*, April 21, 1978.

20. Curry Kirkpatrick, "Ice Man Scoreth and Cometh," *Sports Illustrated*, March 6, 1978, 14.

21. Pluto, *Loose Balls*, 311.

22. *Longshots: The Life and Times of the American Basketball Association*, directed by Ross Greenberg (HBO Films, 1997).

23. *Longshots*.

24. Pluto, *Loose Balls*, 310.

25. Pluto, *Loose Balls*, 310.

26. Paul L. Montgomery, "Nets Beat Spurs, Tie Series," *New York Times*, April 19, 1976; Ray Evans, "'Rustled' Spurs Face Nets in New York," *San Antonio Light*, April 19, 1976.

27. The two other ABA franchises agreed to fold: the Kentucky Colonels, who were bought out for $3 million by the four ABA franchises and the owners of the Spirits of St. Louis, received the greatest settlement of all: four-sevenths of league television money in perpetuity, making them millionaires thrice over.

28. Jan Jarboe, "Major Expansion Ok'd for Arena," *San Antonio Light*, July 1, 1976.

29. John Trowbridge, "'Baseline Bums' REAL Spurs Fans," *San Antonio Light*, February 2, 1974.

30. Dave Anderson, "Dancing Harry and Earl the Pearl," *New York Times*, January 6, 1973.

31. Ray Evans, "New York Edges Spurs, 112–109, Before 11,717," *San Antonio Light*, November 16, 1976.

32. Pluto, *Loose Balls*, 310.

33. Dan Balz, "'Bums' Rush to the Aid of Their Spurs," *Washington Post*, May 13, 1983.

34. Bob Ostrom, "It's Ok to Boo, but Not Harass," *San Antonio Light*, November 6, 1976.

35. Randy Harvey, "A Big Test for the Baseline Bums," *Los Angeles Times*, May 13, 1983.

36. Paul Attner, "Crowd Becomes 6th Man at HemisFair," *Washington Post*, April 18, 1978.

37. Travis Hale, "The Comfort of Feeling Small," NBC Sports, accessed March 12, 2020, http://sportsworld.nbcsports.com/san-antonio-spurs-and -the-comfort-of-feeling-small/.

38. Kirkpatrick, "Ice Man Scoreth," 14.

39. Kirkpatrick, "Ice Man Scoreth," 14.

40. Bob St. John, "Spurmania," *Dallas Morning News*, February 20, 1977.

41. Ray Evans, "Drossos Must Serve Two Masters," *San Antonio Light*, July 12, 1976.

42. O'Lene Stone, "Female Fans Find It Fantastic," *San Antonio Light*, October 11, 1973.

43. Bill Simmons, *The Book of Basketball: The NBA According to the Sports Guy* (New York: ESPN Books, 2010).

44. Bob Ostrom, editorial, *San Antonio Light*, July 1, 1976.

45. Skip Bayless, "Fitting a Team to the City," *Dallas Morning News*, February 18, 1979.

46. Ray Evans, "Gervin's 63 Puts Crown on 'Ice,'" *San Antonio Light*, April 10, 1978.

47. During the first few years in the NBA, the Spurs were placed in the Central Division of the Eastern Conference due to the imbalanced configuration of teams after the merger.

48. Ray Evans, "Moe Sees NBA Title in Future," *San Antonio Light*, April 30, 1978.

49. John Papanek, "He Surely Is the Spur of the Moment," *Sports Illustrated*, February 5, 1979.

50. Papanek, "Muy Loco"; Ray Evans, "Spurs Do It, Do It, Do It," *San Antonio Light*, May 3, 1979.

51. David DuPree, "Gervin and Company Have Revenge in Mind," *Washington Post*, May 4, 1979.

52. Ken Denlinger, "Hayes: Put Dandridge on Gervin," *Washington Post*, May 12, 1979.

53. "1979 NBA Finals Bullets @ Spurs—7 game [George Gervin 42 points, Bob Dandridge 37 points]" YouTube video, posted July 9, 2017, by Ser Gold, https://www.youtube.com/watch?v=SViJFJ5REhs.

54. Paul Attner, "Dandridge Shot Sinks Spurs," *Washington Post*, May 19, 1979.

CHAPTER 8: SLAMMIN' AND JAMMIN' IN HOUSTON

1. Hakeem Olajuwon with Peter Knobler, *Living the Dream* (Boston: Little Brown, 1996), 78.

2. For more on migration and cultural and racial change in Houston, see Tyina L. Steptoe, *Houston Bound: Culture and Color in a Jim Crow City* (Berkeley: University of California Press, 2016).

3. Robert D. Jacobus, *Houston Cougars in the 1960s: Death Threats, the Veer Offense, and the Game of the Century* (College Station: Texas A&M Press, 2015), 72.

4. Eddie Einhorn with Ron Rapoport, *How March Became Madness* (Chicago: Triumph, 2006), 37.

5. "Bruin Cagers to Play in Garden, Astrodome," *Los Angeles Times*, May 4, 1967.

6. Einhorn, *How March Became Madness*, 40.

7. Olajuwon, *Living the Dream*, 105.

8. Einhorn, *How March Became Madness*, 39.

9. Olajuwon, *Living the Dream*, 99.

10. Olajuwon, *Living the Dream*, 101–102.

11. Curry Kirkpatrick, "The Liege Lord of Noxzema," *Sports Illustrated*, November 28, 1983, 106–128.

12. Olajuwon, *Living the Dream*, 101.

13. *Phi Slama Jama*, directed by Chip Rives (ESPN Films, Texas Film Crew Productions, 2016).

14. Clyde Drexler with Kerry Eggers, *Clyde the Glide: My Life in Basketball*, foreword by Jim Nantz (New York: Sports Publishing, 2004), 9–19.

15. Seth Davis, *When March Went Mad: The Game That Transformed Basketball* (New York: Times Books, Henry Holt, 2009).

16. Davis, *When March Went Mad*, 8.

17. Olajuwon, *Living the Dream*, 120.

18. Jerry Ratcliffe, "Lewis Apologizes for UH's Showing," *Houston Post*, December 17, 1982.

19. Thomas Bonk, "Stuffs to Build Coogs' Dream On," *Houston Post*, January 4, 1983.

20. Kevin Sherrington, "Cougars Win Barn Burner," *Houston Post*, March 4, 1983.

21. Jerry Kirshenbaum, "Scorecard," *Sports Illustrated*, February 25, 1980, 11.

22. Charles H. Martin, *Benching Jim Crow: The Rise and Fall of the Color Line in Southern College Sports, 1890–1980* (Urbana: University of Illinois Press, 2010), 94.

23. "04/02/1983 NCAA National Semifinal: ME1 Louisville Cardinals vs. MW1 Houston Cougars," YouTube video, posted October 28, 2013, by thacozzman89, https://www.youtube.com/watch?v=mBlynKTeLBk.

24. Olajuwon, *Living the Dream*, 135.

25. Robert Weintraub, "Jamfest for the Ages," ESPN E-Ticket, March 29, 2007, http://www.espn.com/espn/eticket/story?page=jamfest83.

26. Weintraub, "Jamfest for the Ages."

27. Weintraub, "Jamfest for the Ages."

28. Weintraub, "Jamfest for the Ages."

29. Robert Falkoff, "Faithful Gather to Greet UH," *Houston Post*, April 6, 1983.

30. Michael O. Emerson, Jennifer Bratter, Junia Howell, P. Wilner Jeanty, and Mike Cline, *Houston Region Grows More Racially/Ethnically Diverse with Small Declines in Segregation: A Joint Report Analyzing Census Data from 1999, 2000, and 2010 Data* (Houston: Kinder Center for Urban Research and Hobby Center for the Study of Texas, 2012).

CONCLUSION: THE REVOLUTION UNDONE

1. David Whitford, *A Payroll to Meet: A Story of Greed, Corruption, and Football at SMU* (Lincoln: University of Nebraska Press, 2013), 200.

2. Michael A. Lutz, "Southwest Conference Fades into the Sunset: Is That So Bad?," *Los Angeles Times*, February 27, 1994.

3. "Cowboys Are Sold; Landry out as Coach," *Los Angeles Times*, February 25, 1989; Joe Nick Patoski, *The Dallas Cowboys: The Outrageous History of the Biggest, Loudest, Most Hated, Best Loved Football Team in America* (New York: Little Brown, 2012), 489–524.

4. Michael Oriard, *Bowled Over: Big-Time College Football from the Sixties to the BCS Era* (Chapel Hill: University of North Carolina Press, 2009), 157–166.

5. Douglas Looney, "Jackie Hits the Jackpot," *Sports Illustrated*, February 1, 1982, 26–29.

6. Robert Reinhold, "Increasing Jobless Rate in Texas Shakes Its Politics and Confidence," *New York Times*, October 12, 1982; Robert Reinhold, "Texas in a Tailspin," *New York Times*, July 20, 1986.

7. Jane Wolfe, *The Murchisons: The Rise and Fall of a Texas Dynasty* (New York: St. Martin's, 1989), 395–415.

8. Jane Gross, "Miss Lopiano, a Leader in Women's Sports," *New York Times*, January 8, 1980; Deborah Cannon, "End of an Era," *Austin American-Statesman*, March 13, 2007.

9. Sundiata Djata, *Blacks at Net: Black Achievement in the History of Tennis*, vol. 1 (Syracuse, NY: Syracuse University Press, 2006), 88–106.

10. "Five More Former Cheerleaders File Suit, Claiming Mistreatment," *New York Times*, June 1, 2018.

11. Lois Romano and George Lardner Jr., "Bush Earned Profit, Rangers Insiders Deal Say," *Washington Post*, July 31, 1999.

12. Patoski, *Dallas Cowboys*, 637–641.

Index

Note: Italicized page numbers refer to illustrations.

All-England Club, 133

American Basketball Association (ABA): All-Star teams of, 279; challenge to NCAA's domination of basketball talent, 270; competition with NBA, 262, 263; in Dallas, 135; documentary on, 273; franchises of, 260, 262–263, 278–279, 281, 378n27; legacy of, 262–263; and Moses Malone, 311; merger with NBA, 260, 280–281, 285, 287, 291, 292, 312; racial integration of, 262, 264; and San Antonio Spurs, 8, 259, 260, 261, 267–268, 269, 278–280, 287, 289, 291, 293, 298, 299; scouting in, 270–271; underdog status of, 278

American Football League (AFL): Lamar Hunt as founder of, 1–2, 45, 48, 51–52, 262; merger with NFL, 1–2, 48, 53–54, 135, 173–174, 219; racial integration of, 68, 363n11

American League, 176–178, 180, 182, 186, 198, 199, 207, 209

Americanness, meaning of, 4

American Tennis Association (ATA), 152

Anders, Benny, 317, 327, 336–339, 337

Anders, John, 98–99

Anthony, Susan B., II, 239

Apache Belles, 30–31, 32, 77, 220, 221, 224, 237, 255

Appleton, Scott, 42

Arledge, Roone: and ABC News, 157; and ABC Sports, 2, 84, 104, 157–158, 228, 243; and Battle of the Sexes match, 157–158, 160, 167; *Monday Night Football* created by, 2, 158, 229, 230, 232;

and Richard Nixon, 182; storytelling skills of, 157, 229

Arlington, Texas, 171, 178–179, 181, 182–184, 212, 349

Arlington Park Corporation, 187

Arlington Stadium: attendance at, 188–190, 193, 198, 199, 206–207, 210–211; management of, 187; refurbishing of, 171, 185–186, *185*

Armstrong, Harvey, 124

Armstrong, Otis, 119

Ashe, Arthur, 132, 134–135, 143, 144, 152

Askey, Gil, 38

Associated Press, 101, 243

Astro-Bluebonnet Bowl, Houston Astrodome, 91, 109, 123

AstroWorld, 155

AstroWorld Hotel, 155

AT&T Center, San Antonio, 261, 286

athletic laborers: black male athletes as, 6, 8, 82, 83, 86, 87, 104, 124, 127, 316; blacks and whites playing with each other, 124; and college basketball, 340; and college football, 22, 82, 83, 86, 87–88, 98–99, 104, 110, 119, 124, 125, 127, 343; and college sports, 345; commodification of, 316, 321; Latinos as, 8, 192; NFL cheerleaders as, 252, 255, 257; and professional baseball, 174, 192, 193, 200–201, 204; and professional sports franchises, 78; and tennis, 130, 140–141; upward mobility for, 50; women athletes as, 6, 8; and women's professional tennis, 140–141, 144, 145, 151

Atkins, Joe, 45

Atlanta, Georgia, 173

Schramm, 52, 216; and US Open, 158

Cedeño, César, 364n30

Central Catholic High School, San Antonio, 264

Chamberlain, Wilt, 267, 271

Chaney, Don, 68, 304–305, 308

Chapin, Kim, 148

Chapman, Bill, 245

Chapman, Ron, 239

Chargettes, 246, 250

Charles, Lorenzo, 339

Charlie's Angels (television show), 245

Charlton-Pollard High School, Beaumont, 37

Chass, Murray, 206–207

Chastain, Jane, 227

cheerleaders: beauty queens synonymous with, 214; and black high school and college football, 38; male cheerleaders, 213–214, 240; NFL attitudes toward, 213, 246–253, 255, 257, 347; and regional and national levels of competition, 8; sexual revolution and NFL cheerleaders, 213, 246–251, 253, 255–256, 257, 347; women athletes steered toward cheerleading, 32, 33, 214–215, 256. *See also* Dallas Cowboys Cheerleaders

Chemstrand, 12, 63, 77

Chicago Bears, 52, 242, 246

Chicago Bulls, 285, 299

Chicago Cubs, 191, 194, 197, 198, 199

Chicago White Sox, 125, 305

Chiles, Eddie, 210

Christian values, 107–108

Civil Rights Act, 4

civil rights movement: and baseball, 192; and gender roles, 33; and racial integration of teams, 3, 49, 83, 181–182; and Second Reconstruction era, 4; sit-in movements, 54, 57, 106; and tennis, 131; violent resistance to, 276

Clay, Cassius. *See* Ali, Muhammad

Clemente, Roberto, 208

Clements, Bill, 349

Cleveland Indians, 199

Clyde, David, 188–190

Cockrell, Lila, 281

Coconut Grove, Los Angeles, 49

Cole, Thomas, 58

Coleman, Ornette, 38

Coliseum Relays, California, 37

College All-Star Game, Chicago, 30

college basketball: and black male athletes, 68, 303, 304–305; championship games in dome stadium settings, 305–306; and coaches' salaries, 345; commercialization of, 304, 305–306, 317, 320, 321, 340, 341; Final Four games, 303, 305, 306; and March Madness, 304, 306; racial integration of, 45; television coverage of, 70, 303–304, 306, 320–321, 322, 327–329. *See also* University of Houston basketball; *and specific universities and players*

college football: all-black segregated games, 23, 34–35, 38; and athletic laborers, 22, 82, 83, 86, 87–88, 98–99, 104, 110, 119, 124, 125, 127, 343; authoritarian structure of, 96–97, 99; black quarterbacks, 113–115; and bowl games, 18–19; and coaches' salaries, 345; masculinity in, 100; national notoriety of Texas, 18;

college football (*continued*)

and oil industry, 19, 84, 125; popularity of, 84, 320; racial integration in 1950s and 1960s, 20, 22–23, 42–43, 44, 83–85, 87, 97–99, 107; recruiting for, 316–317; and sports management, 84, 95, 104; and standardized competitions, 20; and "student-athlete" myth, 110, 125; and student protest movement of late 1960s, 99–100; television coverage of, 2, 30, 95, 114, 115, 230–231, 320. *See also* Cotton Bowl Classic; *and specific universities and players*

collegiate sports: amateurism in, 345; commercialization of, 84–85, 95, 127, 128, 317, 320, 343; exploitation of athletes in, 97, 99, 100; hyper-profiteering from college athletes, 5; racial integration of, 44; segregation of, 14–15; television coverage of, 2, 6, 12, 30, 70; and Texas public, 49; Texas's impact on expansion of, 4, 5. *See also* college basketball; college football

Collier's magazine, 25

Collins, Bobby, 127

colonization: and Anglo elites, 39, 40, 50; emergence from, 13; role in development of Texas, 6, 15, 17, 33; and Texas-Mexico borderlands, 39, 290

Colt 45s, 57, 60

Colt Stadium, Houston, 60

Connor, Eugene "Bull," 276

Conover, Al, 99

conquest, role in development of Texas, 6, 17

Conradt, Jody, 347

Conroe, Texas, 36

Continental Baseball League, 176

Convy, Bert, 244

Cooke, Jack Kent, 175, 200, 370n3

Cooke, Sam, 35

Cooper, Marvin, 283–284

Corbett, Brad, 7, 190–191, 193, 199, 200–211, *201*

Cork Club, Shamrock Hotel, 137–138

Cosell, Howard: and Battle of the Sexes match, 155, 158, 160–164, 165, 167–168; as *Monday Night Football* announcer, 1, 2, 4, 10–11, 12, 158, 232, 233

Cotton Bowl Association, 14, 22, 23–24

Cotton Bowl Classic: as annual college football post-season game, 14, 19, 80; and breaking of racial segregation customs, 22–23, 24, 34; and Cotton Bowl Stadium, 71; and Fair Park Stadium, 19; and high school band performances, 14–15; and Kilgore Rangerettes, 14–15, 30, *31*, 32; and "Negro orchestras" in minstrel costumes performing in fairgrounds, 15; "Old South" cotton-related festivities of, 14–15; and promotion of Dallas, 19, 48; segregation of black fans in, 24; and Southern Methodist University, 21, 80–82, 127; and University of Houston, 110–111, 114, 115–116, 120; and University of Texas, 14, 41–42, 96, 103

Cotton Bowl Stadium, Dallas: aerial view of, *72*; and Dallas Cowboys, 31, 220, 221; expansion of 1948, 22; exposure to climate, 75, 76–77, 78; Fair Park Stadium renamed as, 19; and Jerry LeVias,

Erving, Julius "Dr. J.," 267, 271, 278–280, *280*, 294, 318–319, 372n22
Erving, Turquoise, 319, 372n22
Erwitt, Elliott, 30, 32
ESPN, 306, 321, 322, 344
Esquire magazine, 241–242, 247, 249
Evert, Chris, 152, 169, 347
Ewing, Patrick, 323, 341

Fairbanks, Chuck, 102
Fair Park, Dallas, 34
Fair Park Auditorium, Dallas, 27
Fair Park Stadium, Dallas, 19, 23, 31
Fallon, Frank, 331
fans. *See* spectators and spectating culture
Farr, Mel, 37, 88, 89
Farr, Miller, 37, 68, 88
Fawcett, Farrah, 241
Fellowship of Christian Athletes, 107–108
feminism. *See* second-wave feminist movement
finance industry, and college football, 84, 121, 125
Fingers, Rollie, 195
Finley, Charlie, 201
Fonde Hall of Fame, 311
Fonde Recreation Center, Houston, 310–313, *312*, 315–316, 318, 332, 334
football: impact of Texans on, 2, 9, 17; manifestations of performance and spectatorship, 2, 17, 21; and physical education programs, 17; popularity of, 2, 15; and role of white femininity, 33; and spectating culture, 2, 17, 21, 73, 76, 104–105, 174; two-a-day practices of, 32; violence and militarized culture of, 12, 17; white football hero and white beauty queen, 33. *See also* American Football League (AFL); college football; high school football; National Football League (NFL); *and specific teams and players*
Ford, Gerald, 201, *201*, 239
Foreman, Earl, 267, 271
For Men Only (television program), 230
Forte, Chet, 158, 232, 243
Fort Worth High School, 35
Fort Worth Star-Telegram, 187
Foster, Rube, 17
Fouke, Harry, 106–107, 304–305
Franklin, Alvin, 317, 332, 335–336, 338
Frazier, Charlie, 37
Frazier, Joe, 154
Freeman, Donnie, 263
French Championships, Roland Garros, Paris, 132, 150, 151
Freytag, Arny, 249
Friedan, Betty, 239
Fry, Hayden, 87–88, 90–93, 104, 119

Gallagher, Jack, 109, 116
Galloway, Randy, 187, 200, 210
Garner, Janice, 248, 249
Garnett, Ervin, 98
Garrison, Zina, 170, 318, 347
Gavitt, Dave, 321–322
Geary, Joe, 263–264
gender conventions: and Battle of the Sexes match, 156–157, 160–161, 163, 164, 167–168; and Babe Didrikson, 26–28; and Kilgore Rangerettes, 31–32; and patriar-

chal society, 13, 31; and second-wave feminist movement, 28, 33; in South, 15; of tennis, 132, 134, 136, 140–141, 146, 147–148, 153, 160; and white feminine ideals, 26, 32, 33, 140, 146; and white masculine ideals, 26, 33, 49, 100, 131, 290. *See also* women athletes

gender equality, 11, 212–213, 214, 239

gender subordination, 33

Gent, Pete, 100

George, Phyllis, 6, 227–229

Georgetown University, 322, 323, 330, 340

Georgia Tech University, 43

Gervin, George "Iceman": on All-Star team, 279; athleticism of, 278; and Larry Brown, 259–260; Detroit shooting style of, 271–272, 278; finger roll shot of, 271, 274; jump shot of, 271, 272; league scoring titles of, 292–293, 294, 298; nickname of, 272; retirement of, 299; as San Antonio Spurs star, 267, 269–270, 272–273, 282, 292–298, 299, 300, 345; as shooting guard, 271–272; and James Silas, 274, 276; style of play, 271–272, 273, 296–297; traded to Chicago Bulls, 299; traded to San Antonio Spurs, 267, 276; and Virginia Squires, 267, 270–271, 272; weaknesses of, 272; working-class background of, 270

Gettys, Reid, 317

Giants Stadium, 74

Gibson, Althea, 132

Gibson, Pat, 81

Gifford, Frank: and Battle of the Sexes match, 158–160, 163, 166, 167, 353; as *Monday Night Football* announcer, 2, 3, 10, 12, 232, 233

Gilbert, Chris, 105

Gilbert, Dan, 193

Ginobli, Manu, 260

Gipson, Paul, 105–106, 109

Glieber, Frank, 6

Golden Cyclones (women's basketball team), 27

Golden Triangle region, 17, 36, 88, 90

Goolagong, Evonne, 152

Gordon, Lancaster, 330, 333, 335, 338

Grand Prix professional tennis circuit, 135

Grand Slam tournaments, 132, 135

Green, Mike, 294

Greenberg, Hank, 16

Greene, "Mean" Joe, 36

Grevey, Kevin, 287

Griese, Bob, 1, 9–10

Griffith, Calvin, 176, 182, 201, 371n14

Griffith, Darrell, 330

Grossman, Sandy, 227

Grzenda, Joe, 180

Gulf Oil, 63

Gunther, Marc, 232, 375n25

Hadnott, Janis, 266

Hadnott, Jim, 266

Hagan, Cliff, 263

Haines, Kris, 116

Halas, George "Papa Bear," 52

Hall, Evelyn, 28

Hall, Jeff, 330

Hall, Rosemary, 224

Hardin, Paul, 119

Hardin, Wayne, 42

Houston Oilers (*continued*)
Jerry LeVias, 91; and NFL play-
offs of 1978, 1, 2, 9–11; rebrand-
ing as Tennessee Titans, 12,
350; segregated seating at home
games, 55, 56, 58, 363n11; strike-
shortened season of, 324
Houston Post, 109, 144
Houston Racquet Club, 129–130,
142–144, 145, 169
Houston Rockets: and George
Gervin, 273; and HemisFair
Arena, 287; and Moses Malone,
299, 312–313, 324; and Hakeem
Olajuwon, 341, 345, 348; San
Antonio Spurs compared to, 261,
298
Houston Sports Association (HSA),
46, 47, 51, 57, 58–59, 63–65, 155
Houston Stratford High School,
118
Houston Tennis Association,
141–142
Houston Tennis News, 138
Houston Texans, *351*, 352
Howard, Chuck, 158, 230–232
Howard, Frank "Hondo," 171–172,
179–180
Hudson, Buddy, 268
Hughes, Robert, 36
Humble Oil, 84
Humphrey, Hubert, 155, 175
Hunt, H. L., 48, 51
Hunt, Lamar: and Dallas Tex-
ans, 45, 52–53, 215, 229; finan-
cial decline of, 346; as founder
of American Football League,
1–2, 45, 48, 51–52, 262; on Jim
Crow segregation, 217; and Kan-
sas City Chiefs, 53, 57, 74; and
merger of AFL and NFL, 1–2, 48,
53–54, 135, 173–174; photograph

of, *53*; as sports entrepreneur,
1–2, 5, 7, 26, 45, 48, 51, 84, 134;
and World Championship Tennis, 134–136, 169
Hunt, Norma, 136
Hunter, Billy, 203–204, 206–209
Hunter, Jim "Catfish," 195–196,
198–199

Iba, Henry, 326
Illinois Athletic Club, 27
I. M. Terrell High School, Fort
Worth, 36, 38
Indiana Pacers, 263, 264, 268, 276,
281, 284, 285
Indiana State University, 320–321
insurance industry, 121
International Lawn Tennis Federa-
tion (ILTF), 132, 133, 134, 135
International Women's Year (1975),
238–239
Irvin, Michael, 348
Irving, Texas, 183

Jackson, Keith, 104
Jackson, Reggie, 195, 203
Jackson, Ronnie, 284
James, Craig, 118, 123–124, 126
Jefferson High School Lassos, San
Antonio, 30
Jenkins, Delores, 193–194
Jenkins, Ferguson "Fergie," 191,
193–199, *197*, 202, 206, 209
Jenkins, Ferguson, Sr., 194
Jeppesen Stadium, racial segrega-
tion policy of, 55, 56, 68
Jim Crow segregation: Dallas Cow-
boys' management of desegre-
gation, 217–218; demeaning lan-
guage of, 35; emergence from,
13; Hayden Fry's attitude to-
ward, 87; Guy Lewis's break

King, Billie Jean (*continued*)
feminist movement, 159–160,
213, 239, 353; style of play, 146,
149; and Virginia Slims Invita-
tional tennis tournament, 142,
144, 369n19; and Virginia Slims
Tour, 151–152; on whiteness of
tennis, 131
King, Kenny, 102
King, Larry, 146, 158
King, Leon, 45
King, Martin Luther, Jr., 93–94
Kingdome, Seattle, 340
Kirkpatrick, Curry, 272, 288–289,
315
Kirkpatrick, Terence, 314, 316
Kirksey, George, 57, 64
Kirschenbaum, Jerry, 328
Klein, Gene, 250
Klosterman, Don, 68
Knievel, Evel, 64
Koufax, Sandy, 188–189
Kramer, Jack, 132–135, 141–142,
153, 158–160, 169–170
Kuhn, Bowie, 178, 203

Ladd, Ernie, 56
Laettner, Christian, 303
Lagos State University, 314
Landry, Tom: as coach of Dallas
Cowboys, 40, 52, 74, 210, 216,
217, 235, 256–257; and Fellowship of Christian Athletes, 108;
Jerry Jones's firing of, 256, 344;
and Mission High School, 40;
and Southwest Conference, 20;
and Super Bowl victory of 1972,
215; and Duane Thomas, 219
Latin America, nonsegregated
baseball leagues in, 17
Latinos: as athletic laborers, 8, 192;
and Houston Astros, 364n30;

and racial integration of base-
ball, 192, 207–208, 212. *See also*
Mexican Americans
Lattin, David, 36
Laughead, Jim, 25
Laver, Rod, 136
Lavergne, Robert, 111
Layne, Bobby, 18, 20, 21, 37
Layne, Dick "Night Train," 36
L. C. Anderson High School, Austin, 38
Leaks, Roosevelt, 86, 101
Leavell, Allen, 311
Lemon, Jim, 176
Lenglen, Suzanne, 132
lesbians, 239
LeVias, Jerry: Eric Dickerson compared to, 126, 127; as "exemplary" Negro, 93; family members' football playing, 88;
Homecoming 1968, *93*; kick return of, 9, 81, *82*; Warren McVea
compared to, 83; professional
football career of, 91; racist verbal and physical assaults against,
90, 92–94; running style of, 89;
and Southern Methodist University, 80, 86, 88–89, 91–94, 107,
113, 118, 123, 125, 229; sports
media on, 81, 89, 90–91, 92; and
Texas A&M game in 1966, 80–
82, 90
Lewis, Guy V.: as basketball coach
for University of Houston, 68,
70, 106, 303, 304–306, 308, 316,
319, 323–324, 326–327, 340;
and dunk shot, 308–309, 317,
324; and Fonde Recreation Center, 311; and Louisville-Houston
semifinal of 1983, 336, 339; and
Hakeem Olajuwon, 313–314;
Phi Slama Jama teams of early

Walker, Doak (*continued*)
sports media portrayals of, 25–26, 37; touchdown runs of, 9, 21
Wallace, George, 276
Walton, Bill, 267
Warner, A. E., *59*
Washington, Joe, 102
Washington Bullets, 275, 287, 293, 295–298
Washington Post, 251, 272, 284, 287
Washington Redskins, 181–182, 212, 370n3
Washington Senators, 171, 172, 175–182, 349
Washington State University, 88
Waterman, Texie, 222–225, 234, 235–236, 237, 239–240, 245–246
Webster, George, 68
Weintraub, Robert, 334
Wells, Lloyd C. A., 56
Wells, Willie, 17
Wesson, Ricky, 104, 119
West: colonial ideologies of, 33; integrated college football teams of, 37, 89
West, Jerry, 175
Westbrook, John, 88, 91, 94, 113
West Side Tennis Club, Forest Hills, 139, 140, 142, 145, 151
West Texas State University, 218–219
Wharton County Junior College, 39
"What's My Name?" affair, 69–70
Wheatley High School, Houston, 37, 38, 55, 309
White, Mark, 349
White, Randy, 236
White, Thelma, 44
white coaches: and black male athletes, 3; changing role of, 96–97;

prevalence of, 41; and terms of inclusion, 7
Whitehead, Eddie, 329
white men: privileged position of, 4, 6, 41, 348; re-creation of racial and gender exclusion in Texas, 15; sports management opportunities of, 6, 95, 126, 348; as team owners, 3, 7, 11; and tennis, 131–132. *See also* gender conventions
white supremacy: Jerry LeVias's challenge to, 93–94; Guy Lewis's challenge to, 303; South Texas challenges to, 41; and Southwest Conference, 113
Whitfield, Shelby, 176–177, 190
Whitford, David, 86
Whittenburg, Dereck, 339
Whittier, Julius, 101
Whittington, Arthur, 119
Wichita Falls, Texas, 36
Wichita State University, 88
Wide World of Sports (television program), 157–158, 230, 241
Wiley College, 35, 37, 88
Wilkerson, John, 170, 318, 347
Williams, Clancy, 88
Williams, Cleveland, 69
Williams, Delvin, 9
Williams, Gus, 330
Williams, Ray, 330
Williams, Richard, 170
Williams, Rob, 317, 319, 322–323
Williams, Serena, 170
Williams, Ted, 171–172, 176–177, 186, 192
Williams, Venus, 170
Wills, Bump, 205
Wilmot, George, 81
Wilson, Bobby, 33
Wilson, Tim, 9

Wimbledon, 132, 133, 134, 146, 151, 153, 160, 347

Winningham, Geoff, 64

Winter, Max, 52

Witt, Wayne, 288

women: opportunities for, 4, 145; reproductive rights of, 239; rights of, 238–239; segregated participation in sporting culture, 15; social control of young women, 238; as sportscasters, 227–228; as sportswriters, 187. *See also* gender conventions; gender equality; second-wave feminist movement; working-class women

women athletes: aspirations for freedom, equality, and recognition, 11, 214; as athletic laborers, 6, 8; cheerleaders as, 32, 33, 214–215, 256; influx of, 4; and National Women's Conference, 239; and regional and national levels of competition, 8, 26–28; and social change in sports, 6, 11; and tennis, 132, 133, 134, 136; and Title IX, 212, 228–229; and white feminine ideal, 32. *See also* black women athletes; Title IX; women's professional tennis

women of color: rights of, 239; and social change in sports, 6–7

women's professional tennis: cash prizes for, 140–141; and Gladys Heldman, 129–130, 131, 136–137, 141, 142–144, 145, 151, 169, 347; Original Nine, 142, 151, 169, 347; and Philip Morris Tobacco Company, 129, 143–144; and sexual harassment, 151; and tobacco industry, 8, 129–131, 143–145, 159,

169; tours and tournaments, 129, 134, 142–145, 151–152, 153, 169. *See also specific players*

Women's Pro Tour, 153

Women's Strike for Equality, 140

Women's Tennis Association, 169

Wooden, John, 70, 305, 320, 329–330, 335

Woolridge, Orlando, 317

working-class athletes, 270

working-class fans: of Dallas Cowboys, 71–72; of Major League Baseball, 66; of San Antonio Spurs, 259, 261, 289–290, 300–301

working-class men, 6

working-class women: and Dallas Cowboys Cheerleaders, 236; as NFL cheerleaders, 253; and women's professional tennis, 145, 147

World Championship Tennis (WCT), 134–136

World's Fair of 1968, 265, 287

World Tennis, 137–138, 140, 144, 152

Worthing High School, Houston, 36, 309, 317

Worthy, James, 323

Wright, Elmo, 109

Wright, Stan, 36–37, 55

Wussler, Robert, 227–228

Wynn, Jimmy, 68

Yankee Stadium, 74, 191

Yates High School, Houston, 36, 37, 38, 55, 85, 317

Yeoman, Bill: and Danny Davis, 114; and Chuck Fairbanks, 102; as football coach for University of Houston, 105, 106–110, 113–